THE UNITED NATIONS UNIVERSITY/THIRD WORLD FORUM

STUDIES IN AFRICAN POLITICAL ECONOMY

SADCC
Prospects for
Disengagement
and Development in
Southern Africa

THE UNITED NATIONS UNIVERSITY/THIRD WORLD FORUM

STUDIES IN AFRICAN POLITICAL ECONOMY
General Editor: Samir Amin

The United Nations University's Project on Transnationalization or Nation-Building in Africa (1982–1986) was undertaken by a network of African scholars under the co-ordination of Samir Amin. The purpose of the Project was to study the possibilities of and constraints on national autocentric development of African countries in the context of the world-system into which they have been integrated. Since the 1970s the world-system has been in a crisis of a severity and complexity unprecedented since the end of the Second World War; the Project examines the impact of this contemporary crisis on the political, economic and cultural situation of Africa today. Focusing on the complex relationship between transnationalization (namely, the dynamics of the world-system) and nation-building, which is seen as a precondition for national development, the Project explores a wide range of problems besetting Africa today and outlines possible alternatives to the prevailing development models which have proved to be inadequate.

TITLES IN THIS SERIES

M. L. Gakou
The Crisis in African Agriculture
1987

Peter Anyang' Nyong'o (editor)
Popular Struggles for Democracy in Africa
1987

Samir Amin, Derrick Chitala, Ibbo Mandaza (editors)
SADCC: Prospects for Disengagement and Development in Southern Africa
1987

Faysal Yachir
The World Steel Industry Today
1988

Other titles in preparation.

THE UNITED NATIONS UNIVERSITY/THIRD WORLD FORUM

STUDIES IN AFRICAN POLITICAL ECONOMY

SADCC
Prospects for Disengagement and Development in Southern Africa

edited by
Samir Amin
Derrick Chitala
Ibbo Mandaza

The United Nations University
Zed Books Ltd.
London and New Jersey

*SADCC: Prospects for Disengagement and
Development in Southern Africa* was first published in 1987
by:
Zed Books Ltd., 57 Caledonian Road, London N1 9BU, UK, and
171 First Avenue, Atlantic Highlands, New Jersey 07716, USA
and:
The United Nations University, Toho Seimei Building,
15–1 Shibuya 2-chome, Shibuya-ku, Tokyo 150, Japan
in co-operation with:
The Third World Forum, B.P. 3501, Dakar, Senegal.

Cover designed by Andrew Corbett.
Typeset by EMS Photosetters, Rochford, Essex.
Printed and bound in the United Kingdom
by Biddles Ltd., Guildford and King's Lynn.

British Library Cataloguing in Publication Data

SADCC: prospects for disengagement and
development in Southern Africa.——(The
United Nations University/Third World Forum
studies in African political economy).
1. Africa, Southern——Economic
conditions——1975–
I. Amin, Samir   II. Chitala, Derrick
III. Mandaza, Ibbo   IV. Series
330.968'063   HC900

ISBN 0-86232-748-2
ISBN 0-86232-749-0 Pbk

Contents

Tables

Figures

Editors and Contributors

Editors

Professor Samir Amin Co-ordinator of the Third World Forum (Africa Office).

Dr Ibbo Mandaza Formerly lecturer in Political Science, Universities of Botswana and Dar es Salaam. Secretary, Ministry of Planning, Zimbabwe.

Derrick Chitala Lecturer, University of Zambia.

Contributors

Dr Jumanne Hamisi Wagao Senior lecturer in Economics, University of Dar es Salaam.

Benedict Stephen Mongula Lecturer, IDS, University of Dar es Salaam.

Denny H. Kalyala Lecturer in Economics, University of Zambia.

Clever Mumbengegwi Lecturer in Economics, University of Zimbabwe.

Dr Daniel B. Ndlela Head of Department of Economics, University of Zimbabwe. His main interest has been in industrialization and economic planning.

Dr Gilbert Mudenda Lecturer, University of Zambia.

Dr Chiselebwe Ng'andwe Lecturer in Economics, University of Zambia.

Acknowledgements

This book was produced in the framework of the United Nations University (UNU) African Regional Perspectives project, conducted by the African Bureau of the Third World Forum (TWF) and the network of African researchers associated with it. We would like here to thank the UNU, which met a large part of the financing of this programme, and the Swedish agency SAREC, which gives generous and constant support to the African Bureau of the Third World Forum. But, of course, in the hallowed formula, the opinions expressed here are those of their authors only and in no way commit the institutions mentioned.

Preface

Samir Amin

This book in our series is the fruit of collective discussion and reflection within the framework of one of our working groups built around the problematic of the SADCC (Southern African Development Coordination Conference). The aim of the group was to analyse the development policies of the states confronting South Africa, stressing regional cooperation among them, and, from that, to answer the following questions:

(1) Are their policies likely to strengthen their internal cohesion and resistance capacity in the face of South African expansionism and its destabilizing acts of aggression?

(2) Do these policies reduce the historic dependence of these countries on South Africa by 'delinking' them from South Africa?

(3) Do these policies also aim at initiating a policy of 'delinking' the region from the global imperialist system?

Such systematic reflection as ours was already underway several years before the people of South Africa, in the early summer of 1984, obliged all parties involved to undertake a total review of their strategies by carrying its struggle against the apartheid regime to an irreversible level, heralding the end of the regime.

For a century, imperialism had established a system of total domination of the Southern African region in which the white settler colony of South Africa played a key role. The discovery of the mineral riches of the region (such as gold and diamonds in South Africa, copper in Katanga and Northern Rhodesia) just when capitalism was entering a new stage of monopolistic expansion inspired a particular form of colonization – that of 'the economy of the reserves'. That is, a partition of the country and the forcing of the African peasantries back into reserves deliberately planned to be inadequate so as to ensure the failure of subsistence in earlier traditional forms; consequently it would have to re-emerge as a proletarianized migrant labour force for mining capital. The agricultural economy of European plantations in South Africa and Southern Rhodesia, and then later manufacturing industry, also benefited from this system.

Apartheid was thus always an intrinsic part of this form of the expansion of peripheral capitalism, whose peculiar features we have demonstrated elsewhere, in contrast to the forms established in other regions of the continent, notably, the colonial trade economy in West Africa.[1] Contrary to a deep-seated prejudice, it was not the Boers who, in an excess of racism peculiar only to them, invented this system. The Boers had until then elaborated only a crude conception of their society – then agrarian and patriarchal – which involved the conquest of land and the driving back, or wiping out of its occupants rather than integrating them into an efficient capitalist exploitation. In short, a plan similar to the one the Zionists contemplate for the Palestinians. But the defeat inflicted on them by British imperialism gave them a new place and functions in the system invented by English rulers brought up on an interpretation of the ranking of classes and races inspired by a Cambridge reading of Plato. The British established the system of apartheid, and then claimed that it was the Boers who had invented it. They also encouraged the popular misconception that apartheid is a 'vestige' in conflict with the needs of capitalist expansion: on the contrary, it fitted in perfectly with that expansion.

Bourgeois ideology attempts to justify the 'progressive' character of capitalism by claiming that the legal equality of individuals and electoral democracy are absolute hallmarks of this mode of production. Reality tells a different story, which, among other things, stresses the qualitative distinction between centres and peripheries in this global capitalist expansion. For, while in the centres the struggles waged by the bourgeoisie against the absolutism of the *ancien régimes*, and later those waged by the working class did indeed impose bourgeois democracy, as we know it, in the periphery the functions allotted to the conquered peoples called for brutal forms of exploitation – slavery in America, apartheid in South Africa, colonization (and the negation of basic rights which defines it) are necessary forms of capitalist expansion. If today apartheid is being called into question in South Africa, it is not because this form constitutes an obstacle to capitalist expansion, but because the struggles of the black South Africans who are its victims, make it unworkable.[2]

From the end of the 19th Century until 1984, the system functioned well with no major crises calling into question the dominant interests of monopolistic capital. The collapse of British and Belgian colonization in the 1960s did not lead to the destruction of the regional system of imperialist domination. The respective national liberation movements in the region, like others all over the continent, were persuaded or forced to bow to basic 'Western' interests. Of course, depending on the class nature of the alliances that made up these movements, and the vicissitudes of their political and ideological evolution, the range of post-colonial attitudes and practices was very wide, ranging from the open neo-colonialism of Malawi, Swaziland, Lesotho and Zaïre to the national efforts of Tanzania or Zambia. But these latter remained vulnerable and fragile, as the facts have amply demonstrated.

The subsequent collapse of Portuguese colonialism in 1974 and of the Smith regime in Southern Rhodesia in 1980 did, however, constitute a threat to imperialist interests. However, neither in Angola nor in Mozambique, had the West definitively lost the battle. The internal limits typical of the capacities of new nationalist governments obliged them to respect the interests of monopoly capital (as with oil in Angola), or to maintain the system of dependent economic relationships which governs the capitalist world as a whole. Furthermore, the Soviet Union has been neither able nor even disposed to replace Western partners in this area. In Zimbabwe, the independence negotiated by the Lancaster House Agreement prolonged the survival of the previous economic system practically intact in both the rural areas (no agrarian reform liquidating the settler lands in favour of the peasantry) and in the industrial arena (respect for the predominance of the interests of local private capital in partnership with globalized capital).

Nonetheless, it remains the case that the regimes in Angola, Mozambique and Zimbabwe, like those in other frontline states (Tanzania and Zambia) remain 'rather unreliable' in the eyes of the West. Hence the West has considered it positive and useful – for itself – that South Africa has, since 1974 in Angola and Mozambique and since 1980 in Zimbabwe, carried out destabilizing acts of military aggression there. These are complemented on the economic level by the destabilizing aggression of the IMF, acting for the global account of imperialism, turning the weaknesses and errors – sometimes very serious ones – of local policies to advantage. The results of this strategy, aimed at establishing openly neo-colonial regimes, are not at all disappointing for imperialism. Angola was obliged to call for Cuban military assistance to deal with South African attacks, Mozambique to sign the Nkomati Accord, Zimbabwe to show scrupulous respect for the Lancaster House Agreement, Tanzania and Zambia to submit to the humiliating terms of the IMF. The 'Soviet presence' in the region, and the presence of the rear bases of the liberation movements of Namibia and South Africa (SWAPO, ANC, PAC), are no more than excuses, and not the real reasons for the West's offensive strategy. For these presences are the result – and not the cause – of the refusal by the West to accept regimes in Africa that are other than neo-colonial, and, down to the present day, to contemplate the decolonization of Namibia and South Africa.

But since 1984 things have been changing. The struggle in which the people of South Africa have been engaged since then raises the question of the future of the region in terms of new alternatives – global neo-colonialism for Southern Africa, or popular national liberation?

On this I would like here to make six general observations that seem to me useful in throwing light on the nature of the issues and possible strategies:

1. What is in direct, immediate and violent crisis in South Africa is the political regime of apartheid and the denial that it involves of any respect for the basic rights of the African majority. Although, because of the size of the urban proletariat the relations of exploitation typical of capitalism constitute the potential issue in the crisis, the main force of the blow is borne by the demand for majority rule (majority rule against minority rule and apartheid). This characteristic of the movement is, of course, altogether natural in current conditions.

2. In these conditions, and if the struggle does not develop to the point of a real challenge to the relations of production, a neo-colonial solution is not ruled out, even in South Africa. After all, a sort of Lancaster House arrangement would be quite acceptable to the West. No doubt some white settler interests in South Africa would be sacrificed in it; but so they were at the time of the defeat of the Boers at the beginning of the century! There is no point in going any further in attempting to predict possible scenarios. These may well include, in favour of African interests, more or less extensive agrarian reforms and a greater or lesser degree of political representation and, in favour of settler interests, more or less precise and strong 'guarantees'. The essential thing for imperialism is to safeguard capitalist production relations in industry and the mines and the international 'specialization'

of the region that flows from it.

There is, in this perspective, no avoiding heavily qualifying the overly facile arguments that such an outcome would be totally 'impossible'. There is no black bourgeoisie in South Africa, apartheid made it impossible for one to emerge, it is said. That may well be so, but so it was in many African countries and yet a political bourgeoisie was soon able to take over. South Africa's nuclear capacity rules out any compromise, it is said, because the West will never accept that a black government have access to this weapon. Have people ruled out the prospect of this capacity being dismantled, if that proved to be necessary? South Africa is the sole possible supplier of strategic minerals, if imports from the Soviet Union are ruled out. True, but does not the neo-colonial solution aim precisely at ensuring the permanence of those supplies? Finally, the argument that white power in South Africa has an autonomy that enables it to reject any 'plans' that it thinks ask it to sacrifice too much. The analogy with Israel, which could also indefinitely cock a snook at the West as well as force it to give it unconditional support, or even do without it, is frequently put forward. We doubt the strength of this argument. In our view South Africa would stand up poorly to sanctions, even simply economic ones, and the present white regime would collapse even faster if they were to be adopted. Perhaps the spread of the war inside the country will, on its own, lead to such a collapse.

3. It is idle to hope for differences to emerge in the strategies pursued by the various partners in the imperialist system. Certainly imperialism, such as Lenin knew and analysed in his time, was in economic, and even military, conflict (the evidence is the two world wars). But the changes that followed World War II altered the nature of inter-imperialist relations and have apparently ruled out recourse to inter-imperialist wars. But they have also led to a new stage of deeper globalization of the interpenetration of interests. The European Community, the United States and Japan, particularly in regard to the key mining sector in South Africa, deploy perfectly integrated strategies of firms and states.[3] The argument that the EEC, anxious to maintain its African friendships, might detach itself from its American rival and ally scarcely stands up to an examination of the facts, for the subordination of neo-colonial regimes, on the one hand, and the vulnerability of those who attempt to challenge the existing order, on the other, have so far made it possible for European interests to sleep peacefully on their laurels.

4. The neo-colonial outcome is no more an inevitable solution than the opposite – national liberation with a popular content and a socialist vocation. What happens will depend, in the main, on the strategies of struggle deployed in South Africa. If these were to set themselves the sole target of 'majority rule' and actively seek negotiations on that basis, the neo-colonial compromise might perhaps be secured more quickly than might seem possible. But, if the strategies were to be based on an increased emphasis on social objectives (that is on the struggle for workers' control of the means of production and peasant warfare for the recovery of land), it would certainly not be the same. Herein lies all the historical responsibility of vanguards.

5. A question poses itself, namely – is it a struggle for the eventual building of socialism (in the most optimistic hypothesis of the development of the struggle), or a struggle which, on this hypothesis, would simply result in popular national rule

with only a potential socialist vocation? The debates on this issue appear to me to be confused and distorted by the predominant thesis of the 'revolution by stages' (national democratic and then socialist). This is doubtless not the place to analyse these debates in detail; I shall therefore simply formulate a few general thoughts on this issue:[4]

(a) This thesis put forward by recent (post-World War II) vulgar Marxism – which seems to me to be neither truly Leninist, nor Maoist (but, in the last analysis, it matters little whether it is or not) – is little more than the expression of the legitimization of the practices of post-revolutionary governments: first big reforms (including agrarian ones), then 'collectivization' reduced to the substitution of the forms of public ownership (state and cooperative) for private ownership. The vulgar thesis stops there, i.e. it completely glosses over discussion of the content of ownership. Public ownership is treated as if it were socialism, whereas it is only the first condition of it; there is no attempt to look at whether the real functioning of society allows control of the means of production by the producers (through an advanced social and political democracy).

(b) Reality disconfirms the thesis. Is not socialism confronted with the repeated revival of relations of production capable of ensuring greater efficiency in the development of productive forces? Fifty years after the victory of socialism in the USSR (i.e. after the liquidation of the NEP and collectivization) the question of the 'market' is back on the agenda. Twenty years after the Cultural Revolution in China had, it was said, settled the problem, here we are again with these same relations that had been 'abolished' being re-established. In such conditions, is it not necessary to get shot of the dogmatic and empty old saw of the 'national democratic' stage to be followed by 'the stage of building socialism'?

(c) Instead of this misconception, I see that the overthrow of dominant capitalist rule in the conditions in which real history actually makes it happen, i.e. following the unequal development immanent in capitalist expansion, from the peripheries of the global system, calls into question the vulgar theorization of the transition. The objectively necessary task of developing the producing forces, the inevitable conflict with the global logic of world-wide capitalist expansion, the complex internal class relations produced by 'incomplete' capitalist development (the peasant question, the question of petty bourgeoisies and middle classes, the limitations of the labour movement, etc.), call for a long transition. In this period the forces of socialism, capitalism and a statism that I think cannot be reduced to either, combine, and conflict, in forms that are specific to each country and each stage, without one 'general line' – whether desirable or real – being able to constitute a sort of 'model'. It is for this reason that I have preferred to describe the societies in question as 'popular-national', rather than 'socialist'. In so doing, I intend to stress their 'delinking' from the world-wide capitalist system (whence the 'national' character), and the conflict-laden nature of their social content and potential evolution.

These observations are made here because I believe that there is nothing to enable us to say that the issues in South Africa are different from those that this analysis makes it possible to isolate.

6. So long as the popular national construction is not underway, in South Africa

and in the region, relations between the countries that constitute the region will continue to be marked by the inequality inherent in capitalist expansion, both in their relations with imperialism and in their relations with one another. As a result, the global neo-colonial solution involves the segmentation of local and regional ruling classes, and hence conflicts of interest between them. A South African pseudo-'expansionism', the vehicle and expression of globalized capitalist expansion, would thus remain a possible, and even probable reality. But does the popular national solution eliminate this possibility? Here again the dogmatic and vulgar proposition of the coming together of all popular interests precludes analysis. The (real) conflicts between popular national (so-called socialist) regimes, between the USSR and Eastern Europe, China and the USSR, China and Vietnam, are not the product of 'ideological deviations'. The specificity of their nature (since these are not conflicts produced by the unequal development of capitalism) does not mean that they do not exist. The contradiction, and hence the solution to it by various means (cooperation or conflict) according to concrete circumstances, governs post-capitalist society just as it governs pre-capitalist and capitalist societies.[5]

Can we go beyond these general strategic thoughts to look at different possible ways in which the situation might evolve? The forces in conflict owe it to themselves to do so. So we shall suggest the four considerations that follow:

1. The global strategy of imperialism must, if it is to arrive at the neo-colonial outcome sought, act in directions that appear to be contradictory, but in fact converge. In this framework, it is necessary to understand that the apparent contradiction between, on the one hand, the pressure applied on Angola and the other frontline states by active support to South Africa and its local allies (UNITA, RENAMO, etc.), and, on the other, the application of pressure on South Africa to induce it in turn to negotiate, is only apparent.

2. Fissures are appearing within the white South African front, at the level of society and perhaps even at the level of government. But it seems likely that the existing regime would be unable to survive even the beginning of serious negotiations (i.e. ones that went beyond empty pseudo-reforms over which it retains the initiative). Does this mean that an internal *coup d'état*, in some form or other, will be necessary in order to make such negotiations possible? It is perhaps idle to speculate on any evolution like this, but it is worth pointing out that it is possible, so as not to be so surprised by it as to lose the initiative in the waging of the struggle.

3. The pursuit of the neo-colonial solution does not oblige imperialism to lay down all its cards straightaway. At first an attempt may be made with individuals who may appear to be puppets – Buthelezi here playing the role that Muzorewa played in Zimbabwe. That may constitute a means of 'pressure' on the more radical forces in the movement (ANC and PAC).

4. There is sometimes talk of the danger of a 'Vietnamization' of the situation in the sense of a direct military commitment by the United States in the event that the struggles in South Africa were to become threatening for the vital interests of the West. The question being, obviously, not on the agenda for the immediate future, might this not be a softening-up campaign designed to reinforce the very attitudes of compromise that are sought by the Western powers?

The people of South Africa, in the battle that they are now embarked on, have begun to take up the challenge with which the whole of Africa has been confronted for a century, if not more. It is essential to help them to do so, by contributing to create the conditions which make it impossible for its victory to be snatched away from it, and thus open to the peoples of the continent the path to its national and popular development.

Notes

1. We have suggested a typology of the forms of colonial exploitation in Africa in 'Underdevelopment and Dependence in Black Africa', *Journal of Modern African Studies*, 10, 4, 1972.

2. We have defended this viewpoint – that, contrary to liberal ideology, apartheid was not 'dysfunctional' to capitalist expansion, in two articles published in 1971 (*Tiers Monde*, 48, 1971, and *L'Homme et la Société*, 22, 1971); then in a paper presented to the University of Dar es Salaam in 1974 and published in the *Journal of Southern African Affairs*, 2, 3, 1977 (University of Maryland) entitled 'The future of southern Africa'.

3. This theme of the unification of the interests and strategies of imperialist firms and states, *inter alia*, in the mining area, is developed by Fayçal Yachir in his book *Mining in Africa* (Zed, forthcoming).

4. See: Samir Amin, *La Déconnexion* (La Découverte, Paris, 1985), Samir Amin, 'L'état et le développement', article to appear in *Socialism in the World* (Belgrade, 1986).

5. We categorically reject the ideological thesis (propounded by Jaurès) that 'capitalism bears war within itself like the cloud the storm', and *a fortiori* the crazy notions about 'the natural expansionism of dictatorships' (USSR or China or Vietnam). Clausewitz's thesis (adopted by Lenin) is more realistic. He states that war is the pursuit of politics by other means, that is that all societies and governments (pre-capitalist, capitalist and post-capitalist), riven with contradictions, attempt to resolve those contradictions by various means that they judge sufficient, which may be violent (including war) or less violent. Only concrete analysis of these contradictions and the strategies of those involved, governments in the main, can make it possible to understand when recourse to violence is sought.

Introduction

The origins of the Southern African Development Coordination Conference (SADCC) comprising the nine independent states of Southern Africa (Angola, Botswana, Lesotho, Malawi, Mozambique, Swaziland, Tanzania, Zambia and Zimbabwe) are still obscure. For some researchers its foundation started at a meeting in Botswana in May 1979 of foreign ministers of the five frontline states (Angola, Botswana, Mozambique, Tanzania and Zambia) following intensive lobbying by Botswana.

It is now, however, widely recognized that the SADCC was not solely an initiative of the frontline states. On the contrary, there was strong encouragement from Western countries who wished to draw the region closer to the West, and, by creating a diversion from undiluted confrontation with South Africa, to prevent the frontline states from giving greater support to the ANC and SWAPO. Leys and Tostensen (1982) have argued that the SADCC project was seen by Western countries as a programme of reconstruction in Southern Africa after years of war – a kind of Marshall Plan for the region.[1]

Certainly, too, the shared political activity of the frontline states (FLS) between 1974 and 1979 provided the impetus to extend their relationship into the economic sphere. This, however, was the result of external inducement: from the very beginning, the SADCC idea has been dependent on the blessings of imperialism in general. Recognizing that national and regional integration was essential for the 'harmonious' development of Southern Africa, the ministers of the SADCC countries agreed to convene a conference in Arusha, Tanzania in July 1979 with donor governments and international development institutions to discuss a regional programme of economic development. The Arusha meeting (known as SADCC I) provided the SADCC with an opportunity to explain to potential investors the main parameters of such investment and the policy assumptions on which it was being constructed. Studies conducted by foreign interests were presented covering the following areas of potential regional cooperation: transport and communication; agriculture, forestry and fisheries; energy, water and minerals; trade and industry; employment and skills. It was also agreed that the other majority-ruled countries of Southern Africa should be invited to participate in the drawing-up of the Lusaka Declaration on Southern African Development Coordination.

On 1 April 1980 the leaders and representatives of the independent states of

Southern Africa came together in Lusaka and signed a declaration entitled 'Southern Africa: Toward Economic Liberation'. The declaration acknowledged the humiliating dependence status in which Southern Africa was engulfed. It said that

> Southern Africa is dependent on the Republic of South Africa as a focus of transport and communications, as an exporter of goods and services and as an importer of goods and cheap labour. The dependence is not a natural phenomenon nor is it simply the result of a free market economy. The nine states and one occupied territory of Southern Africa (Angola, Botswana, Lesotho, Malawi, Mozambique, Namibia, Swaziland, Tanzania, Zambia and Zimbabwe) were, in varying degrees, deliberately incorporated – by metropolitan powers, colonial rulers and large corporations – into the colonial and sub-colonial structures centring in general on the Republic of South Africa. The development of national economies as balanced units, let alone the welfare of the people of Southern Africa, played no part in the economic integration strategy. Not surprisingly, therefore, Southern Africa is fragmented, grossly exploited and subject to economic manipulation by outsiders. Future development must aim at the reduction of economic dependence not only on the Republic of South Africa, but also on any single external state or groups of states.

The declaration also contained an appeal for external cooperation and international support.

Furthermore, the summit meeting issued a 'Programme of Action'. Mozambique was charged with the task of establishing a regional commission for transport and communications; Botswana to prepare a project for regional control of foot and mouth disease, and for the establishment of an International Crops Research Institute for the Semi-arid Tropics (ICRISAT) to serve the region; Zimbabwe to elaborate a Southern African Food Security Plan; Swaziland to review existing training facilities in the region and make recommendations for their better regional utilization; Tanzania to formulate a strategy aimed at harmonizing the region's industrial development; Zambia to undertake studies leading to proposals for the establishment of a Southern African Development Fund; and Angola to formulate proposals for the harmonization of energy policies in the region.

The second summit conference (SADCC 2) was held in November 1980, in Maputo, Mozambique. It was essentially aimed at winning investors and was a major gathering of representatives of 30 foreign capitalist governments and 18 multilateral organizations. The SADCC countries presented an outline of 97 projects in transport and communications prepared by Danish consultants. The projects included: rehabilitation of the railway line from Nacala to the Mozambique border, and of the Botswana railway; upgrading roads in Lesotho; road-building in Tanzania; deepening and increasing the capacity of the ports of Beira and Maputo; and building new terminal facilities at Harare Airport. These projects account for $US1,007 million of the total $US1,946 million requested.

Altogether $US650 million was pledged, of which $US273 million was committed to specific projects in the field of transport and communications. The largest single pledge, $US384 million spread over 1982–6, came from the African Development Bank. The European Community pledged $US100 million already earmarked under the Lomé convention. The United States pledged $US50 million, the Netherlands $US32 million, Sweden $US22 million, Italy $US15 million, and West Germany a token $US2 million, to improve the SADCC's planning capacity.

The summit meeting at Salisbury in July 1981 reviewed the progress of the projects presented at Maputo and endorsed the SADCC's institutional framework of summit meetings, a council of ministers, commissions, a standing committee of officials and the proposed secretariat.

The relative success of the Maputo Conference led to the holding of another conference in November 1981 at Blantyre, Malawi. The conference brought together officials from SADCC member states and 32 invited governments and agencies to discuss progress in four areas of the SADCC's regional cooperation: transport and communication; food and agriculture; manpower development; and industrial cooperation. Further pledges were given. The Kuwait Fund promised $US37 million, Portugal $US30 million and West Germany increased its pledge to $US15 million. Furthermore, a regional plan of industrial cooperation was approved at the conference. The main thrust of the plan envisaged to develop minimum-needs industries in the areas of food, clothing, housing, health, water supply, power, transport and education. Development of basic industries such as iron and steel, fertilizers, pharmaceuticals, pesticides, and capital goods industries also formed an integral part of the regional plan. Like the Maputo Conference, the 1983 Maseru Conference was also a pledging conference. The main focus of the conference was on industrial development and food and agriculture. An estimated sum of $US489 million was pledged. This trend of 'pledging' continued at the 1984 and 1985 conferences held in Lusaka, Zambia and Mbabane, Swaziland, respectively.

The administrative organs of SADCC are:

1. the Summit of Heads of Governments;
2. the Council of Ministers;
3. a small secretariat; and
4. sectoral commissions for each sectoral programme.

None of these institutions has power to make binding decisions for the region. This reflects the SADCC's unique character as a loose regional grouping which emphasizes national priorities as the starting point in any cooperative effort. This position is underscored by the chairman of the SADCC Council of Ministers, who is also Vice-President of Botswana, Mr P. S. Mmusi:

> The baseline for SADCC's growth in the coming years will remain the perceived interests of our member states, their own measure of what must be done, and their own order of priorities. We now have a good programme of cooperative actions underway which will, when implemented, further integrate our national economies.

While the principal function of the secretariat is liaison work within the SADCC and with donor countries and institutions, the sectoral commissions have some responsibility for planning and implementing regionally coordinated programmes within their respective sectors, subject of course to the SADCC baseline of the supremacy of national priorities. Sectoral commissions have been decentralized such that each member country is responsible for one sector. The transport and communications commission is under Mozambique, while energy is coordinated by Angola. Apart from structural problems, the SADCC's institutional framework is not conducive to regional planning and coordination of transport, communications and energy resources. National sentiments are bound to dominate regional considerations, and this appears to have been the case in the first five years of the SADCC's activities.

In assessing the first five years as a basis for planning the activities of the future, the SADCC Secretariat has discerned the following features for the current programme:

1. In the appraisal of projects, the objective of reducing economic dependence does not appear always to have been observed.
2. Data gathering and preparatory studies have tended to dominate some of the sectoral programmes at the expense of concrete project implementation.
3. Insufficient attention has been paid to the role of productive and commercial enterprises and institutions.
4. There has been inadequate emphasis on the mobilization of the SADCC's own resources – financial and human – and an excessive emphasis on attracting external funding and personnel.
5. Though the approved list of SADCC projects is already lengthy, and the implementation rate is still low, new projects continue to be added at a rate which, if unchecked, could eventually undermine the credibility of the whole programme.
6. Planning and programming of activities have tended to lack a long-term perspective.

Thus, for the next five years and beyond, when the programme emphasis should be on project implementation rather than on preparation, the following SADCC principles will guide sectoral policies and strategies:

1. There should be a mutually supportive relationship between SADCC objectives and programmes and those of the member states.
2. Strategies and programmes should reassert the priority given in the Lusaka Declaration to operational projects for the production of goods and services and for the mobilization of the SADCC's own resources – in particular the development of skills.
3. There should be equitable regional development.
4. There should be decentralized responsibility for project implementation.
5. There should be adequate consultation among SADCC member states and institutions at every stage of planning and implementation. The smooth functioning of a decentralized organization such as the SADCC depends on an effective network of communication and consultation.
6. The realization of the SADCC objectives requires an active participation of all sectors and levels of the communities – particularly the productive and commercial enterprises and institutions in achieving the objectives of SADCC.
7. Maximum coordination and rationalization between related sectors is essential.
8. Programmes should not focus on physical projects alone. Attention should

also be given to operational coordination; and the improvement and harmonization of systems for the optimum realization of the region's economic potential.

9. Parameters should be established within the sector as a whole and also for each project, to measure progress towards achievement of objectives. Pledges of foreign assistance do not by themselves constitute an adequate measure of progress.

Two significant features coming out of the appraisal of the first five years of SADCC's operations are (a) the emphasis on a regional approach in future programmes, and (b) the mobilization of the SADCC's own resources for regional development. While it is recognized that the SADCC has no strong institutional capacity to effectively determine and implement regional programmes, the policy emphasis on a regional approach in project planning and implementation is significant. Given the SADCC's abundant political goodwill, it is possible for sectoral commissions to plan and implement projects with a regional perspective.

With regard to resource mobilization, past programmes have been almost completely dependent on donor resources. While a certain level of dependence on donors may be inevitable, wholesale dependence renders the SADCC's objectives vulnerable to distortions. Even where the donors have the best intentions, development can be distorted through the professional and subjective biases of the advisers from these donor countries and agencies. Moreover, most donors, with the notable exception of Nordic countries, have ideological or commercial interests to promote in any collaborative effort with the SADCC. Such interests are bound to compromise the SADCC's objectives. This is particularly so in view of the organization's loose institutional arrangements which permit purely national projects to compete with legitimate regional projects for donor assistance. The SADCC's flexibility may be an important element in its ability to attract funding as Turner has observed: 'Much of SADCC's success so far in attracting what – compared with other parts of Africa – could be viewed as "disproportionate" amounts of aid finance, is attributed to its openness to discussion of its programmes' (1978). It is important that mobilization of aid finance by SADCC is undertaken with the fullest awareness of the possible negative consequences for its legitimate interests. It is the capacity for mobilizing internal resources that will ultimately reduce the dangers of over-dependence on external donors.

1 The Political Economy of the SADCC and Imperialism's Response

Derrick Chitala

After several experiments in regional cooperation in Africa, Southern Africa is showing a new interest in such cooperation and particularly since the independence of Angola, Mozambique and Zimbabwe. Perhaps the best known attempts on the continent are the now defunct East African Community (EAC) and the Economic Community for West African States (ECOWAS). Further experiments are still being attempted with several multilateral bodies arguing that this is the only way in which problems nurtured by 'smallness' can be solved. The UN General Assembly and the more specialized agencies such as UNCTAD and the Economic Commission for Africa (ECA) have for instance consistently argued for regional and sub-regional integration in order to bring about economic development and growth in Africa. In May 1973, the OAU adopted an 'African Declaration on Co-operation, Development and Economic Independence' where African countries were encouraged to set up inter-African cooperation, particularly in the monetary and communications fields.

The SADCC approach on regional cooperation significantly differs from those that seek common market and customs limitation like ECOWAS and the Southern African Customs Union (SACU). SADCC adopted a structure that has been termed 'sectoral programming'. Advocates of this trend have not been happy with the use of the term 'integration' but see a trend towards self-reliance among developing countries on a so-called 'South–South' basis which is in itself a part of the wider struggle to bring about a redistribution of world production, control over the creation and allocation of surplus and the power to make decisions on matters that affect their societies. To that extent, collective self-reliance implies restructuring the links between underdeveloped and developed countries through the creation of new links among developing countries.

As a policy, sectoral programming limits itself to a particular sector of activity in order to deepen rather than widen the integration movement. The desired goals are to create net benefits in the region by expanding productive capacity, to permit equitable distribution of benefits by allocating production among member countries and designating roles of local participation. Several scholars have supported this approach to regional cooperation. Vaitsos (1978) for instance has contended that integration among developing countries should concentrate on specifically identified areas or projects, this to be backed up by a programming approach broadly developmentally oriented.

This chapter attempts to put into focus the position of the SADCC programme from a broad perspective. In order to shed light on the form of imperialist domination prevailing in the region, the first part examines the nature of South African corporate power, showing in detail the genesis of South African capital. The second part examines the nature of dependent links that bind the SADCC economies to South Africa, and by extension to imperialism, and exposes the disturbing vulnerabilities of the SADCC countries. The last section analyses the contending forces in which it is shown how imperialism in general has helped South Africa to thwart the SADCC challenge and how the historical links that bind several SADCC countries to South Africa cannot be removed without transforming the post-colonial state in a revolutionary manner.

This essay seeks to ascertain the problems and prospects for SADCC and, in so doing, poses the thesis that the ultimate way forward for Southern Africa is through a victorious struggle against the combined corporate power of South Africa and imperialism and through the socialist transformation of the region's states.

Imperialism and the South African State

Theoretical advances to the understanding of Southern Africa as a regional sub-system or a sub-imperial complex have taken various approaches.

One approach, which can be characterized as belonging to sub-systems theory, emphasizes the interdependence and unity of Southern Africa as a region. It contends that Southern Africa is constituted by a permanent constellation of interdependent variables. This approach stresses racial and tribal factors rather than class relations. By ignoring the labour process and class exploitation, this approach has generally been found to be profoundly ahistorical and deficient.

The other approach views the Republic of South Africa as a regional hegemonic power. Nkosi (1967) argues that low wages for blacks (who constitute over 70% of the population of South Africa) place inherent limits on the domestic consumer market and that South Africa is now in the classic imperialist position of the manufacturing country seeking outlets for its capitalist goods.

This view is also held by the African National Congress of South Africa (ANC) and the South African Communist Party (SACP), which view South Africa as a case of 'colonialism of a special type' where South Africa is characterized as possessing all the features of an advanced capitalist country with an insatiable need to expand beyond national boundaries in search of raw materials and areas of profitable investment. Nyati (1975) for instance examines South African imperialism from the perspective of the need for capital accumulation to expand beyond its national territorial boundaries. Apart from the import of foreign migrant labour, Nyati argues that South Africa also exports capital and administers Namibia as a colony. He observes that state settler capitalism has developed within South Africa, and argues that South African capitalism is, however, still dependent for the instruments of production and strategic inputs and that most of its resources are still owned by Northern Atlantic countries. This, according to Nyati, means that South African imperialism is a sub-imperialism whose role is to sustain North

Atlantic capitalism. This sub-imperialist thesis has, however, been criticized.

Yash Tandon (1977), for example, has attacked it, arguing that there is no historical evidence that finance capital indigenous to South Africa ever arose. For Tandon, what on the surface appears to be South African capital, is, in essence, a fraction of international finance capital, even though there has emerged in South Africa a local *petit-bourgeoisie* with local interests.

His assertions concur with the observation of Nabudere (1979), who has argued that in South Africa the main contradiction is between imperialism and the black oppressed masses and that the white bourgeoisie act as agents for imperialism. Nabudere, in criticizing the Trotskyist theory of the dominance of national capital over imperialism, offers a leftist position which does not conform to the reality of the South African situation, as our analysis will substantiate. South Africa is not simply an agent of finance capital, as he argues, but is itself deeply involved in the criss-cross of imperialist relations which give it its key position. The flaw in the analyses of Tandon and Nabudere is that it sidesteps the urgent issues of praxis. In the anti-Amin struggle in Uganda, for instance, it was this position which led to wrong tactics being pursued by revolutionaries who saw the struggle only from an international perspective of fighting imperialism and overlooked imperialism's concretized form in the political economy of Uganda.

Samir Amin (1977) has shown correctly the two tendencies of capitalism. In surveying changes in the international division of labour, Amin argues that South Africa represents a backward form of capitalism. It depicts 'the hideous picture of what the world imperialist system would increasingly be if it continued to develop according to its own logic'. According to Amin, the division of the world imperialist system between dominant imperialist centres and dominated peripheries has led to the overdevelopment of the tertiary sector of the world economy and its concentration at the centres of the system. This is made possible by super-exploitation in the periphery of the primary sector. For Amin, therefore, South African capital has largely been forced by the political hegemony of the local bourgeoisie to establish an integrated auto-centred structure, and not an externally oriented structure as in the Third World. It is in this light that Amin concludes by posing this question:

> Having gone from subjection to foreign capital to alliance with it, cannot the state become stronger and open the way to an autonomous capitalist development? Autonomous (not autarkic) capitalism, integrated into a network of interdependence (no longer qualitatively asymmetrical dependence) even if it is unequal interdependence?

Without doubt, capitalist investment in the South African formation has been a fact running through the whole historical phase of capitalist development up to the present when United States finance capital abounds. Ann and Neva Seidman (1977) in their study on multinationals and the South African state have shown in detail the links and interrelations between South African capital with finance capital, showing conclusively the relative autonomy of South African capital.

South Africa serves not only as a workshop for several monopoly corporations who have transferred production from the high-cost centres of the European and

American base to the low-cost South African sector but has also built its own technological capacity.

Another study, by Duncan Innes (1984), has also shown conclusively the nature of South African capital, particularly as represented by the Anglo American Corporation group, which is by far the biggest monopoly maintaining its leadership in all sectors of the South African economy. The group, though formally based in South Africa, is in content based on the world system of imperialism. Although 56% of Anglo's shares are held locally to the extent that the Oppenheimer family who control the corporation are local, their share is intertwined with considerable British and US finance capital.

Anglo's dominance over the South African economy is best shown by the fact that her overall assets in 1974, for instance, were estimated at $US7.4 billion, accounting for more than a quarter of South Africa's entire GDP. It produced a quarter of South Africa's coal and a quarter of its uranium, and controlled a sizeable portion of its manufacturing. In 1976, for instance, the Anglo group of companies held top positions in every one of South Africa's economic sectors. In mining, the top five companies were all Anglo companies; in manufacturing, Anglo either controlled or held a substantial minority shares in five of the top ten industrial concerns (such as SA Breweries, and AE & CI) and, to extend the list, in twelve of the top thirty. Furthermore, five Anglo companies were among the top ten industrial companies in terms of turnovers and eight among the top fifteen in terms of market capitalization value.

As far as finance is concerned, Anglo had interests in seven of the country's top twenty banks, owned one of the top three life assurers in the country, and had an interest in the country's largest short-term insurers. Anglo's overall financial power in the South African economy can also be demonstrated by the fact that, in 1976, the group not only controlled the country's top three market leaders (De Beers, Anglo American Corporation and AMGOLD), it actually controlled ten of the top fifteen. Altogether the group either controlled or held an important stake in 31 of the country's top 50 market leaders.

Anglo's monopoly position also extends to the agricultural sector. In addition to its many timber interests and its holding (through the Tongaat group) in large sugar plantations, the Soetvelde Farms, formed in 1969, has been the main subsidiary consolidating and developing the farming interests of the Anglo American Corporation and the De Beers Groups. Two of its subsidiaries, Dawn Orchards and Debshan Ranches, are involved in extensive vegetable and ranching operations.

All of the above trends intensified over the next decade so that by 1985 Anglo held 21.1% of all non-state corporate assets in the economy. This process of concentration and centralization was highlighted by Anglo's takeover of South African Breweries, the South African operation of the Ford Motor Company and, in 1986, the South African subsidiary of Barclays Bank.

Ann and Neva Seidman and Duncan Innes in their studies on South Africa's corporate power have also shown the links with interlocking directorships of the Anglo group, showing that the Anglo American group is itself a multinational institution. Its tentacles include Charter Consolidated, based in London, where it undertakes investments on a world scale, and a spread of holding companies located outside South Africa, such as Mineral and Resources Corporation (MINORCO), Zambia Copper Investments, Anglo American Corporation of Canada (AMCAN) and Australian Anglo American (AUSTRAM). In short, as Ann and Neva Seidman conclude (1977):

> the Anglo American Group is, in itself, a multinational corporation which, although based in South Africa, has investments in several continents through dozens of subsidiaries. At the same time, it has direct links through its board of directors with some of the largest financial multinationals in the world.

This account of the Anglo American Corporation is important because, to a large extent, the study of the Anglo group depicts the nature of South African capital. Anglo's direct links with finance capital explain why the South African state is an imperialist state that serves imperialism in general.

Without doubt, capitalist penetration of the South African social formation has also facilitated the emergence of indigenous Afrikaner capital. The largest of the Afrikaner monopolies, Sanlam, controlled in 1985 assets of over R.58 billion and is the second largest monopoly in South Africa after the Anglo American Corporation, while another Afrikaner monopoly, Rembrandt–Volkskas, ranks fifth amongst the conglomerates which today dominate South African capitalism.

In addition to Afrikaner capital, the state too has taken a leading investment role. Since the formation of the first parastatal corporation ISCOR (Iron and Steel Corporation) in 1928, the state has had an expanded role in the economy, enhanced by the active collaboration of international finance capital. Over the last two decades the so-called public corporations Iscor, Escom (electricity), Sasol (oil from coal), Armscor (weapons development), SATS (transport) and Foskor (chemicals) have expanded to the extent that state corporations dominate in the provision of infrastructural facilities essential for the economic growth of the country – energy, transport and cement, steel, power, armaments and chemicals. By 1985, the top 10 state corporations had assets worth R.91 billion.

In all this, there is ever prevalent a link between South African capital and the world capitalist economy. For the decade 1970–80, public corporation investment requirements were quoted as a minimum of $US12 billion, the major share of which would have to be financed from abroad. This provides the clue to the strong links established between the racist state and large numbers of the TNCs and financial institutions in capitalist countries. For example, the Swiss Banking Corporation arranged a $US25 million loan for ESCOM in January 1978 and, in the same year, ESCOM raised another loan of $US9.4 million from Commerzbank of West Germany. ISCOR raised a total of $US49 million via the Beyerische Vereinsbank in 1978 and the Deutsche Bank of the FRG organized another loan of $US2.2 million for South African Railways and Harbours in June of the same year.

ISCOR is the backbone of South Africa's Iron and Steel Industry, with assets in excess of $US3.5 billion and production capacity of 3 million tons a year. Most of ISCOR's development finance has emanated from international banking consortia.

The United Nations Survey in 1982 identified 181 lending banks from 18 countries which provided a total of 57 loans amounting to $US2,756.8 million. Almost two-thirds of the total loans went towards financing the state-owned corporations and the government budget. ISCOR received $US893.2 million, the Department of Posts and Telegraphs $US28.0 million, the Industrial Development Corporation $US45.8 million, the Strategic Oil Fund (SOF) $US108.5 million, SAR and H (now the South African Transport Services – SATS) received $US370.4 million and the state itself borrowed $US376.8 million.

As can be seen, the interests of imperialism in general and those of the South African state coincide. On the one hand, the South African state ensures that the supply of labour is sustained and easily controlled, so that all attempts to challenge the rights of capitalist exploitation are thwarted. It legislates and intervenes to maintain wages at minimum levels using its vast repressive state machinery. All this facilitates the joint super-exploitation of labour by both the multinational corporations and South African capital. In other words, their huge profits are guaranteed.

For instance, profit rates are estimated at between 20 and 25% in South Africa compared with 12 and 14% in the developing countries generally, and much lower in imperialist countries themselves. This explains why the representatives of imperialism in general (notably Reagan and Thatcher) unashamedly back the South African regime. Profitable capitalist investment is not the only reason for the unholy alliance. Imperialism justifies its support for the South African state and economy on the basis of its struggle against Communism. Hence, South Africa is viewed as of strategic importance. For instance, during the year ending 1978 South African ports provided repair and support facilities for 12,552 ships from capitalist countries. On average, 2,500 vessels sail around the Cape every month.

Investment by foreign capital is distributed over wide sectors. The 1973 South African census on foreign investment revealed that 7.5% of all direct foreign investment was concentrated in mining and quarrying, 43.8% in manufacturing, 14.2% in trade and 26.5% in finance. In total, 92% of all direct investments was placed in those sectors of the economy which accounted for 40% of total gross domestic product foreign investment.

For a long time, Britain was the leading foreign investor in South Africa. In 1972, it accounted for some 66% of all foreign investments in South Africa, with the USA accounting for 19%.

British companies from the 1960s dominated private holdings in the mining sector as a whole, accounting for 60% of all private holdings. British-based transnationals such as Rio Tinto Zinc (RTZ), Consolidated Goldfields, Charter Consolidated and Lonhro dominated the RSA mining economy. Consolidated Goldfields, through its associate Goldfields of South Africa, has derived enormous profits from the group's gold-mining operations, which provide 20% of South African gold output.

In all, there is a mutually supportive relationship between South African capital and the world capitalist economy. In appearance non-South-African companies dominate manufacturing. The American corporations (Ford and Chrysler) supply over 50% of the country's motor vehicles. The provision of capital goods is dominated by foreign companies. In 1975, for instance, South Africa imported almost 50% of machinery needed in the domestic sales. According to Clarke (1980) nearly 80% of private industrial production is either controlled by foreign companies or influenced by them. Singh (1984), quoting a survey conducted in 1974, observes that 74% of manufacturing firms indicated that they were dependent for 90% of their technology on foreign-owned and controlled companies. This phenomenon is neither surprising nor unusual. Bienefeld and Innes (1978) have argued that South African manufacturing is essentially of the import-substitution variety. Its industrial expansion 'continues to be import-oriented' while at the same time its export earnings continue to be limited by the fact that

> her access to the export markets is still largely confined to a restricted range of primary commodities such as paper and board, glass and metal working machinery. Outside this, only the export of diamonds, basic inorganic chemicals, unworked metals, and the least advanced iron and steel products found access to major international markets.

On the basis of such reasoning, Nabudere (1979) concludes that South Africa is basically a raw material producer with very limited markets in manufactures outside its borders and that it cannot therefore have its own colonies in this era of intensified monopolistic competition in multilateral markets. This is an incorrect and naïve view of forms of imperialist hegemony. Nabudere overlooks the simple fact that imperialism accumulates on a world scale. To say that South Africa only 'attract[s] technology through joint ventures, licences and so on' without at first being a leader in research and development of high technology (which allegedly would assure it a monopoly of outside markets – a leverage which South Africa does not have) is to view South Africa as standing opposed to the various social forces in the world capitalist system. Without confusing a concrete relationship with abstract theorizing, South Africa is not a 'semi-colonial economy' (Nabudere) but an independent developed capitalist state which has a definite role in the network of imperialist relations.

The picture in finance is equally one of equal integration into the world economy. Banking in South Africa has traditionally been dominated by British banks. Today, British and American finance are most active in the South African economy. The *African Communist* noted that during the recession that hit the South African economy in the 1970s, US banks were able to mobilize nearly $US2.5 billion to rescue the South African economy. The most significant US banks are the two Rockefeller banks – Chase Manhattan and First National City – and the Bank of America. All have entered into mutual relationships with British banks which have enabled America's capital to be infused in the South African economy. For instance, in 1985, Chase Manhattan bought a 15% interest in Standard Bank of South Africa which enabled Chase Manhattan to have access to the more than 890 branches of Standard Bank in South Africa.

There are also European banks active in South Africa. Although British and American banks prevail to the extent, for instance, that capital loans raised specifically by British banks on the Euro currency markets between 1970 and 1976 amounted to nearly $US1,854.5 million, a Christian Council of South Africa study indicates that other European and Japanese finance houses also continue to finance the apartheid regime. Today, there are almost 30 international banks with subsidiaries in South Africa. A corporate Data Exchange Survey prepared by the

United Nations in 1982 revealed that between 1972 and 1978, no fewer than 328 foreign banks were involved in loans to South Africa.

The survey further revealed that, despite repeated resolutions of the General Assembly adopted by overwhelming majorities, banks and financial institutions from Western countries – particularly the United Kingdom, Switzerland, the Federal Republic of Germany and the United States of America – have provided no less than $US2,756 million in loans to the apartheid regime of South Africa, the parastatal corporations of the regime, and South African companies.

This investment has been the major catalysing factor in the genesis of a relative autonomous South African capital. It is this relative autonomy that South African capital holds that explains the rise of the South African bourgeoisie and the South African state. Such a theoretical framework also assists in understanding the political economy of South Africa, its effort to expand its exports and the evolution of dialogue and the philosophy of the constellation of South African states as a counter to the SADCC.

The South African State and SADCC Countries

In a classic study, H. J. and R. E. Simons (1969) have shown how the rise of the South African state was inextricably linked with the transformation of capitalism into imperialism. The granting of independence to South Africa in 1910 by British imperialism through a dominion link implied the creation of a union of the privileged to exploit, with the support of juridical legality, the black people in South Africa and this was greatly valued by the local white bourgeoisie. At first, the links were mainly with Britain through the 'commonwealth' of nations but, after World War II, which saw the rise of multilateral imperialism under the hegemony of the US, other imperialist countries with their monopolies got involved in the exploitation and oppression of the African people. In other words, the independent Republic of South Africa was constituted as an 'outpost' for general imperialist plunder and has always played this role. In this global role, South Africa facilitates the transfer of value from her neighbours which effectively allows it, at the same time, to benefit from both its own investments and the trickle-down effects that characterize these relationships with the world capitalist economy.

Several studies have been published that highlight the links that bind many of the SADCC countries to South Africa and by extension to the wider framework of relationships in the world economy. South Africa has huge investments in most of the SADCC countries, particularly in mining, from which immense value is realized by South African-based companies. Munslow *et al.* (1984) have shown that about four out of every five dollars of direct private South African investment abroad was in the sterling area.

Further, two-thirds of its non-direct investment and half of its short-term private capital was also in the sterling area. Though their data was too general to highlight the nature of South African investment in the SADCC countries, it did show that South Africa's foreign investments are in the sterling area of which the SADCC countries form a major constituent. A clearer picture will be seen when the country-by-country relationship is discussed below.

On the whole, the picture on trade, for instance, shows dependence vulnerability very clearly. On both the import and export side, most SADCC countries are greatly dependent on South Africa, as Table 1.1 shows. The BLS states (Botswana, Lesotho and Swaziland), as members of the South African Customs Union (SACU), are particularly so.

Table 1.1
SADCC Countries' Trade with RSA [estimates as % of total exports and imports (1984 estimates)]

	Imports	Exports
Botswana	88	8
Lesotho	90	95
Swaziland	90	20
Mozambique	15	5
Zimbabwe	40	20
Malawi	40	–
Zambia	7	–
Tanzania	–	–
Angola	–	–

Source: Munslow *et al.*, ROAPE, Conference Paper, 1984.

Only Tanzania and Angola have no direct commodity transactions with South Africa, and even they would be affected by any disturbance of the links between other SADCC countries and South Africa. A case in point is the possibility (which has been a continuous demand by the OAU and the SADCC countries) of an embargo on trade with South Africa. Without doubt, in the short run, such a policy would adversely affect the SADCC countries while it would have a very marginal effect on the apartheid regime. Only in very few sectors of South Africa's economy would such a boycott have adverse implications. Leys and Tostensen (1982) for instance observe that in 1979 '57% of South Africa's total exports of machinery and equipment were exported to Africa, primarily to Southern Africa. Comparative figures for the categories artificial resins, plastics and rubber were 54%, stone and glassware 48%, transport equipment and aircraft 35%.' Without doubt, a boycott in such fields would temporarily affect South African industry.

The picture on investment is equally discouraging. The dependence relationships seen in such formal terms as equity ownership shares are of course important, but far more important are the various informal mechanisms of real control by way of management, sales and technical contracts and transfer pricing which in Zambia for example continue to devastate the economy despite the formal 51% indigenization fallacy. In this regard South African capital which is continuously strengthened by capital from Europe and America has had to expand to the neighbouring states. Most of South Africa's capital investment has been to the mining sectors – Botswana (diamonds, copper and nickel), Swaziland (iron ore and coal), Zambia (copper and cobalt), Angola (gold, diamonds, iron ore and oil), Zimbabwe (coal, iron ore, chrome, etc.).

Aligned to mining, South African capital investment has also been in manufacturing and such physical infrastructures as railways and hydroelectric plans, railway construction (Angola, Malawi and Swaziland) and hydroelectric power stations (Cabora Bassa in Mozambique and Cunene in Angola). Such control of these key industries by South African capital will without doubt expand long-term possibilities for manipulation of the affected SADCC countries, particularly as such investments are also supported by South African 'aid' in different forms.

Transport and communication networks have also been centred on South Africa, whose transport network continues to be important for most of the SADCC countries' trade outside the African continent. Six of the SADCC nine (Zambia, Zimbabwe, Malawi, Swaziland, Lesotho and Botswana) are landlocked and have to various degrees been dependent on the efficient South African transport network for their export–import routes. This is the reason why, from the very beginning, the SADCC countries identified the problems of transport and communications as the most urgent items on their agenda. This need for a break with the apartheid regime's network is, however, hampered by many factors. The Benguela Railway route has since its reopening in 1978 suffered interruptions and security problems due to the banditry activities of UNITA supported by South Africa. The TANZAM Railway route suffers from a low capacity of the harbour at Dar es Salaam and also from a shortage of locomotives and rolling stock. It is further impaired by poor administration and maintenance, resulting in a key country like Zambia preferring the southern route via South Africa. In 1979, for instance, Zambia moved 452,000 tonnes on the Tazara line as against 637,000 tonnes via South Africa, despite the fact that the nominal maximum freight on Tazara is 2 million tonnes per year. The same is true for other principal rail networks from SADCC countries that end at either Maputo or Beira.

They also suffer from the problem of worn-down tracks, manpower shortage, lack of locomotives and rolling stock, inefficiency and frequent sabotage operations carried out by the Mozambique National Resistance.

The question of labour is even more intriguing. South Africa's mining and agricultural concerns though deeply dependent on cheap labour provided by the SADCC countries also contribute to the economies of these countries. The total number of workers migrating to South Africa annually in recent years has been estimated at almost 600,000.

By 1973, labour migrants constituted about eight out of ten workers on the gold mines, as Tables 1.2 and 1.3 show. The return of these migrants to their home countries, apart from adversely affecting South Africa, would also devastate such economies as those of the BLS states and Mozambique. For the near future, therefore, this symbiotic relationship will have to continue until certain transformations occur in the economies of the SADCC countries. A country-by-country characterization of the unity of these opposites emphasizes this position.

Table 1.2
Migrant Labour in Southern Africa, 1973

Country of Origin	
Malawi	280,000
Mozambique	220,000
Lesotho	210,000
Botswana	60,000
Zambia	40,000
Swaziland	30,000
Destination	
South Africa	580,000
Rhodesia	220,000
Unknown	40,000

Source: Rhodesian Farmer Publication *Development Magazine*, March 1973.

Table 1.3
Origins of Miners in South Africa

Country of Origin	1969 No. Employed	%	1973 No. Employed	%
Malawi	69,748	18.8	106,860	28.27
Mozambique	99,799	26.9	87,129	23.05
Lesotho	64,925	17.5	76,280	20.18
Botswana	14,840	4.0	17,803	4.71
Swaziland	5,194	1.4	4,573	1.21
South Africa	116,494	31.4	85,050	22.50
Total	371,000	100.0	377,695	100.00

Source: *African Research Bulletin*, vol. 11, no. 5.

Namibia

Namibia has been linked to South Africa in a position of dependence since 1919. South Africa continues to deny Namibia self-determination, distorting its economy and undermining its society as a whole.

After World War II, with the important developments in South Africa's mining and manufacturing industries, the coalition of South African and imperialist capital in general deepened the exploitation of Namibia's economic resources. Its mining sector since then has been dominated by South African capital and finance capital from the US whose two biggest mining companies are responsible for over 90% of all minerals produced in Namibia. Consolidated Diamond Mines of South West Africa (CDM) – a subsidiary of De Beer's which holds 98.43% of its shares and a member of the Anglo American group – produces over 90% of diamonds mined in Namibia.

The Tsumeb Corporation is the second major mining corporation in Namibia. It is controlled by US-based multinational corporations in which AMAX owns 29.2% of the shares and Newmont 29.2%, Union Corporation 15.6% and O'kiep Copper Company (itself controlled by Newmont and AMAX) 9.5%. Tsumeb is the largest employer in the country with 4–5,000 employees. Other small mining companies include the South West African Company (SWACO), which is 90% owned by a consortium of Anglo, Charter Consolidated and Goldfields of South Africa (GSSA). The picture in manufacturing and agriculture is equally one of control by South Africa and finance capital. Murray (1974) noted that the result is that from 1946 to 1962 some 31.7% of Namibia's GDP accrued to foreign capital. It is estimated that one-third of the raw wealth currently generated in Namibia is being expatriated. The Odendaal Report urged the rapid economic development of known and determinable resources (Lazar, 1972). The beneficiary of this rapid exploitation is imperialism in general. The lifespan of Namibian mineral deposits is projected at between 15 and 20 years, at the present rate of mining. When they run out, the economy of an independent Namibia will certainly be crippled.

The BLS States: Botswana, Lesotho and Swaziland

Close economic ties which South Africa forged during the last few decades have inevitably undermined the political independence of these countries. In 1965, South Africa's prime minister, H. F. Verwoerd stated: 'I believe that the one thing which really binds our country in international relationships is common interests. So far as these governments [of Botswana, Lesotho and Swaziland] are concerned, their political interests will be dominated by their economic interests.' (Innes, 1984). Botswana's first president, Seretse Khama, openly acknowledged the strength of Verwoerd's position:

> We fully appreciate that it is wholly in our interests to preserve as friendly and neighbourly relations with the Republic of South Africa as possible. Our economic links with the Republic are virtually indissoluble. Economically, we are directly tied to the Republic for communications, for markets, for our beef export, for labour on the mines, and in many other respects.

Botswana's mining complexes are financed largely by South African and American-based multinational companies. De Beers – an associate of Anglo American – owns Orapa Diamond Mine, whose 1972 exports by value were more than $US30 million. Selebi Pikwe copper and nickel mines are operated by Bamangwato Concession in which 85% of shares are held by Botswana Roan Selection Trust in which the American AMAX/RST own 30% and Anglo Chartered another 30%. There are other smaller mines like Moropule in which various multinational companies dominated by Anglo American have interests.

Botswana's manufacturing sector is also foreign-controlled. The Botswana Meat Commission, which provides one-third of government tax revenue, is dominated by South African interests. As regards trade, Tostensen (1981) observed that in the latter half of the 1970s the 'South African share of Botswana's imports steadily increased from slightly more than 75 per cent in 1974 to close to 88 per cent in 1979 (CIF including customs), whereas the trend for exports has been the reverse, albeit somewhat erratic, diminishing from 37.5 per cent in 1974 to below 8 per cent in 1979.'

For Swaziland, South Africa's private sector is so large that it effectively dominates the economy. Swaziland's tourist industry is also completely dominated by South African tourist corporations. Almost all manufactured goods in Swaziland are imported, with South African imports accounting for 90%. As regards finance, over 60% of Swaziland's revenue is derived from its share of the Southern African Customs Union duties. Its import–export trade is dominated by South Africa. The same is true for Lesotho, a dependence relationship *par excellence*.

Mozambique

The links between Mozambique and South Africa have continued to weigh heavily on Mozambique. Over 86,000 Mozambique citizens are contracted to the South African mines and farms where they earn for Mozambique in remittances over $US60 million annually. Since liberation, Mozambique has not enjoyed a single day of peace. South African destabilization coupled with natural disasters have played havoc with the country. Table 1.4 summarizes estimates of direct losses and reduction of income from 1978 to 1983 due to these catastrophes.

The Mozambican economy is so weak and vulnerable that South African destabilization forced Mozambique to sign the Accord of Nkomati in 1984. In 1980, Mozambique's GDP fell by 9 billion meticals which further fell by 11.55 billion meticals in 1981 and 10.77 billion meticals in 1982 respectively. The GDP was given in 1982 as 90.7×10^9 meticals, which fell to 76.5×10^9 meticals in 1983. The value of Mozambique's exports in 1984 was only about half that for 1980. Since Mozambique's export production was highly dependent on imported inputs, a vicious circle has been created. Lacking foreign exchange, due to reduced export earnings which have further been worsened by the deteriorating terms of trade on the world market, Mozambique has been particularly hard hit by the current global economic crisis.

Zimbabwe

South Africa's investment in Zimbabwe is greater than in any other Southern African economy. In 1976 the total South African investment commitment in Zimbabwe was estimated at £200 million, which rose to £478 million in 1979.

Most of the important industrial companies, though operating as separate managerial entities, have direct ties with South African corporations. For instance, no less than five of Zimbabwe's top ten industries are either controlled by, or associated with, South African companies. These include Zimbabwe Breweries, Hippo Valley, Premier Portland Cement, Plate Glass and BAT. The biggest of these companies, Zimbabwe Breweries, also holds the key to the country's food and liquor industries and is the most ambitious hotel developer. Anglo American is responsible for such key industries as steel (ZISCO), coal (Hwange) and nickel (Trojan-Bindura), and has extensive interests in sugar, citrus and timber production.

In regard to trade, preliminary figures for the period August 1980 to March 1981 gave an annualized percentage of 18.4% for exports destined to South Africa, whereas the import figure is still as high as 32%. Zimbabwe is thus still very vulnerable to South Africa's destabilization. Tostensen (1982) correctly observed

Table 1.4
Mozambique: Direct Losses and Reduction of Income from 1978 to 1983

Description of Actions	Meticals* (millions)	US Dollars (millions)
Effects of colonial economy devasted by war, distorted, highly dependent and in recession	n.a.	—
Economic sabotage and abandonment of enterprises, equipment and vehicles of settlers who abandoned the country	n.a.	—
Southern Rhodesian sanctions and aggressions since March 1976 to February 1980	16,479	556
Damages from Limpopo/Nkomati river floods in 1977	1,099	34
Zambezi river flood damages in 1978	2,095	64
Effects of non-declared war by the apartheid regime against People's Republic of Mozambique	131,986	3,795
(1) Reduction of railway-post traffic from 1975 to 1983	(8,460)	(248)
(2) Non-integral fulfilment of the agreements on miners by South Africa from April 1978	(91,289)	(2,647)
(3) Reduction in official number of the Mozambican miners in South Africa	(19,252)	(568)
(4) Direct aggression and those carried out through armed bandits in 1982/3	(12,985)	(333)
Direct damages from drought in the South and Centre of the country in 1982 and 1983	6,200	154
Effects of the increase in oil prices from 1975	34,069	819
Reduction in the export income due to drought deterioration of internal terms of exchange from 1980 to 1982 and actions of bandits armed by the South African regime	3,659	132
Total	195,587	5,554

* Mozambican currency unit.

Source: National Planning Commission, Mozambique *Economic Report*, Maputo, Jan. 1984 and also quoted in B. Munslow et al., 1984.

that 'Zimbabwe may be said to be dependent on South African capital, perhaps not so much as a reflection of equity holdings, but rather by way of technology, management and marketing. . . . It would be a delusion to think that simple nationalisation would significantly reduce vulnerability dependence.'

The present global economic recession has further exacerbated Zimbabwe's problems. In 1982, the Gross Domestic Product declined in real terms by 2%, by 3%

in 1983 and probably a further 2% in 1984. Given a population growth rate of 3.5% p.a., this means that GDP per head has fallen 15% in three years.

From a positive net reserve balance of 68 million Zimbabwean dollars in 1981, Zimbabwe's reserve position declined to negative 162 million Zimbabwean dollars in 1983. This economic malaise was only given relief after the IMF loaned Zimbabwe a standby facility of $ZM160 million in 1983.

Zambia

South African investment in Zambia has been concentrated in its copper mining industry through the Anglo American Corporation. In 1984 Zambia Consolidated Copper Mines (ZCCM) held total assets of K2,538.4 million and employed a labour force of 60,178. Anglo American held 27.3% of the assets while the Zambian Government owned 60.3% through ZIMCO, and the American multinational AMAX held the other 6.9%. Anglo American and AMAX, though minority shareholders, also control the management and technical consultancy in the company, which further increases their corporate control of Zambia's mines.

Like all the other SADCC countries, Zambia continues to suffer badly from the world economic recession. Its GDP per capita fell a dramatic 11.5%, 0.2% and 3.9% in 1979, 1980 and 1981 respectively. Deficit on current account was $US566 million in 1980, $US654 million in 1981 and $US600 million in 1982. At the end of 1983, the total foreign debt outstanding was $US3,752 million, of which $US667 million represented use of IMF resources, $US537 million other debt to international financial institutions, $US1,528 million debt to foreign governments, $US570 million medium-term debt to foreign banks and suppliers, and $US450 million short-term debt to foreign banks. The persistent economic crisis has led to an accumulation of arrears on foreign commercial payments which reached $US738 million in 1983 and was expected to rise to $US788 million in 1984. This economic decline continues with little sign of recovery, deepening Zambia's dependence on imperialism in general and vulnerability to South Africa's pressures.

Malawi

Dr Hastings Banda's regime is an open collaborator with apartheid South Africa. Though South Africa's investment in Malawi is minimal because of Malawi's predominantly agrarian economy, South Africa's links to Malawi are significant. Malawi has received South African assistance in building its new capital at Lilongwe, the construction of a rail link from Malawi to Nacala in Mozambique, plus hotel and tourist resort prospects.

Malawi's total imports from South Africa in 1979 accounted for 41% of her imports while her exports to South Africa were 4%. Though relatively better off than her neighbours, Malawi too has suffered from the global recession. Her GDP per capita fell by 2.2% in 1980, and 3.2% in 1981, but showed a small positive growth in 1982 estimated at 0.4%. Deficit on current account was $US117.6 million in 1982.

Angola

Angola is the only oil producer in the SADCC region. Like Mozambique, it has not enjoyed peace since independence. Estimates of the economic cost of South Africa's military invasion in 1975–76 and her destabilization schemes in the 1976–81 period total a staggering $US7,614 million, or more than twice the GDP of Angola for the year 1980.

According to an UNDRO (Office of the United Nations Disaster Relief Co-Ordination) report published in 1982, almost three-quarters of a million of Angola's people were displaced by the middle of 1981 and thousands were killed or injured. Since most of her savings were used to finance the war, Angola has been experiencing severe economic difficulties. Her total reserves fell from 10,920 million kwanza in 1978 to 3,467 million kwanza in 1981, rising only slightly to 3,667 million kwanza in 1981 and 3,667 million kwanza according to preliminary figures for 1982.

Angola's debt servicing (as per cent of debt payments to exports) increased from 9.5 to 17.4% between 1980 and 1981. Over the same period, Angola's trade deficit went from 3,215 million kwanza to 4,989 million kwanza.

Tanzania

Of all the SADCC countries, Tanzania is the least dependent on South Africa. Despite its utopian socialist outbursts, it is still tied to, and adversely affected by, the global capitalist economy. At 1980 prices, Tanzania's per capita GDP fell by 6.6% and 7.8% in 1981 and 1982 respectively. The deficit on current account was $US350 million in 1979, which rose to $US530 million in 1980 but fell to $US280 million in 1981 but again rose to $US300 million in 1982. Her external debt rose by 12.7% p.a. from 1978 to 1982.

For the SADCC countries, the statistical figures presented above emphasize the deteriorating position of these countries. Tables 1.5, 1.6 and 1.7 further indicate this desperate position.

Table 1.5
SADCC Terms of Trade

(1979 figures given by the World Bank)

Net Barter Terms of Trade (1976=100)

	1960	*1970*	*1979*
Malawi	115	99	85
Mozambique	90	88	75
Tanzania	98	103	102
Zambia	115	227	100
Angola	60	68	113

Income Terms of Trade (1975=100)

Malawi	40	83	112
Mozambique	89	167	32
Tanzania	118	154	104
Zambia	99	238	91
Angola	30	93	102

Source: World Bank, 1983, Munslow, B. *et al.*, 1984.

Table 1.6
SADCC Debt Ratios (Payments on Public Debt as % of Exports of Goods and Services)

	1979	1980	1981
Angola		9.5	17.4
Botswana	1.6	1.7	1.5
Lesotho	0.9	1.4	2.9
Malawi	15.9	18.5	24.5
Swaziland	2.7	3.2	3.6
Tanzania	7.5	8.8	20.30[a]
Zambia	18.0	22.2	24.0
Zimbabwe	1.2	2.6	4.4

[a] Estimate
Source: Bhagavan (1985), p. 87.

Table 1.7
Balance of Payments of SADCC Countries (in current $US million, unless otherwise stated)

	1979	1980	1981	1982	
Angola	–5,430	–1,030	–18,469	–6,200	(in million kwanzas 30=$US 1.0 1982 is preliminary)
Botswana	36.9	–79	–272		
Malawi	9.0	67.2	–76.5	–117.6	
Mozambique		–9,000	–11,550	–10,770	(in million of current meticals; $US1=38MT)
Tanzania	–345	–534	–278		
Zambia	–11	–566	–654	–600	(1982 is provisional)
Zimbabwe	–73.9	–156.7	–439.6	–532.9	(Million of current Zimbabwean dollars)

Lesotho's 1979 balance on current account before debt payments was $US22 million.

Swaziland had a balance of trade on visible exports and imports of –E 221.58 million (when E 1 = $US0.9 approx.) in 1982.

Source: Lloyds Bank group Economic Report on: Botswana (1983); Malawi (1983); Tanzania (1984); Zambia (1983); Zimbabwe (1984).
UNIDO, *Country Economic Report on Mozambique*, 1984.
Bhagavan (1985).
World Bank: *Accelerated development in Sub-Saharan Africa*, 1981 appendix, table 17.
Central Bank of Swaziland, *Quarterly Review*, March 1982.

The World Bank's (IBRD) report for 1983 indicates that the terms of trade of low-income African countries have continued to decline since 1979 and that the terms of trade between manufacturers and non-oil commodities (i.e. SADCC exports, apart from Angola) have moved sharply in favour of manufactures.

An idea of the trend is given by Tanzania's estimated 50% fall in external terms of trade between 1977 and 1982 (in fact mostly since 1979) and 14% nominal decline in Zambia's copper by value between 1979 and 1981. Other countries have of course fared no better. Angola, despite the rising oil prices, has also suffered a fall in terms of trade since 1979. For the seven SADCC countries presented in the above tables, it is clear that countries that kept their deficits fairly stable were already in dire straits. Since 1979, the position of most of the countries has deteriorated, resulting in the rapid growth of the public debt, as Table 1.6, showing the SADCC debt ratios, indicates. This has resulted in a position where much of the export earnings among SADCC countries go to service the debts. Zambia, for instance, in early 1985 was reported to be using over 60% of her foreign exchange earnings to service over $US4 billion external debt. For Mozambique, it has been estimated that its external debt, excluding debts to socialist countries, was in April 1983 estimated at $US3,200 million, or 27 times the estimated value of her exports for the whole of 1983. The ROAPE study observed that 'only if the average interest payable on this debt is less than three and half per cent per annum will current exports cover interest payments quite apart from re-payment of the principal.' The ratio, therefore, must be several hundred per cent. It is perhaps not surprising to find that Mozambique is now joining the IMF and is currently undertaking complex debt rescheduling discussions following the visit to the country by the Paris Club fact-finding mission in May 1984.

The evidence of the data presented above indicates that the position of the SADCC countries as a whole is amongst the worst in the world, in terms of how they are affected by the cumulative effects of the global economic recession. In the next section, we show the possibilities that the crisis brings to the region in general.

Dependence, Transformation and Regional Cooperation

South African Response to the SADCC Challenge

The establishment of the SADCC no doubt poses a great challenge to South Africa. This threat induced policies from both South Africa and the world imperialist circles headed by the United States that have attempted to thwart the SADCC's drive to economic integration. From the outset, South Africa proclaimed the notion of the Constellation of South African States (CONSAS) which was intended to promote interregional economic cooperation with respect to trade, transport, energy, investment and manpower.

Breytenbach (1980) has noted that Prime Minister P. W. Botha has proclaimed that 'the constellation of states does not primarily denote a formal organisation but rather a grouping of states with common interests and developing mutual relationships and between which a clear desire to extend areas of co-operation exists.' (1980, pp. 13–16). Breytenbach further observes that although conceived

'to exclude a satellite relationship among any of the constitutents', the explicit reference to the customs union, the Rand Monetary Area and SAA, CCUS [forming] the basis for further co-operation, shows that the intention was clearly to extend, intensify and solidify the operation of the already existing clientalist regional system, only this time including the 'Bantustans' . . .

as separate entities in the constellation. CONSAS is essentially, therefore, a part of the 'Total Strategy' thesis first used in the 1977 white paper. The strategy is a relatively flexible counter-response by South Africa to a series of crises emanating both from the liberation struggle and the challenges posed by the SADCC. As Adam and Gilomee (1979) observe, it does not in any way represent a decisive shift from capitalism based on national oppression to a capitalism that is aimed at buying off the black petty bourgeoisie. On the contrary, the 'Total Strategy' is an admission by South Africa that the regime has to change due to sharpening pressures, both internal and external. The conditions that gave rise to the 'Total Strategy' are well-known. From the early 1970s, black workers began to organize themselves and formed trade unions. This resurgent demand of black workers to form workers' combines culminated in the Soweto uprising of 1976.

On the other hand, the South African ruling class faced a severe economic recession which further weakened the regime. This situation was worsened by the anti-apartheid policies of the Carter administration in the US which induced a massive outflow of foreign capital that had hitherto played a key role in sustaining the boom of the 1960s. It was also at this time that Frelimo and the MPLA smashed Portuguese colonialism in their territories. The 'Total Strategy' thesis therefore came to represent for South Africa a response to an organic crisis and an attempt to reconstruct the conditions of a stable bourgeois rule.

The strategic shifts in South African policy have had both an internal and an external aspect. Internally, there has been relaxation of certain apartheid rules. Indians and coloureds have now been incorporated in the political process. The new industrial legislation has also conceded the right of Africans to form independent trade unions. However, despite these cosmetic changes, the CONSAS idea has been rejected by all the independent SADCC states. South Africa, however, has not abandoned the CONSAS idea and continues to use both legal and illegal methods to subjugate the SADCC countries.

Examples of South African machinations abound, such as blowing up strategic bridges and cutting the vital Beira–Umtali road and rail link at a spot 54 km from Beira on 28 October 1981. On 13 November 1981, saboteurs destroyed navigational buoys in the Beira port access channel, making the port inaccessible until repairs were completed. Further, South Africa also embarked on punitive economic measures against Zimbabwe in particular, abolishing a trade treaty, withdrawing 24 locomotives from Zimbabwe on loan from South Africa at short notice and thus worsening the problem of exportation of Zimbabwe's maize. South Africa also caused panic in Zimbabwe when it announced that work permits for an estimated 20,000 Zimbabwean Blacks in South Africa would not be renewed.

South Africa has also been pursuing policies aimed at driving a wedge between SADCC members. Here, Malawi has been the weak link, accepting several loans from South Africa. In December 1981 a package of aid was given to Malawi which included a soft loan of R1.2 million for the National Seed Company of Malawi, finance worth R415,000 to help Malawi transport wheat from South Africa and a grant of R417,000 for research on breeding and distribution in the country's fisheries industry. Malawi also remains the only SADCC country with diplomatic relations with South Africa.

Lately, SADCC countries have been forced to sign non-aggression pacts. Armed intervention in a variety of forms has been used to subdue the SADCC countries. Military intervention has varied from outright invasion, as in Angola (1975, 1981), and commando raids (Matola) or outright assassinations of the perceived enemies. A more destabilizing element has been South Africa's use of ethnic mercenaries. In Angola, UNITA rebels are used and a virtual civil war continues to rage in Southern Angola. In Mozambique, Samora Machel's country was forced to sign a non-aggression pact with South Africa. The Nkomati Accord came in the wake of activities of the MNR who since independence have caused immense havoc to the stability of Mozambique. The ANC statement observed that the Accord had been signed in order to

> isolate the ANC throughout South Africa and to compel the independent countries of our region to act as Pretoria's agents in emasculating the ANC . . . to liquidate the armed struggle for the liberation of South Africa . . . to gain new bridgeheads for the Pretoria regime in its efforts to undermine the unity of the Frontline states, destroy the SADCC and replace it with a so-called constellation of states and thus to transform the Independent countries of South Africa into its client states.

Lastly, Swaziland has for several years been guided in her relations with South Africa by a 'secret' accord.

Whatever the outcome of military adventures such as Matola (1981), hot pursuits of guerrilla forces, destruction of physical infrastructure, assassinations (Abraham Tito, Joe Quabi, Ruth First), massacres (Kassinga, Angola, May 1978), invasion and financing of insurgents MNR (Mozambique), UNITA (Angola), LLA (Lesotho), Matebeleland rebels (Zimbabwe), Mushala gang (Zambia) and so on, all these measures and the facility with which they are implemented relate to the economic vulnerability of these countries.

South African destabilization manoeuvres are further supported by imperialism in general and in particular by the Reagan administration, which has further strengthened South Africa's intransigence to global demands by progressive mankind. The Reagan administration offers token support to SADCC countries while continuing to strengthen its support of the apartheid regime. During fiscal year 1984, the Reagan administration for instance requested $75 million in economic assistance for Zimbabwe, $10 million for Lesotho, $8 million for Tanzania, $20 million for Zambia, $8 million for Swaziland, $10 million for Malawi and another $10 million for the South Africa Regional programme. It also pledged approximately $180 million to the SADCC and declared US willingness to respond to the legitimate security concerns of Angola and Mozambique. At the same time, the administration facilitated a $1.1 billion IMF loan to South Africa, eased export–import bank loan guarantee restrictions for US corporations operating in South Africa, relaxed trade restrictions on US export sales to the South African military and police and failed to apply pressure on South Africa to stop its aggressive attacks on neighbouring states. Such imperialist schemes clad in the theory of 'constructive engagement' can be easily explained. Deborar Toler (1982) observes correctly that the logic of these contradictory policy initiatives carried out under the rubric of 'constructive engagement' is within the bounds of expansionist capitalist prescription. An expansionist capitalism calls upon the US to use its power to guarantee access to raw materials for its industrial and military plants, access to export markets for the products and particularly to promote favourable climates for US private investment in foreign lands.

Constructive engagement is a more subtle policy of the blatantly imperialistic policies of the US right wing aimed at thwarting the liberatory upsurge threatening South Africa and Namibia and the Southern Africa region in general; bolstering South Africa as an ally in the imperialist plunder of the region, thus ensuring that the independent African states' attempt to break their dependency and socialize their economies is thwarted. This policy further ensures that any severance of capitalist trade and investment will lead to severe economic dislocations and political instability in the whole region.

This combined imperialist assault on the SADCC has raised questions about the efficacy of the SADCC idea. Fears about a danger of new dependency relationships developing have been raised, particularly when the investment pattern is analysed.

The Danger of New Dependencies

The Lusaka Declaration states that the SADCC 'must aim at the reduction of economic dependence not only on the Republic of South Africa but also on any single external state or group of states'. As of now, the SADCC's preoccupation with South Africa leaves an entire range of unresolved issues with imperialism in general. There is no explicit statement on the measures that will be taken to mitigate the effects of external dependence. At present, the SADCC cannot generate investment finance from its own sources and is totally dependent on external financing. An illustrative point is in the transport and communication sector, where at the Maputo pledging forum, $US650 million out of $US1.9 billion requested was pledged.

Transport and communication is often favoured by imperialist countries because it does not disturb the usual roles assigned to client states. On the contrary, it satisfies donor countries' commercial interests. Donor countries will ensure delivery of their own manufactures of locomotives, rolling stock, trucks, electronic equipment and, not least, consultancy services, which are imported cost elements. The more disturbing fact in relation to the SADCC is that the projects that so far have been chosen tend to consolidate existing physical infrastructural networks that continue to serve the import–export trade, the sort of relationships that were established during colonial times to link mining and commercial agriculture of SADCC countries to the world market rather than to internal markets. So far, donors have not provided finance to projects that serve internal markets.

Of interest is the United States' participation whose interest in the SADCC to a great extent serves as an alibi to cover up its relationship with South Africa which it supports both politically and economically. At the Maputo Conference, the US pledged $50 million. The US approach is to favour a bilateral, instead of a multilateral, approach to aid. Hence it favours a selective country strategy in favour of what it views are friendly governments. At present, Zimbabwe appears to be the most favoured recipient. For instance, of $139.5 million bilateral development aid during fiscal year 1983 to individual SADCC states (minus Angola and Mozambique), $75 million went to Zimbabwe. Zimbabwe as a market for commodities and investment is no stranger to the US private sector, and the lifting of sanctions resurrected expanded interest among US firms. US aid programmes are, however, not designed to promote socialism. They are explicitly geared to strengthening the role of indigenous private sectors and to facilitate US investment.

What comes out clearly is that the ownership and control of key sectors in the SADCC are still integrated vertically with corresponding sectors in imperialist countries resulting in the fragmentation of national economies. It is for this reason that Clive Thomas (1975) points out that *laissez-faire* integration schemes have often resulted in an increase in dependence as the large multinational corporations in the regions reap most of the benefits of integration at the expense of existing or potential indigenous enterprises.

Judgement on the success of the SADCC will take some time; its new institutional structures must be allowed to operate long enough to make an impact. None the less it seems that for the SADCC to succeed in reducing dependence, it should adopt regional measures to regulate foreign investment and the transfer of technology, including the designation of certain sectors of the economy in which foreign participation will be limited or totally excluded. This is important because, firstly, it will otherwise be impossible for the SADCC to exercise effective regional regulation over economic activity and, secondly, transnational corporations as usual will try to foster nationalistic influences by playing off member countries against each other in competing for the benefits of investment.

Dependence, Transformation and Regional Cooperation

What grounds are there for assuming that the SADCC will succeed in a way that other regional integrative efforts have not? It is generally acknowledged that economic cooperation does not by any means automatically contribute to the gaining of economic independence. Under certain conditions, it may even favour an increase or stabilization of dependence on imperialism.

Finance capital is generally interested to benefit from the liberalization of intra-African trade, for after all it will utilize the expanded markets provided by such groupings. An analysis of subregional economic groupings in Africa that are extensively influenced by imperialist interests shows clearly that the imperialist countries reap greater benefits from the measures of liberalization in the field of intra-trade or from common market investments. This was most true for instance of the now defunct East African Community.

The possibility of the SADCC falling into this trap is there. Two theoretical positions have been advanced in the literature. The first position recognizes the high level of active hostility to South Africa of all the nine SADCC members and argues that all the nine countries have an immediate interest in breaking with South Africa as soon as possible and that the problems of the SADCC thus consist merely of finding sufficient funds to finance various national development projects that will delink these countries from South African corporate power. The second position asserts that most of the SADCC states are ruled by petit bourgeois elements who are inherently pro-capitalist and hence have no real interest in breaking with South African capitalism. This viewpoint therefore argues that the SADCC will inevitably be doomed, and the pro-capitalist elements in power in these countries will inevitably betray the SADCC objectives. In both viewpoints, an implicit assumption is that the SADCC is not the answer to the problems that affect the region. One reason for uncertainty has been summarized by Leys and Tostensen (1984) who have observed that reducing dependence on 'big brother' is only one of the SADCC's objectives. The more conservative regimes see advantages in the SADCC quite distinct from their relationship to South Africa. They are more interested in the specific projects in which they see an economic advantage. Whether such projects reduce their dependence on South Africa is, to them, not so important.

There are clear economic and political differences which in the long run will no doubt engender conflict. The SADCC countries, for instance, are basically heterogeneous. Member states differ in their political orientations and styles which, to a large extent, is a reflection of their relationship to the world economy. Angola and Mozambique espouse a socialist ideology and are governed by Marxist–Leninist parties. Zimbabwe, Tanzania and Zambia espouse socialist rhetoric but are capitalist in content. The BLS states are dominated by different shades of 'free enterprise' under South African hegemony.

A further factor is that some countries are more favoured in terms of resource endowment, market size, geo-political location and so on than others and so will inevitably have an advantage over others. Zimbabwe in particular is relatively well-endowed with a large industrial base.

It is clear therefore that for the SADCC countries, as progress is made and the areas of cooperation multiply both in depth and breadth, requiring a greater degree of harmonization of external and internal policies, the possibility of open conflict will arise. The historical role of finance capital to divide and rule will come into play with the expanded SADCC programme of industrial cooperation in which some countries will be willing to give more concessions to external capital than others. In the same vein, if intraregional trade is to be expanded, policy issues related to tariffs and quotas will be raised. In this respect too, it will be necessary to harmonize the fiscal and credit policies to promote joint ventures in productive sectors. All this will be difficult to reconcile. It is at this point that the complexity of negotiation will increase and differences in approach to the private sector will manifest. At the moment, as Davies and O'Meara (1984) note, the SADCC cannot succeed in achieving its strategic objectives if it becomes merely another project financing body, but only if it defines a long-term strategy and tactics capable of producing the types of restructuring envisaged in SADCC policy documents, namely: restructuring of internal economic relations of each of its nine member states; restructuring of economic relations between the nine; and restructuring of relations between the nine and the world economy. Each of these spheres involves struggle, on which the efficacy of the SADCC idea will depend.

Global experience shows that the major instrument of social transformation is the state. The process of transformation in countries such as North Korea and Albania occurred almost entirely within the confines of the nation-state because it is on this level that popular support can be mobilized. Therefore, it follows that, given the central importance of the state, regional cooperation can only play a supportive role, namely, that regional cooperation can assist in promoting regulated trade, efficient transport and, to some degree, industrial specialization. Clive Thomas (1975) has argued that, with the proper strategy of socialist transformation, even the smallest and most dependent countries can industrialize. They do not have to depend on regional integration to develop.

Obviously, the successes and failures of the SADCC can only be viewed in the long term. The current political differences will no doubt sharpen as finance capital cajoles with them. Should the weaknesses of the SADCC prove too great, the SADCC will, like the EAC, either wither away or continue to exist as a regional outpost for imperialism in general. As of now, the SADCC has certainly made a slow but steady beginning and it can only be hoped that the unity so far shown can grow in depth and breadth to include all the people in the region in the struggle against dependence and underdevelopment.

2 The Manufacturing Sector in the East and Southern African Subregion, with Emphasis on the SADCC

Daniel B. Ndlela

A Theoretical Basis for the Development of the Manufacturing Sector in the SADCC

In broad terms the theoretical basis of regional integration in the subregion, represented by the SADCC and the Preferential Trade Area (PTA), results from the search for the practical solution of the subregion's political, economic and social problems, all of which are closely linked with the historical roots of the development of imperialism in Southern Africa. The accumulation processes in the region have been historically structured in a manner that favours world imperialism in general and South Africa in particular, which acts as a sub-metropolitan state in the region.[1]

It is often suggested that what is needed in the co-operative effort of the developing countries is the establishment of a set of institutions which facilitate the division of labour between a group of countries at the same level of development. Institutions such as transport and communications, credit facilities and monetary arrangements would be adapted to the pattern of exchange of goods and services in the new forms of the division of labour. While such institutions are generally welcome, as a regional organization the SADCC sees itself merely as a cooperative agency with high regard for the national sovereignty of its members. Thus any form of supranational body is seen as anathema to national sovereignty. As will be seen below, while preservation of national and economic sovereignty is an indisputable demand, it should not be synonymous with a weak and uncoordinated decision-making which weakens the regional organization. On the other hand, regional cooperation through the PTA preferred a relatively strong secretariat which acts like a supranational body, but there is no sign that it does or will in future interfere with the national sovereignty of member states.

Each country, depending on its size, income level and the decisions it makes regarding economies of scale, will determine its own degree of participation in the regional division of labour. Other factors, such as the available natural resources and the levels of skills and technology, may determine the strategy each country follows. Non-economic factors, too, such as the political will and the ensuing political structure and the level of administrative skills, often play a more important role than is recognized.

The particular constellation of interests and willingness to integrate will itself be the result of the economic, social and political history of the countries forming the respective integration zone. In addition there may be complementarities or conflicts between integrating countries and the world division of labour. This is particularly true of the SADCC industrialization strategy, whose appropriateness seems to depend on regional class interests, policy options, raw material availability and the controversial role of South Africa and the converging interests of the Western capitalist world.

Also paramount in the SADCC has been the need to implement the objective of equitable distribution between participating countries. One important interpretation of the economic rationale of the goal of the 'creation of operational and equitable regional integration'[2] is that it is meant to protect the least-developed member states, who may actually, both in the short and long term, pay more for imports from the more developed countries of the subregion than for imports from industrialized countries. The regional division of labour may therefore have to be accompanied by specific policies to assist the least developed members of the group. Regional specialization in certain lines of production may help to distribute the benefits of regional integration. This is something at present lacking in the SADCC. There exists only a loose arrangement in which the member states do not set themselves binding operational targets to be followed, but rely on individual country choice in decision-making.

One can argue that the SADCC needs to be clearer about its objectives and social and political relations before it can properly attend to its methods. In its first five years of existence the SADCC's policies seem to have been arrived at on an *ad hoc* basis, a feature that is now recognized in some official pronouncements by the Executive Secretary. It has recently been stated that the SADCC has begun to formulate medium and long term plans which 'would enable the region to move away from *ad hoc* planning to a more sustained and long-term approach'.[3]

Another important question is – how does the SADCC operate as a regional organization coming into being during this particular conjuncture of an international division of labour shaped by world imperialism? At present both the reduction of dependence and the creation of more equitable regional integration seem to be realized through a major involvement of private commercial and institutional agencies, mainly from Western donor countries.

It may be argued that it is not the mere reduction of direct dependence on South Africa, by whatever means, that is important. Rather it is the process of accumulation adopted in the reduction of dependence that will decisively shape the region's industrialization strategy. At present there is very little indication, if any, of an industrialization strategy that points to particular forms of accumulation. In the narrow sense, whether strategies adopted will be import substitution, export-oriented, resource-based or any mixture of them, for the SADCC region it will be crucial to identify existing and potential opportunities for the manufacturing industry that will be based on well-defined processes or modes of accumulation. An industrialization strategy that seems to squeeze the maximum benefits from international flows might be meaningful in the short term, if only in terms of sparing local resources that are already overstretched in the balance of payments, debt-servicing and sustaining local social and economic infrastructures. But the failure to sustain minimum programmes using indigenous modes of accumulation renders the group members weak, both individually and collectively.

The role of the state and other social factors in the development effort have not yet evolved to a point where they favour the development of a genuinely collective, self-reliant economic and social base that is designed to reduce dependence on imperialism in general and the South African sub-metropolitan state in particular. Indeed some SADCC projects include 'in a few cases offers from South Africa, which will be accepted in several states if they are financially more advantageous, despite being politically disagreeable' (Hanlon, 1985).

In a narrow sense the SADCC's reduction of dependence envisages an improvement in the region's under-utilized manufacturing capacities for basic consumer goods and intermediate goods as well as concentrating on supplying those goods that are currently being imported from outside the region, particularly from South Africa. This will be realized through increased cooperation and regional division of labour, especially in the region's manufacturing sector, which is the most dynamic part of productive forces.

However, for this reduction of dependence to be realized without being eroded by imperialism in general and South Africa in particular, it should be understood in the wider sense, i.e. as 'a radical change in the historical patterns of accumulation in the Southern African region' which is 'clearly the *sine qua non* for the implementation of any development programme capable of satisfying the needs of the masses of the region' (Davies and O'Meara, 1983).

The conditions for the transformation of the region's economies will not only depend on the forces taking place at the regional level but also on the specific conditions for achieving transformation and the role of the state in the individual member countries, as well as on their respective roles in the international division of labour. At present SADCC member states range from a mainly labour-exporting economy (Lesotho), to Mozambique, whose major foreign exchange earnings derive from port and rail charges, to single commodity exporters (Angola, Botswana and Zambia), to those economies in which a single commodity accounts for over one-third of total exports (Malawi, tobacco; Swaziland, sugar; and Tanzania, coffee), and to Zimbabwe with a more diversified economy, with manufacturing accounting for 26 per cent of GDP in 1981 (Thompson, 1985). This diversity is crucial in the planning priorities of each country with respect to the regional industrial programme.

The present noticeable absence of well-formulated strategies and plans for industrialization in each of the SADCC countries will only contribute to the difficulties of formulating a regional industrial strategy. This confusion is at least apparent in the *Economist Intelligence Unit* paper:

> The strength of SADCC is that it is the industry ministers meeting together who voluntarily set a regional industry strategy. They are not bound by policy, but they can do the swaps needed to ensure that every country gets some industry, as they will know what other countries' plans are so that if two decide to go ahead to build the same industry at least they cannot expect to export to each other (Hanlon, 1985, p. 38).

It is clear from this observation that a sound theoretical basis for regional development cannot depend on *ad hoc* 'swaps' of projects at the SADCC regional meetings, without relying on policy to guide the long-term and medium-term strategies of the region. The main advantages of such a system are its flexibility and economic handling of the designated sectors by the coordinating country. Its potential weakness is that the sectors may develop at varying speeds and levels of complexity and possibly in overlapping or even contradictory directions. The question is, can SADCC afford a loose form of transformation of its economies in the face of the present international division of labour and the particularly threatening position of South Africa in the region?

At its inception SADCC defined its principal strategic objective as being to reduce economic dependence on, but not exclusively, South Africa. In order to achieve its main objective, three levels of transformation can be discerned: first, a transformation at the level of the economies of each of the individual member states; second, a transformation in the internal relationships between SADCC member states; and third, a transformation in the relationship between the nine states as a group and the outside world.

A critical factor in the transformation at the level of each member state and in the reduction of all forms of external dependence for the group lies in the nature of the region's industrial cooperation programme, particularly its manufacturing sector. There is, however, very little indication of the first and second transformations referred to above having taken place. The region's production structures still reflect the colonial forms of dependence of these economies on the Western capitalist countries and for some states this includes continued dependence on South Africa. The first of these transformations, i.e. a transformation at the level of the economies of each of the SADCC states, would require room to manoeuvre as far as economic policy is concerned. The individual member states would require an ability to respond to disruptions in sources of supply caused by international disruptions, including recessions, and more particularly the disruptive activities of South Africa. Such an ability would inevitably require the setting up of some industries with forward and backward links, which is usually not an option for typical colonies or neo-colonial set-ups.

An industrial strategy for SADCC cannot be built on a loose cooperative arrangement in which there is no consideration of moves towards effective integrative mechanisms such as deepening the region's division of labour through specialization. Even on a purely economic rationale, which is obviously a very narrow basis for regional integration, economies of scale can be gained in such production lines as chemical plants, iron and steel, and pulp and paper plants.

The third transformation does not only seem to be occurring but is becoming a measure of success for SADCC programmes. It would be no exaggeration to say that this kind of transformation is not based on individual member countries' internal plans for the creation of self-reliant production structures that stand to benefit the region collectively. Rather, it tends towards collective dependence on Western economies, albeit with some disengagement from direct links with the South African economy.

In order to bring about the three transformations, SADCC launched a multilateral and multi-sectoral development programme, concentrating on infrastructural development, particularly the transport sector and food security. The SADCC's action programme also identified a number of other strategic areas in which activities for economic development could be undertaken on a regional basis.

A key variable in any transformation of the SADCC will be what happens to the region's manufacturing sector. Issues of dependence, or regional collective self-reliance, will depend on whether or not the integration enhances the regional divisions of labour in the area of commodity production or only certain aspects of economic and social infrastructure that are meant to attract and benefit extra-regional interests.

Both the institutional arrangements and the decision-making procedure of the SADCC, as enshrined in its founding concept, are co-ordinated regional development. Policy-making is located in the regional political forums, in which decisions are taken by national representatives by consensus. As shown above, the SADCC does not have a supranational body where responsibility for the execution of its programmes falls. This is the function of the member states acting on behalf of the SADCC as a whole in accordance with the division of sectoral responsibilities. The chief function of the national bureaucracies is to co-ordinate and enhance those aspects of national development efforts to which regional cooperation is beneficial, and to mobilize the resources with which to perform the co-ordinating function. The initiation and implementation of projects and programmes, including cooperation with SADCC member states and extra-regional partners, is a national responsibility.

The sectoral responsibility of industry was allocated to Tanzania. The latter became the coordinator of SADCC's manufacturing programmes, including the responsibility to establish consultative machinery with other governments and the procurement of appropriate technical expertise. A SADCC Industrial Development Unit (IDU) was established within Tanzania's Ministry of Industry and Trade. The role of the IDU lies in the coordination and promotion of investment in industrial projects. But in practice once projects have been selected and foreign investors have been identified, negotiations for project implementation become the responsibility of the country concerned and the foreign firm and foreign country.

The Structure and Potential of the Manufacturing Sector in the SADCC

Some Comparative Features

SADCC's regional share of manufacturing value added in GDP in 1980 was 12%, which was somewhat above the World Bank average for sub-Saharan Africa (8%) and low-income countries (10%), though well below the averages of middle-income oil importers and the newly industrializing countries (23 and 24% respectively).[4]

The region's MVA of about $US3.1 billion in 1980 was one-sixth that of South Africa. The region's per capita MVA was a mere $US55, a small fraction of South Africa's (9%). This low level of the development of the region is, however, in sharp contrast to the fairly well-endowed and diverse resources shown in Table 2.5, at the end of this chapter. Given this wide diversity in natural resources, a large population (of more than 60 million) and a large geographical area (49 million km), the fundamental obstacles to industrial development seem to be more historical than environmental.

Some Structural Features of the Manufacturing Sector

SADCC member states are very dissimilar in terms of size, economic structures, potential and level of development, and in economic and social philosophies. The differences are even more glaring when the region's distribution of manufacturing activity is considered. In 1981 Zambia and Zimbabwe, the most industrialized of the SADCC countries, contributed nearly two-thirds of the regional MVA, which is well above their 36% of regional GDP and their 21% of the regional population. Conversely, the remaining seven countries, with 60% of the region's GDP and nearly 80% of the population, contributed only 36% of regional MVA.

The countries with the three largest manufacturing sectors in the region are Zimbabwe, Zambia and Tanzania, which together with Malawi contributed 82% of regional MVA in 1980 at current prices. The production structure in these countries is mainly geared to the domestic market, although manufactured exports also play an important role, especially in Zimbabwe and Zambia. Of the four, Malawi has the smallest and least diversified manufacturing sector. The light industry sector (food, beverages and tobacco) contributed as much as 53% of total MVA. This sector is also high in Tanzania (food – 36%, textile and clothing – 19%, leather and footwear – 5%). Machinery production accounts for only 7%. In both Zambia and Zimbabwe the production structure is much more diversified than in other countries of the region and branches are more evenly balanced.

The heavy industry subsectors are to be found in Zambia and Zimbabwe. Zambia is relatively advanced in clothing (11%), non-basic chemical products (9%), rubber (6%) and fabricated metal products (10%).

Zimbabwe has the most diversified structure of production in the group, ranging from light industry subsectors to heavy metals and metal goods. In 1980, of total MVA, food products and beverages accounted for 19.2%, tobacco, textiles, clothing and footwear 23.4%, and iron and steel, non-ferrous metals, metal products excluding machinery, electrical machinery and transport equipment 31%. Though Zimbabwe's production of capital goods sector is mainly geared to the domestic market, manufactured exports for the region have always played an important part. In 1981 Zimbabwe's exports of capital goods represented only 11.5% of her total exports of manufactured products to the region. From a regional point of view it is possible that Zimbabwe could specialize in the production of capital goods, including machinery and transport equipment. The production of capital goods was emphasized in 1984 by SADCC, with specific reference to machine tools, irrigation pumps, mining equipment, and railway wagons, rolling stock and other rail equipment.

The second group of countries, contributing 4% of regional MVA in 1981, comprises Botswana, Lesotho and Swaziland, all of which are small countries adjacent to (and, in Lesotho's case, surrounded by) South Africa. In each case the manufacturing sector is so small and fragmented that a number of branches are not represented at all. Their dominant sectors of production are mainly geared to exports and their branch structures reflect the products of their larger exporting plants: meat in Botswana (57% in 1975), textile/clothing and furniture in Lesotho (23 and 13% respectively in 1975), food products (canned fruit, meat and sugar), industrial timber, wood pulp, and fertilizer in Swaziland (38, 7, 29 and 9% in 1980). Botswana also manufactures fabricated metal products (11%) and there is a recent growth of textile manufactures, while Lesotho also has printing and non-metallic mineral products (21 and 15%) and a recently established electronics assembly industry.

The third group of countries comprises Angola and Mozambique. These countries have had their economies severely dislocated since the mid 1970s by South Africa's attempts to destabilize them. According to the 1970 breakdown, Angola had a heavy concentration of food products (49%) and textiles (20%). The Mozambican manufacturing sector during the early 1980s, before the renewed disruptions, had fertilizer and soap, tyres, machetes, steel manufactures, hoes and bicycles.

In terms of economic structures the SADCC is characterized by the general lack of complementarities in production and industrial structure among the member countries. This is seen in the sort of horizontal production structures, i.e. similar range of products such as food, textiles, beverages and lack of vertical production structures among the region's branches of production. This factor militates against the regional processing and manufacture of products whose raw material base is readily available, as shown in Table 2.5, at the end of this chapter. Instead, the regional pattern of trade of SADCC reveals a historically determined vertical linkage in production structures between the metropolitan countries and South Africa on the one hand, and SADCC states on the other. The SADCC is, therefore, in the immediate term aiming at replacing historical infrastructures which link all production and marketing in the region to South Africa.

The Supply and Demand for Manufactured Goods

An analysis of the components of supply and demand for manufactured goods, distinguishing the sources of domestic supply (local production and imports) and its disposition (between exports and domestic consumption) is helpful in pointing out the trends and development of the manufacturing sector in the region. Table 2.1 shows that seven SADCC countries are heavily dependent on imports for the satisfaction of manufactured goods. Over $US4,900 million, or nearly 46% of domestic consumption, is met by imports. Between them Zambia and Zimbabwe have an import dependence ranging from 27 to 35%. On the other extreme, Botswana, Lesotho and Swaziland accounted for between 90 and 96% of dependence on imports for the satisfaction of their domestic consumption. It is quite obvious that in order to increase exchange of goods within the SADCC there has to be an increased level of manufacturing in the region.

According to the UNIDO database the structure of imports of manufactured products in the SADCC reveals that metal products, machinery and equipment (ISIC 381–4) accounted for 42% of the region's overall imports in 1980. Ratios of

Table 2.1
Domestic Supply and Disposition of Manufactures of Seven SADCC States
($US million in current prices) for 1980

| | | Supply | | Disposition | |
Country	Dom. Prod.	Imports	Total	Dom. Cons.	Exports
Botswana	180.7	639.6	820.3	709.9	110.4
Lesotho	30.9	413.7	444.6	430.9	13.7
Malawi	363.9	417.6	781.5	692.9	88.6
Swaziland	380.5	477.6	858.1	531.3	326.8
Tanzania	874.4	973.4	1,847.8	1,731.2	116.6
Zambia	2,917.2	892.2	3,809.4	2,528.5	1,280.9
Zimbabwe .	3,702.0	1,122.8	4,824.8	4,199.2	625.5
Total	8,449.6	4,936.9	13,386.5	10,823.9	2,562.5

Source: UNIDO Database. Tables on supply and disposition of manufactures are based on ISIC categories.

Notes: Exchange rates used here that are based on UNIDO's database are: 0.776P; 0.778M; 0.812K; 0.7778E; 8.195Sh.; 0.789K and 0.6437$ per $US for the respective currencies.

imports as a proportion of domestic consumption were 37% for fabricated products and over 85% for non-electrical machinery and transport equipment. The seven SADCC countries in which data was available imported around $US2,240 million of capital goods type of products (ISICs 371, 372, 381–4), representing 47% of these countries' total imports of manufactured products (see Table 2.2). Thus, for Tanzania, Zambia and Zimbabwe, capital goods imports were up to between 43 and 46% of total imports of manufactured goods. Though in terms of value the smaller countries like Botswana, Swaziland, Lesotho and Malawi imported less, this group of products represented important imports for these countries as well.

Though SADCC and the PTA region as a whole are still weak in both metal fabrication and machine building, these capacities are already there in Zimbabwe and Zambia and could represent a crucial nucleus for long-term regional development for self-reliance. The main question is how does the region as an integration grouping respond to the opportunities for supplying this important class of products? Studies of the Zimbabwean capital goods sector indicate the existence of a dynamic resource potential in this sector in the form of the learning processes involved in the development of the skills, especially the engineering skills. Dynamic efficiency is also gained in the production of machinery and equipment, new product designs, new technology processes which find their application in all the other sectors of the economy.[5]

Official SADCC documents state that the selection of SADCC projects should accord with the objectives defined in the Lusaka Declaration of 1980. It is, for instance, recognized that an increase in the capacity of the region's manufacturing sector could be utilized to produce for export within the region, thereby increasing production, employment and export earnings of the productive member states. There are, however, no precise criteria by which to identify what exactly is a

Table 2.2
Supply and Disposition of Manufactures by ISIC Category, 1980
($US million in current prices)

Country	ISIC	Domestic Product	Import	Total	Exports	Domestic Consumption
Botswana	371	—	22.4	22.4	—	22.4
	381	1.3	52.8	54.1	0.3	53.3
	382	12.1	78.7	90.8	1.9	88.9
	383	0.6	39.2	39.8	0.4	39.4
	384	—	78.3	78.3	7.8	70.5
Lesotho	371	—	11.1	11.1	—	11.1
	381	0.4	21.3	21.7	—	21.7
	382	—	16.8	16.8	—	16.8
	383	—	43.9	43.9	0.7	43.2
	384	—	2.1	2.1	0.1	2.0
Malawi	371	—	30.3	30.3	0.5	29.8
	381	—	19.3	19.3	0.1	19.2
	382	—	40.1	40.1	5.8	34.3
	383	—	40.3	40.3	—	40.3
	384	—	67.9	67.9	4.4	63.5
Swaziland	371	—	18.9	18.9	—	18.9
	381	14.8	27.4	42.2	11.9	30.4
	382	2.3	23.5	25.8	0.3	25.5
	383	13.8	15.1	28.9	12.5	16.4
	384	—	60.8	60.8	—	60.4
Tanzania	371	6.4	42.1	48.5	—	48.5
	381	15.2	40.0	55.2	1.2	54.0
	382	—	212.5	212.5	—	212.5
	383	17.2	66.1	83.3	2.7	80.7
	384	—	152.2	152.2	0.2	152.2
Zambia	371	17.5	53.1	70.6	0.1	70.5
	381	136.8	33.8	170.6	0.3	170.3
	382	44.2	191.2	235.4	2.0	233.4
	383	54.5	64.2	118.7	0.7	118.0
	384	36.0	131.9	167.9	1.1	166.8
Zimbabwe	371	396.0	57.3	453.3	187.6	265.6
	381	228.6	17.4	246.0	16.9	229.1
	382	98.0	175.2	273.2	14.5	258.7
	383	99.4	115.2	214.6	7.0	207.6
	384	90.5	222.9	313.4	8.4	305.1

Source: UNIDO Database.

SADCC regional project. In fact the project 'may be purely national both in its location and benefit, for as long as it reduces dependence particularly on the Republic of South Africa, or it may cover two or more member countries resulting in a move towards regional integration.'[6]

It is quite clear that a regional industrialization strategy that has a tendency to make each national economy look internally for the markets of its output does not contribute to a regional harmonization programme. Instead, it would appear that more integration has generally been established with overseas suppliers of hardware and other intermediate inputs than within the SADCC itself. The question is for whose interest is this form of integration? In the *Report of the Workshop on Implementation of SADCC Industrial Projects* it is stated:

> For 55 projects for implementation and 33 projects for study in the sectors of salt, textile and textile chemicals, insecticides and pesticides, wool and mohair, tractors, and farm implements, fertilisers, pulp and paper, cement, electrical distribution and transmission equipment, envisaging foreign exchange assistance of about $US618 million. The commitments are in respect of supplies of capital goods, technology, engineering, lines of credit and other commercial inputs for implementation of core projects relating to fertilisers, pulp and paper, textiles, and salt and for several small industries for farm implements, powerlooms and formulations . . . The workshop . . . was the first of its kind in the SADCC region in providing a forum for investment collaboration and co-operation from commercial and institutional agencies in countries which included Sweden, Australia, India, United Kingdom, France, Italy, West Germany, Romania and from international organisations including EEC, UNIDO, and the Commonwealth Fund for Technical Co-operation (CFTC).[7]

As the nature of the projects and the supply lines from the more developed countries (with the exception of India) shows, there seems to be a bias against the development of capital goods industries. Whilst mention is made of developing capital goods in the region, only one project on *The Expansion of Special Steel and Billet Casting Unit – Zimbabwe* has been identified but not yet found a confirmed funding agency. Other projects under the capital goods subsector are in the manufacture of hand tools, animal-drawn implements and carts in Angola, Botswana, Lesotho, Tanzania, Zambia and Swaziland. This syndrome of 'appropriate technology' and its clearly duplicative effort undermines a meaningful development of the capital goods sector in the region. As will be shown below, a bias against the development of capital goods sector prevents a balanced growth of the internal market and along with the implicit use of capital-intensive techniques, increases dependence of underdeveloped countries both individually and collectively on the importation of specialized machinery and other capital goods from the developed countries.

An absence of specific strategy for the development of the manufacturing sector at the regional level may militate against coordination since many of these countries have a similar economic and social base. Even at the national level, their economic and political structures have not yet evolved into the internal cohesive social structures necessary for effective participation in regional cooperation. The development of this objective precondition, however, would be enhanced by an initial attempt to co-ordinate and learn from each other's national development plans.

The case for iron and steel development and its links with other sectors, particularly the capital goods sector, is discussed below. The importance of the development of this sector justifies the handling of the subject at the subregional level in which the potential of both SADCC and PTA member states is brought under review.

Iron and Steel Production in the East and Southern African Region

Resources and Capacity

It is our view that the existing and potential development of the iron and steel industry and its 'downstream' production industries, the capital goods sector, are crucial for a regional industrial strategy both for the SADCC and the wider East and Southern African region making up the Preferential Trade Area (PTA). If we take the UN ISIC 371 as a proxy for steel, the domestic production figures for seven countries belonging to SADCC (cf. Table 2.2) show that only $US420 million was produced in these countries. This is compared to an import figure of iron and steel products of $US235 million, which shows a surplus production of iron and steel products in the region.

However, there is an acute maldistribution of the production of iron and steel in the region. Zimbabwe accounts for 94%, with Zambia producing 4% and Tanzania 1.5% and the remaining countries (Botswana, Lesotho, Malawi and Swaziland) not producing any steel products.

African leaders in the region have often given high priority to iron and steel production. At the sixth meeting of the Council of Ministers of the Lusaka-based MULPOC, held in Mbabane, Swaziland in February 1983, the following projects were approved:

1. Upgrading and diversification of products from ZISCOSTEEL to meet the present iron and steel requirements of the subregion up to the year 2000.
2. Expansion of existing and development of new electric and arch furnace (EAF) steelmaking plants based on available scrap and sponge iron to be made available within the subregion to meet the crude steel requirements of the subregion up to the year 2000.
3. Construction of direct reduction (DR) plants to produce sponge iron in Angola and Mozambique to meet the subregional demand for sponge up to the year 2000.
4. Integration of EAF steel plants with rolling mills to ironmaking units of the region where demand will have reached a high enough level to justify integration.

As Table 2.3 shows, the region is fairly well endowed with iron ore, and its ferrous content is generally quite high. There are, too, sizeable coal reserves under exploitation in the region (see Table 2.4), although coking coal is found only in Mozambique and Zimbabwe. In addition most countries in the group have considerable hydroelectric potential.

Table 2.3
Iron and Steel Industry Raw Materials

Country	Iron Ore m tons	Fe content in %	Coal m tons	Gas billion cu m	Petroleum m tons	Hydro-electric m watts
Angola	1,220	35.5–40.11	—	62.8	164	11,031
Botswana	—	—	15,200	—	—	—
Ethiopia	12.5	—	—	—	—	12,790
Kenya	42	—	—	—	—	12,274
Madagascar	405	39.1–50	84	—	—	73,059
Malawi	—	—	810	—	—	91
Mauritius	—	—	—	—	—	13
Mozambique	250	30–60	8,000	60	—	10,310
Somalia	180	38	—	—	—	—
Swaziland	477	34–5	977	—	—	—
Tanzania	125	62	1,500	41	—	18,995
Uganda	98	68	—	—	—	16,439
Zambia	306	40–60	90	—	—	3,500
Zimbabwe	3,738	40–69	27,953	—	—	4,566
Total	6,853.5		53,884	163.8	164	163,068

Source: ECA Metal Industry Development Programme paper presented to second meeting of ESASDC Addis Ababa, October 1983, and country sources.

Table 2.4
Coal Reserves in ESASDC Countries

Not under exploitation		Commercial reserves under exploitation	
Country	Quantity million tons	Country	Quantity million tons
Botswana	708	Zimbabwe	22,500
Angola	8	Zambia	20
Ethiopia	10	Tanzania	1,511
		Swaziland	5,150
		Mozambique	700
		Madagascar	50

Notes: ESASDC represents East and Southern African Steel Development Committee.

Source: United Nations ECA/MULPOC/LUSAKA/IV/6, 4 December 1980.

Zimbabwe has particularly large known reserves of iron ore, with very high ferrous content in places and, at the projected rate of exploitation, these should last 35 years. Zimbabwe also has known reserves of coal estimated at 22,000 million tonnes, about 6,500 million tonnes of which are commercially exploitable, over 200 million tonnes of limestone reserves and a good quantity of other fluxing materials. Clay for the production of refractories is also available in Zimbabwe. Coking coal resources amount to 478 million tonnes.

The only existing integrated iron and steel plant in the subregion is the Zimbabwe Iron and Steel Company (ZISCO) at Redcliff in Zimbabwe. ZISCOSTEEL is an integrated producer of semi-finished and finished steel products. Its maximum capacity of one million tonnes is considered to be an overestimate. The best annual production achieved in 1980 was 804,000 tonnes. Of the 1980 output 75% was exported. A recent British Steel Corporation (Overseas Services) Ltd study suggests that hot metal and oxygen supplies constrain current output to a realistically estimated maximum level of 850,000 tonnes.

The other countries in the region (notably Angola, Kenya, Madagascar, Mozambique, Tanzania and Zambia) have in recent years been developing varying projects for the production of primary steel (pig iron) and secondary steel. Angola has a plant with an installed capacity of 30,000 tonnes per year. In addition Angola has plans for a project of crude steel production envisaged to expand from 30,000 to 500,000 tonnes per annum. Kenya envisages installing crude steel production of 300,000 to 500,000 tpa. This capacity will mainly be produced by semi-integrated plants melting scrap in electric furnaces.

Tanzania has an estimated 49 million tonnes of titaniferous iron ore at Liganga and coal reserves in Mchuchuma estimated at about 1,500 million tonnes. Some quantities of limestone and fluorspar have been recorded. Energy supply is, therefore, not a constraint to the exploitation of iron and steelworks in Tanzania.

Uganda's iron ore deposits are mainly of magnetite type in Sukulu mines – Tororo in Eastern Uganda and in Western and Southern Uganda there are substantial deposits of high-grade ores. In addition Uganda has sufficient hydroelectric power, limestone and charcoal for the establishment of an iron and steel industry. As yet there are no studies carried out to determine the existence of sufficient deposits of fluxes and raw materials for the refractory industry.

Kenya's known iron ore deposits are less than 42 million tonnes, and they are generally of very low grade. Other raw materials in support of an iron and steel industry are limestone deposits (8–10 million tonnes), fluorspar (15 million tonnes), silica (1.4 million tonnes) and manganese (443,000 tonnes). Kenya thus faces the problem of importing large amounts of iron ore from the world market. Yet another problem facing Kenya is developing an alternative fuel energy source such as charcoal from eucalyptus trees since metallurgical coal is not available in Kenya.

Zambia has iron ore occurrences all over the country, coal depots and major fluxing and refractory materials. It is one of the few countries in the East and Southern African region with iron and steel production. In 1978 production was slightly over 31.8 million tonnes. The existing plants are foundries based on scrap.

In the second meeting of the Eastern and Southern African Steel Development Committee (ESASDC) a framework for the development of iron and steel industry in Angola and Mozambique was outlined as follows:

1. For Angola short-term measures would involve the rehabilitation and

reactivation of iron ore mines, and the rehabilitation of the existing scrap-based steelworks in Luanda. In the long-term Angola would develop a pelletizing plant project including integration with DR plant and an EAF steelmaking.
2. In the short-term Mozambique proposed a mining project, DRI, EAF steelmaking, continuous casting and rolling mills which would boost their present production capacity from 45,000 tonnes per year to 200,000 tonnes per year by 1986 and to 400,000 tonnes per year by 1990.[8]

Uganda's existing steel plant has an annual capacity of 25,000 tonnes producing bars, rods and sections. The internal steel production depends on imported billets, ingots and local scrap. At present the only alternative to using scrap, which is difficult to collect, is the production of sponge-iron. Uganda has tentative plans for producing sponge-iron from small-scale electro-steel-making. This is based on the assumption that the blast furnace oxygen converter route would be preferable for large-scale production.

Uganda has plans to increase capacity to 100,000 tonnes per year, utilizing local high grade iron ore deposits. There are also plans to begin the expanded programme from 1986, possibly with the local participation of approximately 30% and the remaining share being taken by multinational sources through subregional cooperation programmes under the auspices of the Industrial Development Decade for Africa (IDDA).

Ethiopia's iron and steelworks account for 35% of the output with the remaining 65% feedstock being made up of imported billets, coils and small amounts of bedstead angles. Ethiopia's product range consists of reinforcing bar, fencing wire, bedsprings and bedstead bases and nails. The steelplant is based on scrap. Its rod mill has a rated capacity of 24,000 tonnes per annum and a best performance to date of 18,000 tonnes. It has a wire-drawing capacity of 4,500 tonnes per year.

The Case for 'Downstream' and 'Upstream' Links between Iron and Steel and the Capital Goods Sector

The conventional measures for the domestic market for iron and steel consumption are size of population and per capita income. It is often assumed that at an earlier phase of economic development the share of building and civil engineering construction is high, usually around 40–60% of iron and steel utilization. In the next phase of economic development, this falls to between 20 and 30%. During this phase fabrication and manufacture of transport equipment takes the leading share in the apparent steel consumption, at around 40%. Only in the higher stage of economic development is the major use of steel in the manufacture of machinery and metal products. At this point the engineering industry has begun self-sustaining development on the basis of domestic production for the home market.

The main factor that determines the consumption of steel and flat steel products is the per capita level of the GNP and its development. The population of the East and Southern African subregion is about 170 million. The average GNP per capita of the countries in the region is very low – about $US300–400 in 1981. The situation is further aggravated by the recent declines in GNP figures since 1981, and in some cases since 1980.

Though the population index cannot be minimized in its influence on iron and steel consumption, it does not constitute a central place in the strategy for self-reliance based on the development of the iron and steel industry and the capital goods sector. As will be seen below, the links between the steel industry and the capital goods sector are at the centre of a coordinated development in which a capital goods industry plays a major role.

According to this criterion, Zimbabwe's average of 42 kg per capita consumption of iron and steel is low for a country with a per capita GDP of around $US800. On this basis it is, therefore, assumed that Zimbabwe's economy has yet to move into the rapid industrialization that is accompanied by heavy spending on infrastructural improvements, a trend that has so far been delayed by a number of factors, including the colonial racial discrimination in which the country's majority was left out of the developmental infrastructural improvements, and more recently by world depression and the recent prolonged drought. An upturn in the domestic economy following the end of drought, the international depression and improvement in the country's foreign exchange earnings is expected to lead to higher consumption of steel-intensive infrastructural projects and housing affecting the country's majority of citizens. Iron and steel utilization may be reflected in more production of farm implements such as small-scale agricultural equipment, wire, fence posts, etc.

While eventually leading to more intensive use of iron and steel products, this approach is less geared to a structural transformation of the production system using iron and steel as a 'push' factor. More important is the development of capital goods industry (including intermediate goods) as a 'pull' effect in the end-use of steel production producing internal dynamics in the economic system.

The existence of iron and steel and metallurgical industries in the Eastern and Southern African countries provides 'downstream' industries with a continuous supply of metals needed by the capital goods. As the hub of the engineering industry, capital goods manufacture provides a base for self-sustaining industrialization, and serves as a focal point for the development of technical and managerial skills. It also creates production and design capabilities and improves organizational methods of production.

The engineering core industries for the manufacture of capital goods service both industry and other priority sectors, e.g. agriculture, construction, transport, mining and energy and telecommunications. They are required for the production of building and construction materials, agricultural tools, spare parts, implements and machinery, and other products which are essential for the development of a diverse mix and complex production covering a wide range of sectors in the economic system. The capital goods sector is important in determining the viability of the economic system as a whole, technological change and absorption and displacement of labour. This is because an economy without well-developed metal products, machinery and subsidiary industries cannot produce enough capital goods and thus invest a high proportion of its income, however high its potential saving propensity may be. Such an accumulation path is not only meant for closed economies as is often the case in models of the Feldman–Mahalanobis type. Open and trading economies are vulnerable to the adverse terms of trade resulting from their lack of capacities in the production of capital goods and the associated deficiencies of shortage of skilled manpower, facilities of the learning processes and external factors.

What use can be made of the economic surplus depends on the material structure of the productive system. Even if savings in developing countries are improved to quite substantial levels, there is still the structural inability to convert these savings or economic surplus into investment. This situation results in the usual phenomena of 'conspicuous' consumption, hoarding, capital flights, etc. Thus, the existence of a capital goods sector is crucial for the physical technical aspects, that cannot be replaced by purely financial aspects of savings and investment. If this sector is to be understood as a necessary though not sufficient condition for autonomous industrialization, it should be considered a political issue of the highest order, involving a strategy of 'selective delinking' and the time horizon over which technological autonomy can be achieved. Basic support facilities such as foundry, heat treatment, forging, machine tool shop will be needed for the production of components, spare parts and other products required for the manufacture of capital goods.

The Capital Goods Sector in the Subregion

Zimbabwe

Zimbabwe has the most developed capital goods sector in the SADCC and the PTA subregion. The structure of output of capital goods in Zimbabwe comes under the metals and metal goods group which is Zimbabwe's largest product group in the total manufacturing sector in terms of gross output, net output, number of firms and employment. This is also the most diversified product group in terms of the range of commodities produced, product specifications, product designs and different end-users of the products and processes in the economy. The interlinkages between this group and all other sectors of the economy are probably the most developed and yet the subsector still has the greatest potential for further development of linkages.

The group's products are used as intermediate goods, machinery and equipment by the manufacturing sector itself, agricultural sector, mining, construction, transport, energy and telecommunications. Zimbabwe's capital goods sector provides 'backward integration' for ZISCOSTEEL feedstock as these units use blooms, billets, bars, rods and coils.

Examples of machinery production, machine tools and equipment in Zimbabwe include the production of machinery for agriculture, construction, mining and other areas of activity. The manufacture of railway rolling stock represents a significant import substitution in the production of capital goods.

The metal products, machinery and equipment other than electrical subsector is the largest subsector in metals and metal products group with gross output in 1982 representing 47% of the group's total output, 54% of total net output, 48% of wages and salaries and 51% of employment. Firm activity in this subsector includes the heavy engineering firms involved in design and production of machinery equipment and spares for other industries. There is also a great deal of general jobbing and maintenance activity.

Agricultural implements production includes a wide variety of products including tractor-drawn implements for the large-scale commercial farming sector, irrigation equipment, agricultural boilers for tobacco farmers, coffee processing machines, tobacco curing equipment and implements for the small-scale peasant sector. Zimbabwean firms have built up a reputation for original design in production of agricultural implements and equipment that is suitable to local conditions. Firms in this group have been exporting to neighbouring countries. Most of the steel used in the production of agricultural implements is locally produced. Imported sheet steels are used for the manufacture of specialized parts of implements but this represents a small proportion of the implements both by mass and value.

The electrical machinery and equipment and communications equipment subsector's production includes electrical machinery, industrial electrical goods including geysers, cookers and stoves, communications equipment, and electric cable and wire, which come under capital and intermediate goods.

In 1982 the motor vehicle manufacture and reconditioning subsector accounted for 78% of both total gross output and employment of the transport equipment group. Its major commodity outputs were motor vehicle bodies (61%), trailers for trucks and other vehicles (15%), motor spares and accessories (10%), metal products, machinery and spares (6%), and assembled motor vehicles (5.5%) and caravans (2%). The main activity of the subsector is motor vehicle bodies, which has a growing local content.

The other vehicle and equipment subsector includes the manufacture of railroad equipment, and other transport equipment, especially heavy equipment and machinery coming under the capital goods. There is great scope for growth in this sector for the refurbishment of the railways programme in the region including the electrification programme of the National Railways of Zimbabwe (NRZ).

The Capital Goods Sector in Other Eastern and Southern African Countries

As shown above, domestic production and exports of capital goods in the ESASDC countries, as measured by the three digit classification ISIC 381–4, is insignificant (cf. Table 2.2). Nearly 60% of this production is concentrated in Zimbabwe, about 31% in Zambia, and the rest thinly spread in the remaining five countries. However, judging from the high level of imports and total domestic consumption of the products of the capital goods, of about $US1,949 million, there is scope and potential for the production of this class of products in the region.

Outside of SADCC, Kenya has relatively developed metal engineering workshops and foundries in the region. In a study of the undercapacity utilization of the Kenyan foundries and metal engineering workshops over 90 firms in this sector were interviewed (Coughlin, 1984). The capacity utilization of only 25% for foundries and 34% for metal engineering workshops was found. There were many reasons cited for this undercapacity utilization, including lack of planning of both investments and demand, shortage of material inputs used in production (Ibid, p. 4).

The Kenyan capital goods sector also needs selective investments to improve the scope of the metal production, casting and engineering. It is, however, clear that the availability of resin-and-sand and shell-mould casting and some iron moulds for mass production of non-ferrous castings provide the basis for foundry industry. The largest foundry and workshop in Kenya is the Railway Nairobi Workshop which employs some 2,600 people. But the rest of the foundry and engineering sector facilities are grossly under-utilized. It has about 9% of the centre lathes in the country and 60% of the turret lathes which are designed for mass production (Ibid, p. 13).

The railways workshop has produced 6–10 tonne sugar crusher rollers. However, this is not done on a regular basis because the Kenyan Railways Act does not allow the workshops to engage in commercial production unless specifically directed to do so by the Government. Another thing that inhibits the production of capital goods in Kenya as 'downstream' industries is the proliferation of makes and models. There are too many makes and models of trucks, cars, tractors, water pumps and other machinery and equipment that are imported into the country. Kenya assembles more than 90 models of trucks and buses and has about 60 makes of sedan cars. Kenya also imports more than 260 models of water pump. This proliferation inhibits the local manufacture of components and spares, increases inventory costs and encumbers labour training.

In the case of Uganda, steel consumption and demand are still low and the domestic market has limited product mix. Local production is mainly for the construction industry. Consumption of direct and indirect steel was 57,477 tonnes in 1980 and this is projected to 90,000 tonnes in 1990 (Ibid, p. 4).

The Uganda Steel Corporation established in 1974 was charged with the responsibility of manufacturing steel from iron and steel products. Though there is no production of capital goods in Uganda, the import structure of indirect steel as engineering products indicates a potential for the manufacture of metal products, agricultural machinery and equipment, and transport equipment and machinery. These categories of production are possible at the early stages of the development of capital goods industry.

An integrated development of iron and steel industry and capital goods is quite possible from a resource endowment approach. From a dynamic perspective, the capital goods sector further provides the organic link between the engineering industries and the sectoral structure of the economy. Dynamic efficiency can also be understood from the viewpoint of the transfer of technology. This requires capturing advances in the accumulation of physical capital and skills in the form of learning process on one hand, and the development of externalities and linkages over time on the other. This is provided in the development of the iron and steel industry with 'downstream' industries manufacturing intermediate and capital goods, which further provides the most developed forward linkages with the rest of the economies at both the national and regional levels.

Some Consequences of the Subregion's Industry Sector's International Links

The objective historical conditions of the development of the manufacturing sector in the East and Southern African subregion are multi-faceted in terms of its dependence on South Africa, parallel production structures heavily biased towards the supply of similar products of the light industry sector, unequal distribution of MVA in the region, an insignificant supply of capital goods stemming from the region, low per capita income levels and economic disruptions caused by South African destabilization of the SADCC countries. There is, thus, a strong case for the development of regional integration with emphasis on the development of the manufacturing sector. Centrally, such regional programmes explicitly call for national and collective self-reliance.

The concept of core industries under Industrial Development Decade for Africa (IDDA) involves an ongoing programme of the development of national core projects and multinational/subregional core projects that take into account the following aims:

1. providing inputs into the priority sectors selected in the Lagos Plan of Action and the Final Act of Lagos, i.e. food, transport, communication and energy;
2. providing effective integration and linkages with other industrial and economic activities and infrastructures in the subregion;
3. utilizing and upgrading, to the maximum extent, local natural resources (raw materials and energy) so as to benefit first the subregion, second other African countries and third non-African countries;
4. engaging in the production of intermediates and engineering goods including parts and components for further processing or fabrication in an increasing number of established and planned industries, particularly related to food production and processing, building materials, textiles, energy, transport and mining;
5. catering, first and foremost, directly and indirectly to the basic needs of the people in the subregion and, if required, to those of other African countries;
6. involving
    (a) economies of scale;
    (b) complex technology or upgrading of technology;
    (c) large investment; and
    (d) markets beyond the reach of individual countries in the subregion;
7. offering scope for cooperation, especially among the African countries, in the long-term supply/purchase arrangements for raw materials; intermediates and final products; subcontracting; barter; equity share holding, etc.
8. contributing to reducing the region's heavy reliance on external factor inputs.

At the national level there are programmes to strengthen national capabilities, particularly in the area of increasing the utilization of installed capacities, promotion of product diversification and upgrading of existing facilities in various engineering products.

The objectives of industrial cooperation in the subregion are spelt out in both the SADCC and PTA policy documents. It is quite explicit according to SADCC documents that the region's industrial strategy is based on the processing of locally produced raw materials to meet the basic needs, the upgrading and utilization of existing manufacturing capacity with a view to expanding intra-SADCC trading links. The region's plan of industrial cooperation was approved at the 1981 Blantyre Conference. Thus, according to the Harare Industry Workshop report:

The main thrust of the plan was to develop minimum-needs industries in the areas of food, clothing, housing, health, water supply, power, transport and education. Development of core industries such as fertilisers, pharmaceuticals, pesticides, iron and steel and capital goods industries also formed an integral part of the regional plan (SADCC, 1984a).

The regional responses to these problems cannot be left to an unplanned and loosely coordinated industrial strategy and the situation will be even worse if the forces of international capital are allowed to influence the course of development of the region's manufacturing sector. It can, however, be argued that the course of the development of the manufacturing sector of SADCC has not come to grips with the transformation demands of this sector so that it faces the challenge of supplying the demand structure of the region's economies. One of the main factors of the region's failure to evolve regional policies that are designed to transform the regional economy may be the overt and covert influences of the extra-regional elements. This is particularly relevant in the case of the SADCC.

It is clear that from the outset the SADCC seems to have allowed decision-making in the selection and implementation of projects to be a domain of external technical assistance with growing involvement of direct and indirect investment by large oligopolistic corporations and consortia, the transnational corporations. Outside sources will finance 75% of SADCC industry budget. Nearly $US5 million in studies is being coordinated by the Commonwealth Secretariat Industrial Development Unit. The Commonwealth Secretariat also provided technical assistance on the basis of which the present regional strategy for industrial development has been developed.

In the extreme case, which cannot easily be dismissed, the SADCC's development plans can no longer be realized without the prior approval of foreign interests. It is quite clear that the selection and eventually the approval of projects follows the powerful presence of foreign private interests. For example, at the Harare SADCC Workshop, textile, electrical and telecommunication equipment and salt interests were represented by, respectively, Simon Engineering (UK), Saksik of Cogelex Co-EE Alshthom (France) and Cheethan Salt (Australia). Further, the Report of the Workshop (1984a) states:

> It was made clear that updating of project reports and any specific work of filling up gaps in particular aspects of projects could be taken up with the assistance of agencies who offered to help in the implementation of these projects.

One can also argue that far from establishing a regional harmonization programme in the manufacturing sector, the present industrialization programmes were based on the satisfaction of the internal markets of the member countries establishing these programmes. For example, in the textile sector six member countries – Botswana, Lesotho, Malawi, Swaziland, Zambia and Tanzania – each have power loom projects, while Malawi, Mozambique, Zambia and Lesotho each have knitting projects. A similar pattern is repeated in the assembly of tractors, the production of agricultural implements and other projects currently underway. Only two of the 88 projects presented at Maseru in January 1983 have so far failed to find a confirmed or interested foreign donor.

In the opinion of the Commonwealth Industrial Development Unit, interest has been coming more from 'technology investors' rather than from 'portfolio investors', which is much more suitable for the SADCC because it involves a real transfer of technology. However, if one views the nature of the main forces behind the subregion's decision-making, this claim represents a naked falsification of what a real transfer of technology is about. If technology transfer should be understood as the provision of new information and knowledge that is used effectively in industrial operations in the sense of knowledge 'embodied' in new pieces of machinery and in 'disembodied' knowledge in the form of consulting services and technical assistance, or indigenous effort in human capital training and activity, the very dominant and paramount presence of the Commonwealth and EEC circles in technical assistance militates against the 'real transfer of technology', and therefore renders the claim false.

As shown above, the countries in the ESASDC have reached different stages of development in the area of iron and steel production and capital goods. The region is endowed with ample raw materials in which coordinated and planned programmes on a regional level could lead to rationalized production structures.

Zimbabwe has developed a capital goods sector in the region, an important basis for the development of indigenous capacities in technology. Other countries, like Kenya, Tanzania and Zambia, are also at various stages of the development of casting/foundry/forging production activities and production of agricultural tools, implements and machinery. At the present stage of development ZISCOSTEEL products will serve as feedstock in the production of intermediates and capital goods in the regional economy.

On a regional perspective planning and coordination of iron and steel production is a crucial variable not only for achieving self-reliance but even more importantly if these countries are to avoid over-production and subsequent under-utilized capacities in this area of production. In the developed countries such over-production has in certain cases resulted in complete steel plants being closed down with resultant mass unemployment, and associated ripple effects.

Coordination and cooperation in the specific areas of training of personnel and developing of specific modalities for regional development are necessary for both the medium-term and long-term development strategy. ZISCOSTEEL has undertaken to provide training of personnel in the region involving 'shop floor' expertise. A part of this programme involving a UNIDO consultant team have already worked on the Ugandan and Ethiopian mills.

From the viewpoint of positive externalities the region's intermediate and capital goods sectors should be related to the sectoral structure through the pattern of commodities produced within the individual branches or subsectors of the metal-working industries and their end-use in different sectors of the economy. These relationships call for several aspects in the identification of the main problems to be dealt with in perspective planning, namely:

1. the necessity to consider feasible and desirable qualitative changes of the structure of internal demand;
2. the need to evaluate and analyse improvement in quality and reliability of existing products;

3. the planning of the internal dynamics of the introduction of new products which may increase the satisfaction of the internal demand structure and export needs.

The plan for the introduction of new products which may increase the satisfaction of the internal demand structure and exports constitute the dynamic elements of the development of the intermediate and capital goods sectors. Technical progress in industry is a dynamic element of its growth and that which occurs in other branches of the national economy may help industry since labour previously carried out in other sectors will be transferred to industry. Our concern with growth is with interactions over time among producers, consumers and investors in interrelated sectors of the economy. Investment is considered more profitable in related sectors because of horizontal and vertical dependence, than in the same sectors considered separately. This approach is particularly suitable for the sub-Saharan region, which has the raw materials for sustaining its own development, provided regional coordinated programmes are taken more seriously.

A scientific evaluation of these factors can provide the basis for the region's division of labour. For example, the SADCC has a potential for a resource-based industrialization (see resource structure in SADCC in Table 2.5 at the end of this chapter) in several subsectors of the manufacturing sector. Tanzania, Zambia, Zimbabwe and Swaziland possess pulp and paper industrial raw materials. Mozambique, Angola, Zambia and Zimbabwe have cement and other raw materials for the building industry. There is a relatively developed iron and steel industry in Zimbabwe while other countries in the region have medium-term and long-term potential for foundry industries, machine tool spares, and machine and hand tools. Further import substitution in the region has its basis on the wide range of material resources from the mining, agricultural and energy sectors. An analysis of the existing and potential demand and supply conditions in the SADCC should precede formulation of a regional industrialization strategy or strategies.

The absence of a policy of industrialization in the subregion will propel the SADCC to develop purely in the interests of international monopoly capitalism as a source of raw materials and market for manufactured goods. Such a policy does not seem to be either in the interests of the national bourgeoisies of these countries or of socialist development. Regional self-sufficiency regarding the manufacturing sector is vital for the attainment of both SADCC and PTA objectives, but this cannot be achieved through an *ad hoc* shopping list of industrial projects.

Table 2.5
Industrial Raw Material Sources in the SADCC

Product	Short-Term Supplier	Medium-Term	Long-Term
Pulp	Swazi.	Tanz.	—
Paper	—	Tanz. Zamb.	Swazi.
Plywood/Veneer	Zimb. Tanz. Mal. (?)	Zimb. Botsw.	—
Tea chests	Tanz. Mal. (?)	—	—
Fibreboard	Zimb. Tanz. Mal. (?)	—	—

Packaging mat. Cardboard, Sacks, etc.	Tanz. Zimb. Botsw.	—	—
Rayon staple Fibre	—	—	Swazi. Zamb.
Textiles	Mal. Tanz. Leso. Moza.	—	—
Garments			
Shirts	Mal. Tanz. Zimb.	Moza.	—
Suits	Zamb. Zimb.	—	Tanz.
Woollen	Leso.	Leso.	Leso.
Leather shoes	Tanz. Zimb. Moza. Leso.	—	Botsw.
Wheat	—	Zimb.	Leso.
Vegetable oil	Zimb. Moza.	Botsw.	Leso.
Sugar	Moza. Swazi. Ang. Zimb.	—	—
Cocoa	Tanz.	—	—
Tea (packaged)	Tanz. Mal. Zimb.	—	—
Coffee (instant)	Tanz. Ang. Moza.	—	—
Tinned fish	Ang. (?)	Nam.	—
Tinned meat	Botsw. Zimb.	Nam. Tanz.	Leso.
Coal	Moza. Zimb.	Swazi.	Botsw. Tanz.
Crude oil	Ang.	—	—
Refined Petroleum prod.	Tanz. Moza.	—	—
Bitumen	—	Zimb.	Ang. Moza. Tanz.
Cement	Tanz. Moza. Ang. Zamb. Zimb.	Moza.	Nam. Moza
Sheet glass	—	Tanz.	Moza.
Pig iron	Zimb.	—	Tanz.
Steel	Zimb.	—	Tanz. Ang.
Steel sheet	Tanz.	Ang.	—
GCT sheets	Tanz. Zimb.	—	—
Steel rods	Tanz. Zimb.	—	—
Steel pipe	Tanz. Zimb.	—	—
Foundry prod.	Zimb. Moza.	Botsw. Tanz.	—
Machine tool Spares	Zimb.	—	Tanz.
Machine tools	Zimb.	—	Tanz.
Mining mach.	Zimb.	—	Tanz.
Hand tools	Zimb.	—	Zamb. Nam.
Refrigerators	Zimb. Moza.	—	Tanz. Moza.
Fans, etc.	Tanz. Zimb.	—	—
Radios	Tanz. Zimb. Moza.	Botsw.	—
Copper	Zamb. Zimb. Moza.	Nam.	—
Copper wire, Cables	Moza. Zamb. Zimb. Tanz.	—	Nam.
Lead	Zamb.	Nam.	—
Lead pipe	—	—	Nam.
Aluminium sheet	Tanz.	—	—
Corrugated sheet	Tanz.	—	—
Aluminium circles	Tanz.	—	—

Aluminium foil conductors	Tanz. Zamb.	—	—
Aluminium extrusions	—	—	—
Fertilizer compounds	Swazi. Zimb.	—	Moza.
Ammonia	—	—	Tanz. Moza.
Urea	—	—	Tanz. Moza.
Coal-base chemicals	—	—	Tanz. Zimb. Moza.
Insecticides (pyrethrum base)	Zimb.	—	Tanz.
Vaccine	Botsw. Moza.	—	—
Farm implements	Tanz. Zimb.	Moza.	—
Light tractors	Swazi.	—	—
Bicycles	Tanz. Zimb. Moza.	—	—
Bus and lorry bodies	—	Tanz. Moza. Zimb.	—
Railway wagons	Moza. Zimb.	Moza. Ang.	Tanz.
Explosives	Zamb. Zimb.	—	—
Caustic soda	—	—	—
Soda ash	—	Botsw.	—
Carbon dioxide	Zimb.	Tanz.	—
Mining chem.	Zimb. Zamb.	Zamb. Nam.	—
Plastic feedstock/pases	—	—	Tanz. Ang. Moza.
Tyres & tubes	Moza. Tanz. Zimb.	—	—
TV sets	Swazi. Zimb.	—	Botsw.
Pit props	Swazi.	—	—
Sawn timber	Moza. Swazi. Botsw. Zimb.	—	—
Trailers	Moza. Zimb.	Moza.	—
Electrical pumps	—	—	—
Automotive batteries	Moza. Zimb. Zamb.	Tanz.	—
Dry cell batteries	Tanz. Zimb.	—	—
Mining safety equipment	Zamb. Zimb.	—	—
Lime	Zamb.	Moza. Botsw.	—
Bottles	Zamb. Tanz.	Moza. Botsw.	—
Aluminium conductors	Zamb. Zimb.	—	—
Pharmaceuticals	Zimb. Zamb. Leso.	Tanz.	Moza.

Source: Record of the Meeting of Trade and Finance Ministers, Arusha, United Republic of Tanzania 26–27 October 1983.

Notes

1. South Africa is treated as a sub-metropolitan state in the sense that although it wields imperialist tendencies in the subcontinent, it is essentially dependent on the

larger metropolitan centres in Europe and North America for the maintenance of its hegemonic power.

2. SADCC, Report of the Workshop on Implementation of SADCC Industrial Projects, Harare 10–11 January 1984, p. 1.

3. The *Herald*, Harare, 2 March 1985.

4. World Bank, World Development Report 1982, 'Toward Sustained Development in Sub-Saharan Africa', Table 3. The percentage for Sub-Saharan Africa is for 1982. See also UNIDO, Industry and Development Global Report 1985, United Nations, New York, 1985.

5. D. B. Ndlela 'The Capital Goods Sector in Zimbabwe', paper presented for the project 'Nation Building or Transnationalisation in Africa' within the framework of the Regional Perspective Project of the United Nations University, Dakar, 25–27 January 1983. 'The Capital Goods Sector and Implications for Planning Industrialisation in Zimbabwe', paper presented at the Conference on Economic Policies and Planning under Crisis Conditions in Developing Countries'. University of Zimbabwe, Harare, 2–5 September 1985.

6. See I. Simba, Makoni, 'Organisation and Operational procedures of the Southern African Development Coordination Conference', unpublished paper, p. 27.

7. 'Southern Africa: Towards Economic Liberation: A Declaration by the Governments of Independent States of Southern Africa' made at Lusaka on 1 April 1980 (London: SADCC, 1980).

8. ZISCOSTEEL Report by Economic Commission for Africa 'Second Meeting of the Eastern and Southern African Steel Development Committee' (ESASDC), Addis Ababa, 24–28 October 1983.

3 Food and Agricultural Cooperation in the SADCC: Progress, Problems and Prospects

C. Mumbengegwi

The central theme in SADCC regional cooperation in the sphere of food and agriculture is the increase in agricultural production, with the overall objective of achieving food security and self-sufficiency both at the national and regional levels. Although the sector has been divided into seven subsectoral programme areas, an analysis of these subsectoral objectives shows that these are no more than an attempt to secure an operational framework for achieving the larger objective. Food and agriculture occupy the centre stage of SADCC cooperation programmes because the majority of member states find themselves unable to produce and guarantee a stable and sufficient supply of food for their growing populations. With the exception of Malawi, Zimbabwe and Tanzania, the SADCC states now face a food crisis of unprecedented proportions. This refers not to the frequent food shortages in drought years, but to an enduring deficiency characterized by a dynamic growth in food demand and requirements[1] far outstripping the growth in food production, and this is likely to be a more or less permanent feature of the region in the foreseeable future.

With the benefit of hindsight, it might appear that the crisis could have been anticipated given the domestic agricultural policies pursued by member states. Whatever the historical, political and socio-economic roots of the policies and strategies pursued in agriculture, their common denominator is the systematic neglect of the small farmer shouldering the burden of food production. This is true whether under socialist, state farm cum co-operative collectivization or large-scale capitalist-based modernization schemes and, if continued, this neglect will deepen the food crisis.

Such an observation is not an ideological idealization of the small farmer, but arises out of a cool-headed appreciation of the structural features of the region's food production and supply systems. The majority of farmers in the SADCC are small peasant producers and their failure to make a significant contribution to the goal of food self-sufficiency is as much a product of the region's technological backwardness as it is of the anti-agriculture, anti-peasant economic policies pursued in the past. SADCC has at last woken up to this reality:

> Present food production is largely in the hands of small farmers . . . and the failure of general policies . . . to address the problems of the small farmers has been a major part of the more general problem of declining agricultural production. [SADCC 1986, pp. 2–3]

This chapter examines SADCC programmes and projects in the food and agricultural sector. Its main focus is an examination of the nature of regional cooperation and its consistency with the sectoral goal of achieving food security and self-sufficiency. Does the SADCC framework for regional cooperation and coordination collectively redress the past neglect of small farmers? What are the implications of the SADCC framework on the region's future ability to become self-sufficient in food? What are the problems and future prospects in agricultural cooperation? These are some of the issues and questions addressed in this chapter. Of thematic relevance to this book is the issue of the SADCC's dependence on food aid and imports, especially from South Africa. Is the cooperation likely to arrest and break the cycle of food import dependence or will it result in a mere shift away from South African sub-imperialism into the lap of global imperialism? What role does the agricultural sector and food production in particular play in the SADCC's desire to disengage and delink from global imperialism and is such delinking feasible or desirable?

The first part of the chapter gives an overview of the agricultural and food crisis in the region. The second part examines in detail the philosophical framework, the objectives, scope and progress in regional agricultural cooperation in the SADCC since its formation. The third part is a critical assessment of the achievements, problems and future prospects for the SADCC. The final part gives the summary and main conclusions.

The Food and Agricultural Crisis in the SADCC: An Overview

The economies of SADCC states exhibit a strong structural dependence on the agricultural sector for overall growth and performance. Regionally, agriculture accounts for 34 per cent of GDP, 26 per cent of total export earnings and 79 per cent of employment. Although the importance of agriculture varies from country to country, it is true that for all of them (with Botswana perhaps being the exception), poor performance in this sector spells difficulties for the entire economy. Thus a healthy agricultural sector is both politically and economically desirable.

For the majority of SADCC states both per capita food and agricultural production have experienced a decline while population and food demand have been escalating over the past twenty years. Table 3.1 shows the population, food and agricultural production and food demand growth rates for the decade prior to the SADCC's formation (1971–80).

Only Swaziland and Tanzania achieved a growth rate in food and agricultural production that was marginally above that of population growth and, even so, Tanzania's position has recently declined. This implies that in per capita terms, the SADCC population was fed less well at the turn of the eighties than the seventies. Taking into account all factors affecting growth in food demand – such as incomes, prices, tastes and consumer preferences – food demand growth was greater than domestic food production for all countries except Tanzania and Zambia. For the region as a whole demand outstripped population growth, implying that rising levels of income or changing patterns in its distribution have had a considerable

Table 3.1
Population, Agricultural and Food Production and Food Demand
Growth Rates for SADCC Countries 1971–80

Country	Population Growth %	Agricultural Production	Food Production	Food Demand	Food Gap
Angola	2.6	–3.9	0.4	2.9	–2.5
Botswana	3.1	–3.7	–3.7	6.5	–10.2
Lesotho	2.5	—	0.5	6.0	–5.5
Malawi	3.4	–2.8	2.0	4.5	–2.5
Mozambique	2.7	–2.1	–1.7	0.6	–2.3
Swaziland	3.1	4.0	3.2	4.2	–1.0
Tanzania	3.2	2.3	3.9	3.4	0.4
Zambia	3.4	2.1	2.1	2.0	0.1
Zimbabwe	8.5	1.2	1.2	2.2	–1.0
SADCC	*3.1*	*0.3*	*0.9*	*3.6*	*–2.7*

Source: FAO, *The State of Food and Agriculture 1983* (extracted from Tables 1.23 and 1.24 pp. 58–61).

impact on food demand. The gravity of the food crisis can also be seen in the growing gap in domestic food supply, which is then translated into a demand for food aid or imports.

Table 3.2 shows the (1980–82) levels of cereal output and imports per capita for SADCC countries classified by the FAO as being relatively more affected by food shortages. Although cereals are only a component of the food basket, the figures nevertheless indicate the order of magnitude of food shortage in the region and the extent of food import dependence. This exerts further pressure on the foreign exchange gap facing the majority of these countries. Terms of trade for cash/export crops produced in the region have been declining, implying rising unit costs of

Table 3.2
Cereal Output and Imports per Capita: Selected SADCC Countries 1980–82

Country	(kilograms per capita)			Imports and Aid as per cent of output
	Output	Imports	Food Aid	
Angola	51	41	10	100
Botswana	46	75	15	196
Lesotho	119	86	26	94
Mozambique	46	30	14	96
Tanzania	150	18	11	19
Zambia	160	62	20	51
All Countries	95	52	16	72

Source: FAO, *The State of Food and Agriculture 1984*, p. 33.

imported food in foreign exchange terms. Some of the recent increases in cereal imports represent a shift in consumption patterns away from traditional grains to rice and wheat, partly due to polarizing income distribution in favour of urban élites and changing consumer preferences. On the production side, these increases are symptomatic of an inability to respond quickly to changing consumer tastes. Thus food deficiency is as much related to the levels of production and demand as it is to their patterns.

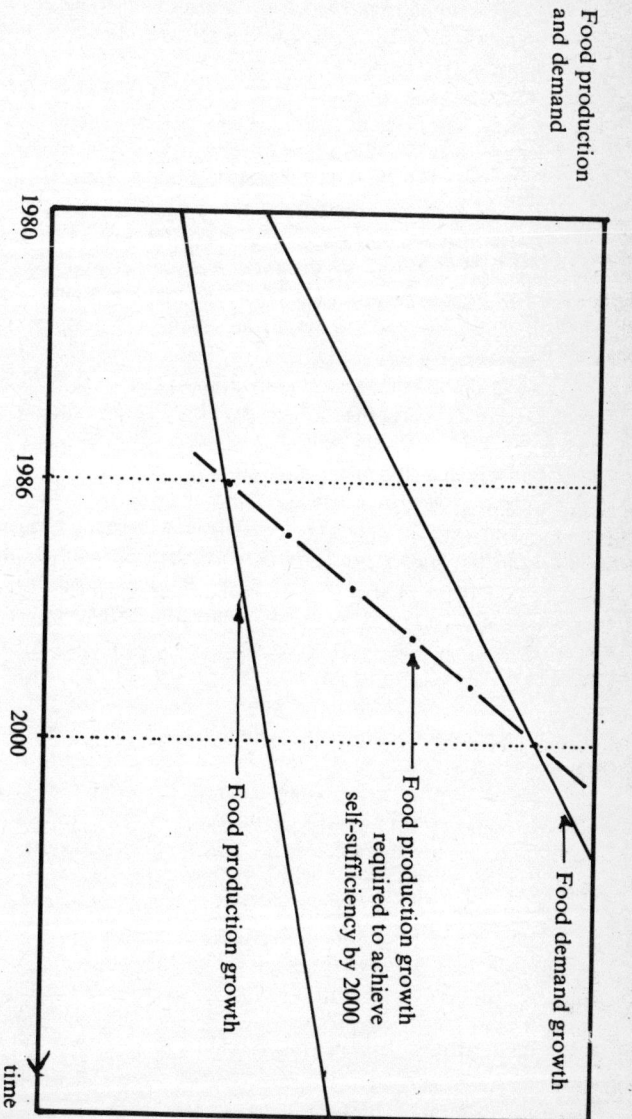

Figure 3.1

Figure 3.1 illustrates the potentially disastrous nature of the growth relationships discussed above. Starting from a position of moderate food deficit in 1980, the diagram illustrates that if food production and food demand continue to grow at the rates of 0.9 per cent and 3.6 per cent respectively, the food crisis will reach unmanageable proportions by the year 2000 if no corrective action is taken promptly to increase domestic production. The dotted line beginning at 1986 to the year 2000 shows the order of magnitude of the required rate of increase in food production if the SADCC were to achieve self-sufficiency by the year 2000. For the SADCC, this is not going to be an easy task considering the bottlenecks confronting their agricultural sectors.

The root cause of this growing malaise is, simply, the failure of SADCC agriculture to keep pace with population and growth in food demand. There are several explanations for this. SADCC takes a technological–determinist view of this failure while we emphasize a political–economic explanation. However, the truth is that both explanations have an important bearing on the root cause of the crisis. In its documents, the SADCC has catalogued what it considers the major constraints on food and agricultural production. Almost all the constraints mentioned are technological or natural ones. Poor soils with low moisture retention capacity compounded with low and unreliable rainfall for large proportions of the region which is prone to intra-seasonal and seasonal droughts are the natural setting for poor performance. Financial constraints and technological backwardness make irrigation development a dream for the future. Currently less than one-eighth of the regional irrigation potential has been exploited.

Other natural constraints in crop and livestock production are pests and diseases. The most serious affecting livestock are foot and mouth diseases, trypanosomiasis, east coast fever and rinderpest. Crops are also destroyed by such diseases as rusts and mosaics and pests like quelea birds, army worm locusts and the larger grain borer. These natural constraints are aided by the low level of technological skills, knowledge and expertise to eradicate them. Generally, with the exception of Zimbabwe, agricultural research institutions have never been strong, and where they have been, they have concentrated on cash/export crops to the exclusion of domestic food production research. The shortage of qualified personnel for research, extension, planning and policy formulation, coupled with the inadequacy of agricultural manufacture and the shortage of foreign exchange to finance the import content of domestic production completes SADCC's view of what has gone wrong. It is therefore not surprising that agricultural research and exchange of technical information, animal disease control, soil and water conservation and land utilization form the central elements of agricultural cooperation in SADCC. The above is only a partial reflection of the production constraints facing the SADCC region. There are several other policy-induced constraints to agricultural performance, especially in relation to food and the small producer.

In the absence of a common agricultural policy, it is noteworthy that each of the SADCC countries has adopted food self-sufficiency as an explicit objective of domestic agricultural policies, although the approaches and specific policies differ according to the current level of self-sufficiency, economic development and ideological persuasions of the incumbent governments. Table 3.3 summarizes the food self-sufficiency levels in 1980 and the stated policy objective for each country.

Table 3.3

Food Self-Sufficiency and Policy Objectives in SADCC Countries

Country	Level of self-sufficiency	Stated policy objectives
Angola	Serious decline in production since mid 70s. Severe food shortages exist despite substantial imports of cereals.	Immediate priority to ensure adequate food supplies; in medium term to increase production especially marketed production.
Botswana	High dependence on food imports, particularly staples. South Africa a major supplier.	Attain greater degree of self-sufficiency in major staples through developing arable agriculture.
Lesotho	High dependence on food imports, particularly staples. South Africa a major supplier.	Reduction of imports and increase of domestic food production, especially through mechanized production.
Malawi	Generally self-sufficient in most foods except after drought years.	Build up stocks in good years and pursue self-sufficiency in wheat.
Mozambique	Serious food shortages exist with rationing imposed despite considerable imports of cereals.	Immediate priority is adequate food supplies. Self-sufficiency in major staples by late 1980s.
Swaziland	Imports high proportion of maize requirements. South Africa a major supplier.	Self-sufficiency in maize by 1983 but concern about feasibility and economic wisdom.
Tanzania	Probably declining production of staples. Commercial and aid imports of staples and milk.	Immediate priority is adequate food supplies. Self-sufficiency at national and regional levels for major staples in the medium term.
Zambia	Considered self-sufficient in staples in good years but recently production declining and imports increasing.	Priority is to increase and stabilize crop production to achieve self-sufficiency at national and provincial levels.
Zimbabwe	Self-sufficient in wide range of food commodities with export surpluses in maize and cattle.	Achievement of sustained food self-sufficiency and regional food security.

Source: SADCC: A Regional Inventory of Agricultural Resource. Base: The Assessment of Food Self Sufficiency Potential. Vol. 2, p. 16. Ministry of Agriculture, Zimbabwe, November 1982.

The SADCC Framework and Approach to Cooperation

The SADCC approach to cooperation is as unorthodox as it is innovative. It is based on realistic political goals and a strong appreciation of the pitfalls in regional cooperation. The SADCC describes its approach as a 'step by step' process which does not

> entail from the outset a high degree of integration of domestic policies on the part of member states . . . Experience has shown that joint ventures between groupings of states to promote long term regional and sub-regional food security goals risk failure if they are over ambitious or are aimed at promoting uncompensated investment transfers from one country to another (SADCC 1986, p. 9).

All too often academic evaluation of the SADCC has analysed SADCC methods in terms of conventional forms of cooperation such as economic integration, customs unions and common markets. While elements of these could at a later stage be incorporated without much difficulty, at this juncture it is incorrect to judge the SADCC by using an analytical framework to which it does not belong. The SADCC is no more than what its founders intended it to be: a rational, gradual and practical approach to coordinating *national* development efforts within a regional framework. Thus its main priority is coordination of national efforts rather than integration of national economies into a supranational economic entity. It relies on the political commitment of member states to the narrowly defined SADCC objectives and the existence of areas of common interest from which mutual benefit can be derived through coordination and regular consultation. Behind the SADCC philosophy of regional cooperation lies a strong nationalistic fervour which has determined the framework for cooperation. A leading founder of SADCC recently made the following observation:

> SADCC is probably the strongest and most active Regional Organisation on the continent now. This may be partly because its structure takes account of the separate nationalisms of its member states while organising for understood and clearly necessary cooperation among them. But the basic reason for SADCC's strength is the political commitment that underlies its existence. For SADCC was created by the Front Line States out of their own felt need; although it now has a somewhat wider membership, the Front Line States still provide its core, are still the guardians of its objectives, and are still its main energisers.[2]

SADCC is a unique attempt at achieving regional cooperation which is based on a correct diagnostic assessment of why other forms of regional cooperation in Africa have either failed or are faltering. This diagnosis is:

1. lack of political will and commitment by participating states;
2. overambitious targets that overshoot themselves and land on the side of failure; and
3. inequity in the distribution of benefits from regional cooperation.

Thus the SADCC framework and approach to cooperation is an attempt to mitigate the potentially harmful effects of these factors. In recognition of the ideological, political and economic diversity among the member states comprising the organization, special effort has been made to take into account the members' 'separate nationalisms'. Emphasis is on commonly agreed areas of cooperation. As shall be shown below, projects and programmes are designed and agreed upon within the broad framework of regional consultation, but their implementation is a national rather than regional responsibility. This raises a question as to when a project is a SADCC project and when it is a national project. As noted earlier by Daniel Ndlela, a flexible approach to this question has been adopted.

Since emphasis is on coordination, this gives scope for accommodating a variety of projects under the SADCC umbrella. Where the interests of all member states coincide necessitating all members' participation a *SADCC Regional Project/ Programme* is designated. Such regional projects/programmes largely aim at removing production constraints common to all members by the 'establishment of a comprehensive network of institutions to strengthen SADCC's capacity to respond, at a regional level, to problems which have undermined the ability of member states to achieve food security' (SADCC 1984, p. 4). However, where a constraint faces a member state more acutely than others, and a project to ease it is likely to benefit non-participating members, a National Project with Regional Impact is hatched. Such projects are supported on the grounds that their implementation is not inimical to the interests of other member states and is deemed likely to make a significant contribution to 'the achievement of SADCC's overall food security objectives' (Ibid., p. 4).

Variations involving some but not all member states are permissible as Regional Projects if the projects have regional implications for achievement of SADCC goals. Thus the SADCC framework is flexible, non-alienating and open to bilateral bargaining, and a certain amount of give-and-take according to the political sensitivities and sensibilities of member states.

At the implementational level, cooperation in the SADCC is through sectoral programming, with each member state designated a coordinating function for all the national efforts pertaining to a particular sector. Zimbabwe is responsible for the Food and Agricultural sector. Within each sector, subsectoral programmes are then designed and member countries again allocated coordinative responsibility under the umbrella of the overall coordinator of the sector. Each programme area is then split into distinct and discrete projects which are then implemented at the national level. This organizational structure for the Food and Agricultural sector is depicted in Figure 3.2.

Altogether, there are seven subsectoral programme areas constituting the SADCC Food and Agricultural sector. These are:

1. Food Security (Zimbabwe)
2. Agricultural Research (Botswana)
3. Livestock Production and Animal Diseases Control (Botswana)
4. Forestry (Malawi)
5. Fisheries (Malawi)
6. Wildlife (Malawi) and
7. Soil and Water Conservation and Land Utilization (Lesotho)

SADCC Global Objectives in Food and Agriculture

SADCC objectives can be discerned at three levels: the sectoral level, the programme (subsectoral), and the project level. In essence the programme and

Figure 3.2
SADCC Food and Agricultural Sector: Structure of Cooperation

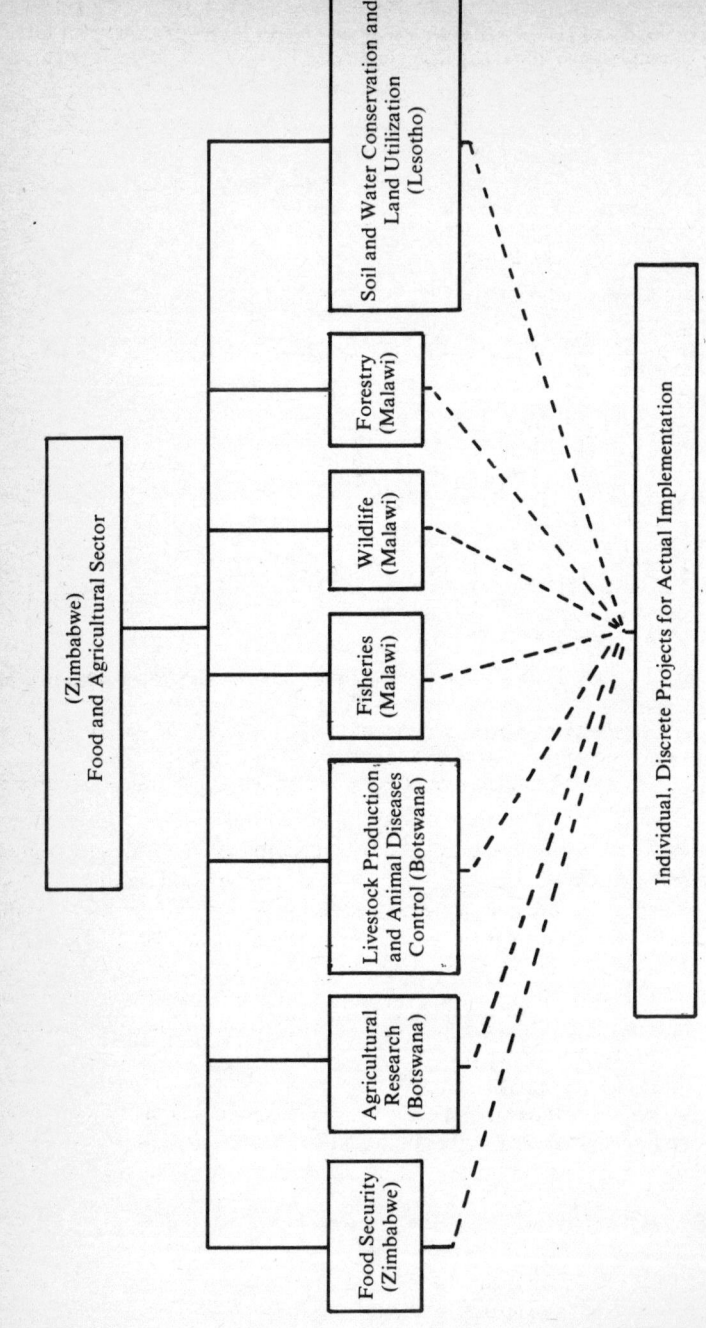

project objectives are no more than an operational basis for implementing the sectoral objectives. At the sectoral level, the objectives of agricultural regional cooperation in the SADCC are twofold:

1. to strengthen national policies and projects aimed at achieving food self-sufficiency and ensuring that agriculture becomes a dynamic sector in each national economy;
2. to increase agricultural production at both the national and regional levels.

The objectives of the former shall be examined in greater detail as we discuss the progress with implementation.

Subsectoral (Programme) Objectives and Progress with Implementation

Food Security Programme (Zimbabwe)

In the light of chronic and persistent food deficits in the region, food security (defined by the SADCC as being 'achieved when a country can assure all its citizens of both physical and economic access to food of an appropriate nutritional quality') has been given priority ranking in the region's programmes (SADCC 1986, p. 9). It is the cornerstone of the SADCC's collective efforts and all the other programmes have been designed largely to facilitate the achievement of the objectives of this subsector, which are:

1. to satisfy the basic needs of the entire population of the region irrespective of their economic status;
2. to achieve national and regional self-sufficiency in food supply in order to reduce dependence on external sources of supply; and
3. to eliminate the periodic food crises which affect areas or countries in the region.

There is no other subsector in which the nationalistic fervour of the SADCC framework comes through so clearly as in the food security sector. Food production is deemed a national responsibility. While the benefits from specialization and intraregional food trade are recognized, SADCC prefers the nationalistic route to regional food security and self-sufficiency irrespective of the efficiency costs involved. To SADCC, regional food security is a function of the achievement of national self-sufficiency. Thus, cooperation is merely an attempt to reinforce each nation's capacity to produce food 'in accordance with national policies and priorities' (Ibid, p. 9). With regard to infrastructural development for food storage, marketing and distribution systems, 'upgrading of such facilities will primarily be undertaken within the context of national development programmes' (Ibid, p. 11). This nationo-centric approach may have some adverse long term implications for the achievement of SADCC's goals, as we shall see later.

Progress. In line with the priority attached to the goal of food security, progress in this subsector is far more advanced than in all the others. Altogether twelve regional projects have been identified, seven have either been completed or are under implementation and five are as yet to be implemented although pre-feasibility and feasibility studies have been undertaken. These projects are tabulated in Table 3.4.

These regional projects have in common the fact that they are not concerned with aspects of production, but with setting the conditions conducive to food production and achievement of food security. However, they also vary in focus. Projects 1 to 4 focus mainly on systematization and exchange of already available information. Through collating, storage processing and analysis of data available, the projects are intended to provide comprehensive information necessary for the design of national policies and programmes and to enable the member states either individually or collectively to respond quickly to impending food shortages. The rest of the projects are concerned with information generation, research, training and building up the SADCC's capacity to effectively implement food production and security programmes at the national level.

In addition, there are also 23 national projects with a regional impact which are supported within the SADCC framework, and there is every indication that the

Table 3.4
SADCC Regional Food Security Projects by Major Focus

Coordinated Exchange of Information	*Coordinated Information Generation, Research and Training*
Projects under Implementation	
1. Technical assistance programme designed to achieve coordination and cooperation on all agrarian issues.	6. Regional post production. food loss.
2. An early warning system for regional food security	7. Regional food-processing technology.
3. A regional resources information system.	10. Recruitment and retention of professional staff in the Ministries of Agriculture in SADCC countries.
4. A regional inventory of agricultural resource base.	
Projects yet to be Implemented	
	5. A regional food reserve.
	8. Regional food-marketing infrastructure.
	9. Food aid.
	11. Study on seed production and supply.
	12. Education and training for irrigation and water management.

number will increase as time and need arises. The focus of the projects varies according to specific circumstances and national priorities. Broadly, they are in the areas of infrastructural development, building food storage facilities, grain reserves, pest control, irrigation, seed production and general rural development. However, national projects have not been very popular with donors and thus progress has been extremely slow. The SADCC has therefore requested the member states concerned to reformulate them with an appropriate 'regional' sugar-coating to make them more palatable to donor financiers.

Overall, for both regional and national projects, implementation is still in the early stages of feasibility studies and, at most, establishment of the necessary administrative units and recruitment of qualified regional personnel. Except for project 1, which started in 1982, all the other projects started in 1984/85 or are as yet to be implemented. National projects are largely still on paper seeking possible donors.

Financing. SADCC is an ambitious attempt at stimulating regional development based on foreign funding. Tables 3.5, 3.6 and 3.7 give summary statistics on the proposed financing structure for food security projects.

Table 3.5
Regional Projects (Combined)

No. of Projects	Estimated Cost ($US million)			Secured Finance	Balance yet to be Secured
	Total	Foreign	Domestic		
12	17.884	16.119	1.765	11.755	4.364

Foreign finance component as % of total cost = 90.1	Secured finance as % of foreign cost = 73

Source: SADCC: Food and Agriculture, 30–31 January 1986 Conference Report, Harare.

The following points deserve particular mention:

1. Regional food security projects are estimated to cost $US17.884 million of which 90 per cent is to be secured through foreign aid. Seventy-three per cent of the foreign finance requirements have already been raised while the balance is still under negotiation with various donors (Table 3.5). The major donors in order of importance/contributions are Denmark (38 per cent), Canada (25 per cent), Ireland (18 per cent), USA (7 per cent), UNDP/FAO (3.6 per cent), Commonwealth Fund for Technical Cooperation (CFTC) (3.4 per cent), EEC (2 per cent), Australia (1 per cent).
2. National food security projects are estimated to cost $US223.401 million, 86 per cent of which is seeking foreign finance. Only 14 per cent of the foreign finance requirements have so far been secured, with little or no interest among donors to finance the balance (Tables 3.6 and 3.7).

3. Although national projects have raised more than twice the amount of foreign funds in absolute terms as regional ones, the latter have performed much better in proportionate terms (1:5). This may be largely because of their lower overall costs and fewer overheads associated with their implementation. All in all, regional projects are only 7.4 per cent of the overall food security subsector's estimated financial requirements of $US241.285 million. Foreign finance

Table 3.6
National Projects with a Regional Impact

Country	No. of Projects	Estimated Cost ($US Million)			Secured Finance	Balance yet to be Secured
		Total	Foreign	Local		
Angola	4	19.729	19.729	Nil	Nil	19.729
Botswana	0	—	—	—	—	—
Lesotho	1	9.958	Nil	9.958	—	Nil
Malawi	1	13.75	13.75	Nil	Nil	13.75
Mozambique	6	37.837	25.132	12.705	11.946	13.186
Swaziland	0	—	—	—	—	—
Tanzania	3	41.833	33.532	8.301	Nil	33.532
Zambia	1	4.021	4.021	Nil	4.021	Nil
Zimbabwe	7	96.723	96.723	Nil	10.75	85.973
Total	23	233.851	192.887	30.964	26.717	166.17

Source: SADCC: Food and Agriculture 30–31 January 1986 Conference Report, Harare.

Table 3.7
SADCC: National Projects: Foreign Financial Proportions

Country	Foreign Finance Requirements as % of Total Cost	Secured Finance as % of Foreign Requirements
Angola	100	Nil
Botswana	—	—
Lesotho[a]	?	?
Malawi	100	Nil
Mozambique	66.4	47.5
Swaziland	—	—
Tanzania	80.2	Nil
Zambia	100	100
Zimbabwe	100	11.1
Total	86.1	13.9

Source: SADCC: Food and Agriculture 30–31 January 1986 Conference Report, Harare

[a] Proportion of foreign and local financing requirements not indicated although the indication is that all could be local finance if foreign finance is not forthcoming.

components are, however, marginally lower for national projects (86 per cent:90 per cent).

4. For national food projects, Zimbabwe accounts for 43 per cent of the total financial costs or 50 per cent of the foreign financing requirements while, when Tanzania and Mozambique are included, the three account for 79 per cent of total costs or 92 per cent of foreign financing requirements.

Agricultural Research Programme (Botswana)

The SADCC has identified the constraints on improved food production as:

1. poor soils that are either nutrient deficient, acidic or structurally prone to erosion;
2. variability and unavailability of rainfall and inadequately developed irrigation facilities which reduce yields;
3. inadequate application and high cost of inorganic fertilizers;
4. pests and diseases which are estimated to reduce food availability by between 30 and 40 per cent;
5. lack of improved seeds;
6. labour supply constraints and low level of development of non-labour means of production which delay planting, weeding and harvesting leading to substantial losses in productivity;
7. farmers' reluctance to adopt new technologies;
8. poor infrastructure, marketing, credit and input supply systems.

Similar constraints for livestock production are outlined as:
1. low carrying capacity of pastures
2. lack of supplementary feeds and fodders
3. overgrazing and land degradation
4. prevalence of livestock diseases and parasites (Ibid., p. 12).

Having adopted this technocratic view of the causes of poor agricultural performance, the SADCC Agricultural Research Programme seeks to alleviate these natural constraints by removing the SADCC's present technological deficiency to effectively deal with these issues. Thus, the objectives in this subsector are:

1. to develop 'technological packages which combine improved drought and disease resistant varieties' of crops with appropriate pest management systems;

2. to strengthen the agricultural research capacity of the region by:

(a) re-orientation of national research institutions to shift away from cash/export crop research bias towards addressing the major problems affecting the bulk of producers, i.e. small farmers,

(b) training of SADCC nationals in relevant fields of crop and livestock research, and

(c) wider dissemination of new and existing research findings throughout the region.

Progress. Five projects have been identified of which two are now fully operational. The coordinating member is Botswana. The central project is the Southern African Centre for Cooperation in Agricultural Research (SACCAR), based in Gaborone, which started in 1984 and is an ongoing project. It performs a dual function:

1. to service national research institutions by acting as the regional documentation centre for all research activities in the region; and
2. to coordinate all research activity within the SADCC framework.

Although SACCAR does not administer or handle funds for other regional research projects, it has the chief coordinative role, with all other projects feeding data, information and research findings into it. SACCAR also administers research grants and scientific training schemes for nationals of the SADCC region.

The other operational project (which started in June 1984) is the Regional Sorghum and Millet Programme, whose main aim is to produce germ plasms for national breeding programmes (notably drought-resistant strains) and to train scientists in sorghum and millet improvement. Altogether 65 scientists at MSc or PhD levels will be trained in ten years.

Three other projects in Grain Legume Improvement (awaiting funding), Land and Water Management Research and Agricultural Research Resources Assessment (completed in 1984 but needs constant updating), have been formulated but implementation is yet to commence. In some cases, funding has not yet been secured. It is significant that all the projects are designated as regional with no national projects in this subsector as is the case in the food security sector.

Financing. Table 3.8 summarizes the estimated financial requirements for the Agricultural Research Subsector. Since the programme is still in its infancy, with every possibility of initial phases of the projects generating more demand for financial resources, the $US51.4 million can only be a very small proportion of the final requirements of the sector. All of this is to be funded from foreign sources, of which $US27.4 million or 53.3 per cent has been secured with the balance yet to be pledged.

Table 3.8
Summary Data on Agricultural Research Financing

No. of Projects	Estimated Cost ($US Million)		Secured Finance	Balance yet to be Secured
	Foreign	Local		
5	51.4	Nil	27.4	24

Source: SADCC Annual Progress Report July 1984 to June 1985, p. 30.

Livestock Production and Animal Disease Control (Botswana)
The original objective was to control and eventually eradicate livestock diseases such as foot and mouth disease, rinderpest, east coast fever, trypanosomiasis and

various diseases carried by tick and tsetsefly. However, with the redesignation of the subsector from Animal Diseases Control to Livestock Production and Animal Diseases Control in January 1986, objectives have been expanded to include broader issues of livestock production, proper range and pasture management, improvements in livestock breeds and breeding techniques; piggery, dairy, poultry and small stock production. In this respect, the subsector is now closely linked with the Agricultural Research Programme. Again the main focus is easing the SADCC's technological deficiency in controlling diseases and natural phenomena. SADCC estimates these to be responsible for 20–35 per cent mortality in sheep and goats, 20–30 per cent retarded weight gain in livestock, and reduced fertility and calving in cattle.

Progress. Altogether, there are 23 projects; six regional and 17 national projects with a regional impact. All were formulated prior to the redesignation of the subsector and hence are purely concerned with animal diseases control. Projects on livestock production are as yet to be formulated and presented. Progress with implementation is also still at an early stage. Of the regional projects, one (a study) has been completed while five are either awaiting funding or are still under negotiation for funding. Eight of the national projects are under implementation, a similar number are awaiting funding, and one (a border fence) has been completed. Next to the food security sector, projects in this area have experienced significant progress. Botswana is the co-ordinating country.

Financing. Summary data on proposed financing arrangements for both regional and national projects is given in Table 3.9.

Table 3.9
Summary Data of Financing Arrangements for Animal Diseases Control

	No. of Projects	*Total*	*Foreign*	*Local*	*Secured*	*Balance*
		\multicolumn{3}{c}{*Estimated Cost ($US Million)*}			
Regional	6	16.045	16.045	Nil	0.5	15.545
National	17	75.164	72.346	3.918	37.315	35.031
Total	23	91.209	88.391	3.918	37.815	50.576

Source: SADCC: Annual Report July 1984 to June 1985.

Of the $US91.209 million budget for the sector, 17.4 per cent is for regional and 82.6 per cent for national projects. Ninety-six per cent of the sector finances is being sought from foreign sources of which 43 per cent has been secured. The balance (57 per cent) is still under negotiation with donors. National projects have had relatively more success in raising donor funds, especially in those cases where a number of member states are involved in the same project. Of note is the active involvement of the EEC in animal disease control funding in view of its imports of beef from the region.

Soil and Water Conservation and Land Utilization (Lesotho)
Environmental degradation, depletion of vegetation and forests, soil erosion and the threat of desertification are seen by the SADCC as serious constraints on crop and livestock production. Thus, soil and water conservation and land utilization constitute an obvious area for regional cooperation. The objectives of the programme are: 1. to achieve a coordinated regional approach to environmental protection; 2. to assist member states to improve their soil and water conservation efforts; 3. to restore the balance between the demands for land for agricultural activities and protection of the environment; 4. to develop policies and farming practices orientated towards conservation issues; and 5. to mobilize and sensitize relevant institutions to the problems of conservation.

These objectives are to be pursued through coordinated sharing of information, training, data, technical expertise and regular joint practical conservation programmes in the field.

Progress. This is a fairly recent area in SADCC cooperation and implementation is at a very rudimentary stage. Three initial national projects with regional impact have been presented to the SADCC and consultations are continuing regarding implementation. These are a Pilot Project to Test Conservation Techniques on Steeply Sloping Land (Malawi), Rainfall Simulator Tests (Lesotho) and Afforestation (Lesotho). While these projects are national in character, their results are of relevance to the entire region given the complexity and diversity of conservation problems confronting the SADCC.

Financing. Since the projects are largely at formulation stage (presented at Harare, January 1986), accurate financial estimates in final form are not yet readily available for analysis. Only financing of the Maseru-based Coordinating Unit has so far been secured or pledged.

Fisheries, Wildlife and Forestry Subsectors (Malawi)
These sectors complete the SADCC's areas of cooperation in agriculture but are not really central to the goal of achieving food security and self-sufficiency. The objectives are to achieve a coordinated, efficient exploitation and development of natural resources in inland and deep-sea fishing, forestry and wildlife to augment national and regional dietary food supplies and utilization of by-products.

Progress. Again, these are new areas of expansion in SADCC cooperation consistent with the 'step by step' approach when time and need arise. Projects were presented as recently as the 1985 Mbabane Conference, and little implementational progress has taken place. There are eleven fisheries projects (six national and five regional), four regional wildlife and eight forestry projects; most are under financing negotiations.

Financing. Table 3.10 summarizes the proposed financing requirements for these subsectors. The three subsectors have a combined budget of $US43.128 million of which $US37.182 million or 86 per cent needs foreign funding. Only 17 per cent of this has so far been raised, mainly in the fisheries subsector. Eighteen of the projects are still under financing negotiations.

Table 3.10
Summary Data on Financing for Fisheries, Wildlife and Forestry Products

	No. of Projects	Estimated Cost ($US Million)			Secured	Balance
		Total	Foreign	Local		
Fisheries	11	7.748	7.682	0.066	4.230	3.452
Wildlife	4	2.58	0.2	2.38	Nil	0.2
Forestry	8	32.8	29.3	3.5	2.0	27.3
Total	23	43.128	37.182	5.946	6.230	30.952

The Food and Agriculture Sector as a Whole

SADCC cooperation in agriculture covers all the important aspects arising from natural and technological constraints on food production in the region. At the financing level, the whole sector presently requires $US430.422 million for all the identified projects to be implemented. Ninety per cent of this is to be foreign-funded, of which only 29 per cent has so far been raised. This raises a number of issues pertaining to the conception of SADCC as a body to foster regional cooperation to achieve collective self-reliance and break the cycle of dependency on South Africa and global imperialism. It is the examination of these and other implications to which we now turn.

Problems and Future Prospects for SADCC Cooperation in Agriculture

The SADCC region holds great potential for the achievement of food security, richly endowed as it is with unexploited agricultural potential. The diversity among member states in natural resources, climate, soil and agro-ecology makes it possible for the region as a whole to produce a wider range of crops than is possible in any single country alone. It follows that regional cooperation would make it easier for member states to achieve food security. Cooperation opens up possibilities for specialization according to comparative advantages, and prospects for increased intraregional trade in food. A number of member states, either due to their size or agro-climatic endowments, are aiming to achieve national self-sufficiency in all but a few food items in the foreseeable future. This could be achieved, but only at the cost of resource allocation inefficiency and heavy capital investments in irrigation and/or land improvements.

The origins of SADCC are more political than economic, and political considerations run strongly through all major SADCC decisions. Despite its claim to political strength and unity, the very framework of cooperation chosen indicates the shaky foundation on which SADCC is built. Desire for collective independence from South African domination is one thing but commitment to regional integration is another. SADCC member states are unwilling to substitute one dependence with another. Consequently, cooperation in SADCC is a loose arrangement from which a member state can opt out without any serious repercussions on its domestic economy. Thus SADCC's claim to political strength and unity is its economic weakness, and the policy choices pursued in the Food and Agriculture sector clearly demonstrate this.

While SADCC recognizes on paper the benefits from specialization and intraregional food trade, political considerations have necessitated an approach to cooperation that prevents their realization. For SADCC countries, pursuit of national food self-sufficiency is not merely an economic necessity; it is a desirable political goal. National independence could not be guaranteed, and control over domestic policies could be easily compromised, if a country depended on its neighbours for basic food requirements. Thus SADCC has consciously made a policy choice to pursue regional food security through the achievement of national self-sufficiency, despite the economic inefficiency this involves, and despite the unattainability of this goal for some member states.

The kind of economic cooperation required of SADCC for maximum efficiency demands mutual trust and confidence among member states. Given the differences in ideological and domestic policy orientations in SADCC, this can only be a dream for the future. SADCC's reluctance to cooperate on production underscores the potential weaknesses in the organization and the fact that economic integration of domestic economies is not one of SADCC's objectives.

A further illustration of the above observation can be drawn from an analysis of SADCC regional projects. The emphasis in the food security subsector is on coordination in generation and supply of information to member states to build up their own individual capacities to produce food. However, the capacity to produce food is dependent on domestic economic policies, technological capacity and agricultural resources. SADCC's strategy conveniently sidesteps any issues relating to domestic economic policies. Although there is increasing awareness of the important role played by small farmers, little has ever been done to articulate a coherent regional policy on reversing the previous neglect of small farmers. Instead, a technocratic-cum-technological diagnosis of the problems constraining food production in the region has been emphasized. The agricultural research programme is geared to producing technological packages to raise production. But to embark on higher-level production, peasant farmers require a more solid tenure system that provides them with security against the vagaries of a market-orientated production system. Peasants do not need enlightened benevolence from governments, but clear policies and institutional arrangements to ensure adequate protection in a constantly changing world.

In an enlightening analysis, the Food Policy Analysis Group outlined a framework that best illustrates the limitations in SADCC's approach to increasing regional food supply. They define three potential ceilings to agricultural output. The first is the actual ceiling defined as the maximum output level achievable under existing technology, farming methods and resource endowments. The second is the economic potential ceiling which is the maximum output that maximizes farmers' returns given a 'set of prices and technological relationships between inputs and outputs'. Clearly this output can be varied by appropriate adjustments to input and output prices, credit, marketing, extension and land tenure policies. The last is the technical potential ceiling which defines the maximum technically feasible level of output in a constraint-free environment. This assumes absence of technological bottlenecks in production and of economic policy constraints on achieving this potential. The three ceilings are illustrated in Figure 3.3, in which t_t, e_t and a_t are the technical, economic and actual production ceilings respectively. Over time, t_t can be raised by technological improvements and a_t by the adoption of these innovations by farmers, whereas e_t can be raised through economic policy instruments. On the assumption that a country is initially in food deficit at time t_o, actual food production is constrained along ceiling a_t until time t_j when technological packages are introduced and adopted by farmers. Food production growth then accelerates along line F_p. Self-sufficiency can then be achieved at time t_i where food demand equals supply. However, this can only be achieved on the assumption that economic policy adjustments are introduced to raise the economic potential above the self-sufficiency level. Short of this, food production growth will be blocked off at the economic potential (e_t) level, making self-sufficiency unattainable despite the introduction of technological improvements in production methods.

The above analysis can be applied to illustrate the limitations in SADCC's approach to food self-sufficiency. Its strategy of increasing food output through removal of technological constraints to production and neglecting domestic economic policy reform is unlikely to yield lasting results. If the food self-sufficiency level is above the output levels that would be economically remunerative to farmers, the narrowing of the food gap can only be short-lived, and the attainment of self-sufficiency indefinitely postponed unless economic policy changes are introduced to complement the technological improvements taking place. This is a challenge that SADCC as a region and at the national level has got to appreciate. It must make appropriate domestic economic policy reforms to make food production attractive to farmers. A coordinated regional approach to agricultural policy would go a long way towards achieving this goal.

Perhaps the most important SADCC food and agriculture objective is to break the cycle of food import dependence, in which South Africa plays a dominant role, especially for the BLS states. SADCC's failure to enter into agricultural production coordination can only help to sustain this dependence. Aiming at food self-sufficiency on a national level can only ensure that South Africa will remain a guaranteed and cheaper source of supply for food imports. Moreover, by adopting this nationalistic approach to food security, SADCC member states have demonstrated that they are no less reluctant to be dependent on regional partners than on South Africa, thus leaving room for lucrative bilateral dealings with the latter where an individual member state stands to be advantaged by such deals.

The importance of food self-sufficiency for the region cannot be overemphasized if economic liberation is to be achieved. However, the dependence of SADCC projects on foreign finances means that de-linking from global imperialism is only a political objective, but in economic terms, SADCC is moving towards greater integration with world imperialism. Progress with implementation can only take place at the pace dictated by SADCC's 'cooperating partners', which can distort the patterns of production and make member states vulnerable to extra-regional

Figure 3.3

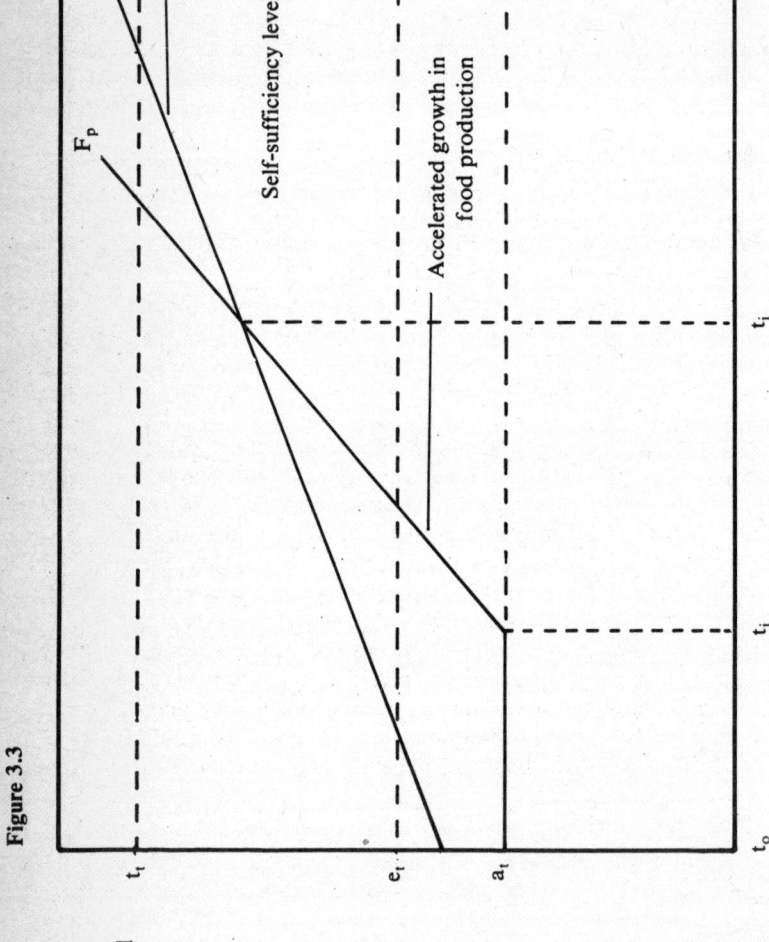

influences. Thus, SADCC's weakness is its lack of control over the financing of its programmes – a problem whose negative effects will become more apparent as progress moves away from feasibility studies and setting up of institutions to the actual task of production. Already, those projects that are nationally based and production-orientated are finding difficulty in attracting foreign funding. This is an issue to which, sooner or later, SADCC has to address itself.

Summary and Conclusions

This chapter has outlined the serious dimensions of the food crisis in the SADCC region and examined the scope and methods of food and agricultural cooperation in the region. A number of important points need re-emphasis.

1. In the short term, SADCC has deliberately substituted financial dependence for food import dependence by launching an ambitious programme to revitalize its agricultural sectors without domestic counterpart finance to carry the programme through. The prospects for disengagement from global imperialism seem unattainable on account of the SADCC's heavy reliance on donor financing to implement its programmes. What began as an attempt at collective independence from South Africa is fast slipping into collective dependence on other imperialist powers.

2. There is little or no indication of domestic economic policy reform towards agriculture. Although each of the nine countries has adopted food self-sufficiency as an explicit objective in domestic agricultural policy, there has been failure at the regional level to articulate a regional agricultural policy that would ensure that this becomes a reality. Although casual reference is made in SADCC documents to the problems of the small farmer, the content of SADCC cooperation is farmer-neutral. It can only be at the level of economic policy that small farmer problems can be specifically addressed rather than at the level of agricultural research, coordination and information exchange.

3. Although SADCC possesses the potential to produce enough food for its growing population, the future prospects for achievement of self-sufficiency lie in regional allocation and planning of production responsibilities according to each country's resource endowments and cost considerations. Individual national attempts at self-sufficiency are not only economically undesirable but practically unfeasible.

Notes

1. A distinction should be made between growth in food demand and food requirements. The former is determined by population growth, incomes, prices, tastes and preferences. Thus it is purely a market concept which bears little relationship to the required nutritional needs of the population. The latter is determined by population, age and workforce composition. It is the food required

to sustain a given population composition in basic physical health to ensure production and its own reproduction. It is thus a biological concept independent of market forces.

2. Julius Kambarege Nyerere, speech delivered at the University of Zimbabwe on being awarded the degree of LL.D. Honoris Causa, 7 June 1986.

4 Limits to Development in Southern Africa: Energy, Transport and Communications in SADCC Countries

Benedict S. Mongula and Chiselebwe Ng'andwe

The basic challenge of SADCC is the promotion of collective self-reliance through reduction of economic dependence, particularly – but not only – on the Republic of South Africa. This entails increased production of the various goods and services needed within the SADCC. It also entails increased intra-SADCC mobility of the factors of production as well as the goods and services. Energy is a basic input in any production process, while transport and communications facilities are basic requirements for the desired increased economic interactions among SADCC members. Thus the physical improvement and rationalization of SADCC transport and communications was included as a specific fundamental strategy of SADCC in the original Lusaka Declaration of April 1980 that created SADCC.

Since the oil crisis of the mid-1970s, the energy problem has attracted special attention both in developed and developing countries. Since then there has been concerted action by governments and the private sectors of many countries with a view to finding appropriate and alternative energy sources while promoting economy and conservation in the use of those already available. The oil crisis has had a particularly severe effect on the economic performance of the non-oil-producing Less Developed Countries (LDCs) where technological inadequacies do not augur well for immediate switching to alternative energy sources or more efficient production techniques.

In Africa, the energy crisis has been crowned by acute poverty and the pressures of rapid economic and social change. Modern production technologies and consumption habits have created new demands and pressures for energy in Africa where traditional human motive power and firewood are still the predominant forms of energy for production and heat respectively. Rapid modernization of production methods and urbanization have created demands for appropriate energy resources which cannot be procured within the available resources.

SADCC's substantial hydroelectric potential has not been fully tapped because of the high opportunity cost. The inevitable heavy dependence on oil has made the SADCC very vulnerable to the worldwide oil crisis. All SADCC members except Angola import either crude oil or refined oil products or both. These countries spend between 30 and 60 per cent of their foreign exchange earnings on quantitatively diminishing oil imports. Moreover, this high relative expenditure on oil comes when most SADCC members are facing severe foreign exchange constraints. The worst hit are Mozambique, Tanzania and Zambia, who for the past years have been unable to pay on their own, even for essential imports like industrial raw materials and intermediate goods, spare parts, basic mass consumption goods and replacement machinery. They have had to depend on 'import support' from friendly governments for their meagre supplies of these items. The industries in these countries are working at about 30 per cent of their capacity. The transport fleets are grinding to a halt, and their roads and railways are in utter disrepair.

The present underdeveloped state of SADCC transport and telecommunications systems are both a symptom and a cause of underdevelopment. As pointed out by Balassa (1965), the task of raising these systems to the desired level often involves a very high opportunity cost which tends to be prohibitive for individual countries as well as for regional integration programmes.

The major historical factor affecting the transport and communications systems of SADCC is the colonial past. During the colonial period, the development of transport and communications facilities was aimed at promoting the flow of trade between the individual colonial states and the colonizing state. Thus there was no deliberate effort to develop transport and communications links between two or more colonies. Indeed, even within individual colonies, there was no deliberate effort to promote cohesive national transport and communications systems. The colonial pattern of transport and communications aimed only at linking those areas in colonies identified as sources of raw materials or concentrated markets for manufactured goods with the metropolis. This pattern was fortified by the international division of labour under which the colonial power produced manufactured goods for sale in the colonies, which in turn produced raw materials to be used in the manufacturing factories of the colonial master.

Since independence there have been attempts by African countries to change the colonial pattern of trade, and this has involved improving transport and communications. The major constraints on this effort have risen from the different timings of independence for various countries in Southern Africa, and in Angola, Mozambique and Zimbabwe from the upheavals of liberation wars. This situation prevented a regionally coordinated policy until 1980.

Thus at the time of formation, SADCC's member countries did not have a regionally planned policy on production, consumption, trade, transport and communications, and energy. Moreover, the member states have irrational transport structures which are also very unequally distributed across their territories. The countries are characterized, too, by inappropriate technology in production, transport and communications, and in energy consumption. Thus SADCC's development is most vulnerable to the worldwide energy crisis and the national and regional constraints of transport and communications.

It is recognized here that the problems affecting the SADCC countries today are partly due to worldwide economic factors: oil price rises, the fall in the real prices of primary commodities and real terms of trade, and the recession in the advanced capitalist countries. But two other major factors could be singled out as peculiar to the SADCC region and responsibile for its alarming state of affairs. The first is the landlocked character of most of the countries and the geopolitics and security relations in the Southern African region as a whole. The problems of the SADCC region in energy, transport and communications are over and above compounded by this constraint. The other is Southern Africa's dependence on the Republic of South Africa.

As indicated by the Lusaka Declaration, Southern Africa is dependent on the Republic of South Africa as a focus of transport and communications, as an exporter of goods and services and as an importer of goods and cheap labour. This dependence is not a natural phenomenon nor is it simply the result of a free market economy. The nine SADCC states and one occupied territory of Southern Africa were, in varying degrees, deliberately incorporated – by metropolitan powers, colonial rulers and large corporations – into the colonial and sub-colonial structures centring in general on the Republic of South Africa. The development of national economies as balanced units, let alone the welfare of the people of Southern Africa, played no part in the economic integration strategy. Not surprisingly, therefore, Southern Africa is fragmented, grossly exploited and subject to economic manipulation by outsiders. Future development must aim at the reduction of economic dependence not only on the Republic of South Africa, but also on any single external state or group of states.

Thus the problems of SADCC have to be viewed in a historical context and within the broad framework of global capitalism, colonialism and neo-colonialism. SADCC countries have been producing primary commodities for export and importing industrial products. Their economies are dependent on the world capitalist system as a whole, and in the case of Botswana, Lesotho and Swaziland, on the South African subsystem in particular. Furthermore, the South African subsystem has to be understood to be an integral part of the global system of capitalism. That is why for example the world leaders of imperialism have continued to lend support to the illegal regime of South Africa despite popular international condemnation of that regime. This, therefore, calls for a very close scrutiny by the SADCC countries of the advances made to it in the form of foreign aid from the Western capitalist countries.

The task of achieving collective self-reliance for the SADCC as a subregional grouping will thus require fundamental restructuring of production and trade patterns so as to make the SADCC economies more complementary. In this restructuring process, energy will play a pivotal role in promoting and sustaining the desired rapid growth in output, while transport and communications will have a similarly critical role in promoting and sustaining intraregional trade. This chapter examines energy, transport and communications as limiting factors on the SADCC's objective of collective self-reliance and regional development.

The practical challenges require effective policies aimed not only at quantitative and qualitative improvements in energy, but also at optimal national and regional distribution of available energy resources. Major distribution problems can arise from inadequate transport and communications infrastructure, and from inadequate mechanisms for settling cross-border trade. In the absence of regional institutional facilities for settling intra-SADCC trade the bulk of this trade is cleared through hard currencies. Given the foreign exchange difficulties of most

SADCC members the absence of a SADCC trade settlement mechanism is a binding constraint on the regional distribution of energy. Thus, while quantitative improvements in energy may solve national problems, they may not automatically contribute to regional self-sufficiency because of regional distribution problems. For instance, 90 per cent of Angola's oil is exported to non-SADCC members while other SADCC countries import oil from outside sources.

Thus the section on energy in this chapter focuses on both quantitative improvements and distribution problems of energy. The chapter first outlines the energy situation in the SADCC and indicates development prospects. Then it examines the transport and communications situation. The final section summarizes the practical and policy constraints and suggests policy options with regard to both energy, and transport and communications.

The Energy Crisis in SADCC

Within each individual member country of the SADCC region, there is a deepening energy crisis. When the Minister for Energy and Petroleum in Angola says only that 'the Energy situation in this region has not developed as well as it should or even could have done' (SADCC 1984, Lusaka), his words do not really capture the magnitude of the problem. The situation is really best described as 'disturbing', as correctly stressed in the Lagos Plan of Action with respect to African countries as a whole. (Lagos Plan, p. 116.)

Energy needs in the region have grown far greater than supplies, which is causing a lot of strain on the socio-economies of those countries. This crisis stems from a number of factors. In the first place, it is an extension of the global energy crisis which began in the 1970s with the sharp rise of world oil prices. Following the price rises from about $US3 per barrel in the 1960s to around $US38 or more in 1980, most oil-importing countries have had to spend greater shares of their foreign exchange earnings on the importation of oil. For the poor SADCC countries, most of them with export earnings of somewhere around $US100 million or so (except Angola, Zambia and Zimbabwe) and which were already experiencing balance of payments problems, the sharp rise in oil prices worsened the problem. All SADCC countries today spend over 20 per cent of their export earnings on oil imports alone with Tanzania, Mozambique and Botswana spending somewhere between 30 and 60 per cent.

But a number of other factors have served to make the energy situation much worse. The first is the economic relations between SADCC countries and the industrialized countries. SADCC countries have been experiencing a decline in their terms of trade with the outside world, mainly the advanced industrialized countries. This of course means that they have less leverage with which to cope with the new problems in the energy sector. But worst of all it has meant that any more expenditures on oil would seriously undermine those countries' capabilities to secure basic consumption needs and techno–industrial inputs.

The other factor is the geo-politics of the region. SADCC countries, most of which belong to what are referred to as the Frontline States, have, because of their opposition to colonialism in Namibia and apartheid inside South Africa, been subjected to frequent attacks by the South African regime. These attacks have mostly aimed at the destruction of economic infrastructures such as roads and railways and have seriously disrupted the transport system in the region. This has affected the flow of energy, especially petroleum, to the landlocked countries of the region. For example, the Benguela Railway which runs through Zambia, Zaïre and Angola has been made almost impassable due to attacks in the territory of Angola. The same applies to roads and other railways, especially those in the Southern part of Mozambique.

This problem, however, is magnified by the reliance of the SADCC member states on South Africa. Botswana, Lesotho and Swaziland for example depend entirely on South Africa's transport routes. This situation makes SADCC members very vulnerable to South Africa's economic and political pressures. Indeed, South Africa uses the opportunity to blackmail SADCC countries. Recently, for example, when some SADCC countries supported campaigns opposing South Africa, Pik Botha stated: 'I hope they [the Black African States neighbouring South Africa] will note the fact the [UN] Security Council, with the help of Soviet Union in the lead, will have to be blamed if that infrastructure [namely transport routes] is no longer available for their imports and exports (*Tanzania Daily News* 31/7/85). Those words of course meant much more than a mere intention to restrict South Africa's transport routes; they also meant that South Africa was going to intensify its attacks on the roads, railways and other economic and social infrastructures of those countries.

The impact of the energy crisis on the economies of the SADCC countries is even more far-ranging when we consider the opportunity cost of the expenditure that goes into oil importation alone. Because of increased oil expenditures, possibilities for domestic capital formation and debt-servicing have become extremely curtailed, resulting in slow economic growth and further indebtedness, particularly for those SADCC countries which have resorted to high commercial interest rates and short-term loans from international financial markets in order to pay for oil.

But while the energy problem in the SADCC region has been an important restricting factor, there have been several others. Neither is energy the only sector which has been in crisis. Most countries are experiencing a severe food crisis. Furthermore, most of them have been subject to an overall crisis characterized by such structural problems as imbalances in the national budgets, external trade and demand for and supply of money, as well as inflation, unemployment and shortages of goods and services. Worst of all, those countries are also facing a debt crisis, even though their debts in absolute terms are nothing when compared to those of Latin American countries. The future of the energy situation in the SADCC region is not encouraging unless bold measures are initiated to regulate the demand and supply of energy resources. In the first place all the countries are expanding their industrial capacities. Indeed they are now opening up or expanding more energy-intensive industries than before.

P. M. Ritz (1985) indicates the energy cost per dollar's worth of final demand of different industrial products is as follows: chemical industries 0.263; plastic and synthetics 0.159; primary iron and steel 0.133; paper and allied products 0.120;

stone and clay 0.109; primary non-ferrous metal manufacturing 0.096; broad and narrow fabrics, yarn and thread etc, 0.96. A 1980 World Bank report estimates energy consumption per tonne of output in terms of barrels of oil equivalent to be as follows: smelted and refined copper 3–8; crude steel 4–8; cement 0.5–1.0; ammonia 6–8; petroleum refining 0.4; cracking 10–20; pulp and paper 4–5. This really means that a typical medium-sized cement plant like that at Tanga in Tanzania, which produces 170,000 tonnes of cement per annum will be consuming 85,000 barrels of oil or its equivalent while Zimbabwe's steel plant, which produces over 1 million tonnes, will use between 4 and 8 million barrels. The industrialization programme in many of the SADCC states is now very much incorporating those types of industries. Amongst the industrial developments established during the last decade or so in Tanzania for example are three cement plants, a fertilizer industry, a petroleum refinery, an ammonia plant, a plant and pulp factory, several textile mills, a set of steel products and industries, a machine tools factory, and a truck assembly plant. Zimbabwe, which is more industrialized than any other country in sub-Saharan Africa, has many more energy-intensive industries. Zambia, Mozambique and Angola, and to some extent Malawi, have similar patterns, trends and even ambitions. For example Tanzania, Zambia and Mozambique are all aiming at establishing primary iron and steel industries in their countries. This trend means that in the coming years industrial energy requirements inside the SADCC will rise rapidly.

Household energy requirements will also increase. The population in the region is increasing at a rate of between 2 and 4 per cent per annum. The rate of urbanization is also high, sometimes as high as 45 per cent – in the case of Zambia, the most urbanized of SADCC countries. Given the declining performance of agriculture and declining terms of trade for agricultural products (compared to industrial products) in the region, the rate of urbanization is likely to remain high. Lastly, personal incomes are also likely to increase. All these factors will raise the household demand for energy. Fernandez (1985) indicates income elasticities of demand for energy in Pakistan, India and Sudan to range between 0.357 and 0.783 for commercial energy sources and between –0.08 and –0.246 for traditional energy sources. Those elasticities, however, differ even more widely between that of woodfuel of 0.354, to those of charcoal of 0.122, kerosene, 0.785 and electricity, 1.898. This means that energy requirements as a whole, and commercial energy requirements in particular, are going to increase rapidly with the rise in personal and national incomes.

The Energy Situation in Individual Countries

Angola

Angola is the only SADCC country with known oil reserves. It produces around 6 million tonnes of oil per year. In 1977 it produced 8.60 million tonnes and in 1981, 6.42 million tonnes. It consumes domestically less than 10 per cent of the total oil produced and about 50 per cent of the refined oil, exporting the rest.

Angola also produces much more electricity than it consumes and has large natural forest reserves for fuelwood and other purposes. More than 50 per cent of the country's land area is covered by natural forests. The pattern of energy consumption in 1980 is given in Table 4.1.

Table 4.1
Pattern of Energy Use in Angola

Fuelwood	3,192,400 tonnes
Petroleum	393,135 tonnes
Electricity	628 GWH
Charcoal	154,400 tonnes

Source: Bhagavan, in O'Keefe and Munslow (eds.), *Energy and Development in Southern Africa*, vol. 3, p. 21.

As in all other African countries, almost all fuelwood and charcoal in Angola go to domestic household use. But in that oil-rich country, oil products are also widely used by the domestic sector.

Household use of oil products amounts to 1 million GJ equivalent. While in most SADCC countries transport takes up the greatest share of oil products consumption, in Angola it takes up less than 10 per cent, with 43 per cent going to services and 30 per cent to industry. Angola also relies widely on electricity, most of which goes to its industry services sector (47 per cent and 30 per cent) respectively.

So far, however, export of Angolan oil is mostly to the international market, and very little goes to other SADCC members. Angola has realized this problem and initiated moves towards oil trade with other members. If Angola's oil resources were at the disposal of SADCC, the regional grouping would be almost self-sufficient in oil. Unfortunately the prospects for this are not good. The immediate neighbour is Zambia, while Botswana is close but separated by a thin strip of Namibia on the northern tip of Botswana. Zambia is not directly linked by railway with Angola. The rail link between Angola and Zambia is through Zaïre, and it has become impassable due to South African-inspired guerrilla attacks on the Angolan side of the railway.

Botswana imports refined oil from South Africa, and an appropriate infrastructure exists for this trade. To switch to Angola as a new source of oil, Botswana would need a new transport infrastructure, such as a railway line. Apart from the lack of a common border, such a link would be uneconomical in the foreseeable future. Thus the transport constraint will not permit export of oil from Angola to Botswana. As for Zambia, which already has an oil refinery linked by a pipeline to Dar es Salaam, switching to Angola would entail fresh investment in infrastructure. Apart from the risks of guerrilla disruptions and the financing problems, the investment either in a railway or pipeline would not be economically viable in view of the heavy capital outlay already tied up in the existing pipeline. Apart from this transport constraint, Zambia has such foreign exchange difficulties that it might not be able to pay for Angolan oil on a regular basis. Current oil imports into Zambia have been possible only through IMF facilities or other loan arrangements which may involve predetermined sources of imports, which would probably not permit exports of Angolan oil to neighbouring Zambia, let alone the most distant SADCC members.

Botswana
Botswana is a much smaller country than Angola in geographical size and population. The whole western part of the country consists of either grassland or arid areas, and almost the whole of the country's population lives in a narrow north–south strip extending from Francistown in the north to Gaborone in the south. Botswana borders South Africa directly to the south and the east, and Namibia, which South Africa occupies illegally, to the west. Gaborone, the country's capital city, which is in the south, is only a few kilometres from South Africa.

Botswana's socio-economy has been greatly integrated into that of South Africa. The country, like many SADCC members, provides migrant labour to South African mines. In addition it depends on South Africa in many ways, including on that country's industry, transport and communications. However, Botswana realizes the possible dangers of cooperating with the Republic of South Africa. As a result it now plays a frontline role in the consolidation and development of the SADCC, the headquarters of which are located in that country. Botswana is also slowly delinking from South Africa, though the task is of course an arduous one, given the country's proximity to South Africa and the long-established economic relations between the two countries.

Table 4.2 indicates the pattern of energy consumption in Botswana.

Table 4.2
Energy Consumption in Botswana

Energy Source	Unit: P.J.	Per cent of total
Wood	11.635	40.2
Coal	8.949	30.9
Refined petrol	5.687	19.7
Electricity	1.745	6
Crop residues	0.509	1.8
Dung	0.423	1.5

Source: Wisner in O'Keefe and Munslow (eds.) *Energy and Development in Southern Africa*, p. 92.

As evident in the table, fuelwood accounts for only 40.2 per cent of total energy consumed, a very low percentage compared to many other African countries. Most of that is used up by households. Over 90 per cent of coal consumed goes to the industrial sector. Petroleum goes mainly to the transport sector (over 80 per cent), while electricity, too, finds most use in industry (over 80 per cent).

Botswana's socio-economic set-up, however, is of interest when analysing its energy use. Both the country's population and household incomes are low and the majority of the population lives in rural areas. This makes fuelwood the major basis for household energy consumption. The industrial sector is large relative to the population size, and it accounts for 38 per cent of the country's total energy consumption.

Botswana imports its petroleum and electricity from South Africa. It produces a substantial amount of its own coal requirement, but also imports coal from Zimbabwe and South Africa. Coal deposits in Botswana are estimated to be 300 million tonnes – enough to satisfy all national needs once full exploitation takes place.

There are two remarkable features of energy consumption in Botswana. The first is the significance occupied by cow dung and crop residues in the country's total energy consumption (see Table 4.2). This particular energy generation technology which prevails in Botswana and the other small Southern African states, namely Lesotho and Swaziland, depicts the seriousness of the energy problem confronting those countries and the amount of initiative being taken by those countries to tackle that problem. The other important feature is the share of total energy consumption going to rural borehole water. About 11 per cent of total petroleum consumption and 2 per cent of national total energy consumption is used for that purpose. In fact borehole water pumping comes only next to transport in the use of petroleum, exceeding all other sectors, namely, household, industry, agriculture and service sectors.

The prices of petroleum products in Botswana are amongst the lowest in the world though petroleum uses as much as 50 per cent of the country's export earnings, mostly in the transport sector. Because of these low prices, a lot of that energy resource goes to private motor transportation.

Lesotho

Lesotho is highly dependent on other countries, especially South Africa, for most of its commercial sources. It imports its petroleum, coal and electricity supplies from South Africa. Fuelwood accounts for most of the energy consumed in Lesotho – over 90 per cent of total household energy consumption, supplemented mainly by cow dung and to some extent by charcoal. Cow dung is uniquely important to Lesotho, where it accounts for about 25 per cent of total rural household energy consumption (or a total of 4.69 GJ) and is the second source of energy in that country. Petroleum and electricity come third and fourth.

The socio-economic set-up of·Lesotho, in which industry, construction and mining are very small, makes it a much smaller user of commercial energy than most other SADCC countries. For the same reason, fuelwood, the traditional source of energy used by rural households, accounts for a large proportion of the total national energy consumption. Forty per cent of total petroleum consumed goes to the transport sector.

Lesotho faces numerous difficulties so far as energy is concerned. Forestland is declining rapidly despite afforestation programmes, and this threatens the supply of its largest source of energy. Being an importer of petroleum, electricity and coal, and above all being so highly dependent on South Africa as her exclusive source of those energy sources, Lesotho is very vulnerable to foreign blackmail. Yet, with its borders totally circumscribed by South Africa, it has little option. South Africa has exploited this strategic dependency effectively, and has tried to stop Lesotho from lessening it. It has for example virtually forced Lesotho to import petroleum from South Africa rather than from the world market. Lack of any major river in Lesotho or of significant amounts of coal makes it difficult for the country to delink itself from South Africa both with respect to coal and especially electricity. Some room does exist, however, for furthering trade in some of the energy sources, such as coal, with the SADCC member states.

Malawi

Landlocked Malawi is much larger than Lesotho, and consumes more energy. Being rich in forestland, it relies heavily on fuelwood for household use and for commercial purposes. Over 90 per cent of Malawi's energy requirement comes from this source, of which about half goes to domestic households and the other half goes to the agriculture, industry and service sectors. Tobacco and tea farms in particular consume a lot of energy, as much as 54.86 PJ, mostly from fuelwood. Of all SADCC countries, Malawi is the greatest commercial user of fuelwood.

Malawi consumes a total of only 6.69 PJ of petroleum, over 50 per cent of which goes to the transport sector and 40 per cent to industry. Like the other SADCC countries, except Angola, Malawi imports all its petroleum. Mozambique's Beira and Nancala ports are the main inlets of the oil imports. On the other hand the country generates its own electricity, mainly from hydro-power. The country still has a large unexploited potential in hydroelectricity and coal. Malawi has presently embarked on production of ethanol, thereby raising her energy development potential.

Swaziland

Swaziland is smaller than all other SADCC countries and almost completely circumscribed by South Africa. The country's population is small, as are its industrial and transport sectors. Fuelwood is, as elsewhere in the region, the largest source of energy, but its share of total national energy consumption is quite low. In this country, as in Lesotho, cow dung is the second largest source of energy. Fuelwood accounts for 35 per cent of energy consumed, cow dung/residue 23.8 per cent, petroleum 20 per cent, coal 13.8 per cent and electricity 6.7 per cent. The country therefore is not particularly dependent on one specific source of energy.

Unlike Lesotho, Swaziland produces a significant share of its own energy requirements. It is able to produce 50 per cent of its electricity requirements and almost all its coal needs. However, it imports all its petroleum and 50 per cent of its electricity from South Africa. Its efforts to get oil from elsewhere have been blocked by South Africa, upon whose transport routes imports depend.

The future energy development potential of Swaziland lies mainly in coal mining. The country has about 200 million tonnes of coal deposits – enough to last several decades. The prospects of development of hydroelectricity, however, are rather limited because of lack of major rivers.

Tanzania

Tanzania is one of the larger SADCC countries with a relatively large population and correspondingly large industry and transport sectors. It has abundant forestland, major rivers and some coal deposits. Fuelwood and charcoal account for 90 per cent of energy used, petroleum 7 per cent, agricultural residue 2 per cent and electricity 1 per cent. Over 70 per cent of the fuelwood goes to household use. Petroleum imports alone account for over 50 per cent of the country's meagre export earnings, which has made the government take several bold steps to reduce its consumption. The price of petrol for example is about $US1.20 per litre in Tanzania. Furthermore, for a long time the government had imposed almost a total ban on importation of private cars, a measure which it has now relaxed. But the country still rations petrol sales and continues to ban Sunday afternoon private motoring. These measures are believed to have had positive impacts on the limitation of petrol consumption. Nonetheless, to produce a full impact, those measures should have included restrictions on public vehicle use of petrol and diesel, including that of military trucks.

Tanzania's largest energy development potential lies with electricity. Hydro-electricity is presently produced at Nyumba ya Mungu and Hale on the River Pangani in the north of the country and at Kidatu on the River Ruaha in the east. Construction for another power station is now going on at the Stiglers Gorge on the River Ruaha. This will be the country's largest power station and its completion will make possible wider use of electricity in industries and urban households as well as rural electrification. There are also quite substantial coal deposits in the south-western part of the country. These deposits, estimated to be about 300 million tonnes, are in the same region as the country's yet untapped iron deposits, meaning that the prospects of the country to satisfy her ambition of establishing primary iron and steel industries are considerable. The exploitation of the coal reserves will also be of great economic value to the country, especially given the fact that several large energy-intensive industries have been established, e.g. cement in Mbeya and Iringa, which are near the coal reserves, and the pulp and paper mill at Mufindi.

Zambia

Zambia's economy is characterized by a dominant mining sector and a relatively large industrial sector. Mining accounts for almost 30 per cent of GDP, and the industry and transport sectors about 20 per cent. Copper-mining and copper-smelting are important in Zambia, and these are energy-intensive activities. The country's industrial and transport sectors are large overall. Hence energy consumption, and especially commercial energy consumption, is amongst the highest in the SADCC region. Mining accounts for 33 per cent of Zambia's petroleum consumption, 62 per cent of coal and 80 per cent of electricity.

However, fuelwood is again the largest source of energy, though altogether it accounts for only 42 per cent of total energy consumption. Commercial energy takes up 57 per cent of total energy consumption, composed of the following: petroleum (20 per cent), electricity (16 per cent) and coal (13 per cent).

Zambia refines crude petroleum at Indeni Refinery in Ndola. Crude oil is pumped through TAZAMA pipelines from Dar es Salaam. It has no oil of its own, however, and its heavy commercial reliance on petroleum has exposed it to the oil price shocks in the world market. This has prompted the government and the mining and manufacturing companies to embark on deliberate policies to substitute petroleum use by coal and electricity. There are indications that petroleum consumption is now on the decrease.

Zambia has coal deposits of about 32 million tonnes,[11] although at present it imports some of its coal from Zimbabwe. Zambia's potential for hydroelectricity development is also huge. As seen above, electricity so far accounts for about 16 per cent of total energy consumption. About 80 per cent of it goes to the mining and industrial sectors. Present production of electricity on the Zambesi and Kafue rivers is estimated to be only about 35 per cent of the installed production capacity. Zambia exports surplus electricity to Zimbabwe.

Zimbabwe

The pattern of energy use in Zimbabwe is similar to that of Zambia and Swaziland, in that it does not rely overly on a single source. Fuelwood accounts for 46 per cent of total consumption, coal 31 per cent, petroleum 11 per cent and electricity 10 per cent. The chief difference between Zambia and Zimbabwe lies in the fact that Zimbabwe's second major source of energy is coal, which is obtained locally and is much cheaper than Zambia's second source – imported petroleum. Zimbabwe has the largest industrial sector in the SADCC region, and a large part of that is heavy industry. The country's mining and quarrying sector, which includes gold, asbestos, nickel, copper, coal and chrome mining, is also quite sizeable. Zimbabwe's commercial agriculture is significantly mechanized. Add to this the size of the population and one can see why Zimbabwe is by far the largest user of energy in the region. Energy consumption by sector is as follows: households 47 per cent, industry 22 per cent, transport 11 per cent, agriculture 7 per cent, mining 5 per cent, power 3.6 per cent and others 3.8 per cent.

Zimbabwe is one of the few countries in Africa which has been able to substitute petroleum with coal in such sectors as mining and transport. Her history of such substitutions dates far back to the UDI period (1965–80) when the country was isolated by the international community. The country has coal deposits estimated at over 30 billion tonnes, which at the current rates of consumption is enough to last about 1,000 years.

Zimbabwe is therefore less haunted than the other SADCC countries by the problem of petroleum expenditure. The country's petroleum is imported by road and rail and also through the Beira–Umtali pipeline. The transport sector is so far the largest user of petroleum. Electrification of railroads has started and this will go some way towards relieving petroleum use in the transport sector. The present efforts to produce ethanol and to blend it with petrol for vehicles are also a step in the right direction.

Mozambique

Munslow (1984) indicates the following energy use pattern in Mozambique: fuelwood 77 per cent, petroleum 7.8 per cent, dung/residue 6.4 per cent, charcoal 4.7 per cent, coal 2.1 per cent, and electricity 0.9 per cent. Typical of the region, most of the fuelwood (76.4 per cent) goes to the household sector; other users are industry (16.6 per cent), transport (4.3 per cent), social service institutions (1.4 per cent) and agriculture (1.3 per cent).

Petroleum, mostly crude, is imported and refined in Mozambique's own refinery which, according to Munslow, has an 800,000 tonne capacity. This commodity accounts for 35 per cent of the country's export earnings. The main use is for: transport (40 per cent), industry (25 per cent), and the remainder for commercial, service and household sectors (Munslow 1984).

The source of energy with perhaps the highest potential is hydroelectricity. Munslow indicates that in 1980 the country produced 11,551 GWH, of which over 8,000 GWH (90 per cent) was exported to South Africa. Completion of expansion of the Cabora Bassa dam, which is the largest producer of hydroelectricity in the country, will provide an additional capacity of 1,200 MW.

There is also some coal, but so far the known deposits are insignificant. Oil prospecting is in progress at several places but as yet there is no evidence of any deposits.

Energy Potential and Prospects in SADCC

The discussion above reveals clearly that the energy situation in the SADCC region demands concern and serious action. This is true especially for commercial energy and, in particular, petroleum. In Africa today, petroleum generally accounts for over 90 per cent of the total commercial energy consumption, while coal, hydroelectricity and gas take up the remainder. This picture is more or less the same in the SADCC with the exception of Zimbabwe, Zambia and Swaziland, where coal and electricity account for a considerable part of the total commercial energy consumed. Botswana, though also endowed with huge deposits of coal, is still heavily dependent on petroleum.

Fuelwood and charcoal are also raising concern amongst SADCC countries, most notably in the small states of Lesotho and Swaziland. The rate of depletion of forests has been quite high and threatens serious ecological and climatic consequences. Mothers now trek longer distances in search of firewood and the prices of fuelwood and charcoal have shot up tremendously. To the urban dweller, fuelwood and charcoal are more expensive than kerosene, electricity or gas.

The situation is no different as far as electricity is concerned. Even though investments are being made the region had a surplus capacity of 17 per cent in 1981, it is envisaged that that surplus will have come down tremendously in 1990 because of the slow rate of investments as compared to demand increases.

Thus despite the fact that energy consumption within SADCC countries is low, ranging between Malawi's per capita consumption of 52 kg of coal equivalent and Zimbabwe's 600 kg, as compared say to the US consumption per capita of 9,000 kg, these countries must strive much more to control their consumption. Ironically, the advanced industrial states have been expressing more concern about energy conservation than Africa (including SADCC countries).

Dependence on South Africa for energy, either directly or through its transport network, poses a grave danger to the development of the SADCC countries. This applies especially to Botswana, Lesotho and Swaziland.

A certain amount of trade has been taking place with respect to energy between

SADCC countries. Zimbabwe exports coal to most of the members of the SADCC. Zambia too exports some coal to Tanzania and electricity to Zimbabwe. Tanzania in turn exports refined petroleum to Zambia. The potential for exports of petroleum by Angola to all members of SADCC are hampered by transport and payments problems. Possibilities for exports of electricity by Mozambique to some of the members are great, as is Botswana's potential with respect to coal. The general SADCC energy prospects may be summarized as follows:

Modern Fuels
In the absence of the existing spatial, financial and institutional impediments, the anticipated regional supplies of modern fuel of the SADCC countries together would more than satisfy the region's demand. On a physical aggregate basis, the energy foundation of the region is strong. There are surpluses of electricity, coal and crude oil – 118 per cent of requirements for crude oil. The region is actually capable of producing over twice (i.e. 210 per cent) the quantity needed to meet projected internal requirements of electricity, coal and crude oil. Additionally, the gross output of refinery capacities seems to meet regional demands. The above surpluses are based on projected energy production capability, not on potential economically exploitable resources. For each type of fuel there is additional promising potential in the region for hydro, coal, oil and natural gas development beyond the projected figures for 1990.

In terms of physical availability of modern fuels in the region, there is ample opportunity for regional self-sufficiency. However, this physical supply/demand match in the aggregate overshadows problems within individual countries and in the region related to: 1) the technical and economic feasibility of developing and upgrading transportation and distribution networks to better link source centres with use centres; and 2) the need to create institutional arrangements which would be effective in ensuring mutual benefits to all SADCC countries.

Woodfuel and Biomass
The situation of traditional fuel contrasts sharply with that of modern fuels. Pressure on wood for the rural communities and charcoal for the towns has become so great that there are severe shortages in a number of localities. These shortages are likely to become more widespread in many countries by the early 1990s.

While biomass is likely to play a significant role in supplementing SADCC energy requirements in future, all the SADCC countries are experiencing some degree of forest depletion. There are cases ranging from severe shortages over substantial portions of the populated rural areas (as in Lesotho, Malawi, Mozambique, Tanzania and Zimbabwe), to deforestation near urban areas for charcoal supply (as in Angola and Zambia), to limited local shortages (as in Botswana and Swaziland). Between 10,000 and 40,000 hectares are being deforested each year. The dominant causes for this rate of deforestation appear to be: clearing land for subsistence and plantation agriculture; excessive (legal and illegal) felling of trees for sale as timber in both domestic and foreign markets; firewood for curing tobacco and tea; charcoal production for sale in the urban areas; and obtaining wooden poles for traditional housebuilding.

New and Renewable Sources of Energy
Excluding biomass and hydroelectricity, new and renewable sources of energy are still at the experimental and demonstration stages. The successful use of ethanol as part substitute for petrol (gasoline) in Zimbabwe is an exception.

Discussions about energy development prospects and strategies for the developing countries have taken place at various intergovernmental and non-governmental meetings. The Brandt Commission Report for example, noting the problems of energy in developing countries, including those of fuelwood shortage and balance of payments, made several recommendations which are particularly relevant to the SADCC. The report suggested that 'the long term solutions [to the energy problems] lie in the development of alternative and renewable energy sources, but the short term difficulties are acute. Both require nothing less than a global strategy for energy'. (Brandt Report, p. 160.) Noting that multinational companies involved with oil make superprofits, the report calls for a 'special care to consider the reciprocal obligations of MNCs and host and home countries'. The report finally comes out with a policy on energy which includes recourse to alternative energy sources (away from oil) including coal, hydroelectricity, solar energy (mostly for space heating and electricity generation in rural areas), and photovoltaic cells and thermal electricity sources. Of special interest in the report as far as the SADCC countries are concerned is the mention made regarding energy development in landlocked developing countries, noting that 'solar energy is already competitive with other energy sources, and can become more so with further development'. (Ibid. p. 167.) Last but not least the report called for international support for the developing countries in their endeavour to explore oil fuels, develop natural gas, and hydroelectric and geothermal energy.

Another report of special interest is the Lagos Plan of Action drawn up by the Heads of State of Africa at the OAU meeting of 1980 in Lagos. The Plan which noted 'the African energy situation as disturbing' outlined the main problems in energy as: lack of energy policy; non-integration of energy activities in national plans; lack of inventory for energy resources and energy-related manpower; lack of subregional efforts in the development and utilization of energy; lack of funds; lack of standardization in the electricity sector; shortage of manpower and exorbitant prices charged for imported energy and equipment; and lastly, lack of a framework for concerted action and cooperation.

The Lagos Plan therefore recommended the following to be undertaken: increasing energy resources so as to ensure endogenous and self-sustained development; diversifying energy sources; finding a permanent solution to the problem of supply of oil in order to be able to ensure sovereignty of the African countries; and lastly, provision of better living conditions in the rural areas by making better use of energy resources and by achieving self-sufficiency in food. It further recommended more specific measures to be undertaken in relation to each source of energy – i.e. fossil fuels, hydro-power, new and renewable energy sources and nuclear energy.

It is important to note some of the efforts being made in other parts of the world in order to come out with a comprehensive set of objectives and priorities for energy development in the SADCC region. For our analysis let us therefore examine the example of Canada's handling of the energy question.

In 1980 Canada embarked on an energy programme aimed at development of the energy sector to take account of the special sectoral problems since the OPEC price rises in the 1970s. The programme included measures such as subsidization, to reduce dependency on petroleum by encouraging substitution by other sources. The programme aimed at reducing oil consumption everywhere for residential, commercial and industrial purposes by 10 per cent. The programme also provided for grants for research and development in areas related to energy production and energy use. (Canada: *The National Energy Programme*, 1980.)

SADCC countries have sought to answer more or less the same questions posed and answered by the Brandt Commission Report, the Lagos Plan of Action or indeed the Canadian Government's Energy Programme. A statement issued in Luanda in February 1982 regarding energy development in the SADCC region pointed out the need for:

1. diversification of energy sources for rural areas in order to avoid serious ecological impact due to over-reliance on fuelwood;
2. more balanced, more economical and more sustaining ways of using energy, including attaching priority to indigenous sources of energy, and creating integrated electricity networks;
3. an approach to the energy problem through self-reliance – developing domestic resources and skills, and resorting to foreign assistance mainly to supplement domestic efforts and resources;
4. a commitment by the world community to meeting UN aid targets in order to offset the hardships experienced by SADCC countries following oil prices.

The statement also called specifically for: a policy of oil conservation; exploration and exploitation of coal deposits; increased use of hydroelectricity; promotion of small-scale hydroelectricity schemes; resorting to biomass, solar energy, etc., in both rural and urban areas; promotion of energy-related research and training; exchange of information and technology in the SADCC region; increase of intraregional trade in energy; promotion of interconnection of national electrical networks; promotion of afforestation programmes.

SADCC Energy Projects

The member states of the SADCC have asked Angola, the energy sector coordinator, to draw up a detailed document on the programme of national priority projects that might get SADCC support.

There are also on the other hand deliberate projects aimed at regional cooperation and rational utilization of energy resources. These include the three electricity projects outlined below.

The Interconnection of the Botswana/Zimbabwe Grids. This project has been identified on the basis of a technical and economic analysis carried out between July 1982 and March 1983 by Angola.

An interconnection with Zimbabwe would broaden the supply possibilities of Botswana, which can only rely on a stand-by supply from South Africa. If the project is implemented Botswana will get substantial support from Zimbabwe and will be able to face the future more securely. This would constitute safety of supply in the event of an incident in its own generation facilities. Besides, the interconnection would allow both characteristics of their power stations, on the basis of a coordinated planning.

The Connection of North Botswana to the Electricity Grids of Zambia or Zimbabwe. The project was investigated in 1975 when it was considered that isolated diesel generators would be less costly because of the then low level of demand. At that time available capacity from generators was 270 kW and total demand was less; the demand has since increased. It is now in the region of 500 kW (not including suppressed demand) and could increase to 1500 kW over the next five years. It now appears feasible to connect north Botswana to the grid of either Zambia or Zimbabwe, both of which benefit from hydroelectricity generation.

The Interconnection of Southern Mozambique and Swaziland Grids. The master plan project for the electricity supply of Swaziland and the Maputo area is one of the regional projects to have resulted from the desire of SADCC member states to promote the national utilization of their energy resources and regional cooperation, and to reduce their dependence on energy imports, particularly from South Africa. It has been drawn up on the basis of a technical and economic analysis carried out between July 1982 and March 1983.

The interconnection should allow both countries to optimize the size and characteristics of their power stations, based on coordinated planning. It would also allow both countries to allocate better their investment over time, by anticipating new schemes on either side of the border as each case may merit. It would give much more flexibility in programming new power stations. Since at least five to six years are needed for the construction of a power station, and considering that the real growth rate of demand is very uncertain, the interconnection would allow some leeway and would reduce the risk of premature investment in either country. It would make Swaziland less dependent on a stand-by supply from South Africa.

Transport and Communications (see Table 4.3)

The Current Situation

It has been observed that the transport and communication sector is one of the problem sectors in SADCC. Intra-SADCC transport networks are limited and even where they do exist in some of the SADCC countries they are extremely insecure. Most SADCC countries, especially landlocked Botswana, Lesotho, Swaziland and Zimbabwe, are extremely dependent on South Africa's transport system, with the risks which that entails.

The main ports of the SADCC countries are Dar es Salaam in Tanzania, Nacala,

Beira and Maputo in Mozambique, and Mercedes, Lobito and Luanda in Angola. The capacities of these ports range from that of Nacala, which is about 0.8 million tonnes per annum, to that of Lobito, which is about 1.1 million tonnes, Beira, 1.5 million tonnes and Maputo, about 7.6 million tonnes. They provide services both to their host country and the other countries of the region.

Some of the railway lines of the SADCC countries lead to South African railway systems and ports, for example the Harare, Gweru-Chicualacuala railway or the lines running from Mbabane (Swaziland) via Goba to Maputo and from Maseru (Lesotho) to South Africa.

The total length of railway lines in the SADCC is over 20,000 km. The capacity of the various regional railway lines varies widely, between that of Tazara, which is about 2 million tonnes, to Nacala and Benguela with about 3 million each, Machipanda and Limpopo about 4 million, and finally Goba about 8 million. The Machipanda, Limpopo and Benguela lines are presently marked with excess capacities of more than a million tonnes each due to security problems inside parts of Mozambique and Angola.

Presently there are no direct railway lines between a number of neighbouring SADCC states. No links exist between Tanzania and Mozambique, Tanzania and Malawi, Zambia and Mozambique, and Zambia and Angola. Malawi railways extend only about 35 km to the Zambian border. The pattern of railways in SADCC countries depicts the colonial legacies. The lines are running to the east, in Tanzania and Mozambique, and to the west in Angola, linking those countries' ports to export commodity producing areas. In Zambia and Zimbabwe, the lines were also built to cater mainly for external trade.

Angola, Mozambique and Tanzania have the longest stretches of railway lines. But overall the best-serviced countries are Zimbabwe and Mozambique. Zimbabwe, which has a stretch of 2,836 km of railway lines (as compared to Angola's 3,810, Mozambique's 3,843 and Tanzania's 3,449) has over 400 locomotives and 13,000 wagons. Mozambique's three railway systems operate over 200 locomotives and 7,500 wagons. The main problems confronting the railway systems in SADCC countries include shortage of locomotives and wagons, worn-out rails, incompatible or inadequate gauges and, most of all, administrative and managerial problems. Tanzania and Zambia for example are acutely hit by the problem of shortage of locomotives along the Tazara and within their individual countries' railway lines. The lines across the whole region are old, a number of them, such as Tanzania's and the Zambia–Zimbabwe line, dating as far back as 1905. Thus they require a lot of repair and maintenance. Most lines are the single-track type, which cannot sustsain heavy-duty transport. The gauges also vary between countries, restricting traffic between incompatible systems.

In so far as inter-country railway transport is concerned, however, some of the biggest problems are administrative. The most obvious is that of border checks, which in some instances are extremely laborious. The other crucial problem is that of settlement of financial accounts between different countries for railway services rendered. The Tazara, for instance, which is owned jointly by Tanzania and Zambia, has come to a standstill several times because Zambia was unable to transfer funds to the Tazara headquarters in Dar es Salaam. Fortunately the amount of political goodwill and cooperation which exists between the two countries has so far led to a smooth settlement of that kind of problem. The Zambia–Tanzania Road Services Company, which was owned by Tanzania, Zambia and an Italian firm, has been less lucky.

There is also the problem of the capacity of the railway systems and the closely linked one of port handling facilities. The capacities of the railway lines are mainly limited both by the stock of locomotives and wagons and by the type of gauges in those lines. A range of problems also arises at the railway terminals and at the ports. The sudden re-routing of cargo shipments away from South African railway and port systems to those of the SADCC countries has meant congestion at the ports of Dar es Salaam, Nacala, Beira and Maputo, where port handling facilities are still limited. This has in turn led to delays in cargo clearing, rising storage charges and surcharges by shipping lines.

The dominant means of surface transport in the SADCC, however, is road transport. But like railway lines, the length of the roads (all-weather roads made of gravel or tarmac) is limited. Altogether the total road network in the SADCC region could be somewhere around 300,000 km, of which less than 10 per cent is tarmacked; 50 per cent is gravelled and the rest is earth road. Inter-country road links are far from being adequate. Only Zimbabwe could be said to have satisfactory road links with all her neighbours. Malawi is poorly linked to Mozambique, Tanzania, Zimbabwe and Zambia. Malawi in fact conspicuously misses road links to Nacala Port in Mozambique, which is nearest to it. There is no road link so far between Zambia and Angola, nor between Tanzania and Mozambique. The tarmac road extending between Tanzania and Zambia, like the Tazara, was constructed in response to the UDI in Rhodesia (now Zimbabwe) and the need to ship Zambian exports and imports via Dar es Salaam.

Overall road transport, including both passenger services and cargo haulage between the SADCC countries, is extremely limited. The main problem is the lack of good connecting roads, but there are also problems associated with the small fleet of buses and trucks operating between those countries, border checks, poor road maintenance, lack of bilateral and multilateral arrangements, and lack of common road design standards.

As for cargo, the biggest drawback to inter-country road transport is the huge operational costs of trucking industry relative to railway transport. Only where railway transport capacity falls short of demand does trucking really become feasible for long-distance cargo haulage. This is demonstrated by the demise of the Zambia–Tanzania Road Services Company (ZTRS) which failed to compete with the Tazara rail system which was established later. This company was initiated immediately after UDI in Rhodesia as an alternative outlet for Zambian copper and an inlet for that country's imports.

Road transport, which includes urban and rural as well as passenger and cargo, is by far the most dominant mode of internal transport in any country. It is also the only means that could be made accessible to each and every part of a country and the most technically and commercially viable where short distances are involved.

Internal road transport inside the SADCC countries is far from being adequate either. The pattern of roadways is very much like that of railways, namely, one that links export commodity producing regions to the ports, leaving wide sections of the country inaccessible. This is the pattern in Angola, Botswana, Mozambique, Tanzania and Zambia. In Botswana, where only around 1,000 km are tarred, the central and western parts of that country are served by only one good road, the one running between Nata and Windhoek (Namibia), which is not tarred.

Road transport inside the SADCC countries is also heavily constrained by shortage of vehicles. The trucking industry is run variously by public and private companies in the different countries. In Tanzania, for example, the trans-country trucking is largely owned by the state while localities are served by private or cooperatively owned lorries. Trans-country bus transport, however, is split almost in half between state and private ownership, while localities are also largely served by private and cooperative buses. The pattern of ownership is more or less the same in some of the SADCC countries such as Mozambique and Angola. In Zambia, Zimbabwe, Botswana, Malawi, Lesotho and Swaziland ownership is predominantly private. However, irrespective of the mode of ownership, all SADCC countries suffer from vehicle shortages, and poor roads ensure a high breakdown rate in what few trucks and buses there are, making the inadequacy of the transport service even more pronounced.

Road transport difficulties are reflected in the socio-economies of SADCC countries in various ways, including: failures in the distribution of production inputs and collection and distribution of industrial and agricultural products, e.g. fertilizers, crops, sugar, cement, etc.; failures to meet export targets of agricultural and industrial products; high freight charges and passenger fares; and unreliability including unexpected journey cancellations and breakdowns.

Urban transport in SADCC countries is mainly composed of motorized transport buses, minibuses, taxis, pickup vans and motorcycles, and non-motorized transport, mostly bicycles and carts. The high rate of urban growth in the SADCC region over the last two decades has meant a corresponding growth in the demand for transport, without corresponding growth in the infrastructural capacity. This problem has been made worse by the adoption of inappropriate urban transport technologies in a number of SADCC countries. In Dar es Salaam, for instance, one finds a huge concentration of energy-intensive landrovers. Taxis in Dar es Salaam, too, are the luxurious single-passenger-per-trip type; taxis are not usually shared. Lastly the use of carts for transport is still limited despite some indication that residents of Dar es Salaam as well as other Tanzanian towns are making increased use of them. Human-drawn carts are now common at railway and bus stations and market places. In Zambia, inadequate or non-existent public transport encourages excessive dependence on relatively costly private cars.

The other important means of transport is air transport. Each SADCC country has its own airline. Given technical, financial and market constraints, most of the airlines have only few aircraft, some of them less than ten. This in turn implies high unit costs of air services and frequent interruptions of flight schedules. Lack of coordination of the different airline operations also results in a lot of inconveniences.

One other communication problem is that of telecommunications. Tele-communications in the region are predominantly made of telegraphic, telephone and telex services employing both terrestrial and satellite links. The services are inadequate, both for internal and external communications. Some SADCC countries do not have direct links between them but have to route calls outside the region, for which they have to pay high transmission charges. The system is also hampered by maintenance problems, scarcity of satellite earth stations and low-capacity terrestrial bearers. In some of the countries, such as Tanzania, television services have not yet been introduced, while in most of the countries, telecommunications are heavily urban-biased.

Cooperation between the SADCC countries in the field of transport and communications will have a lot of advantages for each country. The benefits of cooperation in this sphere are evidenced by the former East African Community (EAC), which brought together Tanzania, Kenya and Uganda. The EAC ran joint air, rail and port services, amongst other activities. It was therefore able to facilitate common aircraft and locomotive workshops, and common railway and aircraft personnel training centres, and it was able to mobilize and share external assistance. The common services also made possible market concentration for the East African Airlines and the East African Railways Corporation and easier travel between the three countries.

The EAC had to be wound up in the end, mainly because of a failure to share benefits equitably between members, but also because of political and ideological differences. None the less a careful study of the EAC has a lot of lessons to offer to the successful development of SADCC.

Table 4.3
SADCC Projects in the Transport and Communications Sector

| | ($US Million) | | |
| | Total Cost | Allocated or Committed Funds | |
Projects	1982 Price	Amount	Percentage
Operational Coordination	9.4	3.8	40
Training	2.0	1.6	80
Maputo Port Transport System	552.0	160.0	29
Beira Port Transport System	414.0	58.0	14
Nacala Port Transport System	235.0	101.0	43
Dar es Salaam Port Transport System	339.0	22.0	7
Lobito Port Transport System	90.0	14.0	16
Inter-regional Surface Transport	404.0	41.0	10
Civil Aviation	308.0	49.0	16
Telecommunications	235.0	108.0	45
Total	2,588.4	558.4	21.5

Source: SADCC, *SADCC Maseru*, Mambo Press, 1983, p. 22.

Prospects in Transport and Telecommunications
A look at the planned and actual improvements in SADCC transport and telecommunications indicates an effort to reduce the vulnerability of the

landlocked SADCC members to South Africa's economic manipulations. Documents for the Seventh Annual SADCC Donor Conference of January 1986, covering 111 transport projects, confirm this. This principle of reducing the SADCC's dependence on South Africa has not been abandoned even in the inevitable rescheduling of some projects for the period 1986–90. The priorities will be completion of essential rehabilitation of the regional rail links and to a lesser extent road links and ports. The emphasis is on the three east coast ports of Dar es Salaam, Nacala and Beira, which are crucial outlets for Zimbabwe, Malawi and Zambia in particular. The most advanced of these projects is the $US285 million programme to upgrade Nacala port and its transport links, in particular the 538 km railway to Cuamba on the Malawi border. For a breakdown of projects see Table 6.1 in Chapter 6.

Although the Tazara carries the majority of copper exports, most imports still come in on the southern routes through South Africa because of inefficiencies on the line. The $US157 million three-phase ten-year plan to overcome these is therefore very important. The plan was presented to the donors in April 1985. It attracted $US65.5 million in finance for 15 of the 22 sub-projects, including ten of the priority schemes.

Progress on the rehabilitation of Beira port and its associated transport systems – in particular the Dondo–Zimbabwe railway, the Beira–Malawi railway and the Beira–Chimoio–Zimbabwe road – has been far less satisfactory, with only 27 per cent of the $US581 million total costs funded or under discussion. This compares with a funding of 46 per cent of the $US444 million Dar es Salaam scheme. In an effort to rectify this, the Southern African Transport and Communications Commission (SATCC) has prepared a ten-year implementation plan. It is easy, however, to foresee that the donors may be conditioned at least in part by the current security situation in Mozambique. Acknowledgement of the security problems in both Angola and Mozambique is also partially behind the lower priority given to the Lobito–Benguela and Maputo–Limpopo port and railway projects, both of which are very vital to the region. Although essential rehabilitation work on the Benguela railway will continue during the period, the $US182 million full-scale rehabilitation work is now scheduled from near the end of the decade up to 1994. Similarly, major work on Lobito Port, based on a Danish-funded masterplan, is now scheduled for 1990 and beyond.

The rescheduling or postponement of implementation of projects based in Angola is recognition of the impact of geo-political circumstances on the transport facilities. For instance the Benguela Railway, which links hinterland Angola and Zambia to the seaport, has been rendered a hopeless system by South African-sponsored UNITA guerrilla attacks on the railway system. Under the circumstances, heavy investment in the rehabilitation of such a system may not significantly improve the regional transport system. Thus the difficult geo-political environment tends to distort the development pattern of the regional transport system. Moreover, by forcing SADCC to rely on second-choice routes or ports, the geo-political hostilities, and in particular South Africa's destabilizing tactics, tend to raise the overall cost of regional improvements in transport systems.

Most affected by the SATCC's rescheduling exercise are the national projects which member states were asked to prioritize additionally in terms of their own development goals. The result has been that some projects, like the trans-Kalahari Railway in Botswana have been at least temporarily withdrawn. Others, such as the $US28 million rehabilitation of Zambia's Lusaka–Mongu Road or the upgrading of its provincial airports, are delayed until after 1988. Probably the largest scheme affected by the reappraisal is the 605 km Mtwara–Songea–Mbamba Road in Tanzania. The previous cost estimates of $US355 million have been cut to $US44 million by reducing rehabilitation work in 1986–90 to a 160 km Songea–Mbamba section and subjecting the rest to a feasibility study for implementation in 1991–95.

Concluding Observations

For most SADCC members there is a need for appropriate technology based on available energy resources. Such a strategy would reduce dependence on electricity for rural domestic energy requirements. Perhaps the biggest problem in this task of rationalizing technology arises from SADCC's excessive dependence on donors not only for finance but also for technology.

While quantitative improvements are essential in many areas of energy, SADCC's difficulties are compounded by severe distribution problems. Even within national boundaries, local sources of energy are not available to certain areas because of transportation problems. For instance, while Mozambique and Zambia export electricity to their neighbours, many areas of Mozambique and Zambia have no electricity. The economics of distributing locally available energy resources to all parts of the country are often prohibitive because of the underdeveloped status of some areas. Indeed there is sometimes a vicious circle: electricity or other modern energy will not reach an area because it is too underdeveloped to justify the necessary investment, and on the other hand the area cannot really develop until it has a modern energy supply. Such a vicious circle has to be broken by the supply of appropriate energy for development.

The inevitable risk of unproductive investment must be absorbed by other comprehensive development promotion efforts. In intraregional distribution of energy the transportation problems are even more pronounced and are compounded by institutional barriers to international trade. Payment difficulties also constrain intra-SADCC trade. Thus, even where available energy resources in a region would adequately cover all the regional requirements, transportation and institutional impediments may hamper the distribution of the energy resources from one SADCC country to others. Until these distribution problems are solved SADCC will continue with the situation in which some members are exporting energy out of SADCC, while others are importing it from outside the region. While efforts are being made to improve the regional transport and communications system, SADCC has no policy on evolving some mechanism for settling intraregional trade. This is a major policy omission which needs immediate attention.

The challenge of developing transport and communications was underscored by the creation of the Transport and Communications Commission in the original

SADCC declaration. This is one sector which appears to have enjoyed priority attention from the very beginning. The slow progress in this area is mainly a reflection of financial constraints. The rehabilitation of existing harbours and railway and road systems will involve heavy financial outlays, not to mention construction of new systems. Certain desirable transport links between SADCC members may not even be considered because of the prohibitive cost of infrastructural development. For instance, a pipeline from Angola to Zambia would encourage the flow of Angolan oil to Zambia and other SADCC members, but the cost of such a pipeline would be prohibitive.

Apart from the absolute cost of intra-SADCC transport and communications infrastructure, the economics of such investment is further complicated by the high probability of under-utilization of such infrastructure for intra-SADCC trade. For the present and the immediate future, South African military activities or those of South African-inspired political rebels will tend to destabilize transport facilities in the SADCC region. The remedy to this problem lies in a political solution based on majority rule in South Africa and independence in Namibia. SADCC must continue its comprehensive pressure for a fair political system in South Africa and Namibia which, in turn, will eliminate the geo-political tensions in the region.

Another factor that leads to under-utilization of the intra-SADCC physical infrastructure is that of the trade barriers among SADCC countries. In this respect, the lack of payments and clearing system for intra-SADCC trade is perhaps the most serious constraint which needs immediate attention.

5 The Effects of the World Economic Recession on the Mining Sector in the SADCC Region

Denny H. Kalyala and Gilbert N. Mudenda

The African continent is one of the world's great storehouses of mineral wealth. Indeed some of the biggest producers and exporters of a wide range of minerals/metals are found in the SADCC region. At a global level, excluding East European countries, Zambia ranks fourth in copper production and export and second in cobalt. Zimbabwe is fifth in chromium and eleventh in nickel, while Botswana ranks fourth in diamonds and tenth in nickel. Botswana, Mozambique, Swaziland, Tanzania and Zimbabwe together account for as much as 60 per cent of Africa's coal reserves, i.e. between 2,500 and 3,000 million tonnes of recoverable resources as well as several tens of thousand million potential geological resources.[1]

Despite this impressive record of mineral wealth the Southern African subcontinent still remains one of the least economically developed areas in the world. Among the principal factors is the heavy entrenchment, since the colonial era, of the multinational corporations which 'dominate exploitation, technology and control of the market' (Moshi 1981, p. 1). Apparently even after attainment of political independence by a majority of countries in the Southern African region the status quo appears to persist. The world recession, triggered by escalating oil prices, has compounded the situation.

The aim of this chapter is to highlight some of the major developments in the mining sector in the non-oil-developing countries, especially SADCC members, against the background of world economic recession. Secondly, to show how this sector has been used as an avenue of capitalist penetration and to outline the potential the SADCC region has in this sector which could be used as a basis for strengthening closer economic cooperation and self-reliance.

Imperialism and the Mining Industry

The advent of capitalism which was heralded by the Industrial Revolution gave great impetus to the development of the mining industry. It increased the demand for metals/minerals; increased the number of metals/minerals required by modern industry; and improved the methods used in the extraction of minerals and metals. Similarly, when capitalism reached the imperialist stage in its development, the mining industry was also affected by that development. In effect, one could say that the mining industry provides a very good illustration of Lenin's theses on imperialism. During the latter half of the 19th Century, the mining industry began to restructure itself according to the imperatives of the imperialist stage. First, there was a spate of mergers leading to the emergence of large mining corporations (Rio Tinto 1873; Metallgesellschaft 1883; Phelps Dodge 1885; Amax 1887; Anaconda 1895; and Ascarco 1899). Secondly, these mergers were all backed by finance capital which had by then assumed the dominant role in the international commercial and industrial system. Thirdly, the increasing need for minerals led to a quest for new deposits and this in turn prompted the export of capital to the then backward regions and the mining companies were among the leading avenues for direct foreign investment. These included such well-known companies as Union Minière du Haute Katanga (1906) and Anglo American Corporation (1917). The British South Africa Company (1885), a company interested in the acquisition of mineral rights, was instrumental in carving out Central Africa as its exclusive sphere of influence. It later annexed Malawi, Zambia and Zimbabwe as colonies of the British Crown.

The impact of the mining industry on Southern Africa has had very long-lasting effects, and the colonial experience of the region was very closely connected to the need to valorize mining capital. This is why Southern Africa has been characterized by Samir Amin and Archie Mafeje as the 'Africa of the labour reserve'. The creation of a large reservoir of cheap African labour was accomplished by various colonial policies such as taxation and those that were deliberately aimed at the destruction of the pre-colonial natural economies. At the same time, the labour migration system which was instituted denied the African population security in the urban centres and thereby for the African people to move between town and country. Together these policies ensured a constant source of cheap African labour for mining, and later agricultural, capital. Obviously, the overall effects of this system differed from one country to another. It is, however, safe to say that the most affected countries were Botswana and Lesotho and to a lesser extent Swaziland, Malawi, Zambia, Zimbabwe and Mozambique. Angola and Tanzania did not become large suppliers of labour to the South African mining towns, albeit a few citizens from these countries found their way to South Africa in search of employment.

In countries such as Zambia, Zimbabwe and Angola, where the mining industry developed at a later stage, it was largely dominated by South African based financial and mining interests. For example, the development of large-scale mining operations in Zambia was dominated, as early as the 1930s, by the Anglo American Corporation of South Africa in collaboration with its subsidiary and affiliated companies. Consequently, the economies of the countries in the region, be they mineral-rich or not, were subordinated to interests of South African based mining capital. In those countries where the mining industry was not developed, it was the cheap labour that mining capital exploited, while in the mineral-rich countries it was the minerals and the cheap labour that monopoly capital was after. In this connection, it is interesting to note that it was only after independence that the mineral resources of Botswana and Swaziland were seriously explored and exploited.

Five years after the attainment of independence, Zambia nationalized foreign mining companies operating in the country. This move was part of a world-wide wave of nationalizations in which developing countries attempted to regain sovereignty over their resources. These nationalizations posed a very serious threat to the interests of monopoly capital and the Zambian example portended what was to follow once the other countries in the region gained their independence and national liberation. Monopoly capital had to reconcile itself to this new situation and adopted other means of control. This, as the Zambian example shows, took the form of shifting the area of activity from direct investment to the commercialization of technology: namely, sale of management skills, equipment, process know-how, marketing outlets, etc.

The remainder of this chapter addresses itself to and counterposes the need for monopoly capital to restructure itself within the region and the efficacy of the SADCC initiative which aims at reducing dependence on South Africa, the dominant power in the region. More specifically, it raises these issues in the context of the mining industry and how the SADCC initiatives relating to the mining sector have either succeeded in reducing dependence on monopoly capital in general and South Africa in particular or whether they have in effect aggravated that dependence. Such questions, especially when they relate to the mining industry, are reasonable, because the mining industry is the principal way through which monopoly capital has been able to penetrate the region. In addition, these questions are important because the programmes of coordination and cooperation within the SADCC region are taking place during a period of crisis and it is the base mining industry which has been most severely hit by the current world economic recession.

The World Economic Recession and Minerals/Metals

During the Great Depression of the 1930s the aggregate gross domestic product (GDP) of the Western industrial countries fell by 17.7 per cent, and world trade 26.8 per cent. The situation must have been much worse for developing countries, especially those in sub-Saharan Africa. Since then there have been a further two severe downturns in the world economy's path to recovery.

The first of these came in 1974–75, when escalating oil prices set another wave of economic recession in motion. The effects of this recession on Western industrial countries and the volume of international trade were not as severe as those of the earlier one. Corresponding declines for GDP and world trade were a mere 0.4 per cent and 5 per cent respectively. As for developing countries a common trend is not discernible. Obviously this was a period of high windfall gains for oil-exporting developing countries yet a period of economic austerity for the non-oil-exporting ones. For the latter category the effects of this era have lasted to the present day. Emergence of the second oil shock of 1979–80, the third phase alluded to earlier, has come to compound the situation further. The effects of this shock have been diverse. Although slight improvements in the GDP of Western industrial countries were recorded in 1981–82, world trade continued to decline, albeit at a very slow pace – 1 per cent (World Development Report 1984, p. 20).

On the whole it has been observed that Western industrial countries and Eastern European countries were in 1983 back on a recovery path. In Western industrial countries growth in 1980–81 was on average 1.5 per cent and even went to below zero in 1982, but it then rose to 2.2 per cent in 1983. However, this recovery has not been shared equitably among the countries. Worst affected have been non-oil-developing countries where recovery is still being expected. For instance in 1983 African output was stagnant. Drought in many parts of the continent is, however, said to be among the principal causes.

Turning to the minerals/metals sector it is noticed that the effects of the world economic recession have been quite severe. Whereas export prices of food and non-food agricultural items showed tremendous improvement after 1982, those of metals/minerals and fuels continued to be depressed. Table 5.1 has details on the behaviour of prices since 1965.

It may also be noted from Table 5.1 that the behaviour of fuel prices was rather peculiar after 1982. This can be explained by what is now known as the oil syndrome of 1982, when oil prices started to fluctuate due to disagreements among OPEC members.

Table 5.1
Change in Export Prices for Developing Countries (Average annual % change)

	1965–73	*1973–80*	*1981*	*1982*	*1983*[a]
Food	6.6	7.8	–16.1	–14.1	5.2
Non-food	3.7	10.1	–14.6	9.4	10.3
Metal and minerals	1.6	5.6	–12.0	–8.0	–2.2
Fuels	6.7	24.7	10.5	–2.6	–14.5

[a] Estimated.

Source: 1. Extracted from the World Development Report 1984, Table 2.7, p. 24.
2. Barry Munslow *et al.*, p. 55.

Taking 1970 as the base year, it is observed that prices of fuels, precious and other metals exhibit different trends. Since 1970 fuels and precious metals had for a long time held their value but only to join the general decline after 1980. Among the base metals, tin is one of the few that did not experience a depression in its value, though at the expense of declining volume. The most plausible explanation could be the existence of a central producer, the International Tin Council (ITC). To a considerable extent the council has upheld the value of its product. Apart from tin, zinc is another metal that has not suffered severe declines in its value. For instance, its current (1984) price is as high as it was in 1971. For more details on metal prices, refer to Table 5.2.

In SADCC there is an additional problem with regard to the minerals/metals sector. Most of the minerals/metals in this region fall into either the non-fuel or the non-precious category. These categories encounter worse declines in the face of a deteriorating world economic situation.

As a direct consequence of fluctuating prices of minerals/metals there are fluctuations in export volumes of the same. Table 5.3 helps to illustrate this point.

Table 5.2
Metal Prices 1970–1983 Indexed Back to 1970 = 100

Metal	1971	1972	1973	1974	1975	1976	1977	1978	1979	1980	1981	1982	1983
Copper	74	71	100	115	63	68	60	58	75	73	53	42	46
Aluminium	99	89	85	98	102	100	119	128	140	137	88	65	91
Tin	92	96	115	176	136	143	189	209	225	216	165	140	137
Lead	80	92	123	153	98	102	130	129	212	140	102	71	54
Zinc	101	119	251	153	182	165	128	120	135	121	122	101	101
Nickel	53	55	57	69	58	61	56	49	60	61	50	38	36
Gold	109	149	253	248	323	237	263	319	456	800	545	419	456
Silver	83	88	126	208	181	168	168	181	335	549	253	181	249
Platinum	88	88	92	109	92	86	76	117	177	242	143	99	123

Source: Barry Munslow *et al.*, p. 55.

Table 5.3
Change in Exports from Developing Countries 1965–83 (Average annual % change)

	1965–73	1973–80	1981	1982	1983[a]
Manufactures	14.9	10.6	16.3	–1.6	6.0
Food	1.3	6.0	19.7	5.0	0.9
Non-food	3.7	1.5	2.5	–6.1	1.7
Metals and minerals	6.3	5.9	2.6	–2.1	–1.9
Fuels	6.4	–1.3	–21.9	5.1	6.1

[a] Estimated.

Source: 1. Extracted from the World Development Report 1984, Table 2.9. p. 28.
2. Barry Munslow *et al.* p. 35.

Overall, however, many factors may be cited as being responsible for the gloomy picture painted by Tables 5.1, 5.2 and 5.3. Among these, three deserve particular mention for they appear to be the most overriding. First, SADCC minerals tend to be 'unprotected' with regard to attempts by developed countries to externalize their economic hardships to Third World countries in the form of declining terms of trade. Copper and nickel seem to be the most adversely affected. Between 1970 and 1983 the values of these metals fell by 46 per cent and 36 per cent respectively. World consumption, especially in the West, went down by 9 per cent for copper and 25 per cent for nickel just between 1979 and 1982. Diamonds seem to be the only exception; however, there was a temporary slump in the diamonds market in 1980–1.

Second, precious metals as opposed to other non-precious ones tend to be positively affected by speculation stimulated by uncertainty just preceding an economic crisis. Finally, country-specific dynamics play an equally important role. Over-dependence on mineral exports for foreign exchange earnings by some

Table 5.4
Debt Indicators for Developing Countries in Selected Years, 1970–84
(ratios in %, amount in $US Billion)

Country Group and Item	1970	1974	1976	1978	1980	1981	1982	1983	1984
Low-Income Africa[a]									
Ratio of debt to GNP	17.5	23.8	27.7	26.9	39.8	43.4	47.7	52.0	54.5
Ratio of debt to exports	75.2	99.5	153.3	162.3	175.8	216.5	260.6	279.5	278.1
Debt service ratio[b]	6.1	8.6	8.5	9.6	12.5	13.8	15.7	16.5	19.9
Ratio of interest service to GNP	0.5	0.7	0.6	0.7	1.3	1.2	1.1	1.4	2.1
Total debt outstanding and disbursed	3.0	7.0	10.0	15.0	21.0	23.0	25.0	25.0	27.0
Private debt as % of total	33.5	39.3	36.6	38.9	29.8	29.3	26.9	22.4	18.4
Other Middle-Income Oil Importers[c]									
Ratio of debt to GNP	21.4	20.3	21.1	24.9	29.7	33.4	40.2	47.5	53.0
Ratio of debt to exports	111.0	88.7	98.3	122.7	120.7	136.4	155.4	175.5	183.9
Debt service ratio	13.6	11.4	14.8	20.9	17.2	20.8	22.7	23.1	24.9
Ratio of interest service to GNP	0.8	0.9	1.0	1.3	1.9	2.4	3.1	3.3	3.9
Total debt outstanding and disbursed	12.0	21.0	27.0	43.0	68.0	79.0	89.0	98.0	108.0
Private debt as % of total	42.9	42.1	43.8	47.8	51.0	51.6	51.5	49.6	49.3
All Developing Countries									
Ratio of debt to GNP	14.1	15.4	18.1	21.0	20.9	22.4	26.3	31.3	33.8
Ratio of debt to exports	108.9	80.0	100.2	113.1	89.8	96.8	115.0	130.8	135.4
Debt service ratio	14.7	11.8	13.6	18.4	16.0	17.6	20.5	19.0	19.7
Ratio of interest service to GNP	0.5	0.8	0.8	1.1	1.6	1.9	2.3	2.3	2.8
Total debt outstanding and disbursed	68.0	141.0	204.0	313.0	430.0	488.0	546.0	620.0	686.0
Private debt as % of total	50.9	56.5	59.0	61.5	62.9	64.1	64.6	65.8	65.0

Note: Interest and debt service for 1970–83 are actual (not contractual) service paid during the period. Interest and debt services for 1984 are projections of contractual obligations due based on commitments received to the end of 1982 and take into account reschedulings to the end of 1984.

[a] In the SADCC these include Malawi, Tanzania and Mozambique.
[b] Debt service ratio is total debt service divided by exports of goods and services.
[c] SADCC members in this category are Angola, Lesotho, Zambia and Zimbabwe.

Source: Adopted from *World Development Report 1985*, Table 2.6, p. 24.

countries compels them to attempt to increase their production and sales whenever there are indications of declining prices. All this is done in a bid to circumvent any scaling down on what they often view as vital imports. In the final analysis this brings about an over-supplied 'buyers' market' and, indeed, low prices. The 'syndrome' of lower prices is exacerbated by high interest rates in OECD countries such that Third World countries accumulate huge loans to enable them repay their loans. The need to earn foreign exchange also forces them to maintain or even increase their minerals production levels. At the same time it should be borne in mind that the mining industry tends to be very capital-intensive, requiring importation of capital equipment which must be paid for in foreign currency. In the face of dwindling foreign exchange earnings by these countries this implies that they have to seek foreign aid either in the form of more loans or grants.

We may hasten to add here, however, that the rationale to raise foreign loans does not necessarily consist in rehabilitating or expanding the mining sector. Moreover the mining industry does not seem to afford an attractive field for private investment, more so in Africa. That is, there is a generally unsound investment climate in many African countries. Under the circumstances it is mainly institutions like the World Bank and other multilateral agencies that can be looked to for such investments. Indeed, 'a minerals lending program of $US700–800 million was approved by the Board of the World Bank for the fiscal years 1977–81' (Munslow *et al.*, 1984, p. 38). Apparently, however, due to the unsatisfactory behaviour of the mineral market and the lack of commercially viable projects, the amount committed is half this.

Notwithstanding, under the Lomé II agreement a 'special financing facility' (SYSMIN) had been worked out for purposes of rehabilitating the mining industry in some African, Caribbean and Pacific (ACP) countries. A total of 280 million European Units of Account (ECUs), equivalent to $US365 million at prevailing exchange rates was set aside for this purpose. This programme was intended to cover the entire period of the Lomé II convention, i.e. until the end of 1984. However, due to delays in implementation, it appears to have been rolled over into Lomé III.

Among the first beneficiaries of the programme were Zambia and Zaïre, who in March 1981 lodged applications for 55 million ECUs and 40 million ECUs respectively. In both cases the requests were for boosting copper and cobalt production. Interestingly, this seemed to confirm earlier fears in some quarters that the programme was designed, exclusively, to benefit African copper producers. This was in spite of the insistence of the progenitors that the programme was not established solely to boost copper and cobalt production. Rather it was an all-encompassing programme incorporating five other major minerals – bauxite and aluminium, iron pyrites and iron ore, manganese, phosphates and tin. For this reason later applications by Guyana and Rwanda for bauxite and tin respectively, were seen by the 'architects' of SYSMIN as strong disclaimers, confirming their ideals of non-discrimination in the manner in which all these minerals were being treated.

While efforts are being made by the World Bank and the European Economic Community (EEC) through such programmes as SYSMIN, the desired goal is far from being reached. It is estimated that in the 1980s an average of $US4 million (in 1977 prices) would be required if all the six minerals mentioned above are to be adequately financed (Ibid., pp. 36–40). It is also interesting to note that domestic contribution (i.e. Africa's contribution) is expected to be a mere 25 per cent of this total amount. For the African continent, obviously, this is not comforting politically or otherwise. It simply entails further entrenchment of international finance capital in the African economy, and Africa is already heavily indebted, especially to the Western World. Overall Africa's external debt, excluding that of the Republic of South Africa, rose from $US30.9 billion in 1977 to $US72.1 billion in 1984 – an increase of almost 133 per cent within a space of seven years, reflecting a rise of approximately 20 per cent each year. As a result debt-servicing problems abound in these countries.

Incidentally, developing countries' debt-servicing problems began to be noticed after 1974, following the first oil crisis in the preceding year, which induced foreign borrowing.

During the period 1970 to 1984 the ratio of debt to gross national product (GNP) reached 34 per cent, representing an increase in exports which rose from 14.7 per cent in 1970 to a peak of 20.5 per cent in 1982, before falling slightly to 19.7 per cent in 1984. Interest payments have also been following a similar trend. Table 5.4 shows these points better.

Two other points concerning Table 5.4 deserve particular mention. First, in relation to income and exports the absolute size of Africa's debt is small – $US27 billion in 1984. This may conceal the fact that it is the highest among the developing countries. Second, the share of private capital in Arica's debt, particularly in the low-income category, is among the lowest. Low-income Asia has the least.

Other characteristic features of the world economic crisis in the developing countries concern debt reschedulings and current account deficits. The former have increased tremendously, especially in the 1980s. Between 1955 and 1970 there were seven developing countries caught up in 17 debt reschedulings: However, in 1981 alone there were 13 reschedulings involving 21 countries. Within two years the number reached an all-time high of 31. This phenomenon is attributed to three major factors. First, it is argued that loans have far outstripped equity finance. Second, there has been a dramatic increase in the share of floating interest rates debt, the result of which has been severe impact on borrowers each time interest rates went up. Third, there has been a drastic reduction in the maturity periods, mainly due to the declining share of official capital flows and debt.

Current account deficits have also been growing. The worst affected have been the non-oil developing countries. The current account deficits of these countries as a group reached unprecedented levels in 1981 when they hit the $US78 billion mark or over 5 per cent of their GNP. Six years earlier it had stood at $US833 billion or 4.3 per cent of GNP.

Therefore we may conclude this part of the chapter by noting that, even without spelling out certain peculiarities about the SADCC region *per se*, it is quite evident that it is among the worst affected by the world economic crisis. Although the Western industrial countries have been on a recovery path since 1983, SADCC members and other sub-Saharan countries are still in economic limbo. The drought situation in some SADCC states has compounded the situation further. The wars of liberation in South Africa and its colonial state of Namibia are further depressing factors in the economies of the region.

Mineral Resources of the SADCC Region and Possibilities of Effective Regional Cooperation

As we have noted, Africa is rich in a wide range of mineral resources. There have been few comprehensive studies on the continent's resources, however, and most of our information exists only in terms of production figures. These do not reveal the actual position of a country or region in relation to other countries or regions. At the same time it should be acknowledged that measuring mineral reserves is an intricate business since it depends on a whole spectrum of variables, such as reigning world prices, available technology, and capital – to mention but three.

As illustration of the unreliability of mineral production figures for assessing relative strength, the following may be noted. In the SADCC region, for instance, most members are not exploiting their mineral potential to the full. Lack of capital is often given as the major constraint. On the other hand, we may add that for some minerals such as base metals, iron and manganese, tin and tantalum, it is perhaps just as well that they are not intensively exploited, since the present level of industrialization and the production systems in operation in these countries do not favour such a development. This will become clearer later.

Notwithstanding the above observations, the current contribution of developing Africa to world mineral production of important minerals is minimal. Table 5.5 shows the contribution of developing Africa to total world mineral production. The table reveals that it is only in phosphate rocks that developing Africa's contribution reaches anywhere near the one-fifth mark. Bauxite and copper follow, each accounting for approximately 15 per cent of the world production. It is therefore not surprising that developing Africa has little bargaining power on the world mineral market, the end result of which is deteriorating terms of trade since external forces will operate such that the prices of these minerals are suppressed.

Table 5.5
Percentage of Developing Africa's Contribution to Total World Mineral Production (Selected Minerals), 1980–82

Mineral	1980	1981	1982
Zinc ores	3	3	3
Tin ores	4	3	3
Iron ore	4	4	4
Manganese ore	10	8	7
Copper ores	15	14	14
Bauxite	16	15	16
Phosphate rocks	21	21	22

Source: E/ECA/NRD/SRCDUMRA/7, Lusaka, March 1985, pp. 4–7.

The situation in SADCC is not much different except in diamonds, where SADCC accounts for almost one-third of the Western world's mineral production. Interestingly, however, when South African production of a number of minerals is added, the combined output accounts for a substantially larger proportion of the Western world's mineral production. As a matter of fact the share of the SADCC region plus that of South Africa in world gold production is an amazing 70 per cent. Comparable figures for diamonds, the platinum group, cobalt, and chrome are 86, 87, 57, and 53 per cent respectively. Table 5.6 sheds more light.

Before discussing SADCC's mineral trade and the marketing framework for some of its major minerals, it is worth giving an indication of the region's mineral potential. For reasons mentioned earlier it is only possible to give a cursory treatment to this subject, and simply note that the SADCC region has considerable potential in a wide spectrum of mineral raw materials. Notable among these are agricultural, industrial construction, and communication mineral raw materials. Tables 5.2–5.5 give an illustration of the availability of these mineral raw materials, albeit vaguely – since there is no quantitative indication of the reserves.

Turning to intra-SADCC trade, it can be seen that this is extremely minimal. It is estimated that this does not account for more than 3 per cent of the SADCC region's total foreign trade. With regard to the direction of trade, we find that there is a heavy concentration to and from developed market economies. Socialist countries of Eastern Europe have lately also become important importers of Africa's raw material commodities. The fact that mineral raw materials are by far the most important exports of developing Africa need not be overemphasized. In fact more often than not when the term 'traditional African exports' is used, it is more or less synonymous with minerals. Of course this is not to underestimate the importance of agricultural commodities in the export trade of these countries. For more information on the pattern of mineral/metal trade of developing Africa refer to Table 5.7. This confirms that the developed market economies dominate the trade (exports and imports) of developing Africa. These market economies account for over 80 per cent of both exports to and imports from the African continent. The table also confirms that there is minimal intra-Africa and intra-developing countries trade. This militates against some of the known characteristics of the SADCC region, especially. The region as earlier indicated has such a variety of minerals and mineral products that one would expect a lot of trade to be going on between these countries, but at present most of their trade is with Western industrial countries. The danger with this type of trade is the dependence on industrial activity abroad that the exporting countries have to put up with. Quite naturally when there is a slack period in industrial activity abroad, which actually dominated the late 1970s and early 1980s, exporters experience export instabilities.

It can be argued that there is great scope for increasing intra-regional trade in SADCC if members were to formulate deliberate policies to promote this kind of trade. Looking at the 'balance sheet' of the mineral/metal trade of SADCC, one is struck by the number of possible contra-entries that are at present not exploited. Table 5.8 gives an illustration of the types of minerals and mineral products that the SADCC states trade in.

Table 5.6
SADCC Production of Major Minerals/Metals, 1982 (with Namibia, Zaïre and RSA for Comparison)

Mineral/Metal	Angola	Botsw.	Mozamb.	Tanz.	Zambia	Zimbabwe	Total SADCC	Western World %	Zaïre/ Namibia	Western World %	RSA	Southern Africa	Western World %
Gold (t)	—	—	—	(0.01)	0.4	13.4	13.8	1.4	4.2	2.0	664.3	682.3	70.0
Nickel ('000t)	—	17.8	—	—	—	13.4	31.2	8.0	—	8.0	20.5	51.7	13.0
Copper ('000t)	—	18.0	—	—	530	25.0	573.0	9.0	552.0	18.0	207.0	1,332.0	21.0
Cobalt (t)	—	254.0	—	—	2,300	98.0	2,652.0	18.0	5,608.0	57.0	—	8,260.0	57.0
Chrome ('000t)	—	—	—	—	—	432.0	432.0	9.0	—	9.0	2,162.0	2,594.0	53.0
High carbon ferrochrome ('000t)[a]	—	—	—	—	—	200.0	200.0	12.0	—	12.0	570.0	770.0	47.0
Coal (bit) ('000t)	—	415.0	500	(1)	604	2,969.0	4,488.0	Neg	—	Neg	140,137.0	144,625.0	5.0
Diamonds ('000 carats)	1,400	7,770	—	300	—	—	9,470.0	28.0	11,010.0	61.0	8,850.0	29,330.0	86.0
PGM's (kg)	—	—	—	—	—	145.0	145.0	1.3	—	1.3	94,194.0	94,339.0	87.0

a Figure for 1981. t = metric tonne, bit = bituminous, PGM = platinum minerals, Neg = negligible.

Source: Adapted from Barry Munslow *et al.*, 'The Effects of World Recession and Crisis upon the Southern Africa Coordination Conference', paper presented to a ROAPE Conference at University of Keele, September 1984, p. 53.

Table 5.7

Percentage Share by Origin and Destination of Trade in Ores and Metals of Developing Africa[a]

Partners	Imports by Origin			Exports by Destination		
	1965	*1970*	*1980*	*1965*	*1970*	*1980*
Development Market Economies	86.6	82.9	89.2	94.4	84.2	85.4
Socialist Countries of Eastern Europe	6.9	8.7	3.5	2.2	2.4	5.7
Developing Countries Total	4.8	7.9	6.5	2.7	3.7	7.3
Africa ·	4.2	3.2	2.5	1.4	1.2	2.7

[a] Ores and metals refer to items 27, 28, 67 and 68 in the system of International Trade Classification (SITC).

Source: E/ECA/NRD/SRCDUMRA/7, p. 4.

The mining industry has historically been very concentrated in structure and control and exhibits extensive vertical integration from exploration to marketing of minerals. Anglo America of South Africa and De Beers dominate the mining industry in the SADCC region. These and other MNCs exert their influence directly through ownership as well as indirectly, at different stages of the mineral–metal cycle, ranging from 'inputs (equipment/technology) to the extractive phase, through mineral processing and metals refining, to the marketing of the final product'. (*World Development Report* 1985, p. 2.)

In the final analysis one is left wondering whether MNCs are actually not the ones producing and selling to one another. Table 5.9 elaborates on some marketing characteristics of Africa's major metals. It demonstrates quite clearly the vertically integrated nature of the minerals market. Interestingly minerals such as copper and chrome which are not vertically integrated are vulnerable to market fluctuations. In the case of copper these fluctuations have even led to general decline in economies which are very dependent on it, such as that of Zambia. Zimbabwe, which exports a great deal of chrome, is fortunate in that she has a somewhat diversified mineral base (see Tables 3–6 in the Appendix).

Predominance of primary commodity production and export is by and large the most constraining factor on SADCC economies, since it renders these countries vulnerable to the vagaries of the world commodity market. The mineral/metal market is in fact among the worst affected during times of recession. Given that six SADCC members are virtually mineral economies, the implications are obvious. These countries have to respond to stimuli from their industrialized counterparts. When there is a slump in industrial activity in the latter the result is depressed demand for the products of the former, which in its turn leads to further reductions in production.

It has also been observed that although SADCC countries are relatively heavily endowed in mineral resources, exploitation of these is concentrated in the hands of a few MNCs. Two leading South African concerns, Anglo American and De Beers, have tremendous influence over this issue. The implications of this with regard to

Table 5.8
Current Minerals/Metal Exports and Imports of SADCC Member States, January 1985

Country	Imports	Exports
Angola	Ceramic ware, sanitary ware, cementile products, cement	Quartz, common salt, marbles, granites, crude petroleum, diamonds, iron ore
Botswana	Coal, oils (bituminous materials), petroleum products, soap, copper wire bars & rods, glass containers, lead, zinc, cement products, aluminium sheets & alloys & steel products & washing preparations	Diamonds, copper-nickel matte
Lesotho	Cement & petroleum products	Ceramic ware & building construction materials
Malawi	Iron sheets & steel, steel products, petroleum products	Nil
Mozambique	Cement, petroleum products, metal fabrication & products, coal, fertilizer, chemical products	Coal, gemstones, cement
Swaziland	Petroleum & mineral fuels and petroleum products, fertilizers, petroleum products	Chrysotile asbestos, coal, diamonds, tin, concentrated, iron & steel products and fabricated products
Tanzania	Sulphuric acid, lime-stone, caustic soda, lime, carbide, fertilizers, ammonium salts, insecticides, copper & iron ores, petroleum products, ceramic ware, asbestos products, steel products & sanitary ware	Glassware, cement, fertilizers, paints, explosives, asbestos products, iron & steel products and fabricated products
Zambia	Fertilizers, salt, soda ash, chemicals, metal sheets, metal products	Copper, zinc, cables, lead, cement, gypsum anhydrous, lime, coal, glass containers & cobalt
Zimbabwe	Copper, zinc, lead and steel products	Copper, zinc, lead and steel products

Source: SADCC Mining Development Workshop, Lusaka 8-11 January 1985. Background Paper No. 3.

Table 5.9
The Marketing of African Minerals

Metal	Market Characteristics	Remarks
Iron	Vertical integration	Backward linkage by steel companies.
Aluminium	Vertical integration/ producer monopoly	Market controlled by North American producers. Bauxite producers are trying to combat this through the IBA.
Nickel	Vertical integration/ producer monopoly	Dominated by INCO, whose monopoly is, however, slowly being eroded.
Diamonds	Vertical integration/ producer monopoly	De Beers regulates world production and marketing.
Gold	Closed market/producer monopoly	South African Government restricts sales according to its needs.
Uranium	Vertical integration	North American and British companies dominate.
Platinum	Producer control	Rustenbury Mines and South African companies largely successful in stabilizing price.
Tin	Producer/consumer control	Fifth International Tin Agreement backed by IMF.
Lead and Zinc	—	US market protected.
Copper	Unstable marketing	Producers' cooperative so far without effect; speculators active on market. US Market protected.
Chrome	Unstable marketing	Due to company competition.

Source: G. Lanning and M. Mueller, *Africa Undermined* (Penguin, Harmondsworth, 1979), p. 398.

capital externalization should be quite obvious. The MNCs have sophisticated mechanisms of siphoning resources from LDCs. Given that the mining sector deals in non-renewable resources, this becomes all the more intricate. All in all the non-renewable nature of mineral resources calls for a more cautious approach towards exploitation. Furthermore, the capital-intensive nature of the mining industry is often used as a rationale for the MNCs' involvement. Since they are able to provide capital, they are able to persuade host governments to allow them to operate either as joint ventures or as independent entities. The question of heavy capital investment raises an attendant issue of technology, especially in the form of human capital. MNCs are often called upon to provide technological expertise to Third World countries. The MNCs then use this advantage to manipulate the form of investment and returns thereof.

It has been observed that the volume of trade within SADCC is very minimal. Perhaps this has to do with the fact that most of these countries have remained producers of 'traditional exports' whose markets are predominantly in their former colonial masters' economies. One hopes that as SADCC matures this trend will be reversed. Finally, it has also been observed that SADCC states are characterized by different political systems and some analysts view this as a potential source of conflict. It can only be hoped that the spirit of pragmatism that heralded its formation shall continue to be championed, especially in the mining sector.

The Coordination of the Mining Sector

In spite of the importance of the mining sector to most SADCC countries, it was missing from the first list of areas of coordination adopted by the SADCC at the Lusaka summit. A year later, however, it was included and delegated to Zambia. However, until 1985, this area of coordination did not receive much attention, except for the recognition that there was a need to coordinate the 'training of personnel; downstream processing and metal fabrication; production of mining equipment and of chemicals; marketing and elaboration of better legal frameworks for the sector'. (*SADCC* 1983, p. 187.) And this was all the 'experts' had to say of this vitally important sector.

Since 1985 the mining sector coordinating unit, based in the Zambian Ministry of Mines, has produced a *Five-Year Strategy 1986–1990*. In this document, it is recognized that the mineral resources of the region give a 'good spread between industrial, construction, energy and metallic minerals in addition to precious metals and gemstones'. (*SADCC* 1986, p. 2.) The industrial minerals such as sulphur, salt and soda ash are important in the chemical industry while potash and phosphates are important in fertilizer production. Other industrial minerals found in the region include refractory minerals such as magnetite, kyanite and sillimanite; and abrasive minerals such as corundum and garnet. Furthermore there is a host of other industrial minerals such as bauxite, fluorite, talc, mica, graphite, rare earths, etc.

Iron ore is available and other alloying metals and minerals such as chromium, manganese, molybdenum and vanadium are found in the region. These could form the basis for an iron and steel industry. In addition, there are the other base metals such as copper, lead, zinc, tin, cobalt, etc., which are found in large quantities which could together with the ferrous metals form a dynamic base metals industry in the region. Precious metals produced in the region include gold, silver, and the platinum group of metals, albeit in very small quantities. Gemstones are also mined in the region. These include diamonds, tanzanites, emeralds, amethyst, aquamarine, garnets and tourmaline. Most of the gemstones are ideally suited for small-scale mining. Energy minerals include oil, coal and some uranium.

The broad policies that have been adopted for this sector comprise the establishment of sovereignty over natural resources; development of mineral-based industries, and development of indigenous skilled manpower capability. These policies have been amplified and now contain seven areas of focus for the regional strategy in the mining sector:

1. improvement of knowledge of mineral resources through establishment of adequate inventories of existing and potential resources, creation of better forecasting systems of consumption patterns with a view to rationalizing the utilization of mineral resources and the development of mechanisms for intra-regional trade;
2. establishment of the appropriate scientific, technical and industrial environment required for the development of mineral industries;
3. cooperation among SADCC countries in the exploitation and utilization of mineral resources;
4. training of high-level professional, managerial and technical personnel in all aspects of mineral resource development, with a view to alleviating the shortage of qualified manpower and reducing dependence on expatriate personnel and specialized services from overseas;
5. development of suitable systems of transfer of technological know-how and exchange of scientific, technical and economic data on geology, mining activities and mineral economics among SADCC countries;
6. attainment of maximum diversification of the mining industries bearing in mind the principle of equitable regional development;
7. prioritization of programmes in the light of their feasibility and capacity to deliver maximum benefits to the subregion – for example, operational projects for the production of goods and services can be preferred.

From this strategy a total of 17 projects have been approved for implementation and the sponsors are as follows:

Project 1	Subregional Skilled Manpower Survey (EEC)
Project 2	Small-scale Mining, Processing and Marketing (EEC)
Project 3	Inventory on Geology, Minerals and Mining (EEC)
Project 4	Foundry, Fabrication and Machining Facilities (IDU/CFTC)
Project 5	Mining Machinery and Spare Parts Manufacturing, Repairing and Reconditioning Facilities (IDU/CFTC)
Project 6	Mining Chemicals Manufacturing Facilities (IDU/CFTC)
Project 7	Sharing of Mineral Processing Facilities (under consideration; the French Government has shown interest)
Project 8	Development of Iron and Steel Industry (is being undertaken by UNIDO as a SADCC/PTA Joint Project)
Project 9	Development of Fertilizer Mineral Raw Materials (under consideration and NORAD and ABD are interested)

Project 10	Market Study for Common Salt, Soda-ash, Potash and other Related Products within the Subregion (NORAD)
Project 11	Market Study for Semi-finished and Finished Copper Products within the Subregion (Netherlands Government)
Project 12	Preliminary Study on the Possibility of Establishing a Refractory Industry in the Subregion (UNIDO)
Project 13	Central Isotope Geochronology Laboratory for the SADCC Subregion (EEC)
Project 14	Integrated Exploitation and Processing of Bauxite Deposits within the SADCC Subregion and Establishing an Alumina/Aluminium/Calcination Industry (several governments/agencies have been approached)
Project 15	Processing of Lime in the SADCC Subregion (NORAD has been approached)
Project 16	Remote Sensing Survey of Mineral Resources in the SADCC Subregion using Spot Satellite (EEC)
Project 17	Manufacturing of Diamond Tools in the Kingdom of Lesotho (under negotiation with IDU/CFTC).

Together these projects present the overall strategy for the coordination of the development of the mining sector in the region. Implicit in the strategy is the need to retain and make the already MNC dominated large-scale mining operations more efficient and integrated; and to promote small-scale and medium-scale mining which has so far been ignored by the MNCs. This refers more to industrial minerals and gemstones.

Recommendations for Policy and Planning

It is now evident that the mining industry plays two roles in the economies of the SADCC countries, one negative, the other positive. On the one hand, the mining sector is one of the major mechanisms through which monopoly capital penetrates and dominates the region; it is the major cause of instability due to fluctuating commodity prices, and the major avenue for the continuing technological dependence. On the other hand, subject to strategic policies, the mining sector holds the key to the region's prospects for development. The sector has great potential for foreign exchange earnings and has the capability of being the leading and integrating sector for the economies of the SADCC countries. This positive role largely depends on the region's capacity to reduce the monopolistic control of the MNCs, and on the stabilization of commodity prices. In addition such a capability can only be attained if the region begins to build its own institutions and personnel to counteract the other contrary forces.

The remainder of this chapter outlines some proposals that the SADCC countries may wish to consider in their efforts to coordinate dynamic development of the mining sector in the region.

First, SADCC exploits and exports a variety of base metals mainly as raw material commodities. The existing economic order, of course, dictates that these be exported to industrialized countries to support their growing industries. It will, however, be appreciated that these so-called developed countries were – and to some extent still are – able to set up these sophisticated industrial complexes because they can readily obtain these important raw materials. Needless to say, to achieve this objective these countries employ a variety of techniques to contend with the machinations of the MNCs, and commodity price instabilities. In the light of the foregoing, we are proposing that there is a need for SADCC states to seriously consider scaling down exportation of the base metals, especially if the present trend persists. The basic argument here is that when the time is ripe for the SADCC countries to industrialize they might find themselves in a position where they have to reimport the same minerals, at exorbitant prices, as they will have exhausted them domestically. Admittedly this is a difficult proposal to implement especially for those SADCC members which depend on exportation of such minerals for foreign exchange earnings. Following this proposal would reduce foreign exchange earnings which might be needed for certain imports. Naturally there is no easy way out but, if we are serious about industrialization, certain difficult choices will have to be made, including this one. Besides, the SADCC countries can still enhance their foreign exchange earnings base by accelerating exportation of gemstones and other precious metals, which are also relatively abundant in SADCC.

Second, the SADCC region abounds in industrial minerals, as mentioned earlier. Here efforts should not be spared to increase exploitation. These minerals are the raw materials of a wide range of manufactures and they can also be recovered by using simpler technologies. If developed, this subsector could go a long way to alleviate the foreign exchange hardships by lessening imports of such raw materials. In addition, development of the subsector would enhance industrial development in the region with possible spin-offs of increased regional commodity flows.

Third, the SADCC region is to a great extent characterized by large-scale, as opposed to small-scale, mining. In fact the two are highly complementary. The existing situation is therefore one of lopsided development and needs redressing, particularly since most SADCC members can ill afford large-scale mining, which requires enormous capital investments. The SADCC states should formulate deliberate policies aimed at propping up this sector. Of course, large-scale mining should not be abandoned; rather the issue is one of enhancing complementarity between the two. As an indication of the possible areas of small-scale mining, we may refer to Table 6 in the Appendix.

Fourth, a number of SADCC countries are food deficit areas. Sometimes the deficits are due to poor weather conditions, but at times the shortages are caused by lack of important inputs such as fertilizers. Within the SADCC Tanzania, Zambia and Zimbabwe produce some fertilizers though not enough for their own local demands. Lack of raw materials for industry in these countries is one possible major explanation yet some other members of SADCC have extensive agricultural raw materials including those for the fertilizer industry. Therefore, this is another area where there are prospects to foster regional initiatives or ventures.

Fifth, SADCC needs to focus more attention on developing an iron and steel industry. Needless to say this forms the core of any industrialization process, but especially regarding the development of the iron and steel industry. Thus, much as it is well-known that the Zimbabwean iron and steel industry is operating under capacity, other members of SADCC are also struggling to establish their own. In the final analysis this tends to dissipate regional efforts. This brings us to another point, that is appeal for establishing regional mineral enterprises similar to existing MNCs.

Finally, we cannot overemphasize the role of education and research in this whole process. Until we develop our own technological capabilities we will not only remain appendages of the Western industrial countries but also testing grounds of the sometimes obsolete technologies. By the same token our economies will remain vulnerable to manipulation by those who provide the technology.

A Concluding Note

This chapter has addressed itself to one of the most important and potentially dynamic sectors in the region. The sector is important because SADCC is a highly mineralized region. It is potentially a dynamic sector because a properly developed mining industry has the potential for integrating an economy owing to its many linkages. However, the history of the mining industry in the region has been one of underdevelopment and dependence. Attempts at coordinating this sector have not yet changed this significantly and the most disturbing thing is that the projects being implemented do not portend any major changes, nor do they attempt to build a local capacity that may in future produce more fundamental changes in the mining sector.

Notes

1. For more information on mineral resources of the African continent see *Accelerated Development in Sub-Saharan Africa: An Agenda for Action*, (World Bank 1981); European News Agency, 'The Renewal of the Lomé Convention', 1984; Barry Munslow *et al.*, 'The Effects of World Recession and Crisis Upon the Southern African Coordination Conference', paper presented to a ROAPE Conference, University of Keele, September 1984; and 'Intra-African Trade in Certain Mineral Raw Materials: An Issue paper', E/ECA/NRD/SRCDUMRA/7, February 1985.

6 The Development of a Local Technological Capacity in the SADCC Region

Gilbert N. Mudenda

Let us now face the economic challenge. Let us form a powerful front against poverty and its offshoots of hunger, ignorance, disease, crime and exploitation of man by man. Let us form an African Movement to wage a militant struggle against poverty . . . sharpening new tools, forging new weapons, working out new strategies and tactics for fighting poverty and improving the quality of life of our peoples.

Kenneth Kaunda, April 1980

The African Movement Kaunda was talking about was the Southern African Development Coordination Conference (SADCC). SADCC was born out of the struggle for the political liberation of Southern African countries: it was an extension of this struggle to include economic liberation. In other words:

For the member states of SADCC, reduction of external dependence is an economic necessity, not a political slogan. The warped, dependent subordination of Southern African territories in spheres ranging from transport and communications through production and personnel to trade and finance has, in the past, prevented and still gravely hinders economic development to meet basic needs of the people of Southern Africa.

(*SADCC* 1983, p. 14)

Since its foundation, the SADCC movement has devised strategies aimed at extricating member countries from external dependence, and more especially from dependence on South Africa. Consequently, member states have identified critical areas of coordination and delegated responsibility for them to individual countries.

But if the objectives of the SADCC initiative are to succeed, there is a need for an additional area of coordination. This is the coordination of local technological capacity accumulation. This is so because economic self-reliance presupposes two critical variables: the development of a self-sustaining industrial sector; and the development of high-level manpower. In other words, all areas of coordination require technological resources for their proper coordination and development. And if the ultimate objective of the SADCC is to rid member states of external dependence, then the supply of the resources required ought to be locally generated. Technology here means both embodied technology (equipment, plant and processes) and disembodied technology (knowledge, skills and organization).[1]

Similarly, a local technological capacity will be understood to comprise three component parts: human resources; scientific and technological infrastructure; and a dynamic industrial infrastructure. Thus, the accumulation of a local technological capacity involves the development of local personnel, institutions and those policies which generate, nurture and accumulate technological resources locally.

This chapter is divided into four parts. The first will give a broad picture of imperialism and the commercialization of technology. This is intended to provide a contextual background to our general discussion and argument. The second will review the work, relating to the areas of coordination, that has been done so far. The third will outline and elaborate the demand and supply situation of technological resources in the region. This part of the paper is intended to show the nature and extent of technological resources required in the region if SADCC member countries are to reduce their external dependence. The last part will make some observations and recommendations for policy. The essential part of the recommendations will be the need to found a centre to plan and coordinate issues relating to the development of a local technological capacity in the region.

Imperialism and the Commercialization of Technology

Classical economists such as Smith, Marx and Marshall gave technological innovations pride of place in their analyses of economic progress. Yet, for a very long time, modern economists have treated technical changes as mere 'exogenous variables' in their economic models. However, this orthodoxy began to change after Solow's (1957) seminal paper on *Technological Change and the Aggregate Production Function* and since then, the contribution of technical innovations to economic development has been acknowledged and its pride of place restored. More recently, those concerned about the problems of the developing countries have increasingly come to the conclusion that technology, especially in its commercialized form, is one of the major avenues through which monopoly capital penetrates and integrates the economies of the Third World countries into the capitalist world system. Technology transfer, which is the general term for the commercialization of technology, will here be understood to include: direct foreign investment; agreements on licensing, patents, trade marks, and managerial, technical and marketing know-how; importation of machinery, equipment and blueprints; and the recruitment of foreign technicians, experts and consultants.

It should also be noted that the history of technology transfer generally speaking goes far back to pre-industrial times. The commercialization of technology is, however, almost exclusively a post-industrial phenomenon. This is because prior to the industrial revolution there was no direct foreign investment; and any 'transfer to technology' was largely by way of travellers who observed new techniques used in foreign lands and brought them back to their home countries. It is also interesting to note that during the pre-industrial period, the direction of 'technology transfer' was mainly from the present-day developing countries to the now developed countries. Furthermore, the new techniques that were relocated were not patented and as such they were merely pirated.

Since the advent of the industrial revolution, however, three phases in the commercialization of technology have evolved: the colonial phase; the inter-war period; and the post-colonial phase, which is the current period.

During the colonial period imperialism, in the Leninist sense of the term, was characterized by, amongst other things, the export of capital. As such the principal medium in the commercialization of technology was through direct foreign investment. Consequently, the technology transferred was largely of a proprietary nature and embodied in capital and consumer goods exported to the colonies and semi-colonies and realized in the form of superprofits, which have been extensively documented. During the inter-war years and up to the 1940s it became evident that the demise of the colonial empires was imminent. As a response to this prospect, monopoly capital began to adjust and to employ, more and more, arms-length arrangements in preparation for this eventuality. Thus, the dominant form in which technology was commercialized during this period was that of transfer pricing through the mechanism of intra-company trade. The third and current phase has come as a result of the spate of nationalizations of foreign companies operating in most Third World countries after decolonization and the import-substituting industrialization strategies aimed at broadening the industrial structures of developing countries which the new states adopted. As a response to this situation, monopoly capital has had to devise more subtle and more advanced forms of commercializing its technology, namely the sale of disembodied technology through a variety of technology contracts and agreements.

Odle (1985, p. 11) has summarized this process as follows:

> In this the latest and most modern imperialist phase technology has been made explicit and has become commercially disembodied from capital in order to maximize the profits of the multinational enterprises. This control over technology acts as an effective counter to Third World successes in the last two decades in gaining ownership over the means of production. Generally, the commercialisation of technology in this import substituting period marks a new era of imperialist penetration. It is itself a culmination of previous modes of the commercialisation process in the manufacturing sector . . . the technology supplying multinationals [are] now able to enjoy very substantial rewards without the responsibility involved in the commitment of risk capital.

Thus, monopoly capital has been able to continue to maintain its dominant place and has been able to extract surpluses from the countries of the Third World through the commercialization of technology. The mechanisms through which this process takes place are many and varied. However, the principal means are as follows: 1) declared profits from subsidiaries still operating in developing countries; 2) the use of debt as a substitute for equity in joint ventures; 3) payments of royalties on licences, patents and trade marks; 4) capitalization of know-how in the form of payments for managerial, technical and marketing know-how; 5) capitalization on machinery and equipment supplies, most of which are already completely depreciated; 6) creation of secure markets for intermediate and capital inputs; and 7) control of further technological development by the use of foreign technical personnel, experts and consultants (Vaitsos 1974, appendix 7).

The remaining part of this section will attempt to outline the manner in which monopoly capital has used the process of technology transfer to dominate the SADCC region and incorporate it in the capitalist world system. More specific examples will be drawn mainly from the Zambian experience. In this way, the following question will be posed: is the SADCC initiative an attempt to extricate the region from further imperialist penetration or a mere restructuring and consolidation of the regional market to facilitate further capitalist penetration in line with the changing geo-political and economic situation? What follows is a schematic presentation of the processes of technology transfer in the SADCC region during the colonial and the post-colonial periods.

The Colonial Period

The colonization of the countries which form the SADCC group is very closely associated with the development of capitalism in Europe, especially when that development had attained a mature imperialist stage.[2] While this movement encompasses the whole world, it had two very specific features in the Southern African region. First, and apart from Tanzania and to a lesser extent Angola, the countries of the SADCC region were dominated by monopoly capital via South Africa, which acted as a submetropole within the region. Second, the initial aim of monopoly capital in the region was to create a large reserve of cheap labour to valorize capitalist investments in the mining, plantation, industrial and infra-structural sectors. The precise manner in which this aim was realized in the different countries may differ in form but not in essence. Generally speaking, three forms of colonial rule can be discerned, with Tanzania being the only exception. This is largely due to historical and geographical reasons. The three dominant forms are: the British South Africa Company (BSA) territories (Malawi, Zambia and Zimbabwe); the British High Commission territories (Botswana, Lesotho and Swaziland); and the Portuguese territories (Angola and Mozambique).

The colonization of Malawi, Zambia and Zimbabwe was largely due to Cecil Rhodes, a South African-based mining baron, who in 1885 founded the BSA with the explicit aim of exploiting the mineral and human resources of the three countries. Following the occupation of these countries the BSA alienated some land and took possession of all the mineral rights in these countries. Furthermore, it established an administrative system which nurtured capitalist relations of production and ensured the reproduction of those relations. In 1923 when Company Rule was abolished, the BSA retained both the land and the mineral rights. By that time the economies of these countries had already been turned into large reservoirs of cheap labour for the South African mines and plantations. Subsequently, with the development of the mining industries in Zimbabwe and Zambia, and the growth of settler agriculture in all the three countries, some labour was retained within these countries while the large surpluses were exported to South Africa. It should also be mentioned that most of the capital investments made in these countries, during this period, were mostly connected to South African mining houses. In fact, colonial Zambia was dubbed as 'company territory' because of the inordinate power the BSA and other associated mining companies held in the country.

The manner in which Botswana, Lesotho and Swaziland (BLS states) were colonized remains a poignant monument to British duplicity. At the time, the people of the BLS states were being harassed by Boer expansionism and the British offered protection. It turned out that this was merely a military strategy to enable the British to conquer the Boer Republics and to incorporate the BLS states into the South African economy as suppliers of cheap labour. With the reconciliation of Afrikaner nationalism to the regional intentions of monopoly capital, the BLS states were then effectively turned into the first 'Bantustans' of South Africa long before that notion was ever dreamt of by Afrikaner political theorists. The colonial authorities paid little attention to the development of these territories and their resources remained largely undeveloped so as to ensure a continuing supply of cheap labour to South Africa.

In Europe, Portugal was the first casualty of the theory and practice of regional specialization. By the time of the scramble for Africa, Portugal was already under the influence of British capital. Hence Portugal's colonies in the Southern African region were largely dominated by British capital based in South Africa. Thus, in spite of the long Portuguese presence in the region, the history of Portuguese colonialism in the Southern African region was essentially a history of *rentier* colonialism. The rent Portugal collected from Angola and Mozambique took the form of: mineral rights, company and port taxes, and gold bullion for migrant labour charges. Characteristically, the type of economy which emerged in these two countries (apart from the export of labour) included extractive industries, service industries and export agriculture dominated by settler plantations.

As already indicated, Tanzania is the only country in the SADCC region that had no direct colonial relationship with South Africa. Its only links to South Africa were provided by the few Tanzanian workers who found their way to South African mines or who worked in Zambian and Zaïrean mines dominated by South African capital, and the existence of a Tanzanian diamond mine owned by De Beers. Since the defeat of Germany, the former 'colonial master,' in 1918, Tanzania has been connected to the British East African colonies. As a colony, Tanzania's role in the international division of labour was the production of tropical crops for the metropolitan countries in both large-scale plantations and peasant agriculture. Thus in Tanzania there was a process of peasantization and proletarianization based on agriculture.

During the colonial period, the dominant forms by which technology was transferred were direct foreign investment, the encouragement of European immigration, and later the establishment of subsidiaries and/or affiliates of multinational companies. As such, direct foreign investment was a characteristic feature of colonialism penetrating the SADCC region, especially Zimbabwe, Zambia and Angola, via the mining industry. Agriculture, and later other service industries, did receive some injections of foreign investment. For example, in Zambia, it was only after the advent of large-scale mining operations that the other sectors of the economy such as agriculture, transport, construction and engineering, and various service industries got their impetus for growth. However, this growth was tied to the fortunes of the mining industry.

The encouragement of white immigration was another way by which the colonial governments in the region transferred disembodied technology. This was most pronounced in the designated settler colonies such as Zimbabwe, Zambia, Angola and Mozambique, and to a lesser extent Malawi and Swaziland. The settlers were meant to bring skills required for industrial growth in the region while the African population was largely seen as the supplier of cheap unskilled labour. Towards the end of colonial rule, a third form of transferring technology began to emerge and this was through the establishment of subsidiaries and/or affiliates of multinational companies in the region, thereby facilitating the extraction of surpluses from these economies through intra-company trade and transfer pricing mechanisms. In Zambia, for example, a large number of multinational companies established affiliated companies in the 1950s in order to take advantage of the growing market for technology created by the expansion and rehabilitation programmes which the mining companies embarked upon after the end of the Second World War. Similarly, other international firms entered the region to take advantage of the growing markets in the region so as to ensure or protect their global market share in their particular line of business. This form of technology transfer became even more common during the post-colonial period.

The Post-Colonial Period
Under colonialism there was a territorial expansion in terms of capitalist penetration. In the Southern African situation this penetration was largely confined to the mining and agriculture industries. The post-colonial period, however, saw a growing sectoral penetration of capital into a variety of non-traditional sectors. For example, the Anglo American Corporation, the largest and most powerful multinational company in the region, did not only diversify its mining activities, but also entered into numerous other non-mining industries. The need for this sectoral diversification was partly due to the changing structures in the organization and management of modern firms, as well as to changes brought about by the fact that a number of countries in the region were attaining their independence. These countries could now influence, albeit in a modest manner, the direction of economic activities in their own countries.

The political independence process in SADCC started in 1961 with Tanganyika's independence and ended with the granting of independence to Zimbabwe in 1980. In general terms, this process occurred in each country in one of two ways: some through constitutional means (Tanganyika 1961, Malawi 1963, Zambia 1964, Botswana and Lesotho 1966, and Swaziland 1968), some through armed struggle (Angola and Mozambique 1975, and Zimbabwe 1980). The first group of countries, especially Tanzania and Zambia, with their larger economies, had an early start in attempting to restructure their economies in order to meet the requirements of their people. This restructuring of the inherited colonial economy took the form of nationalization of the 'commanding heights' of the leading sectors of the economy, and the diversification of the economic base through the adoption of import-substituting industrial development strategies. The BLS states were more restricted because their economies were more structurally integrated in that of South Africa through the mechanism of a customs union. Malawi was not very willing to sever her economic relations with South Africa and continued to export labour to that country even after the attainment of independence. However, the restructuring process, particularly in Tanzania and Zambia, resulted in the establishment of new industries which, in turn, raised the demand for externally generated technological inputs.

In countries which attained independence through armed struggle, economic restructuring took two forms. First, in the period which preceded independence, the settler colonial states expanded and diversified the economic base in order to contain the liberation movements. Among other things, this is evidenced by the existence of basic metals and engineering industries in these countries. In addition, they diversified through import-substituting industrial development strategies. After independence in Angola and Mozambique, these countries nationalized foreign companies as part of a socialist-oriented economic development strategy. The independence of Zimbabwe portended a similar development. Thus political independence enabled the new states in the region to embark on ventures which would curtail the economic power enjoyed by monopoly capital, at least the total power associated with direct foreign investment combined with political control. However, both the nationalizations and import-substituting industrialization contained an organic weakness in that implementation required even larger technological inputs, which these countries did not have – thanks to the colonial legacy.

This dilemma is graphically exemplified by the Zambian experience. Between 1968 and 1969, the Zambian Government decided to nationalize all the large commercial, industrial and mining companies in the country. The main reason was their perceived unwillingness to participate in the restructuring of the Zambian economy. The mining industry was the major target. However, with nationalization it became evident that the Zambian State did not have the personnel nor the experience to run a technologically complex industry like the mining industry. Consequently, the international mining companies were asked to provide the management of the newly nationalized companies. The management agreement gave the international mining companies wide powers: to recruit staff; to undertake all engineering, design and consultancy; purchase all supplies outside Zambia; and to market all Zambian metals and their by-products. In return, the international mining companies were to be paid 0.75 per cent of turnover for overall management, 3 per cent of the total cost of a project for technical consultancy, 15 per cent of gross emoluments payable to each expatriate employee's first year of recruitment, 0.75 per cent of total sales for marketing, and 100 per cent reimbursement on all external purchases plus other costs incurred in the process (Bostock and Harvey 1972, pp. 217–39). Additionally, all these service charges, fees and bonds were to be paid in US dollars and exempted from Zambian taxes and exchange control regulations. As a result of this management contract, between 1970 and 1975 the Zambian Government paid the international mining companies a total of £337.71 million (Lanning and Mueller 1979, p. 219). Furthermore, other foreign companies that were nationalized during this period entered into similar management agreements and it is reasonable to assume that they also earned similar benefits. While the management contracts with the international mining companies were abrogated in 1975, most of the contracts with companies in other industries were not. More recently, there has been a move to introduce management contracts in those companies that, so far, have had no such management contracts.[3]

The Zambian experience, it is reasonable to assume, exemplifies the new trend and the new mechanisms used by multinational companies to commercialize their technology in the changing situation in the individual countries comprising the SADCC region. However, to answer the question whether the SADCC initiative is an attempt to stem the further integration of the SADCC countries into the world capitalist system, or an attempt by the imperialist powers to realign and reassert their hegemony in the region, needs more investigation and analysis. In effect, such a question has to contend with the following hypotheses: 1) the independence of Zimbabwe, a relatively industrially developed country in the region, together with the general revolution against apartheid, posed a major threat to the efficacy of South Africa's continuing hegemony in the region; and 2) it was perceived that the socialist posturings of the three newly independent states in the Southern African region would be more effectively contained by the creation of an alternative economic bloc comprising a majority of moderate African states than a continuing reliance on the use of South Africa's economic power.

These hypotheses can only be meaningfully tested by examining the activities of the SADCC since its formation, particularly in relation to technology transfer.

Review of Performance

Areas of cooperation will be discussed individually. It is hoped that by doing this issues of a scientific and technological nature will become apparent; and, at a regional level, a general demand for technology will be indicated. This, it is hoped, will set the backdrop from which the more substantive parts of the paper will be premised.

Transport and Communication

One of the first areas of cooperation identified was the coordination of regional transport and communication networks, due largely to the fact that a number of countries in the region are both landlocked and dependent on South Africa's transport and communication networks. To develop collective self-reliance in this area it was decided to set up the Southern African Transport and Communications Commission (SATCC). SATCC is based in Maputo and is aided by a Technical Unit of experts provided by the Nordic countries and Italy. It addresses problems relating to roads and road transport, railways and railway transport, ports and water transport, civil aviation and telecommunications.

By 1982, about 106 projects had been identified and about $US665 million (487 million external, 178 domestic) had been committed. So far the SATCC projects have been the most detailed projects and have received a continuing interest. They are also the most expensive and difficult because of the differing systems, standards and designs. In addition, it has been said that there is a lack of local technical personnel at professional level in this area.

Food and Agriculture

Agriculture and food security in the region is another area that has been given a high priority by SADCC. Agriculture is severely threatened by the gradual degradation of the environment. Desert areas are expanding and droughts becoming more frequent. This area of cooperation is coordinated by the Zimbabwe Ministry of Agriculture, which has since identified two broad fronts for action: the development and implementation of a regional food security programme; and the development and implementation of national agriculture and food projects. (See Chapter 3, especially Table 3.4, concerning regional projects.)

The national projects are to be carried out by individual member countries, though their implementation should benefit the region as a whole. They include the following:

Mozambique – Production of groundnut and sorghum seed;
         – Establishment of seed security stock;
         – Reinforcement of food marketing network;
         – Reduction of past harvest losses;
         – An early-warning system;
         – Establishment of a network of quarantine stations;
         – Establishment of food security storage.
Zimbabwe – Interim regional grain reserve.
Lesotho – Improvement of food storage capacity.
Zambia – Construction of storage facilities in rural areas.

It should be noticed that all of these projects including those relating to food security, largely consist of feasibility studies which have been undertaken to establish how such coordination could be undertaken and implemented within the SADCC region.

Soil Conservation and Land Utilization

It is well known that African countries are as a whole losing about 6 million hectares of arable land annually. While this problem is more acute in the Sahel region, Southern African countries also lose arable soils (albeit not at a comparable rate) through desertification due to overgrazing and the use of destructive farming systems which cause soil erosion. This is why Lesotho, a small country which has experienced severe soil erosion, is coordinating this area of cooperation. However, as late as 1983, work in this area was still confined to discussions among experts and no specific programmes and projects had been identified for action. It should, however, be noted that a sum of $US1.8 million was indicated as necessary for carrying out initial studies.

Crop Research in Semi-arid Tropics

Most of the countries which form the SADCC region lie in the semi-arid tropic zone. Botswana, the country delegated to coordinate this area of cooperation, is the most arid country in the region. In recent years, the region was severely affected by a drought. However, internationally and in the Southern African region, there is very little attention and research paid to this ecological problem. Thus in 1980,

Botswana sought and was granted a mandate by the other SADCC countries to approach the International Crops Research Institute on Agriculture in Semi-arid Tropics (ICRISAT) and to request that ICRISAT found a regional centre in Botswana to tackle this problem. ICRISAT has since sent a team of experts to investigate the feasibility of such a centre and to work out the specific regional requirements which may constitute the initial programme priorities for such a centre.

Animal Disease Control

Animal husbandry is a major source of livelihood in the region. The region is, however, infested with numerous animal diseases which threaten this livelihood. Botswana has been delegated with the responsibility of coordinating various efforts aimed at controlling and, where possible, eradicating animal diseases in the region. A number of projects which aim at controlling animal diseases have been identified and countries have been assigned various projects. These are as follows:

Tsetse eradication in Northwestern Botswana and Southwestern Zambia
Regional Meat Inspector Training School – Lobatse, Botswana
Establishment of a Zoonosis Centre – Zambia
Regional Programme for East Coast Fever Immunization
Tick and Tick Borne Disease Centre – Malawi
Foot and Mouth Disease Control – Malawi/Tanzania/Zambia borders; Southern Malawi
Regional Foot and Mouth Vaccine Bank
Integrated Animal Disease Control – Tanzania
Control/Eradication of Rinderpest in Tanzania
Equipment of the Biological Substance Laboratory in Mozambique
Annual Disease Reference Laboratory in Zimbabwe

The amount of money required to undertake these projects is in the region of $US62 million. However, by 1983 only FAO and DANIDA had expressed an interest in supporting the Regional Meat Inspector Training School to be based in Botswana.

Manpower Development

From the outset the SADCC countries have realized that the lack of skilled and high-level manpower constituted a severe constraint to the prospects of national regional development. The Lusaka summit adopted and endorsed a document relating to basic guidelines for Regional Cooperation in Manpower Development and Training which was delegated to Swaziland for coordination. The document stressed the interrelationship between national and regional efforts and activities aimed at creating and enhancing the skills of the labour force. Since the Blantyre Conference, which created the Regional Training Council, a number of specific areas of cooperation and coordination have been identified. These have taken the form of studies aimed at appraising the region's skill requirements. They are as follows:

1. Training for the Sugar Industry
2. Technical Training for the Mining Sector (to be funded from the Federal Republic of Germany)

3. Health Training (undertaken by NORAD Consultants)
4. Training of Teacher Educators (Consultancy team funded by SIDA)
5. Comparability of Educational Levels (funding from USAID and Portugal)
6. Regional Manpower Information (funded and Complemented by ILO/SATEP)
7. Management and Public Administration (funding from USAID)
8. Criteria for Success of Regional Training Institutions.

In addition to the studies, two projects have been identified. These are the Zambia Air Services Training Institute and the Mananga Agricultural Management Centre.

The work of the regional training centre has largely consisted of two components: the preparation of projects for external donor support; and the strengthening of regional cooperation through exchanges of students, staff and educational and training materials.

Industrial Development

A large part of the SADCC initiative aims at achieving collective self-reliance among the countries in the region. One, if not the most, important part of that goal relates to increasing industrial production. Castro put it thus:

> Industrialization is a decisive process for the Third World's economic development . . . the industrialization of the Third World is equivalent, in strategic terms, to laying the main technological and material base for development.

In this connection the SADCC countries decided to base and develop industrial production on the basic needs of the people in the region. Manufactured goods identified as basic requirements were grouped into seven categories – food, clothing, housing, health, water supply and power, transport, and education. On the basis of these categories a number of projects in engineering, metallurgy and chemical branches of the manufacturing sector have been initiated. Tanzania was delegated the responsibility of coordinating industrial development in the region and, by 1983, about 53 projects had been prepared for implementation while another 34 were being actively pursued. Together these projects fall under nine industrial branches and are summarized in Table 6.1. These include those aimed at upgrading existing capacities; expanding already installed plants; and establishing completely new industrial establishments.

Energy Conservation and Security

Energy is a very vital component in the development process. The SADCC region is well-endowed with energy sources, namely, oil, coal, hydroelectric power and natural gas. The problem, however, is that these resources are distributed unevenly among the countries, hence the need for coordination. Angola is the sole producer of petroleum in the region, although there is an indicated potential in Mozambique and Tanzania. Zimbabwe, Botswana, Mozambique, Tanzania, Swaziland and Zambia produce coal. Together these countries have 60 per cent of the coal resources in Africa. The region produces about 4,000 MW from the various hydroelectric plants, mainly concentrated on the Zambezi River. Natural gas

Table 6.1
SADCC Industrial Projects

	No. of Projects and Project Costs $US (000)					
	Implementation		Study		Total	
	No.	Cost	No.	Cost	No.	Cost
Salt	8	29.60	4	0.62	12	30.22
Textiles	16	116.57	2	0.50	18	118.07
Wool and mohair	3	9.59	1	0.10	4	9.69
Textile chemicals, insecticides and pesticides	2	7.50	15	5.90	17	13.40
Tractors and farm implements	13	51.51	4	1.12	17	52.63
Fertilizers	4	732.11	1	0.12	5	732.23
Pulp and paper	5	525.10	4	0.12	5	525.51
Cement	2	—	2	0.19	4	0.19
Electrical transmission and distribution equipment	—	—	1	0.25	1	0.25
Total	53	1,471.98	34	8.92	83	1,482.19

Source: SADCC, *SADCC Maseru* (Mambo Press, 1983) p. 73.

resources are mainly indicated in Angola, Mozambique and Tanzania.

The task of coordinating these resources has been delegated to Angola. So far Angola has developed a regional programme of action whose priorities are:

1. to analyse the energy situation in the region;
2. to identitfy energy projects of regional interest;
3. to select the projects and present them to the international funding agencies.

To date, three projects have been identified: Regional Petroleum Development Centre; Zimbabwe/Mozambique Electricity Supply Cooperation in the Central/ Southern Border Region; and Repair, Rebuilding and Extension of Liquid Fuel Capacity at Beira. In addition, a study on how SADCC countries might achieve self-sufficiency in the supply of oil products has been completed.

Fisheries, Wildlife and Forestry
Malawi has been delegated the task of coordinating the development and management of the region's important natural (organic) resources, namely: fisheries, wildlife and forestry. The region is well endowed with these resources, but they are under-utilized. The region has a long coastline, lakes and rivers, all of which are rich in fish. However, there has not been much fishing in either the sea or the lakes. To date, four projects relating to the development of the fisheries have been identified, and these are: Joint Research of Pelagic Fishery Resources of Lake Malawi (Niassa) among the three countries (Malawi, Mozambique and Tanzania) which share the lake; a Regional Survey of Fish Production, Processing and Marketing; Lake Kariba Fisheries Research and Development between Zambia

and Zimbabwe; and a study to identify Regional Projects and Programmes for Production and Commercialization of Fishing and Fish Processing Materials and Equipment in the region.

The region is also endowed with beautiful game parks which offer sanctuary to wildlife. However, there is no overall regional strategy for conservation, management and utilization of wildlife. As a result, a study has been commissioned to gather background information from which projects aimed at standardizing efforts regarding problems of wildlife conservation and management in the region can be formulated. Similarly, efforts at coordinating the management of forestries have merely been identified. These comprise research, training of personnel, mapping and inventory compilation, development of forest-based industries, setting standards, watershed management of multinational river systems and specimen collection.

Mining

The potential of the mining industry is not yet fully exploited. However, the region's mining sector has also been the major sector through which monopoly capital has penetrated the region. Ironically, and because the region is endowed with vast mineral resources, the development and the judicious exploitation of its mineral resources constitutes one of the major ways by which it can attain self-sustaining development. This is so because the mining industry has the potential for earning foreign currency, providing a source of energy, and providing raw materials for the development of such local industries as the metallurgical, engineering, construction, chemical and agricultural.

It is, however, interesting to note that this important sector was not amongst the first areas of cooperation adopted at the Lusaka Summit. This oversight was later corrected by the Council of Ministers which met in 1981 in Harare, and coordination was delegated to Zambia. The coordinating agency, the Zambia Ministry of Mines, initially outlined broad areas of cooperation following the guidelines enunciated in the Lagos Plan of Action. These relate to the establishment of sovereignty over natural resources; the development of mineral-based industries; and the development of indigenous skilled manpower. As such, the areas of coordination identified include: manpower development and training; manufacturing and fabrication of metal products linked to the mining industry; manufacture of machinery, spares and chemicals for use in the mining industry; mobilization of funds for financing mining projects; and formulation of legislation relating to mineral rights, taxation and labour utilization.

In 1984, the Council of Ministers meeting in Blantyre adopted a document, *Mineral Resources Development Strategy*, which, among other things, contained nine programmes (see Projects 1–9 on page 124). In addition to these promotional programmes, the SADCC Council of Ministers meeting in Maseru in 1985 approved other new projects for implementation and these are: 1) Remote Sensing Survey of Mineral Resources Using Satellite; 2) Central Isotope Geochronology Laboratory; 3) Refractory Industry in the SADCC Region; 4) Processing of Bauxite; 5) Manufacture of Diamond Tools; 6) Market Study of Production of Common Salt, Soda Ash, Potash and Related Products; 7)

Feasibility Study on Expansion of Copper Semi-finished Products for Local and Export Markets; 8) Processing of Lime for Chemical, Industrial, Agricultural and Construction Purposes.

All of these programmes and projects, except for two whose funding is still being negotiated, have found donors. Initially, the preliminary studies will cost about $US3 million and implementation about $US8 million. For most of the projects and programmes detailed feasibility studies will be completed by 1988, and by 1990 most of the projects that will require implementation will have commenced. Zambian experts have visited all member states and identified and formulated a number of research proposals which are currently being implemented.

Summary
Some areas of coordination, such as transport and communication, manufacturing and agriculture, have received active support, while work in other areas has been slack. It has also become very evident that, while SADCC aims at attaining self-reliance through this cooperation, most of the work and funding has come from external donor agencies. In other words, most inputs, financial and technological, have been externally generated. This apparent contradiction is due largely to the fact that the region lacks a local technological capacity; furthermore, and more importantly, the SADCC is not doing much to nurture and accumulate such a capacity.

Demand and Supply of Technological Resources

The range of programmes and projects requires enormous technological resources. This part of the chapter deals with the demand for technological inputs; the manner in which that demand has so far been met; and how this relates to technological self-reliance. In other words, it will begin to answer the question whether there is a move towards regional self-reliance in technology-related issues, or whether the experience of SADCC has so far tended to incorporate the region further into the capitalist world system. The underlying assumption is that the commercialization of technology is the prinicpal mechanism by which capitalism continues to penetrate and dominate the developing countries. More specifically, this sort of domination is best realized in relatively large regional markets.

Most projects that have been identified by SADCC relate to surveys, inventories and studies, and only a few aim at establishing physical technical systems. However, feasibility studies require technological resources that are critically important to the whole process of technology transfer. Not only do they indicate the demand for technological inputs but also indicate and recommend the possible sources of the supply of those resources. Furthermore, the feasibility study stage is important in the sense that it sets the tempo and direction of the subsequent phases in the technology transfer process, namely: detailed design; equipment and plant fabrication and procurement; on-site installation; commissioning and production management.

What is interesting to note about the manner in which these technological resources have been supplied is the total absence of local participation. Almost all the projects or studies have relied very much on outside resources in terms of finance, personnel and expertise. Thus while SADCC claims to foster regional self-reliance, the initiation of that self-reliance has been given to Western European countries and personnel. Consequently, the people of the region have not had a chance to participate in that process. It is therefore reasonable to assume that, when it comes to the implementation of SADCC projects, it will most likely exclude the local supply of technological resources.

This raises a question regarding the efficacy of regional self-reliance when regionally based resources are not utilized. For example, Zambia has since independence produced a wide range of high-level technical personnel who could have easily carried out most, if not all, of the studies in the mining industry. However, all the projects implemented so far have been contracted out to outside consulting companies with dubious knowledge of mining technology and industry. Similarly, the transport sector has not utilized local economists and engineers with a better appreciation of the local situation.

It would seem therefore that the current activities of the SADCC increase the region's technological dependence and benefit world capitalist interests more than they promote regional self-reliance.

It is well known that technological dependence leads to high prices paid for foreign technology; it pre-empts the local supply of technological inputs; obstructs adaptation of foreign technology; and reduces the stimulus to build a local technological capacity. The experience of most SADCC projects has confirmed this. For example, the prices of feasibility studies are unreasonably high; no local personnel are involved; and consequently local efforts to contribute to SADCC projects are largely frustrated. Thus, there is a great need to develop a local technological capacity to participate in the planning, coordination and implementation of regional projects if there is to be a move towards regional technological self-reliance and consequently regional independence of South Africa and the other developed countries.

Local Technology Capacity

In general terms, the development and accumulation of technological capacity comprises the development of three components – human resources, scientific and technological infrastructure and a dynamic industrial infrastructure. The development of human resources requires the provision of a modern educational system including technical, industrial and managerial. The development of a scientific and technological infrastructure relates to the production of a community of scientists and engineers, research and development units, engineering and consulting firms, and information systems and networks. A dynamic industrial infrastructure involves the establishment of a number of strategic industries in the economy – basic metals, chemical, metal-working and engineering. In the remaining part of this chapter the components of a local (regional) technological infrastructure and how such elements promote dynamic self-reliance will be outlined. The basic assumption made is that the region cannot hope to be self-reliant without significant industrial development.

A glance at the region's educational system reveals a critical shortage of educational and training facilities, partly due to the colonial heritage and partly to a general lack of appreciation of the importance of manpower development and use in the post-independence period. This is vividly illustrated by the dearth of industrial and management training programmes in the region. For example, Zambia, which has very comprehensive industrial training programmes, especially in the mining industry, has no programme for training management personnel.[4] In general, therefore, the region lacks high-level manpower and this is why most SADCC projects have been carried out by experts from outside the region. Similarly the majority of personnel working in the various regional centres established to promote regional cooperation are not from the member states.

The second component of a technological capacity, that of a scientific and technological infrastructure, is composed firstly of a community of scientists and engineers. Such a community is a product of the modern educational system and should be a centre of excellence, innovation and development. It is often organized around national academies of sciences which plan and undertake basic applied scientific research in order to meet national – and possibly regional – requirements. States in the SADCC group have no such national communities, let alone a regional community.

Applied research aimed at industrial use is often carried out in R and D centres, often owned by governments, inter-governmental organizations and private enterprises. Apart from the small laboratories of the national councils for scientific research and universities, the pilot plants of the companies and the testing units of the standards bureaux, this element of the scientific and technological infrastructure is almost non-existent in the smaller countries of the region. In addition, although there is no data relating to the amount of money spent on research and development in the SADCC member states, it is reasonable to assume that this expenditure is relatively small and most of it goes to agricultural research stations.

The translation of scientific and technological information into operating technical systems is usually done by consulting engineering firms. This work is critical to the implementation of development projects as well as industrial projects in general. As such this capability is an essential component of the scientific and technological infrastructure. In Zambia for example, this element is one of the weakest. The few engineering consulting companies registered in the country are mainly subsidiaries of international firms, or local drawing offices that work in close collaboration with companies outside the country. Since Zambia is one of the most industrially developed and technically sophisticated economies in the region, it is reasonable to assume that most member states also lack this capability.

Lastly, information systems and mechanisms for disseminating scientific and technological innovations and processes constitute a vital element in the scientific and technological infrastructure. Such information networks comprise libraries, technical and/or business libraries, documentation centres and various publishing and marketing outlets for books and journals. This element of the scientific and technological infrastructure provides the link between the local scientific workers and their international counterparts as well as between the activities of R and D establishments and local industry. Again this capability is very limited, witness the low level of development in the printing industry and the dearth of scientific and technological journals, documentation centres and technical libraries. This is largely why most projects carried out so far have been confined to generating data banks (surveys and inventories) on the region's resources and potential.

The last component of a local technological capacity is a dynamic industrial infrastructure. This comprises industries that are strategic to the national (and regional) economy and produce both capital and intermediate goods. More specifically they are the basic metals, chemical, metal-working and engineering industries. It is divided into two parts: ferrous metals (ISIC code 371), comprising iron and steel; and non-ferrous metals (ISIC code 372), comprising copper, lead, zinc, tin, nickel, aluminium, etc. Generally speaking, the basic metals industry involves mining, metallurgy, rolling, extrusion and drawing processes which produce semi-fabricated products which serve as intermediate inputs into the metal-working industry. In spite of the preponderance of mining in the region, it is only Zimbabwe which has a relatively developed basic metal sector. It should be noted that this is one of the major industries responsible for the generation of raw or basic materials to other sectors of the economy.

Recommendations for Policy and Planning

SADCC member states require a local technological capacity, individually and collectively, in order to enable them to manage the processes of technology transfer more effectively. As such there is a need to create another agency whose task will be that of coordinating and planning the development of a local technological capacity. The principal functions of such an agency would be: 1) the planning of the development of scientific and technological inputs required by the other agencies to enable them to execute their mandate; 2) the planning and development of human resources required for national and regional development; 3) the planning and development of a scientific and technological infrastructure at both national and regional levels; 4) the planning and strengthening of national and regional industrial infrastructure; and 5) the development of a mechanism to monitor the transfer of technology in the region.

The first task has already been elaborated. Suffice it to say that all the areas of cooperation that are currently being coordinated require technological inputs. Such inputs need to be systematically identified, analysed and their sourcing strategically worked out. Otherwise, as has been the case up till now, each agency is forced to go it alone. This not only dissipates resources but, in the long run, fails to come up with an integrated science and technology policy in the region. Obviously the areas of concentration would be food and agriculture, natural resources, mining, industry, energy, transport and communication, etc. Hence the agency charged with this task will have to work closely with the other agencies.

The planning and development of human resources is a central component of the development of a local technological capacity. Although this task is provided for under the guise of manpower development, a closer look at the programmes that have been implemented reveals that human resources development includes more than what has so far been done or planned. First and foremost, there is a need to plan the development of a modern education system to meet the challenges of a modern technological society. The importance of the quality of the labour cannot be disputed. Second, there is a need to carry out a comprehensive inventory of scientific and technological personnel available so as to identify the areas in which there are critical shortages in order to devise training programmes aimed at making available such personnel. Furthermore, there might be a need to revise and develop the curriculum so as to strengthen the teaching of science and industrial arts in the school system. In addition, human resources development involves the strengthening of industrial and managerial training programmes as well as the training of science and technology teachers.

The planning, development and coordination of a regional scientific and technological infrastructure forms another important component of a local technological infrastructure. In general terms, it comprises the nurturing of a community of scientists and engineers (in the broader meanings of the terms); the strengthening of the region's research and development capabilities; and the establishment of local project engineering consultancy capabilities. The first could be achieved through the creation of national academies of science and the facilitation of scientific dialogue across national boundaries. Of course the activities of national academies of science and the regional dialogue should be directed at those issues that are relevant to the development of the region. The second would aim at providing answers to the problems of the region by regional institutions. It should be noted here that without such a capability the region cannot aspire to self-reliance. Lastly, the third would aim at designing regional development programmes and projects by experts within the region. For without the use of local personnel, it is impossible to envisage a move towards regional technological self-reliance.

The planning and development of a dynamic industrial infrastructure aims at supplementing national and regional industrial development programmes and projects. This could be accomplished through the deliberate effort of nurturing strategic industries in the region. It is no accident that those industries (base metals, chemical, metal-working and engineering) that are critical to any industrialization process are missing from the region. The region has great potential for developing these industries; what is therefore required is their planning and coordination. It is also known that there are significant benefits to be gained from economies of scale (albeit not to the extent often claimed) and if such industries are planned at a regional level they could be large enough to reap these benefits. However, such industries should also look to the regional market and not to the distortions of the international market.

Finally, and since most of the development effort implies the transfer of technology, the region does require a centre that would monitor processes associated with technology transfer. The centre would thus play two roles. On the regional front the centre would concern itself with the popularization of science and technology; the dissemination of scientific and technological information among countries, sectors and institutions; and the mobilization of regional funds to support the accumulation of a local technological capacity within the region. At the international level, the centre would be charged with the planning of international cooperation, the coordination of scientific and technological policies with international agencies; and the monitoring of technology transfer processes relating to commercialization of technology, transfer-pricing and the establishment of a code of conduct relating to purchases of technological inputs.

Notes

1. Technology is also distinguished or characterized as either being for production or for consumption, and whether it is dynamic or static.

2. V. I. Lenin, *Imperialism: The Highest Stage of Capitalism*, 1975. In his characterization of imperialism Lenin isolated the following features: concentration and centralization of capital to form large business trusts; the merger of commercial and industrial capital to form finance capital; the export of capital; the territorial division of the world by the large trusts into spheres of influence; and the territorial division of the world by leading capitalist powers.

3. The companies which have recently signed management contracts are Zambia Breweries, National Milling and Nitrogen Chemicals.

4. After Independence, Zambia adopted a very comprehensive technical education system offering about 95 certificates and diplomas at artisan, technician and technologist levels. In addition, the mining industry spends about K20 million annually on training. However, there is no scheme for training managers.

7 Trade Relations among SADCC Countries

Jumanne H. Wagao

This chapter does not seek to provide a comprehensive review of SADCC. The limited aim of the present study is to examine one important aspect of the SADCC region, namely foreign trade. In what sense can the level and composition of foreign trade tell us something about a given region's degree of dependence? On the other hand, the paper does pay some attention to the prospects of foreign trade in SADCC's economic development and to the potential constraints on collective approach in foreign trade matters within the region.

The Role of Foreign Trade in SADCC

The nine member states of SADCC constitute a bloc in Southern Africa covering a total area of 4,884,297 sq. km, with a total population of more than 63 million people in 1982 and a combined GNP estimated at $US22,983 million in 1983.

It is generally claimed that the SADCC region has practically all the natural resources required to build a strong and modern economy. The region is said to have known reserves of solid fossil fuels estimated at 4,671 million tons, known hydroelectricity potential of nearly 266,768 gigawatt hours; and in the field of non-fuel minerals there are significant deposits of iron ore, diamonds, chromium and zinc. In agriculture, it is estimated that 223.3 million hectares are suitable for arable farming and animal husbandry.

SADCC cooperation in sectoral activities is now beginning to move from project feasibility studies to project implementation, and it is expected that the SADCC's productive sector will in the near future be producing commodities for trade. The Lusaka Declaration provides for trade development as an area of activity which governments of SADCC states should study in order to build up a sound regional trade system.

More empirical and analytical work has to be done to identify what would be desirable in the development of trade among SADCC countries. Trade between SADCC members is at an extremely low level in relation to their total world trade. For instance, in 1981 intra-SADCC trade exchanges amounted to about $US283.5 million whereas SADCC trade with other countries outside the region was estimated at $US13,220 million. According to some estimates intra-SADCC trade accounts for only about 4 per cent of the total foreign trade of SADCC countries.

While dependence on trading partners outside the SADCC will continue, there is considerable scope for expansion of intra-SADCC trade. However, this will largely depend on judicious and sustained planned investment in new activities as part of the overall objective of restructuring the production pattern of the SADCC region.

Relevance of Experiences in Regional Cooperation

Regional cooperation is not a new phenomenon. Cooperation among nations aspiring towards certain common objectives is a practical strategy towards achieving those objectives. Full economic integration assumes a common currency, free mobility of the factors of production, especially labour. It also assumes free trade in goods and services among integrating countries.

However, a good deal of the literature to date has been academic in orientation because no existing regional cooperation has reached the theoretical model of integrated development at regional level. All the same, it is hardly a disputable fact that, in principle, integration is the most efficient and the most rapid path to bring about effective structural changes in weaker economies. All developing countries have, by and large, very weak and fragile economies. In Africa, for example, most of the countries produce similar export commodities while their manufactures are usually import substitutes and their services are virtually the same. This feature has provided very little opportunity for trade amongst African countries.

With the growing awareness of weaknesses in the economies of developing countries and the increasing economic disparities between developing countries and Western industrialized ones, more and more Third World countries have recognized the potential of regional cooperation. Indeed, regional cooperation in developing countries is vital for the coherent allocation of scarce resources to meet local needs and for the growth of domestic markets. It can also lead to improved locally based research and the growth of indigenous economic institutions.

But experiences drawn from earlier experiments of regional cooperation amongst developing countries paint a gloomy picture of cooperation. The issues which arise in all efforts at economic integration, or even loose regional cooperation, among developing countries are always complex. So far no clear-cut formula has been documented which could have universal application.

Governments of the nine states of Southern Africa decided, in 1980, to utilize their unity and bond of friendship – forged during the struggle for political independence – for two basic objectives: first, the economic liberation of the member states from the historical domination in the region by the Republic of South Africa; second, and more important, joint cooperation for rapid economic and social development of their peoples and the economies of the nine states as a whole.

The SADCC strategy towards development through regional cooperation differs in one way from similar regional cooperation strategies elsewhere. The SADCC did not stop at making high-sounding statements or documents: it laid down a definite strategy which outlined clearly how development would be brought about in the region.

A serious examination of development potential of each country was made and a reasonably short list of priorities was drawn up. These priorities revolved around basic needs, as it was felt that unless a project-by-project approach was adopted in tackling basic needs first, no meaningful and orderly development would be conceivable, notwithstanding the vast resource potential. Such basic needs are broadly defined to include food, clothing, shelter, health, water supply, power, transport and education.

SADCC is in several other ways different from most regional South–South economic coordination or integration groupings:

1. The SADCC is basically self-designed by member states and without the use of the standard neo-classical model based on free trade and preferential trade. Rather, it is seen to be a creation of the SADCC member states based on what they believe are the appropriate objectives, ways and means for a regional development grouping in Southern Africa. Thus SADCC owes little or nothing to the theory of common markets which is at the heart of most South–South regional economic groupings.

2. Operation-wise, SADCC entails two combinations: first, there is harmony in identifying sectoral priorities without the sacrifice of frank dialogue with the obvious result that agreed decisions have both substance and form; second, there is agreement on priorities which leads to action on the agreed list of commitments.

3. The content of SADCC's progamme of action is unusual. For historical reasons, it is based on priority sectors, notably the transport and communication sector. Hence, there is a deliberate delay in the articulation of the trade sector programme.

4. SADCC has placed a high priority on external cooperation within the format which has been designed by the member states in the region. External support is considered to be critical to rapid enhancement of action to implement collective self-reliance amongst SADCC member states. Probably the SADCC's goals can secure external assistance on the basis of dialogue and negotiations without compromising the right and duty of its member states to take final decisions.

5. Absence of rhetoric is indicated by the fact that SADCC did not endeavour to produce a written treatise. Rather, it has so far concentrated on coherent articulation from principles and goals to programmes and projects directly relevant to the political economy of dependence reduction and development enhancement. The SADCC is determined to move in the direction of implementation as rapidly as possible.

This optimism has been suggested by Leys and Tostensen (1984, p. 67) in the following terms: with the 'functionalist and decentralized model, SADCC hopes to profit from mistakes of some of its predecessors'. However, the fate which has befallen earlier regional cooperation endeavours in UDCs leaves much to be desired. At any rate, experiences have shown that regional cooperation is not easy to carry out. Moreover, they show that cooperation is always problematic and sometimes tension can increase to the point of destroying what were meant to be cooperative structures.

The Structure of SADCC's Trade

Intra-SADCC Trade

The main purpose of this section is to summarize and comment on some relevant data pertaining to SADCC's foreign trade.

Some of the basic facts about SADCC are presented in Table 7.1. Angola, Mozambique, Tanzania and Zambia account for more than two-thirds of the total land area. Three countries alone accounted for nearly two-thirds of the total population in the region in the early 1980s. These are Angola, Mozambique and Tanzania.

To obtain a picture of the extent to which the individual countries in the SADCC region participate in intraregional trade, Table 7.1 gives the shares of regional exports and regional imports in total exports and total imports, respectively in 1981. The country contributions to the total value of intraregional trade are summarized in Table 7.2.

Table 7.1

SADCC: Relative Importance of Regional Trade to Individual Member Countries, 1981

	Share of intra-SADCC exports in total exports (%)	Share of intra-SADCC imports in total imports (%)	All exports as % of GNP	All imports as % of GNP
Angola	NA	0.7	NA	NA
Botswana	9	6	50	100
Lesotho	0.4	0	7.4	77
Malawi	10	8	23	29
Mozambique	9	3	16	31
Swaziland	2.6	0.6	59	96
Tanzania	0.9	0.8	12	25
Zambia	4	5	30	33
Zimbabwe	10	6	22	28

NA = Not available.

Source: *A Strategy for the Integration of SADCC Markets*, International Fund Services, S.C. Brussels, 1983.

Tables 7.1 and 7.2 show clearly that Botswana, Malawi, Mozambique and Zimbabwe are the leading regional exporters. Botswana, Zambia and Zimbabwe are the leading regional exporters in terms of their contribution to total value of intraregional trade in exports in the SADCC region. In 1981, the three countries accounted for 76 per cent of intra-SADCC exports. Botswana, Malawi, Zambia and Zimbabwe are the leading regional importers. Namibia's and Lesotho's participation in intraregional trade is at a low level both on the export side and on the import side. This is also true for Angola's participation on the export side and Tanzania's participation on the import side. Table 7.3 gives a summary of the trade structure in the SADCC region in 1981.

Table 7.2
SADCC: Country Share in Regional Trade, 1981

	% of intra-SADCC exports	% of intra-SADCC imports
Angola	0.03	2.5
Botswana	13.0	15.0
Lesotho	0.1	0.6
Malawi	8.0	9.0
Mozambique	11.0	12.0
Swaziland	3.4	1.2
Tanzania	1.7	3.1
Zimbabwe	49.0	38.0
Zambia	14.0	19.0
Total	100.0	100.0

Source: As Table 7.1

In Table 7.4, the relative importance of intraregional trade for the most remarkable bilateral trade relations in the SADCC region has been indicated for the years 1976 and 1979. The following features emerge:

1. Mozambique's trade with both Tanzania and Swaziland significantly increased in relative terms;
2. Trade relations between Mozambique/Angola, Zambia/Tanzania, Zambia/Malawi declined in relative terms;
3. Botswana/Angola trade increased;
4. Bilateral trade between Botswana and Zimbabwe is the leading trade relation in the region; and
5. Zambia/Zimbabwe trade increased tremendously in relative terms.

Interestingly enough, while Zambia/Zimbabwe trade was dominated by Zimbabwe's exports to Zambia during the early 1970s, by the late 1970s trade between them was dominated by Zambian exports to Zimbabwe.

In general, the study reveals three trends. First, Mozambique trade shifted away from Angola and towards Tanzania and Swaziland between 1970 and 1979. Second, Tanzania shifted away from Zambia and towards Mozambique. Third, Angola's trade shifted from Mozambique and towards Botswana.

Dependence on South Africa
In this section we consider the significance of South Africa both as an export market and as a source of imports for member states in the SADCC region. To this end, we

Table 7.3
SADCC: Trade within the Region, 1981, $US million

Destination / Origin	Angola	Botswana	Lesotho	Malawi	Mozambique	Swaziland	Tanzania	Zambia	Zimbabwe	Total Exports
Angola	X	X	X	X	0.99 (1.7)	X	X	X	X	0.09
Botswana	2.98 (41.5)	X	0.03 (1.7)	0.1 (0.4)	8.21 (24.3)	0.01 (0.3)	0.01 (0.3)	1.54 (2.8)	22.81 (21.4)	35.76 (12.6)
Lesotho	X	0.02 (0.1)	X	X	0.16 (0.5)	X	X	X	0.02	0.2
Malawi	X	0.72 (1.7)	X	X	1.49 (4.4)	X	0.05 (0.6)	X	21.69 (20.4)	23.95 (8.4)
Mozambique	0.87 (12.1)	X	X	3.64 (14.8)	X	1.24 (37.8)	3.41 (38.4)	X	21.79 (20.5)	30.95 (10.9)
Swaziland	0.08 (1.1)	X	X	0.1 (0.4)	5.10 (15.1)	X	X	X	4.34 (4.1)	9.62 (3.4)
Tanzania	X	X	X	0.13 (0.5)	2.67 (7.9)	0.01 (0.3)	X	1.88 (3.5)	0.23 (0.2)	4.92 (1.7)
Zambia	X	0.72 (1.7)	X	X	0.08 (0.2)	X	3.39 (38.2)	X	35.57 (33.4)	39.76 (14.0)
Zimbabwe	3.33 (46.4)	41.5 (96.4)	1.74 (98.3)	20.53 (83.7)	16.05 (47.4)	2.02 (61.6)	2.02 (22.7)	51.04 (93.8)	X	138.23 (48.8)
Total Imports	7.18	43.04	1.77	24.53	33.85	3.28	8.88	54.42	106.45	283.48

Note: Figures in brackets refer to % column-wise.
Source: As for Table 7.1.

Table 7.4
SADCC: Relative Importance of Intraregional Trade for Bilateral Trade Relations

Bilateral trade relation	Intra-trade in % of total exports from the two countries	
	1976	1979
Mozambique–Tanzania	0.26	1.04
Mozambique–Swaziland	0.29	1.11
Mozambique–Angola	1.36	0.05
Botswana–Angola	0.00	1.35
Zambia–Zimbabwe	0.01	0.61
Zambia–Tanzania	0.47	0.22
Zimbabwe–Botswana	4.20	2.95
Zimbabwe–Malawi	1.46	0.63
Malawi–Zambia	0.92	0.55

Sources: J. Isaksen and J. Faaland, *Economic Dependence and Regional Cooperation*; G. Sollie, *Trade Patterns and Institutional Aspects of Trade*.

need information to reveal the share of total exports from each country imported by white-dominated South Africa as well as the share of total imports in each country imported from South Africa.

In Table 7.5, the relative importance of South Africa for the SADCC region is presented for the 1970–79 period. It is shown that between 1970 and 1976 the relative importance of South Africa as a trading partner remained constant both on the exports and imports side. However, the relative importance of South Africa as an export market declined slightly between 1976 and 1979. But probably the SADCC region has gradually become closely linked to South Africa on the import side.

The extent of dependence on South Africa is indicated in Table 7.6, where more disaggregated information on a country basis is presented. The table shows clearly that most of the SADCC countries are highly dependent on South Africa, especially as a source of imports. This is true for Botswana, Lesotho, Namibia and Swaziland.

Table 7.5
Relative Importance of Trade with South Africa for the SADCC

	1970	1976	1979	1982
1. Exports to South Africa from SADCC % of total exports from SADCC	7.5	7.4	6.6	6.9
2. Imports from South Africa to SADCC % of total imports to SADCC	28.2	28.8	33.4	20.9

Sources: A. Nse Kela (ed.) *SADCC: Southern Africa Towards Economic Liberation*; J. Isaksen and J. Faaland, *Economic Dependence and Regional Cooperation*; G. Sollie, *Trade Patterns and Institutional Aspects of Trade*; and UNIDO, 'Industrial Co-operation Through the SADCC'.

Table 7.6
SADCC: Relative Importance of Regional Trade to Individual Member Countries, 1981 and with South Africa

	Share of intra-SADCC exports in total exports (%)	Share of intra-SADCC imports in total imports (%)	All exports as % of GNP	All imports as % of GNP	Share of exports to and imports from South Africa (1979)[1]	
					Exports	Imports
Angola	NA	0.7	NA	NA	2.17	11.99
Botswana	9	6	50	100	6.98	87.67
Lesotho	0.4	0	7.4	77	70.0	94.0
Malawi	10	8	23	29	9.75	41.74
Mozambique	9	3	16	31	4.77	14.35
Swaziland	2.6	0.6	59	96	19.2	87.0
Tanzania	0.9	0.8	12	25	0.0	0.0
Zambia	4	5	30	33	0.1	5.78
Zimbabwe	10	6	22	28	16.0	38.0

NA = Not available.

Source: *A Strategy for the Integration of SADCC Markets*, International Fund Services, S.C. Brussels, 1983; Sollie (1984).

[1] The percentages have to be interpreted with caution since a good deal of trade with South Africa is hidden, and hence, does not show up in official statistics.

However, South Africa is probably less important as a source of imports in the cases of both Tanzania and Zambia. More recent data paint the picture as follows. Imports from South Africa accounted for the following: Botswana (88 per cent), Lesotho (90 per cent), Swaziland (90 per cent), Mozambique (15 per cent), Zambia (7 per cent), Zimbabwe (40 per cent) and Malawi (40 per cent). Tanzania and Angola have no direct commodity transactions with South Africa (Leys and Tostensen 1984, p. 58).

On the export side, South Africa is most important to Lesotho, followed by Namibia, Swaziland and Zimbabwe. It is still of no importance to Zambia and Tanzania. It is estimated that South Africa's imports from individual SADCC member states is as follows: Botswana (8 per cent), Lesotho (95 per cent), Swaziland (20 per cent), Mozambique (5 per cent), Zambia (nil), Zimbabwe (less than 20 per cent) and Malawi (4–5 per cent) (Ibid., p. 58).

Owing to the hidden nature of trade links between some SADCC countries and South Africa, the statistics presented in Tables 7.6 and 7.7 are of limited value. Nevertheless, the direction of change in trade links with South Africa is probably closer to what follows: 1) Angola has recently become closely linked to South Africa both on the export side and import side; 2) for Botswana the relative importance of South Africa as an export market has declined markedly during the 1970s, although the country has probably become more closely linked to South Africa as an important import source; 3) Malawi's low relative reliance on South Africa as an export market has been nearly constant, at a low level, but on the import side, the relative importance of South Africa as a source of imports has increased tremendously; 4) Tanzania's trade links to South Africa are non-existent; and 5) for Zambia and Zimbabwe there is a growing tendency to delink from South Africa on both the export and the import sides.

If published data were of an acceptable quality, attention should have been devoted to an analysis of the commodity structure of imports to the region supplied by South Africa. Unfortunately, such data could not easily be traced and compiled.

Notwithstanding the drawback, limited data available in the cases of South Africa's trade links with Swaziland and Zambia reveal that the most important commodity groupings imported from South Africa include chemicals (SITC 5), machinery and transport equipment (SITC 7), fuel and electricity (SITC 3), food (SITC 0) and basic manufactures (SITC 6). Whereas the SADCC's exports to South Africa are composed mainly of foodstuffs and agricultural produce, its exports to the region in a more recent year were composed of precious metal (18 per cent), machinery and equipment (16 per cent), chemical products (13 per cent) and foodstuffs (13 per cent) (Ibid., p. 59).

Commodity Structure of Trade
The qualitative aspects of the SADCC's trade have hitherto largely been neglected. We should now pay some attention to the character of the commodities traded. Since the statistical base is rather weak, trade data will be presented in very aggregate terms, without entering into the details.

SADCC's exports and imports structure. Export trade in the region is still that of a predominantly agrarian economy. Considering the commodity structure of each country's total exports, the following is the picture: In *Angola*, crude oil and coffee accounted for nearly 70 per cent of total exports in 1977 with crude oil as the leading export commodity. *Namibia*'s leading export commodity is diamond (gem), and this, together with uranium and copper/lead/zinc exports, accounted for 84 per cent of total exports. This is also true for *Botswana* where the country's leading export commodity – diamonds – together with meat and meat products accounted for 70 per cent of all exports in 1979.

Wool, mohair and diamonds accounted for 48 per cent of *Lesotho*'s exports in 1977. In 1979, *Swaziland*'s sugar and woodpulp represented 53 per cent of the country's exports. The countries' principal export commodities were wool and sugar respectively. *Zambia*'s copper was 82 per cent of total exports in 1979 while in *Zimbabwe* the share of three commodities – tobacco, asbestos and gold – was 30 per cent. For *Mozambique*, cashew nuts, petroleum products and shrimps accounted for 47 per cent of total exports in 1978. Tobacco and tea formed more than 70 per cent of *Malawi*'s total exports in 1978 while, in the same year, cotton, coffee and sisal represented 50 per cent of *Tanzania*'s exports.

In general one notices three important characteristics of export trade. First, there is considerable variation among countries as to the degree of commodity diversification of exports. Zimbabwe has the most diversified commodity structure, followed by Lesotho, Mozambique and Tanzania. In the case of Zambia, Angola, Namibia, Botswana and Malawi, the degree of commodity diversification is at a low level.

Second, during the latter part of the 1970s the most important change that has taken place in the countries' export trade has been the sudden appearance of crude oil in place of coffee as the leading export commodity in Angola; cashew nuts in place of cotton in Mozambique; diamonds in place of meat in Botswana; and coffee in place of cotton in Tanzania. Finally, for the SADCC region as a whole, diamonds and copper account for 30–35 per cent of total exports.

The commodity structure of the imports in each country in the region in 1979 is presented in Table 7.7, which lists the shares of different commodity groups in total imports. Table 7.8 reveals that in 1979 machinery and transport equipment was the leading commodity group in total imports for most countries, although fuels and electricity were the leading commodity groups in Zimbabwe's import trade. The share of fuels and electricity in total imports has increased sharply for all the countries in the region.

Let us now turn to a survey of the commodity structure of intra-SADCC trade flows in 1979.

Commodity specification of intra-SADCC trade. Botswana supplied Angola with meat and meat products (SITC 01) while Zimbabwe's imports from Botswana included animal and vegetable crude materials (SITC 29), clothing (SITC 841), animal oil and fats (SITC 411), and textiles (SITC 65). Zambia's exports to Angola and Zimbabwe were comprised of maize (SITC 044), unmanufactured tobacco (SITC 121) and electric energy (SITC 351).

Malawi's exports to Zambia consisted of fish and fish products (SITC 03), tea (SITC 074), rice (SITC 042), textiles (SITC 65) and sugar (SITC 061). Imports into Mozambique from Tanzania were dominated by coffee (SITC 071), clothing (SITC 841), textiles (SITC 65), and aluminium (SITC 684). Zimbabwe supplied sugar (SITC 061), textiles (SITC 65), manufactures of metal (SITC 698), fixed vegetables (SITC 421), cement (SITC 661), furniture (SITC 821), articles of rubber (SITC 629), and finished structural metal parts (SITC 691) to Botswana. Zimbabwe's other important trade partner was Malawi, whose imports consisted of medicinal and pharmaceutical products (SITC 541), cement (SITC 661), rubber goods (SITC 629), iron and steel bars, rods and angles (SITC 673), and yarn and thread (SITC 651).

Agencies Controlling External Trade

So far we have mostly dealt with the direct trade dependence of the SADCC's member states. A different, though interrelated, problem is the danger that the region as a whole is probably exceedingly influenced by institutions of foreign origin controlling trade in the respective countries. As some of these may be of external origin, this might signify one important aspect of the more indirect and hidden forms of dependence.

In Angola a state trading organization, Importang, controls a substantial share of the country's imports. Enacomo is the leading parastatal handling foodstuffs and textile imports in Mozambique. Others include Petromoc (petrol), Intermetal

Table 7.7
SADCC: The Commodity Structure of Imports, 1979

SITC	Description of Commodity Group	% of total imports accounted for by							
		Botswana	Lesotho[a]	Swaziland[a]	Zimbabwe	Zambia	Malawi[b]	Mozambique	Tanzania
0	Food	13.52	21.6	8.2	1.77	6.33	3.87	12.29	3.39
1	Beverages and tobacco	2.76	4.6	4.1	0.38	0.22	0.77	0.20	0.07
2	Crude materials (exc. fuel)	1.11	1.0	0.6	3.37	1.85	1.51	0.86	1.59
3	Fuels and electricity	13.26	8.8	12.1	29.53	17.80	11.92	24.59	15.7
4	Oils and fat	0.57	0.6	0.3	0.41	1.69	0.47	0.93	1.37
5	Chemicals	4.71	5.3	8.0	13.91	13.26	11.86	6.87	9.54
6	Basic manufactures	21.71	19.4	10.1	17.21	20.33	24.66	16.13	18.14
7	Machinery and transport equipment	27.23	12.3	20.0	23.06	34.27	37.23	27.99	46.84
8 + 9	Misc. manufactured articles and commodities n.e.c.	15.13	26.3	36.5	10.36	4.25	7.36	10.14	3.36

a 1977-data.   b 1978-data.

Source: G. Sollie, *Trade Patterns and Institutional Aspects of Trade*.

(non-ferrous materials), Intermecano (motor vehicles and agricultural materials), Medimoc (pharmaceuticals and medical equipment), Pescom International (frozen and dried fish including fish meal). In the case of Tanzania nearly 45 per cent of the leading consumer goods imports are channelled through the Board of Internal Trade (BIT). The grain imports are the sole responsibility of the National Milling Corporation (NMC). Steel imports and imported industrial inputs are handled by the National Steel Corporation (NSC) and National Development Corporation (NDC) respectively.

The National Import–Export Corporation (NIEC) is the leading trade agency in Zambia. The NIEC which is owned by Zimco has exclusive control of several commodities, including oil. Indeco and Namboar are responsible for most of the imported input requirements in manufacturing industries and the agricultural sector respectively. It is roughly estimated that nearly 30 per cent of Zambia's total imports are handled by the NIEC, with only a very insignificant share of total imports being channelled through private companies.

Generally speaking, state participation in import activities seems to be more considerable in Angola, Lesotho, Tanzania, Mozambique and Zambia, and is relatively unimportant in Namibia, Botswana, Swaziland and Zimbabwe. In the latter, a good deal of the imports are channelled through TNCs – controlled importing agencies. In fact the same agencies controlling export trade also seem to be most influential on the importation front.

This leads us to the question of control over exports. As already noted, Zambia's export market is dominated by copper. Through Zimco (or Zambia Industrial and Mining Corporation) the Government of Zambia acquired, in 1970, 51 per cent of the country's copper mines. The remaining equity share was exclusively left to the former owners – the RSA-owned Anglo American Corporation (AAC) and the US-owned American Metal Climax (Amax). Prior to February 1975 exportation of this major commodity was handled by Anmersales AG and RSTIM which were owned by AAC and Amax respectively. However, since then a new marketing company – known as the Metal Marketing Corporation of Zambia Ltd (Memaco) – which is owned by Zimco has been in operation.

The independent state of Mozambique has successfully mounted an ambitious programme to establish state-owned enterprises in the external trade sector. Enacomo is the leading export-controlling agency in the country, controlling 65 per cent of cashew nut exports, one-third of cotton, 80 per cent of copra and 100 per cent of tea and sugar exports. Similar state-owned agencies have been in operation on the exports field in petroleum products, shrimps and cement. Most of the exports which fall outside the domain of the state fall largely under the control of private domestic companies.

In Tanzania, a significant portion of the export trade is handled by parastatal organizations. Agricultural exports are fully controlled by the General Agricultural Products Export Corporation (Gapex). Other parastatals handle specific export crops like the Cotton Authority, Tea Authority, Tobacco Authority and Cashew nut Authority.

In the other SADCC states, exports are handled in varying degrees by state-owned corporations, notably in Lesotho and to a lesser extent in Botswana and

Angola; by subsidiaries of TNCs – in Zimbabwe, Angola, Botswana and Swaziland, and by some private domestic companies. Information pertaining to Malawi is hard to come by.

The relative importance of state-owned agencies (SOAs), subsidiaries of Transnational Corporations (TNCs) and private domestic agencies (PDAs) in each country's (other than Malawi's) export trade in 1979 is shown in Table 7.8, where only the leading agencies are included for each of the three categories.

Table 7.8
SADCC: % of Exports Accounted for by SOAs, TNCs and PDAs, 1979

Country	SOAs	TNCs	PDAs	Others
Angola	20.1	32.3	—	47.6
Namibia	—	100.0	—	—
Botswana	18.0	68.7	—	13.3
Lesotho	43.0	10.7	—	46.3
Swaziland	—	77.6	—	—
Zimbabwe	21.2	57.3	4.7	16.8
Zambia	91.9	—	—	8.1
Mozambique	58.7	16.4	—	24.9
Tanzania	74.7	—	—	25.3

Source: As for Table 7.7.

Two features are discernible from Table 7.8. First, in the cases of four countries in the SADCC – Lesotho, Zambia, Mozambique and Tanzania – the share in total exports accounted for by SOAs exceeded the combined share accounted for by TNCs and PDAs in 1979. Second, in the cases of Angola, Namibia, Botswana, Swaziland and Zimbabwe, the share accounted for by TNCs exceeded that accounted for by both SOAs and PDAs. Presumably this is related to the countries' differing ideological stances.

For the SADCC region as a whole, what emerges from Table 7.8 is that the share in the region's total exports accounted for by SOAs equalled that accounted for by TNCs. However, one gets the impression that with time the relative importance of SOAs will probably increase for the region as a whole.

Prospects and Problems of the Trade Sector in SADCC's Economic Cooperation

Time now to return to some issues touched upon in the first section of this study. What is the potential impact of trade on the direction of economic development of member states in the SADCC region? It is unfortunately impossible to provide reliable answers to the potential impact of foreign trade within SADCC. As noted at the very outset, the relationship between foreign trade and development is one of the poorly developed and controversial areas in the literature on economic development.

There is further complication at two levels. First, in quantitative terms, the importance of intra-SADCC trade appears quite insignificant when, in fact, intra-SADCC commodity transactions are extremely minimal, consisting of not more than 2–3 per cent of the region's foreign trade. Second, integration schemes in the developing economies have not been conspicuously successful to date. The intended gains to be realized from the creation of such arrangements, especially in sub-Saharan Africa, have not been realized and intraregional trade increases remained limited. Such experiences leave each SADCC member state with reserved commitment.

However, SADCC remained committed to the policy of intraregional trade promoted by its founding members as reflected in the Lusaka Declaration. It is believed that with regional integration between its member states, the SADCC would be able to take advantage of economies of scale; provide greater scope for investment decisions beyond the limits of the domestic markets; and strengthen economic bargaining power, thereby mitigating a possibility of increasing external dependence.

The broad approach to be taken comprises a number of proposals. These would include: 1) bilateral (or multilateral) trade agreements negotiated annually within a longer term and possibly a regional framework; 2) target levels of trade and indicative lists of goods in the format of countertrade and cross accounts between central banks allowing prompt payments to exporters; 3) preference in import licensing and output allocation to facilitate achieving pre-set target trade levels; 4) specified and agreed upon procedures to handle imbalances through increasing exports by the state experiencing a shortfall rather than through cutting back on total trade or by automatic settlement in hard currency; and 5) exchange of information on tradeable commodities, developing contacts among enterprises, facilitating export credit, harmonization of trade as well as transit documentation and coordination with sectoral programmes aiming at production of goods and services.

Although trade is seen as a consequential means to validate production, the usefulness of trade *per se*, given the prevailing markets (nationally or regionally), does not seem to be the subject of serious dispute in principle. Indeed, with a combined GNP of nearly $US20 billion together with a population of 60 million, the 'larger market' argument seems potentially realistic. Nevertheless, the promotion of trade in the SADCC is bound to encounter several complicating factors. Chief among these will, no doubt, be the dominance of South Africa.

The South African Connection
On the question of greater economic and political independence from South Africa there is virtually no disagreement. However, as noted, on both the import and export side, most SADCC countries are dependent on South Africa to various degrees. This is true especially in the case of Botswana, Lesotho and Swaziland (the BLS states). As members of the South African Customs Union (SACU), the three countries, as Table 7.10 shows, are firmly integrated into South Africa's economic system.

South Africa's regional economic hegemony is real. The GNP of South Africa is more than twice that of the SADCC states, while its industrial base is unsurpassed throughout Africa. As a result of the latter, South Africa is able to account for 78 per cent of all African steel production. 53 per cent of the continent's steel consumption, 30 per cent of all cement produced on the continent and 40 per cent of Africa's industrial production. Besides, South Africa has a well-developed infrastructure; notably its transport and communication networks which continue to be important for most of the SADCC member states' trade contacts outside the African continent. As a result, countries like Botswana, Lesotho, Malawi, Swaziland, Zambia and Zimbabwe are dependent on efficient South African transport and communication networks for their export–import trade. Some of these factors may have lain behind the Pretoria government's proposal of a Constellation of South African States (CONSAS).

The first mention of a Constellation of States was made in March 1979 when the South African Minister of Foreign Affairs suggested that between seven and ten countries in Southern Africa could expand existing ties and develop a common approach in the fields of security and political matters. In November 1979, the South African Prime Minister proposed a CONSAS that would include any country in Southern Africa wishing to expand relationships and regional cooperation. He mentioned the so-called Independent Homelands, members of SACU and 'in due course other countries in the region'.

The origin of the concept is both economic and political. It springs from the deterioration of South Africa's relations with the West, the threat of Communism in Southern Africa, the need to harmonize economic policies and the desire to find solutions for regional development problems.

Furthermore, there is the investment side of the equation expressed in the role played by South Africa within some SADCC member countries in equity ownership, management sales and technical agreements. Sub-imperialist South Africa is the centre for foreign investment in Africa and has to be seen in her close relations with the other Southern African countries of Angola, Mozambique, Zimbabwe, Namibia, Botswana, Swaziland and Lesotho. Also capitalist relations do exist with the Zambian copper industry. Average profits in the South African context are higher than elsewhere. For instance, during the 1960–70 decade, the average world profit rate for direct US investment was 11 per cent, but capital invested in South Africa earned a phenomenal 18.6 per cent, largely because of its connection with the institution of forced labour in Southern Africa and the role the region has been forced to play as a labour reservoir for settler and corporate capital.

Undoubtedly, South Africa's manipulation of its neighbouring states makes harmonized trade within SADCC difficult to achieve. This is also true of the so-called 'external co-operators'.

Dependence on the West

There are well-founded fears that the reduction of South African dominance may not reduce overall dependence but be replaced by new forms of dependence, most probably on the West – albeit in a more diversified form. The dependence on donor countries and agencies constitutes one of SADCC's major weak points. There are cases where major regional programmes cannot be completed due to the absence of

Table 7.9
RMA: Intra-Regional Trade, 1974 and 1982 ($US millions)

Exports from	Swaziland 1974	Swaziland 1982	South Africa 1974	South Africa 1982	Lesotho 1974	Lesotho 1982	RMA[1] 1974	RMA[1] 1982	ROW[2] 1974	ROW[2] 1982	Total Exports 1974	Total Exports 1982
Swaziland	—	—	25.5	113.1	0	0	25.5	131.1	150.6	193.2	176.1	306.3
South Africa	130.2	430.4	—	—	125.6	521.7	255.8	952.1	8,371.1	16,282.2	8,627.5	17,234.3
Lesotho	0	0	14.4	35.4	—	—	14.4	35.4	0	0	14.4	35.4
RMA	130.2	430.4	39.9	148.5	125.6	521.7	295.7	1,100.6	8,522.3	16,475.4	8,818.0	17,576.0
ROW	7.4	89	7,504.6	16,149.1	1.3	5.3	7,513.3	16,234.0	—	—	—	—
Total imports	137.6	519.4	7,544.5	16,297.6	126.9	527.0	7,809.0	17,344.0	—	—	—	—

Source: X. P. Guma, 'The Rand Monetary Area Agreement', Tables 5 and 6.

[1] Rand Monetary Area.
[2] Rest of the World.

interest among donors in financing them. A case in point here is a regionally important project like the Dar es Salaam port-system which could only attract credit assurance amounting to 6 per cent of total costs. Another case is the proposed expansion of the ports at Beira and Maputo whose coverage of total costs involved by foreign donors came only to 18 per cent and 22 per cent respectively.

Thus, one of the most serious problems facing SADCC is whether its attempts at economic liberation from South Africa will lead to new forms of economic dependence. This is especially true once it is recalled that some donors are former colonial powers in the region and hence, they are likely to have significant neo-colonial political, economic and strategic interests. Since SADCC is almost totally dependent on external financing for its work, possibilities of influencing SADCC policy increase.

After the donor countries had dismissed the industrial projects submitted at the Maseru Conference as a 'shopping list of uncoordinated projects', the SADCC states then presented a list of 55 feasible projects at the donors' conference in Lusaka in February 1984. Firm financial assurances were given in respect of 18 of these projects – e.g. salt production and textiles – located in Botswana, Lesotho, Swaziland, Mozambique and Tanzania. The impression one gets from the donors' preferences is that only the most profitable projects stand a chance of gaining external support. And this might not easily fit in with the desire to create a system of complementary industrial combinations that would generate new industrial units as well as a capacity for renewal.

In considering the elements of an appropriate policy framework for trade promotion within SADCC, it is also essential to examine another important drawback: that is, the structure of production in the respective countries.

Dependence on Primary Commodity Exports
Few SADCC countries have actually succeeded in reducing their dependence on primary commodity exports by building up industry. As seen in the section on 'The SADCC's Exports and Imports Structure', diversification by changing from the production of mineral or agricultural commodities to the production of manufactures has proved to be one of the most difficult tasks confronting SADCC countries. The duplication of products makes intraregional trade unlikely to grow. This will greatly hinder the evolution of mutually beneficial trade between the SADCC countries.

This phenomenon is best illustrated when the share of exported manufactured commodities in total exports is considered. The ratios are presented in Table 7.10. Here we have adopted the UNCTAD definition whereby manufactured commodities belong to SITC 5–8, less those belonging to SITC 67 and 68.

The limited SADCC industrial base has had to cope with unhealthy changing world economic conditions. Thus for Angola, Mozambique and Tanzania the share of exported manufactures in total exports has declined, notably in the first two countries. The increases recorded in the cases of Zambia and Malawi were less spectacular.

Some of the most important effects of the slow-down in world economic activity for most developing countries have been the fall in export demand for the

Table 7.10

Exported manufactures % of Total Exports: Selected SADCC Countries

Angola	12 ('70)	8 ('75)
Swaziland		8 ('75)
Zimbabwe	0.1 ('70)	11 ('79)
Zambia	0.1 ('70)	1 ('77)
Malawi	3 ('70)	4 ('78)
Mozambique	9 ('70)	3 ('75)
Tanzania	13 ('70)	10 ('76)

Source: As for Table 7.9.

commodities supplied by them, particularly agricultural and mineral exports; fall in commodity prices and hence adverse movements in their terms of trade; an increase in the real burden of interest and debt service payments and a reduction in aid and other capital flows. All these effects have contributed to the difficulties involved in financing imports, especially the essential imports – e.g. industrial raw materials and spare parts – required for maintaining existing levels of industrial domestic production. Accordingly, the level of industrial capacity utilization has become low and industrial production has slackened, if it has not declined.

The position of the SADCC states has deteriorated in the face of the cumulative effects of global economic recession. Thus:

> the 1973–83 world economic recession has crippled a majority of SADCC economies and present patterns and projections of partial recovery globally suggest that the damage done will not be speedily or automatically reversed. SADCC can reduce vulnerability to extra-regional economic malaise but not eliminate it and substantial results cannot be achieved in less than a decade from 1980 (Green 1985, p. 102).

The tasks that SADCC countries face today are unenviable. Two types of constraint on their industrialization are most pressing. The first is of a short-term nature, namely an insufficiency of the foreign exchange rate that would allow importation of the raw materials, other supplies, spare parts and additional machinery and equipment needed to operate their *existing* industries at high rates of capacity utilization. A central policy question here is: should the scarce foreign exchange available for industry be allocated to all existing industries proportionately so that each can work at a very low level of capacity utilization? Or should one close down some industries and allow others to operate at much higher capacity utilization so that economies of scale can be reaped and costs reduced?

At any rate, the focus during the short term is likely to revolve around revamping the present unused capacity. This move, however, will have to be aligned with the second and more long-term constraint associated with a low level of investment in industry. The problem will then be to reach this goal even when the immediate concern entails restraining the level of imports owing to the current less favourable climate of expanding exports and attracting the required massive inflows of external finance.

The second constraint calls for planned long-term solutions which would entail programmes to identify the import needs of SADCC countries as well as gaps in the industrial structure of the region as a whole and a suggestion as to how they might be filled by joint planning of new industries at the subregional level. This will be necessary in order to make greater use of the SADCC's potential for diversifying and increasing industrial output. A certain amount of rationalization and adjustment in the SADCC productive systems could effect economies of scale and eventually achieve more efficient production too.

But there is one common setback, as insisted generally by Kaldor (1970); that is, the large and increasing differences in the level of development of the integrating countries. Thus the long-term solution to the external vulnerability facing SADCC member states may not be feasible because of the absence of any coordinated regional investment policy as well as the great differences in investment incentives in the various SADCC states, which may only favour those states considered to have instituted the most favourable investment climate.

Besides, one is bound to encounter the political problems of the SADCC: that is, the prevailing political heterogeneity within SADCC member states.

Differing Ideological and Political Stances

The success of the SADCC initiative will depend on the extent of understanding and participation by all member states. At the risk of simplification, it could probably be assumed that the general political philosophy underlying the creation of the SADCC is clear and indisputable. It may also be assumed that SADCC's overall objectives are equally clear to all member states. Indeed, the attempt to allocate priority sectors so as to coordinate efforts has served as a confidence-building measure and may help to avoid a polarization of activities towards the economically more developed states.

Nevertheless, what may not be so clear is how SADCC is structured and how it can carry out its programmes of activity, and develop ideas into viable projects. Instantly, one comes up against the limitations of the institutional framework. So far SADCC has tended to operate through coordinated national action, and no attempts have been made to create multinational or supranational operating agencies. And currently there is no plan to build up such a regional organization. Although sensible in many ways, such a loose institutional set-up also poses a threat to the smooth operation of the SADCC's Plan of Action.

There are additional problems connected with the absence of a clearly defined overall regional political–economic strategy. As is well known, there can be no genuine economic cooperation without political integration. In the absence of the latter, it is not clear how SADCC will keep track of the obvious tendency to subjugate regional objectives to national interests. Because of SADCC's quite specific goals and focus, its continued survival will largely depend upon the extent to which its objectives and actions will be relevant to certain basic goals of its member states. The following warning is relevant: 'in the long run, if SADCC does lead to greater economic integration which requires a greater degree of harmonisation of domestic policies and development strategies, possibilities of open friction exist' (Leys and Tostensen 1984, p. 67).

Finally, one may also mention the dangers that may arise from differences in ideology. It is often the case that ideology acts as the overriding factor militating against regional cooperation and development. Some countries, like Angola, Mozambique, Tanzania and Zambia, profess leftist ideologies while others have shied away from the leftist stance by embracing pro-market ideologies.

No SADCC state acts on the basis of *laissez-faire*, or, conversely, of full-fledged state intervention. Even in the cases of Malawi, Botswana and Lesotho, government intervention in the market place does exist in a mild form, and this is likely to become more pervasive in future. However, 'the differences in capacity and need to intervene, objectives of intervention and instruments used, as well as frequency, pervasiveness and effectiveness of such intervention vary very widely' (Green 1985, p. 109). As might be expected, the articulation of a SADCC programme will be complicated by the impossibility of working out concrete and coordinated economic policy targets and instruments which are independent of ideological questions.

SADCC and PTA: Multiplicity or Complementarity?

Another set-back to effective economic integration of the SADCC region is the multiplicity of institutions dealing with similar issues, which helps to breed tendencies to arrest the attention and the degree of cooperation. Would membership in additional regional organizations or bilateral cooperation schemes be complementary to or competitive with the SADCC?

Within the Eastern and Southern region there are the following additional cooperation and integration arrangements: Kagera Basin Grouping (Tanzania, Burundi, Ruanda and Uganda) with a series of water, power, trade, industry and transport coordinations; Ruvuma Free Trade Area (Tanzania and Mozambique); Preferential Trade Area (PTA) for Eastern and Southern Africa; bilateral cooperation arrangements in the form of Joint Commissions; and Multinational Programming and Operational Centre (MULPOC) for Eastern and Southern African states. Three of these are of interest to us here: Joint Commissions, MULPOC and PTA.

The Joint Commissions are typically bilateral arrangements involving initiation, coordination and supervision of cooperation programmes in economic, scientific and technical fields, trade, industry, transport and communication, and finance. Three types of cooperative trade agreements are prominent in the SADCC region. First, there are bilateral agreements in which emphasis is put primarily on planned trade promotion of specified commodities – e.g. Zimbabwe/Mozambique; Zambia/Malawi, etc. Second, other bilateral agreements are characterized primarily by the existence of preferential duties – e.g. Botswana/Zimbabwe, Malawi; Zimbabwe/Botswana; South Africa; Malawi/Botswana, South Africa, Mozambique, etc. Third, multilateral agreements are dominated by SACU and Lomé Convention arrangements.

Although joint development commissions are potentially complementary to SADCC's objectives, in practice they may not necessarily be perfectly compatible with the countries' commitment to development coordination. Since most of these agreements pre-dated the SADCC, both bilateral and multilateral trade agreements were negotiated outside a regional framework. Hence the potential element of competition between the two.

MULPOC are programmes and operational centres established in 1975 as operational arms of ECA. The Lusaka-based MULPOC for Eastern and Southern Africa is one of the five MULPOCs created by the ECA and the UN Economic and Social Council for West Africa, North Africa, Central Africa and the Great Lakes. The major objective of the MULPOC is 'to promote meaningful co-operation and integration as a prelude to the establishment of the sub-regional Common Market which will eventually lead to regional economic integration' (Ibid.).

The MULPOC at Lusaka was established in November 1977 to service 18 member states in the African subregion. The member states include all SADCC countries. Aside from providing various forms of assistance, MULPOC has carried out feasibility studies and has identified and developed programmes to foster subregional cooperation in sectors like agriculture, industry, natural resources, human resource planning, transport and communication, trade and finance. Thus the broad objectives of MULPOC and SADCC are similar.

The negotiating process that led to the forming of the PTA goes back at least to 1965 under the aegis of the ECA, revived in 1978 with a formal treaty signed in December 1981 by nine member states.[1] Its operation began effectively in July 1984. The PTA has 15 members, covering a total area of 5.013 million sq. km (April 1985) and an estimated population of more than 114 million. Lesotho, Malawi, Swaziland, Tanzania, Zambia and Zimbabwe are among the current SADCC member states which have signed the treaty.

The objectives of the PTA are twofold: first, it is aimed at the growth and expansion of trade through trade liberalization; second, it is intended to promote closer cooperation and integration in many fields of economic activity besides trade. Some of the high priority sectors include industry, transport and communication, agriculture and monetary affairs. It is clear from Article 3 of the PTA Treaty that the purpose of the establishment of the PTA is not simply to foster closer economic integration but also to lay the foundation for the economic development of its members.

In respect of the PTA, SADCC hopes to achieve complementarity because the former involves a broader geographical area, less close coordination over a narrower front (trade liberalization) and using different instruments like tariff and exchange control reduction, and standard clearing with automatic settlement of trade balance in convertible currency. However, because the PTA and SADCC do not necessarily coordinate their activities, there is a high likelihood that a conflict of interests may arise which could have serious consequences to the intended cooperation, subsequently hindering regional development. Complementarity will be hard to accomplish for two major reasons. First, there is bound to arise considerable overlap in many respects and SADCC and PTA approaches could easily clash because they duplicate their fields of operation.

Overlap is potentially visible in the areas of transport and communication, agricultural development and industrial cooperation. It is also interesting to see how PTA handles trade in the case of BLS states which are already members of the SACU. Special provisions have been arranged within PTA as these countries have to coordinate their tariff policy with South Africa. These arrangements are aimed at ensuring 'full and effective participation of Botswana, Lesotho and Swaziland in the PTA with the view to reduction of their dependence on South Africa without dislocation or fundamental disturbances to their economies' (Olwa 1984, p. 15).

Moreover, there is the original SADCC concept which aimed at directing its efforts towards production and merely using trade as a means of attaining other goals. Meanwhile, however, seven of the nine SADCC member states have been pressing to delegate the trade sector, like other sectors, for coordination to a single member state. Negotiations which began in 1982 remain under attention by the Council of Ministers because only Zambia (PTA secretariat) and Zimbabwe (the clearing house for PTA) would like to leave the trade sector temporarily to the PTA. Perhaps the differences in respect to trade arise partly from the awareness of the potential conflict with or overlapping of the PTA of Eastern and Southern Africa.

Secondly, since the PTA tariff reduction of July 1984, joint membership of both the PTA and the SADCC has created conflict between SADCC and PTA obligations for states which are members of both, since they have been obliged to discriminate against non-PTA SADCC members in favour of third parties.

The SADCC/PTA complementarity will remain pure theory as long as SADCC's Ministerial Council fails to gain any consensus about future relations with the PTA. In the meantime, the Council of Ministers has agreed on the directive for the SADCC secretariat not to conduct any talks with the PTA. There is an ongoing study which is seeking to identify areas of potential complementarity and potential overlap between the two bodies.

There are two schools of thought regarding the future of the PTA and SADCC. In the first of these, it is predicted that although there could be a conflict of interests between the PTA and SADCC, it may be that the PTA will become the more dominant organization. This is too simplistic a view in that it fails to recognize that what the PTA amounts to essentially is a renewed effort to lead a neo-classical type of free-trade zone under the known conditions where the necessary prerequisites do not seem to prevail.

What is portrayed by the PTA arrangement is a grouping of countries whose degree of integration is small; the political and economic heterogeneity of interests does not indicate any common denominator for cooperation; and advantages for cooperation are only likely for the most advanced states as a result of easier access to markets.

An alternative view considers the strength of SADCC to be growing faster than that of the PTA, which may affect the future of the latter. Some PTA members may mistakenly regard their organization as an institution dealing with consumer (or trade) integration rather than with cooperation in the broader fields of the economies of the member states. SADCC, on the other hand, could easily be conceived by the same members as a cooperative arrangement that works to foster production. This might make some PTA members give priority to production – and therefore the SADCC, rather than trade – and the PTA, merely on the sound argument, which is explicit in SADCC's Programme of Action, that one has to produce before one can trade.

In view of the points raised above, I would predict that the future of the PTA will largely depend on the political climate of its member states, itself determined by the state of their economies. On balance, SADCC's future stands a better chance, albeit one that will be surrounded by mounting challenges.

The time may now be right for trade to be taken up as a sectoral activity for coordination along with other SADCC sectoral economic development programmes. Since the PTA now exists and is operational, with a majority of SADCC members having ratified the treaty, the best compromise would first be to create a SADCC trade sector, followed by all SADCC members becoming PTA members, at least temporarily. A complementary list of SADCC/PTA programmes in various areas other than trade could be compiled and acted upon immediately. This approach would be politically feasible and likely to minimize conflicts between the two organizations, at least temporarily.

Desirability and Limits of Coordinated SADCC Regional Trade

Coordinated cooperation will remain unthinkable in the absence of complementarity in production and trade. This will be among the essential components of any attempts to bring about structural change and specialization in production. Regional industrial cooperation demands suitable arrangements for both intra- and extra-regional trade to take advantage of economies of scale, particularly with large industrial plants.

Trade, for example, is integral to each of the three levels of industrial coordination in the SADCC strategy – namely: 1) short-term matching of under-utilized capacity to unsatisfied demand; 2) building of interlinked chains of industrial production; and 3) establishment of core industrial plants where economies of scale may require a full-fledged regional market for full capacity utilization.

However, the SADCC has yet to adopt a regional trade policy because, unlike the PTA, whose main thrust is on liberalization of trade, the coordination arrangement has put more emphasis on industrial and agricultural production with regional trade policy coming in later as a consequential arrangement.

The Lusaka Declaration has deliberately adopted a notably cautious and restricted view, stating that:

> For trade development we recognise that many of us have existing bilateral and multilateral trade and customs arrangements. But even within these constraints we believe that there is room for substantial increases in trade among ourselves. To this end existing payment systems and customs instruments will be studied in order to build up a regional trade system based on bilaterally negotiated annual trade targets and product lists.

There is only clouded reference in the Declaration to the question of a regional position on SADCC countries' trade with the rest of the world. In fact, issues concerned with extra-SADCC trade have tended to be treated merely as a function of intra-SADCC trade issues, even if somewhat vaguely.

Although intraregional trade liberalization is envisaged, this is not necessarily treated on a common regional basis. It is seen not as a basic framework for regional economic cooperation but as a means of achieving particular economic goals in the spheres of production and reduction of the region's dependence. Accordingly,

> Regional trade and the development of financial institutions are seen to be important. However, they are perceived to be consequential on prior transport and production coordination and as a means to facilitate such coordination, not as *a priori* requirements or ends in themselves (SADCC 1983, p. 19).

Trade policy remains the subject of heated debate within SADCC. The Council of Ministers directed in January 1983 that Trade and Finance Ministers of SADCC member states should work out proper arrangements for facilitating increased interstate trade within the region. The Council further called for a study by consultants on SADCC intraregional trade. Two internal studies have since then been prepared in the course of 1983.[2] Another study on trade policy had been commissioned by the SADCC Secretariat for presentation by 1986.

Concern for action in the area of trade was also voiced by representatives of the private sector in July 1984 during a SADCC conference sponsored by the Commonwealth Institute in London. Prior to this concern, the issue of trade had received close attention in the 1980 Industry Strategy paper. The central emphasis then was on the pragmatic, step-by-step expansion of intra-SADCC trade and other related aspects of external trade policy. As seen then, industrial coordination strategy 'must include regional trade since coordination of production requires trade to be meaningful' (SADCC 1980c).

It seems that the formulation of intraregional trade policy will soon be in the making. However, for the time being it has been unanimously adopted that existing similar PTA studies should first be examined by the SADCC in an attempt to avoid the duplication of efforts and possible clashes. It is this feeling which, among other things, will precede launching of full-scale and more detailed SADCC trade studies.

The General Pattern of SADCC Trade
Further analysis of the components of domestic supply and consumption of manufactures indicates the inherent weaknesses of the SADCC countries. Firstly, industrial production falls well below domestic consumption in nearly all branches. This is more marked in the more complex manufacturing processes and in capital goods. This feature has induced a heavy, if not total, dependence on manufactured imports from external suppliers.

Secondly, a good deal of the manufactured exports consist of processed raw materials and only small quantities of fabricated products, machinery and equipment have attained competitive levels in external markets. Thirdly, only Zimbabwe can boast a large and integrated manufacturing sector and the dominant regional share in a variety of industrial branches. Zambia's industry is also sufficiently diversified while Tanzania's and Malawi's are heavily concentrated in more basic manufacturing branches like food and textile. Botswana, Lesotho and Swaziland, on the other hand, have little more than their export processing and assembling plants.

The general pattern of trade is strongly characterized by manufactured imports and raw material exports. On the side of exports, several high-volume commodities are upgraded by processing, although most are not. The largest trade flows are to and from the leading industrial market countries, exchanging raw and processed materials for fabricated goods, machinery and other equipment. Taking 1982 as a case, over 80 per cent of regional imports originated from industrial market economies (IMEs). Conversely, 64 per cent of all exports were dispatched to IMEs. Only 5 per cent of the total flow was between SADCC countries themselves, whilst trade with the rest of sub-Saharan Africa was less than 2 per cent in either direction.

The overall direction of trade leaves the region overwhelmingly oriented to foreign markets and suppliers. As can be read from Table 7.11, in 1982 the main suppliers to the SADCC region were South Africa (35 per cent) and overseas industrial suppliers (46 per cent). Import dependence on South Africa was much more general in the three SACU countries, accounting for 88 per cent of the group's total imports. Aside, therefore, from the very low level of intra-SADCC trade, the other most striking feature of the pattern of trade is the large SADCC deficit with South Africa which, standing at $US1,061 million, represented 57 per cent of the total SADCC–South African trade. Thus while South Africa took only 7 per cent of SADCC exports, it supplied 35 per cent of the region's imports. Clearly, the SADCC region is still serving as a foreign exchange generator for the South African economy.

The current pattern of SADCC trade raises two major policy questions. On the one hand, extra-SADCC trade will long remain dominant in trade flows. It will thus be important to consider in what ways regionally coordinated external trade policies might further the achievement of the SADCC's broader developmental goals. On the other, given the constraints imposed by small domestic markets and the limited scope for industrialization led by manufactured exports, market expansion will to an important extent depend on regional cooperation. This, in turn, will necessitate further considerations in trade policy, namely: the viability of intra-SADCC trade liberalization and the protection of regional production against external imports.

I will conclude the study by briefly commenting on the desirability of launching efforts in the direction of trade promotion both within and outside the SADCC region.

Coordinated Extra-SADCC Trade Policy

As already mentioned at the beginning, external exports by SADCC member countries – as in most other UD – are a means of expanding and diversifying the markets and developing the international competitiveness of domestically manufactured goods. Exports will further be needed to generate foreign exchange for importation of capital goods and other essential inputs to industry which cannot be obtained domestically or locally. This might call for concerted efforts in the direction of promoting exports of manufactures, raw and processed primary products.

Exports of manufactures. The current international trading environment is notoriously restrictive. This limits the scope for the SADCC's prospects of raising

Table 7.11
SADCC: Direction of Regional Trade by Major Origins and Destinations, 1982, in $US millions

Exports to (Imports from)	Botswana	Lesotho	Swaziland	Angola	Mozambique	Malawi	Tanzania	Zambia	Zimbabwe
SADCC members	52 (36)	0 (1)	8 (3)	— (7)	17 (36)	23 (24)	6 (12)	38 (51)	128 (101)
South Africa	52 (594)	20 N.A.	113 (430)	— —	10 —	14 (104)	— —	5 —	191 (338)
Other Africa	5[a] (1)	— N.A.	4 —	5 (6)	5 (22)	12 (2)	25 (89)	9 (7)	43 (3)
Asia (excl. Japan)	1[a] (3)	— N.A.	20 —	0 (14)	3 (74)	6 (25)	88 (86)	91 (28)	46 (20)
Others (excl. EEC)	60 (24)	10 N.A.	61 (89)	1408 (584)	208 (464)	66 (54)	169 (441)	540 (383)	523 (489)
EEC	286 (28)	5 N.A.	100 —	318 (390)	60 (196)	111 (82)	192 (418)	376 (270)	345 (471)
Totals	456 (686)	35 (527)	306 (519)	1731 (1001)	303 (792)	232 (291)	480 (1046)	1059 (739)	1276 (1422)

Figures for 1981.
  N.A. = Not available.

Source: Compiled from UNIDO, 'Industrial Co-operation Through the SADCC'.

the share of manufactured products in the total regional exports. If processed raw materials are excluded, intra-SADCC flows far exceed external flows of manufactured exports for all SADCC countries, save for Zimbabwe, and possibly Tanzania. Only Zimbabwe's manufactured exports comprised 20–25 per cent of the country's total and slightly over 60 per cent of SADCC's manufactured exports in the late 1970s.

Beyond first-stage processed manufactures, the scope for regional cooperation in expanding either the volume of exports or the fraction of manufactures in the export bundle is likely to be restricted in both the short and long terms to particular subsectors. Perhaps in cases where demand within the SADCC absorbs only part of the volume of output required for optimal efficiency the coordination of regional production might be extended towards securing export outlets as part of a more broad-based negotiated package.

In the very long term, IMEs will be more important for the SADCC's manufactures. This might point to the fact that reduction of import barriers within IMEs will remain of primary concern. And towards this end, SADCC members as a group probably hold a firmer negotiating position than as a collection of individual nations. Presently, SADCC is not framed as a medium for multilateral negotiations or trade relations. This is an area deserving coordinated considerations in any future formulations of region-wide external trade policy.

Exports of raw and processed primary products. Raw materials currently contribute the bulk of external export earnings and it can safely be projected that they will continue to bear the main burden of generating the finances needed for industrial development and other investment ventures for the foreseeable future. For this reason alone, it will be in the interests of SADCC member countries to improve the prices and terms of access for leading export commodities in IMEs. This could possibly be accomplished by SADCC acting as a group in negotiations with governments and relevant international organizations.

Appendix Table 8 shows clearly that several raw materials, including slightly processed products, accounted for more than 90 per cent of regional commodity exports over the 1970–78 period and for nearly three-quarters of the SADCC's total exports. Furthermore, particular SADCC countries are presently sole or dominant producers of some of the products. This is equally true for some of the relatively minor, but nationally significant commodities. For example, spices (Tanzania), copra and prawns (Mozambique), fish meal (Angola), groundnuts (Malawi), wool and mohair (Lesotho), gold (Zimbabwe), and diamonds (Botswana). For nearly two-fifths of the regional exports, two or more SADCC members are leading producers.

However, one need not overstress the viability of such bargaining attempts. Indeed, SADCC's effective bargaining strength is limited in many cases. Nevertheless, it is notable that SADCC has a substantial share in world exports in as many as half of the commodities we have listed in Appendix Table 8. It may be assumed that some form of regional or inter-country cooperation would greatly benefit the region.

In several other areas, commodity exporters could probably benefit jointly from coordinated endeavours in areas such as shared and improved market intelligence, cooperation between exporters in the marketing operations as well as cooperation in transporting the more bulky commodities to their principal overseas outlets.

Intra-SADCC Trade

A sizeable increase in intra-SADCC trade occurred between 1979 and 1982, largely due to Zimbabwe's pivotal role which doubled its share of exports to other SADCC member countries. Zimbabwe's independence opened up the potential for a rapid increase in intra-SADCC trade and for greater diversion of imports away from South Africa.

The pattern of intra-SADCC trade flows clearly shows that Zimbabwe quadrupled its exports in four years (1979 to 1982), a trend which marked static or declining flows between other SADCC member countries. Indeed, the other significant intraregional trade flows which do not involve Zimbabwe are those involving Mozambique/Tanzania, Malawi/Zambia, and Tanzania/Zambia (Tables 7.12 and 7.13). However, the structure of Zimbabwe's extra-SADCC trade reveals also that a greater volume of its manufactured exports went to South Africa than to the SADCC region. These made up two-thirds of the total exports in 1982, a much higher ratio than Zimbabwe was exporting either to the SADCC states or the IMEs. Further, imports from South Africa were mostly manufactured goods, although IMEs, and especially the EEC, dominated as chief suppliers of machinery and the more sophisticated products.

A breakdown of intra-SADCC trade by commodity of industrial branches is given in Appendix Table 9, wherein it is shown clearly that the range of commodities is reasonably broad – with food, textiles and leather products tending to dominate. The breakdown of the direction of trade flows in 1982 sheds some light

Table 7.12
SADCC: National Shares of Intraregional Trade and Ratios to Total Trade 1979–82 (%)

Country	Imports from the region			Exports to the region		
	1979	1982	Share in total 1982	1979	1982	Share in total
Angola	17	3	0.7	0	—	—
Botswana	19	13	5.2	24	19	7.5
Lesotho	0	0	0.0	0	0	0.0
Malawi	9	9	8.2	5	8	9.9
Mozambique	13	13	4.5	5	6	5.6
Swaziland	2	1	0.6	3	3	2.6
Tanzania	4	4	1.1	21	2	1.3
Zambia	17	19	5.1	19	14	3.6
Zimbabwe	18	37	6.2	23	47	10.0
Total	100	100	3.6	100	100	4.6

Source: As for Table 7.11.

on the composition of trade within the SADCC region. First, under half of the value of trade in the region was in food and beverages. The value of exports in manufactures was only slightly less, and remained dominated by fabricated products, chemicals and machinery. Second, food predominated in exports to Mozambique, whereas manufactures dominated in the import bundles of Botswana and Malawi. Third, fuel comprised the bulk of imports from Mozambique (refined petroleum and coal) and Zambia (electricity); crude materials (ore) and manufactures (textiles) from Botswana; and both manufactures (clothing) and food from Malawi.

Table 7.13
SADCC: Country Matrix of Intraregional Trade 1982 in \$US millions

Origin	*Destination*
Botswana	Angola 3 (1981); Mozambique 8 (1981); Zambia 1.7; Zimbabwe 39.7; SADCC 52.4
Lesotho	SADCC 0.2
Malawi	Botswana 1 (1981); Mozambique 0.5; Zambia 3.4; Zimbabwe 18; SADCC 22.9
Mozambique	Angola 0.5; Malawi 3.1; Swaziland 1; Tanzania 4; Zimbabwe 8.2; SADCC 16.8
Swaziland	Zambia 3.6; Zimbabwe 4.4; SADCC 8
Tanzania	Malawi 0.2; Mozambique 2.2; Zambia 3.2; Zimbabwe 0.1; SADCC 5.7
Zambia	Botswana 0.3; Malawi 4.5; Swaziland 0.1; Tanzania 2.5; Zimbabwe 30.7; SADCC 38.1
Zimbabwe	Angola 3.5; Botswana 35.1; Lesotho 0.7; Malawi 16.4; Mozambique 25; Swaziland 1.8; Tanzania 5.7; Zambia 39.3; SADCC 127.5

Source: As for Table 7.11.

SADCC has always stressed that its primary concerns are investment and production. Cooperation in trade is considered to be a mere instrument for facilitating both investment and production. However, our discussion has abundantly shown that cooperation in trade will be instrumental in the realization of all the dimensions of the SADCC industrial coordination programme. Needless to add, the reduction of intra-SADCC trade and payments barriers will be an essential facilitator. Moreover, protection from external imports will often be necessary for the viability of new and expanded industrial capacity within the broader context of regional production complementarities.

This will, however, be contrary to the current discussion within the SADCC whereby regional trade policy appears to concentrate on intraregional trade issues which are more consistent with industrial coordination in the region. We are tempted to add that external protection is a subject worth serious consideration at this stage. This is needed to assure the viability of certain vital production activities. Indeed, the absence of protective policies will, to some degree, hinder the smooth interdependence of production and supplies in the SADCC region.

Concluding Remarks

It is not to be denied that coordinated intra-SADCC trade can very greatly assist and simplify the tasks of regionally planned production decisions. Neglecting coordinated regional trade policy would very soon defeat the very purpose of the SADCC by causing dislocations of production through supply shortages and non-deliveries of components.

In conclusion, there are additional operational problems that seem worth mentioning in this context, even at the expense of repetition. *First*, there are problems arising from transport costs and bottlenecks. These problems include general lack of adequate transport networks in the area, the insistence by transport firms that they be paid in foreign exchange, poorly maintained roads, losses of goods in transit, varying railway gauges, poor shipping and port facilities as well as poor telecommunications facilities

The regional transport system is geared to primary exports and urban imports. It lacks internal integration in several parts of the region. The expansion and integration of the transport network will lower the cost of imports and exports and is essential for the creation of an interdependent regional production and marketing structure. At present the emphasis in SADCC transport planning is on upgrading railways and ports, which may reinforce the unbalanced production system. Expansion of the road network will need to focus on the medium-term planning agenda to stimulate industrialization and markets for manufactured goods outside the large towns especially on a regional basis. Hence the desirability of harmonizing existing transport networks, railway gauges, development of port facilities and new telecommunications.

It should be added here that although the SADCC attaches great importance to transport and communications, its concentration on the rehabilitation of existing transport systems may encourage the perpetuation and reinforcement of neo-colonial patterns of trade and production. This tendency, unfortunately, is likely to be increased by donor countries' preference for projects which benefit them financially (see Chapter 4).

Second, custom procedures have an important bearing on the functioning of the transport system in particular, and trade in general. These differ radically from one SADCC member to the next and can be cumbersome, inhibiting overseas imports rather less than intra-SADCC trade. Further, there are additional problems of transit, documentation and insurance of goods in transit. There is often unnecessary documentation, a feature which frustrates traders. SADCC member states may wish to consider the feasibility of adopting simple, straightforward and workable trade documentation. Besides, region-wide simplification and standardization would assist the competitiveness of local suppliers against external imports to the region.

Third, there is the problem likely to arise from SADCC's payment regimes. A potential obstacle to the expansion of intraregional trade is the absence of a clearing house for transactions between members – something like the Zimbabwe-based settlement arrangement for PTA member states. There is a clear need for such a facility in the SADCC region.

This, however, will not be enough because under the well-known conditions in which convertible currency is in short supply, the mechanism of the clearing house is unlikely of itself to clear payments backlogs. The problems of balance of payments vary between countries. For example, Lesotho and Swaziland who are still members of the Rand Monetary Area remain subjected to the overall state of South Africa's balance of payments and monetary policy. The position of Angola has been made worse by the disruption of war and the collapse of some of the former leading exports. Mozambique and Tanzania are presently confronted with mounting balance of payments problems which appear unresolvable within the short to medium term.

Thus a common factor in many of the difficulties faced by SADCC countries has been the shortage of foreign exchange, a constraint which has been persistent in eight of the SADCC countries (i.e. excluding Botswana) for the last decade and more severely in the majority. These differences in the balance of payments problems suggest that the potential for expanding intra-SADCC trade will not necessarily be exploited fully. And payments backlogs are likely to remain one of the chief obstacles to the expansion of intra-SADCC trade.

Fourth, a major weakness in export-based manufacturing is the lack of linkage to other producers. In many instances neither local production of the required inputs nor a local market for processed intermediate goods actually exist. Even where they exist on a regional basis, the established ties are often to external products.

For example, in the case of the Tanzanian radiator manufactures the main inputs of copper and steel were imported from Sweden under Swedish subsidy, even though Zambia and Zimbabwe respectively are large regional exporters of these metals. Similarly, instant coffee is produced by Tanzania, but several SADCC countries continue to import an inferior South African chicory mixture. In general, even when linkages have been established, regional possibilities could be more fully exploited.

A *fifth* constraint is inequalities of income distribution, which perpetuate a pre-existing colonial trade bias in favour of a few consumers who possess the financial power, few of whom reside outside the larger towns. Since the income inequalities are more sharply drawn in some SADCC member countries than in others, the existing pattern of income distribution in SADCC may, at best, serve to retard the growth of domestic production. As might be expected, the more affluent SADCC consumers have distinct preferences for imported goods.

Hence the dangers that may arise from the excessive attachment to 'quality'. It is inevitable that locally produced goods, particularly from newly established industries, will on occasion suffer from quality and marketing problems. This is often the outcome of factors such as poor management and/or supervision, inadequately trained labour, variations in the quality of inputs, scarce supplies and irregularities in production. Thus competition against the more established brand names and capturing markets presently being served by TNCs may prove difficult. The necessity, therefore, is for pooled efforts in the direction of maintaining sustained product improvements, with regional support in determining standards and establishing specialized services.

Finally, there are institutional aspects of trade promotion in the SADCC region.

As already mentioned, focus should also be brought to the external factors controlling trade. In this regard, feasibility problems arising from PTA 'Rules of Origin'³ are more than revealing. As one recent PTA-focused workshop notes:

> The rules of Origin of the PTA are too stringent considering that the region is very underdeveloped in the availability of indigenous capital, technology and entrepreneurship. Therefore there is urgent need to either scrap these rules or to revise them drastically, particularly to relax the requirement of domestic content and the management provision . . . The management requirement will tend to discourage foreign investment in the area. This is not good for the PTA member states since it is clear that most of their economies cannot develop much without substantial inflows of private foreign capital . . . The Rules of Origin as they exist now should be shelved until such time when the PTA Member States have developed viable indigenous technological investment and entrepreneurial capacities. (Manundu 1985, p. 53.)

Contrary to this clear submission to TNCs' domination, the same workshop had initially expressed fears of TNCs' penetration into the PTA region. As the participants saw it:

> It is expected that foreign firms and their affiliates can dominate trade in the area . . . because they have enormous resources of capital, human skills and technology which they use as packages to produce (or market) more efficiently than local firms. For this reason, it is possible for such firms to be able to sell profitably in the area even when their products do not get preferential treatment. Thus the emerging market in the region can be captured easily by extra-regional corporate affiliates of multinational corporations who then become the main beneficiaries of the larger market to the detriment of indigenous production elements. (Ibid., p. 36)

Against this fear, some participants held the optimistic view that:

> It is hoped that if Member States adhere to the Protocol on the Rules of Origin then in the long run the nationals of the Member States will have a more firm and stable grip of their economies, which is a desirable goal. (Ibid.)

The practical difficulties arising from PTA 'Rules of Origin' are a clear pointer to the feasibility of SADCC's objective of reducing the region's dependence, particularly, but not only, on South Africa. At any rate, the experience of diamond marketing is one example of the potential practical complexities. At the moment, the SADCC region has surpassed South Africa (excluding Namibia) as a producer of diamonds, and ranks third in the world, after the USSR.

Yet diamonds continue to be marketed through a tightly regulated world monopoly, the Central Selling Organization (CSO), in turn an associate company of the South African based TNC, the Anglo-American Corporation. De Beers/Anglo-American are also strongly entrenched in the two principal diamond-producing states, Botswana and Angola, through the ownership linkages and technical, managerial and marketing contracts. The complex network is illustrated below:

1. In *Tanzania*, South African based De Beers owned 50 per cent of the diamond mine and controlled exclusively management and sales before independence. Since then, the diamond mine was fully nationalized, but advice on management continues to be supplied by De Beers. All production is bought by the Diamond Corporation, a wholly owned subsidiary of De Beers; and sold to the De Beers-owned CSO in London.
2. In *Angola*, diamonds are produced by a 61 per cent government-owned DIAMANG, the rest held by a number of foreign corporations, including South African based De Beers. It is hard to establish the agency which handles diamond sales. In the final analysis, however, all Angolese diamonds are sold to the CSO in London.
3. In *Botswana*, diamonds are produced by De Beers Botswana Mining Company (DEBSWANA) which is partly owned by De Beers and the Government of Botswana. Management of and sales from DEBSWANA are handled by De Beers, who sell the diamonds to the CSO in London.
4. *Lesotho*'s diamonds are produced by De Beers Lesotho, a wholly owned subsidiary of De Beers which sells the diamonds to the CSO in London.

Thus SADCC's diamond production and its marketing are deeply subordinated to South African corporate interests. Similar arrangements, no doubt, exist for a good number of products produced and/or marketed in the region.

In concluding, we might suggest that the process towards the creation of a successful SADCC will be a complex one. The proponents of the SADCC initiative are aware of the complex nature of the strategy. Mwalimu Nyerere said in the late 1970s that every successful effort at cooperation strengthens the whole Third World in its dealings with the developed world. He cautioned, however, that successes would to a large extent depend on whether or not 'it is truly Third World cooperative effort; and that it is designed to strengthen the independence of the economy of the Third World countries' (Nyerere 1979).

It may be too early to evaluate SADCC's initiatives. However, as Green has pointed out 'the pace and depth of (SADCC) consolidation and programme development are critically dependent on four factors beyond member states' control: South African policies, drought, the global economic crisis and flows of external economic assistance'. (Green 1984, p. 481.) As a fifth factor, we might add the region's internal socio-political matrix.

SADCC's main thrust attached less weight to trade. For what purposes, and with what economic consequences, has the SADCC chosen this particular approach? This we don't know. The interpretation that might lie closest to hand if one studies official documents is that regional trade comes in later as a consequential arrangement. But we have attempted to show in this study that a strategy for increasing trade links between SADCC member countries is a prerequisite for the success of regional industrial cooperation. It is in the interests of SADCC that suitable trade arrangements be made and implemented in order to establish a solid base for regional cooperation.

Notes

1. The first nine member states to ratify the Treaty were the Comoros, Djibouti, Ethiopia, Kenya, Malawi, Mauritius, Somalia, Uganda and Zambia. Three more states, Lesotho, Swaziland and Zimbabwe, signed in March 1982. Rwanda and Burundi, and more recently Tanzania, have also signed the Treaty – making 15 signatories in all. On this account alone, the Lusaka-based MULTOC would probably be more willing to promote the PTA than the SADCC's initiative. In fact, two of the leading personalities associated with the PTA have built a negative attitude to SADCC since 1978, characterizing it as 'agent of perpetuation of the division of Africa and of imperialist penetration' (Green 1985, p. 99).

2. These include 'A Strategy for the Integration of SADCC Markets' International Funding Services of Brussels, November 1983; 'Study on Payments and Clearing Between SADCC Member States', IFS of Brussels, July 1984; and R. H. Green, 'SADCC: Towards Regional Trade Development'.

3. Under Article 15 of the PTA Treaty only those commodities are to be accepted as being eligible for preferential treatment which (a) originate in Treaty Member States, and (b) are contained in the Common list during the period of ten years for the definitive entry into force of the Treaty. Under Article 3 (4) (ii) of the Treaty, the Member States are obliged to establish rules of origin to determine if a certain commodity originates in a Treaty Member State. It is stipulated in the Rules of Origin (Annex III of the Treaty) that goods are accepted as originating in a Treaty member state if (a) they are consigned directly to a consignee in another member state; (b) they have been produced in a member state by enterprises, whose majority management is by its nationals and whose at least 51 per cent equity is held by nationals of the Treaty members or governments or government-owned institutions of the member states; (c) they satisfy 'local content' or per cent value added or 'substantial transformation' criteria.

8 Financial Integration and Development in SADCC and PTA Countries

Chiselebwe Ng'andwe

SADCC has as yet no plans to encourage political union among its member countries, which have an assortment of ideological inclinations and which include a kingdom and democracies of various shades. Nor are there any plans to encourage fiscal and monetary union or coordination. Indeed at present there are not even plans for a customs union and emphasis has been on increasing the transport and other communications links within the region and on developing various economic activities based on a national rather than regional basis. Thus SADCC can be said to be less ambitious in its cooperative effort than most regional collaborative efforts that have appeared on the African scene.

The rather loose practical relations adopted by SADCC are a reflection of the over-cautious approach of member states which have at one time or another been members of integrative groupings which involved a dominant partner. This point has been underscored by the Executive Secretary of SADCC, Dr Simba Makoni: 'At the time of the formation of SADCC, all our member states had emerged the wiser from the experiences of earlier integrative regional organisations. . . . The results of these organisations were as we all know the creation of a powerful and dominant centre.' (Makoni 1985, p. 8.)

The question is whether SADCC's practical challenges can be faced squarely with this over-cautious approach. Due to historical circumstances, all SADCC members are economically linked with outside countries rather than with one another. Hence there is a need for fundamental economic restructuring to make these economies more interdependent. In this restructuring process special attention will inevitably be paid to those factors that promote intraregional trade, and other forms of intraregional mobility of goods and services. In view of the fact that most SADCC members do not separately command adequate resource bases for sustained development, intra-SADCC mobility of factors of production, goods and services is fundamental to the SADCC objective of collective self-reliance. Significant factors in the promotion of intra-SADCC flow of goods and services are: 1) SADCC's production structure and pattern; 2) transport and communication facilities; 3) institutional facilities such as monetary and fiscal facilities governing regional trade; 4) organizational and administrative infrastructures for a coordinated approach. SADCC's production structure needs to be regionally rationalized to make member economies complementary rather than competitive in their production lines. Given a sufficiently strong regional coordinating capacity,

SADCC's production restructuring can also be based on the optimal regional allocation of resources. Improvements and rationalization of transport and communications infrastructure are essential for easy flow of materials, goods and services. Appropriate organizational and administrative infrastructures are also essential for sound planning, implementation, and coordination of programmes and projects which have a bearing on regional activities. Monetary and fiscal policies are the principal abstract institutional facilities that govern national and international mobility of goods and services.

This chapter will focus on the monetary and fiscal facilities as they relate to the promotion of intraregional trade. There is no coordinated monetary and fiscal infrastructure for SADCC. Thus the task in hand is to examine the institutional capacity or indeed lack of institutional capacity of SADCC to stimulate and sustain regional economic interactions in the absence of regionally coordinated monetary and fiscal policies. Under the circumstances, the study cannot be empirical, and will thus be only analytical and speculative.

All SADCC members are potential members of the PTA, and indeed only three (Angola, Botswana and Mozambique) of the eight SADCC members have not yet joined the PTA. Thus the SADCC is potentially a subregional grouping of the wider PTA regional grouping. Unlike SADCC, the PTA emphasizes a regional approach, and its programmes are based on supranational institutions with a capacity for regional coordination. It will thus be illuminating to examine the relevant PTA institutions, notably the trade protocol, the proposed PTA Trade and Development Bank, and the Clearing House. Since all these institutions are still developing, this chapter will suggest developments that are most conducive to the promotion of intraregional economic interaction and general development in the region. Special emphasis will be given to trade financing and promotion.

The first substantive section presents a theoretical framework which is amplified by empirical observations from other regional groupings. In the next section we look at SADCC's institutional framework and at other economic units which have a bearing on SADCC. We then look at SADCC's development programmes as they have been planned and implemented. These programmes are analysed with a view to determining their impact on national and regional development as they are operating. The underlying question in making this analysis is whether in the absence of coordinated monetary and fiscal policies, these programmes are being implemented as efficiently as possible. The basic hypothesis presented here is that the fullest development potential for this region can only be exploited by maximizing the interstate flow of resources, goods and services, and that in the absence of coordinated monetary and fiscal policies, meaningful regional collaboration will become difficult to implement. This hypothesis is explicitly or implicitly examined when looking at the SADCC's institutions and programmes of activities. The next section looks at the PTA's facilities for promoting intraregional mobility of goods and services. The chapter concludes by summarizing the institutional improvements necessary to make the SADCC a more effective and realistic economic collaborative effort.

The general conclusion of the chapter is that SADCC's institutional framework is too weak to promote any meaningful economic interaction among the member states. In particular, the absence of a regionally coordinated monetary and fiscal policy makes it difficult for intraregional trade in goods and services to prosper. While improvements in the physical links will facilitate the flow of resources and goods, payment problems could lead to under-utilization of this physical infrastructure. In the absence of effective trade links, industrial and general developments will tend to be based on individual national rather than on a coordinated regional programme. Thus, SADCC will not fully enjoy the possibilities of wider resource base and wider (than territorial) markets which are the major potential advantages of a regional grouping. In order to exploit the fullest advantages of regional cooperation, it may be necessary for SADCC to coordinate their monetary and fiscal policies.

The institutional weaknesses of SADCC are partially compensated for by the PTA's more practical approach to regional economic interaction. The inevitable policy question is whether the region can benefit more by maintaining both SADCC and the PTA or by merging the two regional groupings. Beyond the practical questions of institutional duplications and operational efficiency, the over-cautious approach of SADCC does raise academic and practical questions as to whether it is a realistic instrument of promoting collective self-reliance in the region.

The Theoretical Framework

As long as SADCC's emphasis is on reducing dependency on South Africa and other foreign countries, it follows that practical policy will involve the development of industries that will provide the needs of the regional grouping. As all the member countries are, in terms of resource endowment, too small to be self-sufficient, the strategy of subregional independence will entail mutual interdependence. Indeed, in any such cooperative industrial development endeavours, there is an implicit if not explicit emphasis on intraregional trade. In this respect, communications and energy will have as much emphasis as the primary industrial activities. Macro-efficiency considerations at regional level will dictate selectivity in the development of various national industries, especially those with markets outside the territory of domicile. From the purely economic point of view, the development of industries will inevitably involve regional resources allocation based on competitive advantage.

By pooling the regional resources and creating wider (than territorial) markets, the regional grouping removes some of the major constraints on industrial development. The assumed benefits of industrial expansion include reduction in unemployment, stimulation of other industrial activities, general economic growth, technological advances and strategic benefits. Initially, the industrialization programmes will inevitably involve import substitution. As Yu-Min Chou (1967) points out, the early stages of industrialization will tend to involve a high cost of import substitution and relatively high consumer prices for the goods. In the absence of a formal regional trade agreement, member countries could easily be tempted to buy outside the regional grouping and thus deny the new industry the markets it needs to survive. This problem is particularly significant for industrial projects where technology dictates a minimum size whose output is well above the territorial demand of the country in which the project is established.

In a situation of mutual trade agreements, the regional efforts at industrialization are bound to be well rewarded in terms of a higher pace of industrial progress. However, in the absence of political union, the distribution of benefits tends to be biased in favour of the country that joins the regional grouping with a superior economic base. In addition to national investment resources, the major influences on industrial location are market concentration, economic and social infrastructure. All these factors favour the country with a superior economic base. Moreover, the advantages will tend to be enhanced over time as each new industrial project represents greater purchasing power and positive linkages for fresh industries.

There are some location factors that may not necessarily be biased towards the relatively developed member countries. Some industries need to be located near the sources of raw materials to reduce the cost of transportation. Strategic considerations, need for balanced developments and long-term economic and political considerations – these are among other factors that influence industrial location within national boundaries. However, apart from the raw material factor all these location criteria need a central political authority with legitimacy throughout the grouping. Hence, these factors will not influence industrial location in a loose grouping like the SADCC. Since the raw materials consideration is not enough to counteract the factors that bias location towards the country with superior economic base, the problem of uneven distribution of industrial plants is bound to arise.

Empirically, it is observed within most national boundaries that most industrial plants with the exception of extractive and agro industries tend to be based in the relatively developed and densely populated areas. Significant exceptions to this general pattern are usually those industries whose location is subjectively determined by the central political authority. The biased distribution of industrial plants in regional groupings is observed in the defunct East African Common Market, the West African Customs Union, the Central African Customs, and Economic Union and in the former Federation of Rhodesia and Nyasaland. The experience of the USA with its long period of economic and political integration, also confirms this. As S. Dell pointed out even as late as 1959, 'The early advantages of the Northern States [of USA] appear to have not only been perpetuated but also enhanced industrial imbalance in favour of the North over a period of two centuries. The South still has an industrial structure that is startlingly reminiscent of an underdeveloped country.' (Dell 1959, p. 51.)

With the general acceptance of the inevitability of industrial concentration there has been growing emphasis on the spillover effects. The most likely spillover effects are in the area of employment, lower prices, easy access to manufactured products and the stimulation of other industrial activities. But unfortunately, the positive effects of new industry in LDCs tend to be confined to the countries in which the industries are established. In the absence of free labour mobility across the national boundaries the advantages of new employment opportunities created by new industries are confined to the countries in which the industries are established. The direct employment benefits can only spread to other countries if the regional grouping enjoys common citizenship. Thus, as Dell points out, when the USA experienced industrial expansion in the Northern states, and a recession in the Southern states, at the turn of the century, there were no serious employment imbalances because of the high mobility of labour. Moreover, for the LDCs the indirect employment opportunities that may be created through new demands for food, housing and other facilities will tend to be confined within the country because of transportation problems which dictate reliance on local sources.

With the emphasis on rapid economic development in all LDCs, the reaction to industrial and economic imbalances in regional groupings is often very damaging. As observed by Adedeji (1973), Seidman (1972) and Mytelka (1973), the uneven distribution of industrial development was the major cause of the failure of the UDAO, UNDEAC and EACM. The problem of the underprivileged member countries was stated thus by President Nyerere of Tanzania: 'Tanganyika should not be stopped from having textile, cement, refining and sugar industries just because Kenya and Uganda have them or Tanganyika will end with nothing because everything we want we will be able to find in Kenya or Uganda.' (Nye 1965, p. 46.) Thus, whenever these loose regional groupings continue under these circumstances, there is a proliferation of industries which defeats the fundamental objective of intraregional economic interactions based on an efficient regional allocation of resources; and indeed the cooperation venture is thus dead for all practical purposes.

As observed by Ng'andwe (1982) the most stable regional economic groupings are those that enjoy some kind of common political umbrella. The ideal situation is of course the political union that provides some political intervention in the economic arena to rationalize distribution of economic benefits. It also permits easy mobility of labour and material resources. Above all, its institutions of economic control and coordination enjoy legitimacy throughout the union. In the absence of political union, the best one can expect is a combination of political goodwill and adequate institutional infrastructure for coordinating regional policies and programmes.

Monetary and Fiscal Policies

Monetary and fiscal policies are generally regarded as major instruments of economic control. Trade across the national boundaries and even industrial investment will need some harmonization of monetary and fiscal policies.

Monetary policies. The most effective form of monetary collaboration is that involving a monetary union. The basic requirements of this type of union are: 1) permanently fixed exchange rates and guaranteed convertibility of the currencies; 2) joint monetary policies based on the group decisions of the central banks; 3) a common agency for external exchange rate policy and management capable of controlling a common pool of resources. The ideal situation for a monetary union should involve one central monetary authority and a unified currency. However, there are practical considerations which might militate against a centralized authority for sovereign states. It may be less costly and more practical to use the existing organizational and bureaucratic facilities of national central banks than to set up a new union central bank. Given a large regional grouping especially under difficult communication circumstances, the decentralization of monetary operations may be more efficient than a single central authority. The major practical problem is coordination of national central banks which have been used to guiding their own independent policies. As observed by P. R. Allen (1976), this problem is aggravated when the monetary policies and practices of member nations have traditionally differed. This has been a major problem for the European Community in its efforts to unify banking regulations. And it is likely to be a problem for SADCC.

The advantages of a single currency include the psychological sense of commitment which may be essential, especially for a young, fragile community. It also means low currency administration costs. Factors militating against a single union currency would also involve psychological and political considerations. Habits and national identities may not be conducive to a sudden switch to a different currency.

A Report by the European Community has suggested that the maintenance of national currencies may be desirable for deeply rooted European emotional needs. (European Communities 1973.) The break-up of the East African Community currency soon after the three African countries became politically independent could also be associated with the political sentiments and national pride. For a new community, there could also be practical problems. As Allen (1972) points out, the premature substitution of union currencies could cause widespread confusion, suspicion and consequently inefficiency in the entire financial system.

The usual institution for coordinating monetary policies is the central bank. In a grouping of sovereign states, the multiplicity of central banks will create definite problems for a unified monetary policy. Different currencies, unless they are easily convertible, will create serious inconveniences and definite barriers to intraregional trade. Moreover, under the present circumstances of major foreign exchange difficulties for most SADCC member states, separate foreign reserves are more vulnerable to external fluctuations than joint reserves. Because of distortions caused by uncoordinated policies, the absence of a central monetary authority makes it difficult to harmonize even those policy areas where joint arrangements exist.

It has empirically been observed that an effective joint monetary authority is very difficult in the absence of political union. As long as nations insist on total sovereignty, it is always difficult to surrender a major control instrument of economic policy to an effective joint monetary authority. Thus the EEC has failed in spite of continuous effort to create a unified central monetary authority. In East Africa, the East African Currency Board which served Uganda, Kenya and Tanzania as a kind of a unified central bank while these countries were all under British colonial rule broke up as soon as the countries acquired independence. The former Governor of the Tanzania Central Bank, Mr Mtei, observed that the break-up of the Currency Board and the common currency 'lay mainly in that the Currency Board had not met the full needs of these countries for a central banking institution . . . a realisation that an effective central bank could not function serving three sovereign and independent states'. (Mtei 1972.) A unified central bank for former French (West African) colonies closely linked with the French Central Bank is a hangover from colonial economic relations. Similar historical economic links are seen in Liberia's dependence on the US monetary system, and Swaziland and Lesotho's links with that of South Africa.

In the absence of monetary union, a regional grouping needs coordination of some basic monetary and financial policies to facilitate the smooth flow of goods, services and productive resources within the region on the basis of comparative advantage. Thus the underlying objective of such coordination is efficient allocation of resources in the region. Capital mobility is basic to the flow of goods and services. Hence, integration of national financial policies and all asset markets is fundamental to the promotion of intraregional trade. Here we adopt P. B. Kenen's definition of integration as the most practical. Kenen (1976, p. 9) defines integration as 'the degree to which participants in any market are enabled and obliged to take notice of events occurring in other markets'. While Kenen's definition allows for a broad range of factors our focus here is confined to the impact of financial relations on the integration of goods markets.

Capital mobility among LDCs is sluggish and very slight in absolute terms. The major reasons for this include the paucity of capital in LDCs. Most of the capital flowing into LDCs comes from the large industrialized countries. The absence of capital markets in all but one SADCC country is mainly a reflection of this problem. Other barriers to capital mobility within the SADCC are likely to be national identities and political uncertainties which will strongly bias investment towards the countries in which investible financial resources are available. Such factors will tend to militate against efficient regional allocation of resources. This observation is consistent with the current general view that international portfolio allocation in LDCs is more sensitive to long-term political factors than to the expected financial yields on investment.

Coordinated policies aimed at stimulating mobility of whatever available capital there is within SADCC would help support industrial activity on the basis of comparative advantage. Financial integration is particularly desirable for promoting intraregional trade in goods and services. The minimum requirement here is easy convertibility of the currencies. Like most LDCs' currencies, SADCC's currencies are not easily convertible, and trade between these countries is usually through the medium of the internationally recognized currencies. Thus intraregional trade will tend to be limited to the foreign reserve holdings. In practice this means trade within SADCC, as it is among other LDCs, will be based on surplus foreign spending power after the trade transactions between individual LDCs and their industrialized trading partners have been settled. In other words, trade within SADCC will be confined to peripheral and supplementary transactions rather than forming the mainstream transactions.

This problem is particularly significant in that for historical reasons LDCs' production and consumption patterns have married them with the industrialized countries as the principal trading partners. For new regional groupings like SADCC, the greatest challenge is the restructuring of the production patterns of member countries so as to make their economies more interdependent in a manner that promotes regional self-reliance. In the absence of easy currency convertibility, this challenge will be a difficult one to meet.

A higher degree of financial integration would require fixed exchange rates in addition to easy convertibility. A fixed exchange rate would facilitate joint monetary policy to regulate trade between a regional grouping and the outside world. But even more important than this joint external trade policy management capability is the impact of fixed exchange rates on intraregional trade. Even if there was smooth convertibility, absence of a fixed exchange rate would lead to serious distortions of other policy variables. For instance a change in the exchange rate could nullify policy measures aimed at expanding the volume of exports between member countries.

With regard to internal and intraregional monetary policies, lack of coordination can lead to contradictory signals and counterbalancing policies within the region. Most SADCC members do not use open market operations, and they depend mainly on reserve ratios, interest rates, monetary base, and direct controls on credit to regulate monetary flows. If a member country for instance adopts an expansionary monetary policy it needs similar policies within the region to absorb any excess output and to provide for any increase in demand. Contraction policies in other member countries may frustrate the expansionary policies of the member country and lead only to inflation in the absence of recourse to external trade relations. But such unplanned resort to external trade relations is a frustration of regional objectives. Moreover, uncoordinated monetary policies could frustrate fiscal policies and make it almost impossible to coordinate other policies and programmes.

Fiscal Policies. Fiscal policies are important for influencing the flow of productive resources and consumer items. They can also be a potent instrument for resource allocation in the economy by influencing investment and consumer patterns. They are also important in the redistribution of income among various strata of the economy. But such functional capacity of fiscal policies is only available in an area which enjoys a joint political system. For instance, in the US the Federal Government's financial support to state and local governments is influenced by the state and local needs, regional unemployment imbalances and the national policy of development bias towards the backward regions. Such redistributive measures may not be able to remedy the regional inequalities but can at least remove the obnoxious elements in any regional imbalances. In the absence of political union, harmonization of the fiscal distributive measures across the regional grouping becomes very difficult. It is significant to note here that empirically, fiscal policies are extremely sensitive to the political expediencies of the people in power. Thus in 1962, with local elections looming, Uganda failed to keep her commitments to the EACM on regionally agreed excise tax increases on sugar. The abdication of the regional policy by the Uganda Government was intended to outmanoeuvre the opposition party which had made political issue of the excise duty by saying 'Is Nairobi or Dar-es-Salaam going to make decisions for Kampala? . . . the interests of Uganda is what should be borne in mind and not Kenya and Tanganyika.' (Nye 1965, pp. 53–4.)

In the absence of political union, joint fiscal policies should adopt measures aimed at promoting intraregional trade while protecting regional industries from outside competition. Such measures should involve a common tariff policy and joint policy on excise duty and other taxes. Above all there should be no tariff and other institutional barriers against intraregional trade. The divergence between national and regional interests usually makes it very difficult to adopt such measures with adequate legitimacy throughout the region. Thus, even in the EEC compliance with regionally devised policies has only been possible because of the need felt in the region to have a common political platform. Otherwise, there has been continuing debate, especially in the UK, about the economic wisdom of complying with joint EEC fiscal policies that govern intra-EEC trade.

Even where joint policies are adopted, problems arise with regard to the distribution of benefits and the burden of collaboration. The major burden arises out of trade diversion for countries which have to pay more by buying from within the region at higher prices than they would pay for external sources. Problems also arise from the uneven distribution of income and excise tax revenue that follows the uneven distribution pattern of industrial projects. There must be adequate compensatory mechanisms to absorb any unfair burdens. In some regional groupings efforts have been made to redistribute excise duty throughout the regional grouping in a manner that helps to offset the burden of trade diversion.

But the most effective remedy is to promote a more equitable distribution of industrial plants. Thus for most regional groupings there have been regional development banks with an allocation system biased in favour of the economically weak members. Such arrangements facilitate the harmonization of fiscal and monetary policies to reduce economic imbalances in a regional grouping. But in the absence of political union, such measures have generally failed to reduce imbalances sufficiently to make the collaborative efforts worthwhile for all member states. Thus historically all the regional groupings in Africa except those with political union have either broken up or are existing in name only without a meaningful capacity to achieve their economic objectives. Since the Lagos plan, however, the regional groupings have inspired optimism.

In a regional grouping such as SADCC, where the inevitable emphasis will be on aggressive industrialization programmes, an institutional capacity to influence a regionally efficient allocation of resources is particularly desirable. Such capacity usually involves a variety of measures aimed at influencing effective demands for various items, relative prices of various productive resources and physical infrastructures necessary to sustain the appropriate movements of productive and consumer goods. In a loose collaborative effort such as SADCC, such measures become difficult to coordinate regionally.

For small countries such as the SADCC members, the internal (intraregional) problems of coordination are compounded by the dominant influence of the transnational corporations which seek to preserve their trade ties. Thus in the East African Community, there was an uneconomical duplication of tyre factories because of the influence of transnational corporations. The first tyre factory designed to serve the entire community was established with the collaboration of one transnational corporation in Tanzania. But a rival transnational company arranged to establish another one in Kenya to preserve its market in East Africa.

Such duplication of industrial plants could lead to inefficient allocations of resources, and consequently to a suboptimal economic growth rate for the region. Effective coordination of fiscal policies is essential to contain this and other anomalies in the industrialization programme of SADCC.

The Preferential Trade Area (PTA)

The PTA protocol was enacted on 27 December 1981 and is intended to cover all countries within Eastern and Southern Africa. Thus all SADCC members are potentially members of the PTA. As at 1 January 1986, of the eight SADCC members only three – Angola, Botswana and Mozambique – have not joined. The full list of PTA members as at 31 December 1985 was Burundi, Comoros, Djibouti, Ethiopia, Kenya, Lesotho, Malawi, Mauritius, Rwanda, Somalia, Swaziland, Tanzania, Uganda, Zambia and Zimbabwe.

The basic objectives and specific undertakings of the PTA are given under Article 3 of the Treaty as:

1. It shall be the aim of the Preferential Trade Area to promote cooperation and development in all fields of economic activity particularly in the field of trade, customs, industry, transport, communications, agriculture, natural resources and monetary affairs with the aim of raising the standard of living of its peoples, of fostering closer relations among its Member States, and to contribute to the progress and development of the African continent.
2. The functioning and development of the Preferential Trade Area shall be reviewed in accordance with the provisions of this Treaty with a view to the establishment of a Common Market and eventually of an Economic Community for Eastern and Southern African States.
3. For the purposes set out in paragraphs 1 and 2 of this Article the Member States agree to implement the undertakings set out in paragraph 4 of this Article and as provided for elsewhere in particular provisions of this Treaty.
4. (i) The Member States undertake by way of the Protocol annexed to this Treaty to:

   a) gradually reduce and eventually eliminate as between themselves customs duties in respect of imports of selected commodities produced within the Preferential Trade Area;
   b) establish common rules of origin with respect to products that shall be eligible for preferential treatment;
   c) establish appropriate payments and clearing arrangements among themselves that would facilitate trade in goods and services;
   d) foster such cooperation among themselves in the fields of transport and communications as would facilitate trade in goods and services;
   e) cooperate in the field of industrial development;
   f) cooperate in the field of agricultural development;
   g) establish conditions regulating the re-export of products within the Preferential Trade Area;

h) promulgate regulations for facilitating transit trade within the Preferential Trade Area;

i) simplify and harmonize their trade documents and procedures;

j) cooperate in customs matters;

k) standardize the manufacture and quality of goods produced and traded within the Preferential Trade Area;

l) recognise the unique situation of Botswana, Lesotho, and Swaziland and their membership of the Southern African Customs Union within the context of the Preferential Trade Area and to grant temporary exemptions to Botswana, Lesotho and Swaziland from the full application of certain provisions of this Treaty; and

m) govern such other matters as may be necessary to further the aims of the Preferential Trade Area.

(ii) The Member States further undertake to:

a) relax or abolish quantitative and administrative restrictions on trade among themselves;

b) promote the establishment of appropriate machinery for the exchange of agricultural products, minerals, metals, manufactures and semi-manufactures within the Preferential Trade Area;

c) promote the establishment of direct contacts between, and regulate the exchange of information among, their commercial organisations such as State trading corporations, export promotion and marketing organisations, chambers of commerce, associations of businessmen and trade information and publicity centres;

d) ensure the application of the most favoured nation clause to each other;

e) adapt progressively their commercial policy in accordance with the provisions of this Treaty; and

f) take in common such other steps as are calculated to further the aims of the Preferential Trade Area.

Under Article 29 of the Treaty it is planned that after eight years of enforcement of the Treaty, appropriate measures will be worked out for the development of the PTA into a common market, and eventually into an Economic Community. The achievement of a common market is anticipated after ten years of the PTA's life.

The institutions of the PTA are: (1) the Authority; (2) the Council of Ministers; (3) the Secretariat; (4) the Tribunal; and (5) the Commission, the committees, and such other technical and specialized bodies as may be established or provided for by this Treaty.

The Authority is the supreme organ of the PTA, and it consists of the heads of state and government of member states. The Authority is responsible for general policy and general direction and control of the PTA's activities. The decisions of the Authority shall be taken by consensus.

The Council of Ministers is the second highest organ of the PTA. It consists of such Ministers as may be designated by member states. It is responsible for active review and supervision of PTA activities, and for evolution of proper policies to be adopted by the Authority. The decisions of the Council are binding on all the subordinate institutions except the Tribunal. The Council's decisions are taken by consensus.

The Secretariat is the administrative arm of the PTA. Its Chief Executive is appointed by the Authority. The Secretariat's responsibilities are mainly general administration and technical support to the Authority and the Council.

The Tribunal is the judicial organ of the PTA. Its main function is to ensure proper application or interpretation of the provisions of the Treaty, and to adjudicate upon any disputes in such matters.

The intergovernmental commissions and Technical Committees consist of experts on specific issues as determined by the Council. They oversee the implementation of the provisions of the Treaty.

Unlike SADCC, the PTA's policy orientation is clearly towards strong economic links and effective regional cooperation and coordination of development programmes. Under the Treaty, emphasis is put on a regional approach in the fields of transport and communication; industrial development; agricultural development; trade documentations and procedures; standardization and quality control of goods; clearing and payments arrangements; and general aspects such as information exchange among various private and public institutions on matters of mutual interest. The principal institutions for promoting and sustaining intraregional economic intercourse are the protocol on customs and trade matters, the PTA Clearing House, and the PTA Trade and Development Bank. These are the institutions related to the control and coordination of monetary and fiscal policies on which this paper is focusing. These institutions will therefore be examined separately and in reasonable detail.

PTA Customs and Trade Protocol

Under the customs and trade protocol are undertakings of member states with regard to the liberalization of trade; customs duties; common external tariff; preferential treatment; non-tariff barriers to trade; and general administrative aspects of trade including the list of products to be covered under this protocol.

The liberalization of trade undertaking stipulates that there will be a gradual reduction and eventual elimination of customs duties and non-tariff barriers within the PTA. There will also be gradual evolution of a common external tariff policy.

As a guide to intraregional trade there exists the common list of selected commodities which have export and import interest in member countries, and are produced in the region. The common list shall be amended from time to time by the Council on recommendation of the committee of experts. The commodities covered in this list shall be accorded preferential treatment.

Under article 8, section 3 of the protocol on the reduction and elimination of trade barriers, member states are free to maintain or enter into new preferential trade arrangements with third countries 'provided such arrangements do not impede or frustrate the objectives of this protocol and that any preferences granted to third countries under such arrangements are extended to member states on a reciprocal basis'. (PTA Treaty, p. 48.)

The freedom of PTA members to have preferential arrangements with third countries is partly a recognition of the difficulties that would be encountered by some members if they were to suddenly cut their existing preferential relations with third countries. This applies particularly to the economic ties of Lesotho and Swaziland with South Africa. The spirit of flexibility runs throughout the PTA Treaty, and there is an emphasis on consensus in decision-making. While the long-term objective of the PTA is integration of its members' economies, the process will inevitably be gradual. Initially there are bound to be problems of trade diversion which can only be absorbed by members through adequate long-term positive expectations of the PTA. In the absence of these long-term expectations, the short-term trade diversion problems could undermine the efficacy of the cooperative spirit if there was no flexibility in the PTA programmes of cooperation. The PTA Secretary-General, Dr Bax Nomvete, has underscored this point thus:

> The creation of an integrated subregional economy, if it is to be achieved at minimum political and economic cost, has to be approached in stages. Undue haste will be counter productive. Each of the participating states has to be convinced of the benefits it will derive from the integration process.

In the area of tariff concessions and harmonization, the PTA has adopted a common percentage for the reduction of customs duties to be applied to each commodity. The highest percentage reduction is 70 per cent and is on capital goods (including transport equipment) and consumer items of particular importance to economic development. The next highest are intermediate goods and non-agricultural raw materials whose percentage reductions are respectively 65 per cent and 60 per cent. Luxury goods have attracted the lowest percentage reduction of 10 per cent while food has 30 per cent.

It is not yet clear how effective a common percentage reduction in tariff barriers will be for countries with different tariff patterns. This approach is apparently more expedient than imposing actual common tariff rates for each product. In the actual promotion of intraregional trade the protocol gives appropriate bias towards the mobility of capital and non-agricultural intermediate goods. These items are important in the overall development process. It is noted here that the production of capital goods involves high technology and heavy investment. Hence there is need for a regional approach in these areas. For instance the machine tool industry recently established in Tanzania cannot be expected to be easily duplicated in other PTA countries because of both cost and market considerations. Such plants are only viable if the wide PTA market is open to them. Being a new industry it cannot immediately compete on the PTA market with older industries of the developed world. Hence preferential treatment is essential to support and sustain such regional capital goods industries.

While trade in food and agricultural produce is also to be encouraged, it has been given only modest emphasis in the customs arrangements. This perhaps is a reflection of the fact that all PTA countries are potentially self-sufficient in food and other agricultural produce. Moreover where climatic conditions permit, a policy of territorial self-sufficiency in food and other agricultural produce is economically sensible because most agricultural produce, as mentioned earlier, is high in weight and bulk relative to value, as well as being perishable. This means of course that it does not lend itself to long-distance trade. And indeed, given adequate agricultural potential in each PTA country, it is not economically prudent as a long-term policy to encourage agricultural produce to compete with other items for the limited transport facilities available.

The intraregional trade in luxury items receives only a token encouragement in the customs arrangements. Since PTA countries normally impose duties of 100 per cent or more on these items, the 10 per cent reduction in tariff rates for members is hardly capable of conveying real preferential treatment. It is recognized here that classification of this category if on consensus basis is bound to be very difficult for countries with various levels of development. It is clear, however, that this is an area where PTA countries face serious external competition, and the mere 10 per cent reduction for PTA members will leave PTA markets quite open to external supply sources.

The PTA position here can be rationalized on the basis of encouraging PTA trade in factors which have more direct dynamic impact on socio-economic development. But it must be recognized that some PTA countries' expenditure on luxuries is substantial. And if such expenditure is allowed to go to third countries, it is bound to have a serious negative impact on PTA trade and development. Thus where the customs arrangements fail to convey the anticipated preferential treatment, there should be active recourse to non-tariff facilities.

According to article 5 of the protocol on trade barriers, non-tariff barriers shall be relaxed or eliminated as follows:

	Non-tariff barriers	*Concessions*
(a)	Quantitative restrictions	Preferential treatment in allocation of quotas
(b)	Foreign and import licensing	Preferential treatment in issuing licences
(c)	Foreign exchange licensing	Preferential treatment in issuing licences
(d)	Stipulation of import sources	Preferential treatment
(e)	Prohibition or temporary prohibition of imports	Exempted where possible
(f)	Advance import deposits	Preferential treatment
(g)	Conditional permission for imports	Exempted
(h)	Special charges for acquiring foreign exchange licences	Preferential treatment

These concessions if properly synchronized with the customs arrangements both by individual member countries and at regional level could go a long way towards promoting PTA trade.

The PTA Clearing House
The protocol on clearing and payment arrangements has recognized in its preamble that the absence or inadequacy of machinery for settlement of payments among PTA members has hampered intraregional trade. The Clearing House is intended to facilitate expansion of trade within the PTA by reducing the dependence of such trade on hard currencies. In this respect, use of national

currencies expressed in UA PTA (unit of account for PTA currently equal to one SDR) is encouraged in the settlement of eligible intra-PTA transactions.

The functions of the Clearing House include all clearing operations in respect of eligible transactions, and to regulate and oversee the efficient and speedy transfers of payments between member states. Without prejudice to any bilateral clearing arrangements, the clearing arrangements of this institution are based on multilateral principles. The net debit and credit positions for each monetary authority are determined by the committee on the basis of the volume of trade of each member state within the PTA. The net debit balance outstanding at the end of the transactions period shall be settled in hard currency by the debtor country.

The Clearing House became operational in February 1984 and is at present located in the Reserve Bank of Zimbabwe. It is too early to make a realistic assessment of the Clearing House's performance. Observations on the operations of the Clearing House so far are thus not intended to make a definitive assessment of the institutions, but are part of a critical analysis of the potential of the Clearing House. The Clearing House is facing the usual teething problems. However, an account of some operations of the Clearing House will illuminate the institutional capabilities and weaknesses that are likely to be permanent features of this institution.

Member countries are able to use national currencies in the settlement of payments during a transactions period of two calendar months. Net balances at the end of the transactions period are settled in convertible currencies, i.e. Deutschemark, French franc, Japanese yen, pound sterling, SDR, and US dollar. The limit of each country's net credit (debit) at any point will be equal to 25 per cent (20 per cent) of the average value of the country's total annual trade within the PTA during the previous three years. The limits for the initial period are shown in Table 8.1.

Table 8.1
PTA Countries' Credit and Debit Limits

Country	Credit Limit UAPTA 000's	Debit Limit UAPTA 000's
Burundi	5,310	4,248
Comoros	1,110	888
Djibouti	13,963	11,170
Ethiopia	9,635	7,708
Kenya	57,183	45,746
Lesotho	268	214
Malawi	10,280	8,224
Mauritius	4,203	3,362
Rwanda	11,193	8,954
Somalia	4,455	3,564
Swaziland	1,763	1,410
Uganda	28,255	22,604
Zambia	18,528	14,822
Zimbabwe	23,370	18,696

The unit of account for settlements will be the UAPTA which will be equal to the SDR. Intraregional settlements will be expressed and recorded in terms of UAPTA. Most PTA currencies are pegged to a single currency or unit of account, or based on a trade-weighted basket system. Djibouti, Ethiopia and Somali are pegged to the US dollar; Comoros to the French franc; Lesotho and Swaziland to the South African rand; Kenya, Malawi, Rwanda and Burundi to the SDR; while Mauritius, Zambia and Zimbabwe use a trade-weighted basket. Each monetary authority will quote a daily rate of exchange against the UAPTA. Each monetary authority will undertake to sell or buy its own currency at the quoted rate to other monetary authorities through the Clearing House. Commercial banks can use cross rates in foreign currency dealings with their central banks.

In accordance with rule 9 of the regulations, settlement of all net debits and credits will be made in full in convertible currencies at the end of each transaction period, i.e. six times a year. The facilities of the Bank for International Settlements (BIS) in Basle were originally intended to process actual settlements. So it would be necessary for the Clearing House and each country to maintain an account with BIS in convertible currencies. The Clearing House would inform the members of the exact date of each settlement, and the amounts receivable or payable by each monetary authority. As it turned out, the BIS was not willing to provide the clearing services, and the PTA turned to the Federal Reserve Bank of New York for this service. Thus the settlements are made through the Clearing House account at the Federal Reserve Bank to which debtor countries pay their net debt, and from which net creditors' accounts are reimbursed.

In the event of a debtor member failing to settle on time, interest will be charged at one percentage point above the ruling SDR rate for the first week, after which it will rise by one percentage point for each subsequent week for which the amount remains outstanding. Interest so earned shall be distributed pro-rata to creditors. Defaulters can also be reported to the committee, Council and the Tribunal.

The principal objective of the Clearing House is to minimize dependence on third currencies in the settlement of intraregional trade. If total intra-PTA trade for instance is $US 10 million, in the absence of the Clearing House there will be need for $US 10 million worth of convertible currencies to settle the transactions. With the clearing facilities, it is possible for $US 8 million worth of transactions to be settled in local currencies, with only $US 2 million remaining to be settled in hard currencies.

During the first transactions period, 1 February to 31 March 1984, the total volume of trade through the Clearing House was UAPTA 5.6 million, of which only UAPTA 1.3 million or 23 per cent of total was settled in convertible currencies. In the second period, the volume of business increased to UAPTA 7.8 million, and the foreign exchange component rose in relative terms to UAPTA 5.4 million or 69 per cent of total. During the third transaction period, from 1 June to 31 July 1984, the volume of business rose to UAPTA 9.7 million while the amount of foreign exchange settlement also rose both in absolute and relative terms to UAPTA 9.1 million or 94 per cent of total. By July 1985, in spite of an increase in the number of countries using the Clearing House, the volume of trade settled through the Clearing House was only UAPTA 42.8 million which was 20 per cent of the full potential of the clearing facility.

At its sixth meeting, in July 1985, the Council of Ministers noted that the Clearing House was capable of achieving its objectives, and at low cost to member states. Thus it endorsed the agreement of the clearing and payments committee to renew the interim arrangement for the Reserve Bank of Zimbabwe to perform the duties of the Clearing House for a further period of two years. The committee, which comprises the Chief Executives of the Monetary Authorities, would examine the question of permanent location for the Clearing House after one year.

By July 1985 nine members of the PTA were using the clearing facility. The actual volume of this trade is an insignificant fraction of the total trade of PTA countries. This is not surprising because historically trade among PTA countries has been very low. To make PTA countries better trading partners is a long-term proposition that requires fundamental restructuring in production patterns, transport and communications infrastructure, and institutional facilities. The Clearing House is thus an important institutional facility for this long-term restructuring programme. While promotion of intraregional trade would be very difficult without this institution, it shall be recognized that until other PTA policies and programmes have had a chance to remove some of the structural constraints on intra-PTA trade, the Clearing House cannot realistically be expected to be fully utilized. This observation does not in any way underrate the important catalytic role of the clearing facility even at this stage of its under-utilization.

It can be anticipated that as the PTA economies become more complementary in their trade relations, the volume of trade settled through the clearing facility will rise.

Apart from these structural problems of the PTA, the low business of the Clearing House in its early stages is also a reflection of teething and transient problems. The PTA Secretary-General, Dr Bax Nomvete (1984, p. 5), has outlined these problems as follows.

First, the participating countries have tended to channel more of their imports than exports through the Clearing House. This problem has also been observed in the case of Zambia by the Deputy Governor of the Bank of Zambia, Mr Kwalela Lamaswala (1984). This emphasizes the need for member countries to organize their transactions in a more balanced way.

Second, some countries have insisted on convertible currencies for their exports to other PTA members. This could be a reflection of these countries' desperate need for hard currency. It could also indicate inadequate confidence in, or inadequate understanding of, the clearing facility among member countries. Thus, according to the Secretary-General, this problem emphasizes the need for national workshops on the clearing facility involving monetary authorities, banking and business communities.

The third problem involves the traditional trade barriers such as export or import licences. Bureaucratic delays in such matters hamper PTA trade. This problem can be solved by observing the PTA protocol on the relaxation of non-tariff barriers.

The fourth problem involves the practical problems of opening correspondent accounts by some commercial banks. Some banks have not adjusted their traditional banking relations, and have been slow in opening reciprocal accounts or UAPTA accounts with other PTA member banks. This could be the usual problem of adjusting to a new situation. The proposed association of PTA commercial banks will go a long way in improving operational relations among the commercial banks.

The final problem observed by the Secretary-General is the fact that not all members were using the facility. As fewer members use the Clearing House, the lower is the group advantage of multilateral clearing. As the Clearing House stabilizes, practically all members can be expected to use its facilities.

It has been proposed to have a balance of payments support facility within the Clearing House. A study has already been undertaken by the PTA Secretariat on this, but no decision has yet been made. If and when implemented, this facility needs to be harmonized with the trade financing facilities of the PTA Trade and Development Bank.

Although the PTA trade accounts will be recorded and settled in UAPTA, currency fluctuations will pose some problems. Sometimes there are sudden and violent exchange rate movements in PTA countries. Such changes are often the result of external pressure, notably from the IMF, which usually insists on devaluation, amongst other things, as a condition for its loan facilities. The general instability of the exchange rates in PTA countries will affect both the direction of trade and the payments and settlements capacity of the countries. It is noted here that most PTA members are mono-export economies whose exports are not very sensitive to the exchange rate behaviour. Where the price of such exports are traditionally quoted in hard currency, e.g. copper, currency devaluation does not affect the physical volume or hard currency value of the exports. What may be affected in the short run is profitability of the exporting company if it manages to keep domestic costs – especially wages – low. Otherwise the general import capacity will fall. Moreover by raising the price of imported productive resources, devaluation has a negative dynamic impact on economic activities of developing countries which often do not have immediate local alternative sources for these imported productive resources. Thus different exchange rate regimes will cause some distortions in the operations of the Clearing House.

The question of travellers' cheques and credit cards in national currencies was raised at the fourth meeting of the Clearing and Payments Committee in September 1984. It was resolved that it was not opportune at this early stage for the Clearing House to handle such arrangements. No doubt, the Committee's position is sensible in that it recognizes the practical problems of dealing with travellers' cheques and credit cards which are novel ideas or non-existent even in the domestic transactions of most PTA countries. Yet it must be recognized that intra-PTA travel is one service which provides captive opportunities for the Clearing House.

Intra-PTA business and other travel is quite significant. If this was settled in local currencies, it could go some way towards reducing the overall dependence on third currencies for settling PTA transactions. At present all intra-PTA travel is facilitated in third currency travellers' cheques. Thus after a trip any unspent funds can easily be channelled into trade with third countries. Indeed casual evidence indicates this practice is quite common. Thus apart from the problem of encouraging dependency on the third currency, the current practice of settling travel services gives undue opportunities for shifting funds from potentially captive intra-PTA transactions to outside imports. It is therefore imperative that the question of settling intra-PTA travel services be re-examined with a view to minimizing use of hard currency, and preventing diversion of funds from this PTA captive transaction.

The PTA Trade and Development Bank
The objectives of the Bank are:

1. to provide financial and technical assistance to promote the economic and social development of the member states, taking into account the prevailing varying economic and other relevant conditions within the Preferential Trade Area;
2. to promote the development of trade among the member states conducted in accordance with the provisions of this Treaty by financing, where appropriate, activities related to such trade;
3. to further the aims of the Preferential Trade Area by financing, wherever possible, projects designed to make the economics of the member states increasingly complementary to each other;
4. to supplement the activities of the national development agencies of the member states by joint financing operations and by the use of such agencies as channels for financing specific projects;
5. to cooperate, within the terms of its Charter, with other institutions and organizations, public or private, national or international, which are interested in the economic and social development of the member states; and
6. to undertake such other activities and provide such other services as may advance the objectives of the Bank.

Membership of the Bank is open to all PTA members, and such other states or institutions as may be approved by the authority. The authorized capital stock is UAPTA 400 million, and may be increased by the resolution of the Board of Governors.

Member states shall subscribe to the capital stock on the basis of a formula that takes account of GDP, population and net exports. Weights of 25 per cent have been assigned to GDP, another 25 per cent to population, and 50 per cent to net exports, provided that each member state shall have a minimum of 0.5 per cent and a maximum of 10 per cent of capital stock reserved exclusively for member states. The Board of Governors shall determine the basis of subscription for non-member states whose share of the capital stock shall not exceed one-third.

The Bank will be based in Bujumbura, Burundi, but there is provision for regional offices to be established later. The Bank's administrative organs are: 1) the Board of Governors; 2) the Board of Directors; and 3) the President and general staff.

The Board of Governors is the supreme controlling organ, and consists of one representative from each member of the Bank. The voting powers of the Governors are based on the shares of the members they represent. The functions of this organ include the appointment of the President, and general guidance of the Board of Directors.

The Board of Directors shall consist of not more than seven directors, of whom five shall be appointed by member states on a representation basis and the other two by non-PTA members. This organ is responsible for the conduct of general operations of the Bank. Its responsibilities include: 1) determination of the organization and offices of the Bank, and prescribing responsibilities attached to offices of the Bank; 2) approving the Bank's budget; 3) taking decisions on loans, guarantees, borrowing of funds by the Bank, etc.; 4) determining rates of interests on loans, commissions and fees for guarantees and other financial transactions.

Decisions of the Board of Directors shall be based on voting powers of the members of the Bank represented by the directors. The President shall preside over meetings of the Board of Directors which shall be held at least once every three months. The President is the chief executive officer, and he shall conduct the Bank's business under the direction of the Board of Directors.

There are two principal banking activities, i.e. trade financing and development banking. There shall be a trade financing fund which shall be allocated between 15 per cent and 25 per cent of the ordinary capital resources of the bank. The terms and conditions for operating this fund will be determined by the Board of Governors.

The Bank is due to open in January 1986. Thus there can be no empirical observations on the Bank at this stage. What follows therefore is a theoretical critical analysis of the development possibilities that can be expected from the Bank. We shall examine trade financing and development banking as distinct though related aspects of the Bank. The basic link is that new development projects must lead to greater complementarity among the economies, while trade financing is intended to relax the financial constraints on intra-PTA trade. Thus trade financing may be seen as a tool for the short-term policy management, while development banking is the long-term tool for the same policy objectives.

Trade Financing

The basic objective of trade financing is to promote the intraregional flow of goods and services. Considering the scarcity of foreign exchange, emphasis should be put on counter-trade arrangements on a multilateral basis. Here the limitation of the Clearing House is that net balances must be cleared in convertible currencies at the end of the transactions period of two months. The scarcity of hard currency tends to limit the scope of counter-trade based on multilateral clearing within short periods.

Counter-trade or linked purchases is the general term given to reciprocal purchasing commitments in international trade. This form of trade mainly developed among COMECON countries in their attempt to reduce their indebtedness to Western Europe which had risen from $US13 billion in 1967 to $US65 billion in 1980. When this form of trade involves long-term contracts of economic collaboration, it is generally referred to as cooperation. Among COMECON countries, cooperation is the principal form of trade and import requirements are often prescribed in five-year plans. This arrangement has become important also in trade between COMECON and Western Countries.

On a multilateral basis, cooperation could provide real opportunities for promoting trade among PTA countries. In the first place, the long-term planning of exports and imports provides opportunities for deliberate development of complementary trade relations. Secondly, it reduces reliance on hard currency for settling PTA trade. It is observed here that if centrally, i.e. regionally, planned on a long-term basis, a significant volume of trade can emerge among PTA countries, especially when the development financing programme is also deliberately used to promote complementary relations. In the cooperation arrangements between Western and COMECON countries it has been observed that new sources of supplies have been discovered, and trade opportunities thus enhanced. Such opportunities are bound to be more pronounced in the PTA which has a deliberate policy of deepening trade links, and where mutually advantageous trade opportunities have not been vigorously explored.

It is observed that regardless of how well the trade transactions are arranged there are bound to be deficit and surplus countries at the end of the cooperation period. Such balances will perhaps have to be settled in hard currencies. A possible advantage of cooperation is the reduction in the frequency of resorting to a third currency for settling net trade balances. Let us demonstrate a possible five-year multilateral counter-trade agreement. Zambia supplies UAPTA 100 million worth of electricity to Zimbabwe from which she imports UAPTA 20 million worth of steel. Tanzania imports UAPTA 90 million steel from Zimbabwe, while exporting machine tools worth UAPTA 30 million, UAPTA 20 million, and UAPTA 40 million to Zimbabwe, Zambia and Kenya respectively. Kenya exports agricultural and manufactured goods worth UAPTA 30 million to Zambia and UAPTA 20 million to Tanzania. The total transactions are summarized in the import–export table showing total trade of UAPTA 350. To settle net balances, only UAPTA 40 million of hard currency is required. Because of the seasonal nature of some of these exports, if payments were due in short periods of say two months, total demand for hard currency to settle net balances would have been much higher. Moreover, the foreign exchange constraint could even have reduced the total volume of trade below UAPTA 350 million.

Table 8:2
Sample Five-Year Cooperation Transaction (UAPTA Million)

	Kenya	Tanzania	Zambia	Zimbabwe	Total Exports
Kenya	—	20	30	—	**50**
Tanzania	40	—	20	30	**90**
Zambia	—	—	—	100	**100**
Zimbabwe	—	90	20	—	**110**
Total Imports	**40**	**110**	**70**	**130**	**350**

Net Trade Balances: Credit (Debit)
Kenya   10
Tanzania   (20)
Zambia   30
Zimbabwe   (20)

Total Credit (Debit): UAPTA 40 million.

While the strategy of long-term multilateral trade arrangements would thus encourage PTA trade and reduce dependence on hard currency, it does raise questions of short-term and long-term trade financing. In our example the Zambian suppliers of hydroelectric power which has a steady supply may want payment at least four times a year or even monthly. The Tanzanian suppliers of machine tools, whose supply is very irregular, may get paid maybe four times during the five-year cooperation period. The exporters may thus have various cash-flow needs for which appropriate financing requirements are essential. On the other hand, individual importers need financial facilities to pay for their products while in transit and while in stock. Moreover, the long-term arrangements may not cover all imports, especially those of an emergency nature for which special settlement arrangements may be needed. Thus even in the light of long-term trade arrangements, there will be a need for trade financing involving both local currencies and hard currencies. The Trade and Development Bank should address itself to both aspects of financing. We shall just examine some forms of financing that operate mainly in Western countries, and look at the chances of their active duplication in PTA. Finally, we shall examine possibilities of trade financing that may arise as a result of the PTA's peculiar circumstances.

Trade financing is generally treated as a set of facilities available to cover the risks of non-payment for goods exported, and for non-delivery of goods imported. The facilities include insurance aspects as well as banking mechanisms. The PTA Bank will have to cover both aspects. In this chapter we shall dwell on the banking facilities, while recognizing the insurance aspects as being of equal importance.

In trade financing, there is need to distinguish between consumer goods trade and capital goods trade. Consumer goods trade usually involves only short-term credit, while capital goods trade often involves long-term credit facilities.

Bills of exchange. The bill of exchange is a credit instrument whereby the vendor agrees to deferred payment, and the purchaser acknowledges the liability to pay at an agreed future date. The usual credit period runs between 30 days and six months. These bills are negotiable instruments which can be sold and bought. In a situation of easy currency convertibility, the bill of exchange would be a very convenient form of short-term credit. But currency exchange in PTA countries is too complicated a process to make this form of credit a reliable one for cross-border trade. The Trade and Development Bank can facilitate this credit form by buying and selling these bills. As will be seen later, possibilities do exist for individual short-term credits to be settled without the use of foreign exchange.

Accounts receivable and factoring. Accounts receivable is a short-term financing arrangement that involves a bank providing credit to the supplier (exporter) of goods. The seller's claims against the importer serve as security for the Bank. Normally, the importer is kept out of the debt assignment, and the financing is basically made on the credit worthiness of the exporter. However, in view of foreign business risks such as ignorance of importer's credit worthiness, political and transfer risks and currency risks, this credit facility normally covers 65–70 per cent of the assigned claims.

In factoring the credit recipient is the importer who must be creditworthy. The factor purchases the client's claims and assumes the pertinent commercial risks. Normally cross-border factoring involves correspondent relations with local factoring companies that can assess the economic risks of claims to be assumed by their foreign partners. As a general rule the factoring company in the importing country takes over the commercial risk and collection responsibility from the export factor. Because of currency transfer problems, these forms of financing are not feasible for PTA trade for the short-term needs for which they are traditionally used. The Trade and Development Bank can facilitate these credit systems by providing facilities that solve the foreign exchange constraint.

Trade financing in capital goods. Although some trade in capital goods is settled on cash or short-term credit, the bulk of this trade usually involves medium-term (up to five years) or long-term (five to ten years) credit. As pointed out by R. H. Miller (1981), in the highly competitive world of international trade in capital goods, credit considerations often tend to outweigh other factors such as price, technical specifications and delivery period.

Since supplier's credit is usually short-term, and unlikely to be a significant form of financing intra-PTA trade in capital goods, we shall not dwell on it, but shall focus on financing for the exporter and other buyer credits. Export finance can be grouped under three categories; these are dealt with below.

The first form of credit is that where the exporter bears all the risk. Examples here are foreign currency credits, secured bank overdrafts, and discount of trade receivables either in local or foreign currency.

Foreign currency facilities include basic foreign currency loans and forward foreign exchange sales to avoid losses arising from currency fluctuations. The exporter bears the risks. In case of overdrafts, the exporter secures them with his rights under the export transaction by assigning to the bank all negotiable documents. The discount facilities involve the cash purchase by the bank of negotiable bills of the exporter, but the bank retains the right of recourse to the exporter in the event of bills being dishonoured at maturity.

The second form of export finance is that which involves risk-sharing, such as state-controlled export guarantee schemes and private sector credit insurance. State export guarantee schemes normally cover 95 per cent of political risk and 85–95 per cent of the commercial risk. Under these schemes, a large percentage of total value of exports can be given by commercial banks, while the exporter bears the financing responsibility of the other percentage. The private sector insurance scheme underwrites only the risk of buyer insolvency or protracted default; the other risks are borne by the exporter. These schemes are not developed in PTA countries, but they have potential.

The third category comprises those forms of credit which permit the exporter to pass all the export risks to the bank or finance house. Examples include confirming house facilities; buyer credits; export leasing.

Confirming houses act as agents for the buyer by confirming as principals, orders placed with the exporter, and thereby undertaking to pay him without recourse on evidence of shipment. They can also act as merchants by purchasing the goods from the exporter and selling them abroad. Within the PTA the major constraint here would be the currency transfer problem.

Buyer credits are sometimes arranged by the importer in the exporting country. Such credits are often covered by government credit guarantee programmes. The credit relationship is between the financier and the importer. The exporter is generally in a non-recourse situation. This form of credit is particularly common for large capital purchases and is mainly undertaken by specialist banks, major international banks and consortium arrangements. The bulk of finance here comes from Enromarkets, i.e. the pool of funds outside domestic monetary markets. The Trade and Development Bank can secure access to this source of funds for the PTA. Otherwise, within the PTA, the scope may be too limited for generating significant internal resources for long-term buyer credits.

The exporter may sell his product to a leasing company that leases it to the foreign country. Under leasing, technically, you are exporting use of the equipment at monthly rentals. The major difficulty here would be with timely and regular externalization of payments. Otherwise, there are some local and international leasing experiences in some PTA countries.

Development Financing

In the area of development financing the principal challenge of the PTA Trade and Development Bank is to mobilize resources mainly for long-term financing of development projects. The short-term financing needs, i.e. working capital, can very often be financed by local commercial banks, subject of course to the foreign exchange constraint for imported raw materials for which the trade financing facilities of the Bank will be required. The other major challenge is the efficient regional allocation of these resources. In this respect, the overriding consideration must be the long-term promotion of complementary relations in production and trade of the PTA economies. We shall first examine the task of resource mobilization, then that of resource utilization.

The challenge of economic development in the PTA is a monumental one that requires substantial capital resources to tackle. Given the low technological and capital base in most PTA countries, any major industrial and agricultural investment will require imported equipment and sometimes auxiliary professional staff outside the PTA. These will inevitably require external (financial) capital resources to import. The inadequacies of local capital resources are crowned by the widespread foreign exchange constraints in most PTA countries. Very often even where funds for the full project cost are available in local currency project implementation can be delayed or completely frustrated by the foreign exchange component of the project cost.

While the long-term strategy is to increase intra-PTA trade and reduce trade with other countries, it is inevitable in the early stages of the PTA and during the economic restructuring period that the industrialization process will involve substantial imports from outside the PTA. Such imports will usually require credit in foreign currencies. One of the major tasks of the PTA Bank is to mobilize such resources for member countries.

In mobilizing external resources the Bank can use its UAPTA 400 million capital stock as a leverage to borrow additional funds for disbursement to development projects in member countries. The Bank can also facilitate development funding by providing guarantees for export financing that is often raised in the country of exporters of capital goods or projects.

While foreign exchange resource mobilization may be the principal task, mobilization of local currency for both development investment and trade purposes should also be of some concern to the PTA Bank. In practice local commercial banks and financial institutions will be active in mobilizing and disbursing such resources. But the PTA Bank could collaborate with these institutions, especially where local currency is generated by the PTA Bank's foreign exchange facilities.

With regard to the regional allocation of resources there will be various considerations, including equitable distribution of development projects, short-term and long-term yields of investment, national and regional forward and backward linkages, and strategic and political considerations. In terms of the objectives of the PTA the overriding consideration must be the impact of investment on the regional restructuring of the economies. Such regional considerations may be at variance with narrow national objectives. Moreover, the optimal regional distribution of resources may be at variance with the politically determined equitable formula of distribution.

The resolution of these conflicts between regional and national objectives will determine efficiency levels of resource utilization. If national interests are allowed free rein the regional economic restructuring process would be seriously compromised. For instance, if projects like Iron and Steel industries which need regional markets are duplicated because of national pressures, they could become very inefficient and could discourage development through the high prices of their products.

The question thus arises regarding the resolution of conflicts between national objectives and regional objectives in development planning. It is certainly important and fair that each country should be able to identify its priorities. However, it is equally important that such priorities are tempered by regional perspectives. A good number of projects that fulfil national development priorities may not have any significant impact on the regional programmes. But where a national project is bound to create serious distortions of the restructuring programme, the PTA Bank should suggest alternative projects to finance in the same country. Otherwise, its basic objective is compromised.

Apart from conflicts between regional and national considerations the Bank must provide technical support in project identification and feasibility studies. Such services may be needed by some countries even in determining purely national priorities. Such services as a complement to the financing services were emphasized by the former ADB President Mr Willa Mung'omba as being very fundamental to the process of development financing in Africa.

Operational Options for the PTA Bank

Given the technological and capital limitations of all PTA members, major development projects will inevitably involve reliance on imported inputs, including financial resources. Thus in the development financing activities of the Bank, the bulk of financial facilities will involve a corresponding cross-border movement of goods and services both within and outside the PTA. Thus the practical distinction between trade financing and development financing cannot be taken for granted in the context of the PTA Bank. Some capital goods imports from non-PTA countries will involve trade financing facilities of the Bank, although the recipient PTA member will treat such facilities as development funding.

Even apart from the practical problems of definition, a rigid formula for the allocation of funds between trade and development financing may not be conducive to the efficient allocation of available resources. Flexibility would widen the Bank's capacity for meshing the various trading and development activities for any given volume of resources. Such flexibility would lead to more efficient utilization of available resources. To reduce reliance on third currency in intra-PTA trade, the Bank's strategy should be cooperation arrangements based on long-term multilateral counter trade clearing mechanisms. Such arrangements could be supported by guarantees of the PTA Bank. To ensure maximum exploitation of these facilities, they should not be confined to intra-PTA trade, but should be extended as much as possible to trade relations with third countries. In this respect, the Bank's task should involve identification and mobilization of a pool of PTA exportable goods that can be used in these cooperation arrangements with third parties. Individual country's trade deficits and credits with third countries can be meshed and harmonized with intra-PTA cooperation arrangements. The PTA Bank's guarantees may be utilized for most of these arrangements and thus reduce pressure on other capital resources of the Bank.

While the major task of the PTA Bank will be mobilizing foreign exchange resources, it should also be concerned with mobilization of local currencies. One area which needs active examination by the Bank is the local currency that is generated by external injection of foreign currency. Sometimes local currency is available for a project, but foreign exchange is the constraint. In such cases, if the PTA Bank provides the foreign exchange facility it should be free to show interest in the local currency generated by its foreign exchange facilities. The local currencies so generated can form a basis for development funds to finance various local costs.

In its development objectives the Bank should deliberately and actively promote projects which rely substantially on local raw materials. Not only will this approach promote national development programmes, it will also reduce unnecessary pressure on the Bank's trade financing resources. Even where the PTA Bank's resources are passed through the national Development Banks, the PTA can prescribe general guidelines to govern disbursements of its resources. It can also be active in monitoring the efficient utilization of such resources.

The PTA Bank is bound to work very closely with national Development Banks with regard to development financing, with national commercial banks in matters of trade financing, and with central banks in international settlements. As pointed out by M. Khonje (1984), national development banks tend to be biased towards large business houses in urban areas, and tend to neglect small entrepreneurs and rural areas.

The development banks' bias towards large industries poses special problems for most PTA countries where large industries are owned and controlled by non-nationals. Thus such bias tends to support foreign businesses at the expense of nationals. This is clearly not conducive to stable economic growth.

Today, the strategic role of small entrepreneurs and rural development is widely accepted as is evidenced by the creation of specialized institutions for small-scale enterprises, and special rural development programmes in practically all PTA countries. It may be operationally wise for the PTA Bank not to channel all its development resources through the national development bank, but also through the specialized institutions for small enterprises and rural development.

In trade financing the commercial banks have to play a major practical role in the absence of specialized export credit institutions such as exist in Western developed economies. It will be essential for the national monetary authorities and the PTA Bank to work closely together with the Commercial Banks to evolve and standardize institutional facilities for cross-border trading. The Commercial Banks can provide practically all required national services, while the PTA Bank can provide guarantees of foreign exchange. It may thus be necessary to hasten the formation of the PTA Association of Commercial Banks. The PTA Bank should also be active in the promotion of other public or private, national or regional specialized institutions to augment the commercial banks' and PTA Bank's facilities in trade financing.

Concluding Observations

The existence of two regional groupings in the same region does raise questions of possible duplications. Moreover, the different approaches of SADCC and the PTA to the objectives of regional integration do raise theoretical and practical questions regarding the relative capabilities to achieve the stated objectives. SADCC's basic approach is averse to regional central authority. The PTA philosophy on the other hand emphasizes central coordination of programmes while recognizing the practical dangers of hasty centralization of the decision-making processes.

The most fundamental objective of SADCC as originally pronounced in the Lusaka Declaration is the forging of links to create a genuine and equitable regional integration so as to reduce economic dependence on the outside world. In a way, the creation of SADCC reflects growing emphasis on economic issues in the cooperative effort among the Southern African independent states which had previously confined their cooperation to political issues. The SADCC Executive Secretary underscored this point as follows: 'SADCC was launched as a liberation movement, the logical and natural progeny of the political struggle, the translation of the tactics and strategy of the political struggle into the economic struggle.' (Makoni 1985, p. 4.) The late President Khama of Botswana put it thus: 'The strength and effectiveness of coordination action in the political liberation struggle encourages us to believe that a similar dynamic or coordination is attainable on the economic front.' (Ibid., p. 4.)

It is quite clear from various policy pronouncements that SADCC is seeking effective coordination of economic policies. At the same time, it is quite clear that SADCC's operational strategy is based on very loose institutional arrangements such as those which have enabled the Frontline States to wage an effective coordinated political struggle against colonialism and apartheid in South Africa. It must be realized, however, that while political coordination is feasible even with the minimal facility of diplomatic missions, coordination of economic policies among sovereign states requires some basic economic institutions and policy instruments which have legitimacy throughout the region. The current institutional framework of SADCC is clearly inadequate for effective coordination and harmonization of economic policies.

There are no doubts about the practical economic objectives of SADCC, which are to widen the regional resource base and market base to stimulate economic growth in the region. In the words of Dr Makoni:

> The underlying assumption here is that where our national economies are too small and weak, coordinated and integrated development will yield strength, and where our national entities are incapable of providing the goods and services needed by our peoples, the pooling of resources and facilities will yield greater capabilities and competence thus leading to collective regional self-reliance. (Ibid., p. 7.)

In practice, the policy of regional self-reliance requires new industries and an improved intraregional flow of goods and services. While SADCC has a strong policy emphasis on physical links, it has neglected institutional links which, in fact, at present constitute the binding constraint on intraregional trade. In particular the absence of coordinated intraregional trade settlement and appropriate tariff arrangements have tended to restrict trade within SADCC below the capability of existing modest transport and communications facilities.

In its five years of existence SADCC has made reasonable progress, especially in planning transport and communications on a regional basis. Current plans and programmes in other areas will also significantly add to the productive capability of SADCC member countries. It is doubtful, however, under the current institutional framework, if the improved physical links and productive capabilities will be optimally utilized to promote intraregional trade, which is essential to facilitate and sustain the economic linkages necessary for economic growth. Indeed, it is doubtful whether in the absence of a proper payments system and conducive fiscal arrangements, new industries will be operated as truly regional rather than national projects.

While physical links are important, it must be recognized that other factors are also involved in the promotion of the intraregional flow of goods and services. The SADCC has an urgent need to evolve and adopt a realistic institutional framework and control instruments to coordinate economic policies on a regional basis, if it is to realize the full potential of its investment in the physical infrastructure and in productive industries. More specifically it should evolve an institutional capability to coordinate and harmonize the monetary and fiscal policies of its member countries to ensure smooth economic interactions within the regional grouping. While all monetary and fiscal policies need effective coordination and harmonization to achieve 'a genuine and equitable regional integration', the most immediately binding constraint on SADCC is the absence of a regional mechanism for smooth clearance of intraregional trade. This is required to stimulate and sustain regional economic interactions that will in turn sustain the desired long-term restructuring of the SADCC's production pattern on the basis of a regional allocation of resources.

Unlike SADCC, the PTA emphasizes regional considerations, while recognizing the national peculiar circumstances. Moreover, the PTA is seen as a transitional phase leading eventually to an economic community. In its charter the PTA provides for adequate institutional infrastructure for initiating and coordinating development programmes on a regional basis. In practice, the PTA approach recognizes the special circumstances of each member state and where necessary provides special dispensation with regard to specific regional programmes. This flexibility and the PTA's emphasis on consensus in decision-making reflect awareness of the disruptive effects of hasty centralization or rigidity in regional policies affecting countries with various historical and economic circumstances. The implementation of the PTA treaty will be phased over a period of ten years. According to the PTA Secretary-General, the first phase will emphasize

> intra regional trade, without, of course, neglecting the other sectors, especially those on which increase in trade directly depends. The underlying logic behind this approach is that, as sectoral linkages among our countries are established and strengthened through growing and mutually beneficial economic inter-dependence, resulting from intraregional trade, market integration within the PTA will be developed. (Nomvete 1984, pp. 5–6.)

As recognized by the PTA Secretary-General, trade is the key instrument in promoting regional integration.

In summary, the promotion of intraregional trade requires both physical and institutional infrastructure. The key physical infrastructure comprises transport and communications facilities. The principal institutional infrastructure for trade has to do with cross-border payments and settlement mechanisms, and tariff arrangements. The PTA Clearing House, the Trade and Development Bank, and the protocols on customs and Trade Barriers constitute adequate institutional framework for promotion and coordination of regional trade. The protocol on transport and communication will take care of the physical infrastructure.

Unlike SADCC, the PTA appears to have a comprehensive and realistic institutional base for promoting and sustaining economic interaction among its members. Without the dual membership of the majority of SADCC members, SADCC may find it very difficult to achieve its objectives on its own institutional infrastructure. It may be in the interests of the region to consider merging SADCC with the PTA. There are no fundamental differences in objectives to hinder such a merger.

9 Perspectives on Economic Cooperation and Autonomous Development in Southern Africa

Ibbo Mandaza

The chapter begins with a review of theories and philosophies on regional economic cooperation with particular reference to Africa; and in the context of global processes in the era of imperialism and international finance capital. All this poses the basic question: whether organizations such as SADCC will be able to constitute an alternative to – and a delinking from – the centre. But in this respect, SADCC is viewed as the main agency for the attempt towards such an alternative within the Southern African subregion. In as far as the liberation movements of South Africa and Namibia acknowledge its role, SADCC is expected to encompass the entire Southern African subregion in due course.

It will be necessary therefore to outline the historical, socio-economic and political factors inherent in the Southern African situation so as to indicate broadly the parameters and possible line of development of the struggle in Southern Africa. This might also help to explain why so far SADCC cannot be viewed as fulfilling the objectives for which it was established, and in doing so to suggest how Southern Africa might be able to develop autonomously. Essentially, future developments hinge heavily on the struggle in South Africa itself.

Indeed with the likelihood that South Africa will attain majority rule within the next decade, there must come a fundamental change in the conception of SADCC which up to now has been firmly based on the need to delink from South Africa. The possibilities for a neo-colonial solution in South Africa are real, given the strength of imperialism and international finance capital. Yet internal developments in South Africa itself indicate that the new state will have to come to terms with the labour movement and other mass organizations, and will be obliged to concede to demands for democracy and socialist development. This would have a direct impact on the entire subregion, allowing for the full expression of progressive forces in such countries as Angola, Mozambique and Zimbabwe. As one writer has warned, the 'sudden collapse of white rule in South Africa would lead to a catastrophe similar to that of the Russian revolution itself.' (Howard 1985, p. 5.)

Logically, therefore, a liberated South Africa will become the economic, political and strategic base for a future SADCC, regardless of the organization's attitude to international capital. There is also the question of the kind of new relations that a liberated South Africa will have to develop with its historical neighbours, in the interests of genuine economic cooperation. The legacy of uneven and unequal development in Southern Africa could itself be the source of conflict and render any regional cooperation strategy vulnerable to imperialist intrigue. At any rate, the battle for a future Southern Africa – with a liberated South Africa (and Namibia) and a stronger SADCC – is already on. The question is whether in the foreseeable future the SADCC and Southern Africa will be able to break away from domination by imperialism and international capital and work towards autonomous development.

Lastly, the chapter deals with some issues pertinent to the nature of the South African struggle, including the growing international pressure against the apartheid regime, the possibilities and possible consequences (for all in the region) of the imposition of sanctions, and the possible configuration of forces on Day One of South African liberation.

The analysis should help expose some of the shortcomings of SADCC, particularly its current emphasis on mere opposition to South Africa as well as its failure to recognize the contradiction in seeking American and other Western capital as a basis for disengaging from South Africa. It might also help towards a strategy which will include, under the objectives of regional economic cooperation and autonomous development, a liberated South Africa. SADCC and frontline states must quickly move away from the short-sighted conception of an economic and political struggle that sees its goal as merely the downfall of apartheid. Needless to add, it is difficult to see how such a change could develop easily in an organization whose *raison d'être* is essentially opposition to South Africa. Perhaps then, it is fair to expect that only through the liberation of South Africa will the SADCC begin to tackle the overall and more enduring problem of dependence on international finance capital. There is, however, the hope that a change in this direction has begun in the growing involvement in SADCC of the South African and Namibian liberation movements. The challenge is how this involvement can be nurtured and developed positively as the struggle intensifies.

Regional Economic Cooperation in Africa in the Era of Imperialism and International Finance Capital

The problems of regional economic cooperation in developing countries are obvious in that the aims and objectives of regional organizations relate to the struggle of these countries against underdevelopment by (and dependence on) the developed countries. But these problems have been compounded by the tendency of regional organizations to reinforce the dominant features of the neo-colonial relations that exist between most developing countries and the metropolitan countries.

The background to the formation in recent years of regional organizations in Africa has been the *Lagos Plan of Action* (LPA) of 1980. A creation of the African Heads of State, the LPA called for the establishment of an African Common Market by the year 2000. But the origins of the LPA itself go back to March 1977 when the fourth Economic Commission for Africa (ECA) Conference of Ministers established the Multinational Programming and Operational Centres (MULPOCS) whose specific objective was to promote economic cooperation at subregional levels in Africa. These subregional common markets would in turn develop into the kind of African common market envisaged under the LPA. The Economic Community of West African States (ECOWAS) and SADCC were established quickly on the heels of the LPA. But the PTA was also an outcome of these developments, born specifically out of the MULPOC.

As is implicit in the objectives of all such organizations, the argument for cooperation is, as Mkandawire (1985, pp. 93–4) has aptly summarized, based mainly on: (a) the hope that the 'enormous economies of scale' can be attained through cooperation and coordination at regional level; and (b) the belief that regional integration, 'by removing the monocultural nature of individual members', will increasingly reduce the risk of export diversification. Thus regional cooperation would gradually unite a continent that has been hitherto 'balkanized', increase Africa's bargaining power *vis-à-vis* foreigners who have for centuries controlled and used its immense material and human resources, and thereby enhance Africa's political and economic independence.

There are many studies which have sought to address this problem of regional economic cooperation. But among the most revealing, particularly in the African context, is a collection of papers by African scholars of the African Association of Political Science (AAPS) presented at a seminar in Harare in February 1984.[1] Africa has had its fair share of attempts at regional economic cooperation; and, perhaps, no other continent has maintained such faith and optimism in such attempts, even in spite of the evident disparity between the aims and achievements of these organizations. The seminar represented a watershed in the analysis of the theories and philosophies of regional organizations with particular reference to Africa. But the discussion related particularly, of course, to SADCC and the PTA.

As has already been pointed out, ECOWAS, SADCC and the PTA were born against the background of much optimism; with the OAU's *Lagos Plan of Action* of 1980 which called for the creation of an African Common Market by the year 2000; and the developments in Southern Africa itself, particularly the liberation of Zimbabwe in that same year. There was also the hope that these organizations would have learnt for the better from their predecessors in similar attempts at regional economic cooperation, particularly the defunct East African Community (EAC). But the African scholars variously showed that attempts at regional economic cooperation in Africa are largely unsuccessful, even though they do constitute an important dimension in Africa's development and its struggle to regain its history. All pointed to the root causes that stem from Africa's historical relations with Europe and North America, economic dependence and the overall ambitions of imperialism in a continent that is largely given to neo-colonialism.

Writing about ECOWAS, Jinadu (in Shaw and Tandon 1985, p. 41) points out therefore that 'We cannot take it as self-evident that regional integration will promote or facilitate regional development. It may or it may not.' Designed to overcome dependence and enhance intraregional transactional flows and trade, ECOWAS 'is faulty and therefore incapable of the task'. It has been more concerned with finding itself a place within the global structure of economic relations, 'hoping that moral suasion will result in winning concessions here and there, and in improving West Africa's relative position and advantage in international economic relations'. Thus ECOWAS has been concerned more with institution-building (within the framework of neo-colonialism) than with structural transformation (that would lead to autonomous development). (Ibid., pp. 46–7.)

In his account of the now defunct East African Community, Dan Nabudere has shown that the origins of this organization are to be found in British imperialist designs in East Africa at the turn of this century. Determined to exclude other imperialist competitors and thereby consolidate her economic interests in this region, British imperialism had established in 1907 a 'customs union' for Kenya and Uganda as 'one of the first steps . . . to protect its market in these two territories by imposing a tariff against the imports of other powers seeking markets'. (Ibid., p. 55.) Tanganyika was to join this British colonial structure in 1923, after the defeat of Germany in World War I. Tariffs and other mechanisms were subsequently introduced and together formed the basis for both the concentration of the productive powers of British capital and the establishment of white settler agriculture and semi-manufacturing. Included in this was the process of land-grabbing from the Africans, the consequent gradual proletarianization of the African peasantry, particularly in Kenya, and the development of a transportation and communication system, with preferential railway freight rates for settler farmers and therefore altogether designed to facilitate the exploitation of raw materials as required by British metropolitan industry.

With the emphasis on the railways as an important basis for development, there arose the East African Railways and Harbours which

> became the most important of the pillars of British integration of the region with its own finance capital. Upon this were added other institutions like the Currency Board, research institutes, the post office and telecommunications and these together were consolidated into a *system* supervised by the three governors jointly on directives of the Secretary for the Colonies of the British government through a *Governors' Conference*. (Ibid., p. 56.)

Subsequently, other institutions would be created, giving form and content to what became known as the East African High Commission.

Thus, Nabudere's main point is that 'the outlines of what came to be the East African Community' are to be found in these political, economic, and institutional arrangements by Britain, 'in the course of the competitive struggle to assert her interests in the region'. (Ibid., p. 55.) The difference, Nabudere would argue, between the colonial-inspired East African High Commission and the post-colonial East African Community that was formed in 1967, was 'no more than' the sentiment of Pan-Africanism that characterized the latter. But despite the good intentions of the African leaders of the East African Community, 'there were strong, compelling forces at work in the region that negated their honourable intentions'. (Ibid., pp. 58–9.) These forces included US-led multilateral imperialism.

In this new phase, the transnational corporation was becoming a new force of integration of production, distribution and finance on a world scale. The more dynamic of these finance capitals saw no particular value in regional arrangements. Indeed they saw these as old colonial structures advantageous to the former colonial powers only. (Ibid., p. 60.)

If this is true, then the post-colonial period – and the East African Community itself – in fact facilitated the transnationalization of the East African region, beyond the confines of British imperialism and its imperially protected markets. Indeed from the 1960s onwards, Africa began to experience more directly the influence of the US in the 'latter's objective of 'protecting' the former colonies from 'Communist' influence. As will also be outlined below, this US policy is many-faceted. But its main instruments have been 'aid', military assistance to client countries, and the development of such multilateral institutions as the International Monetary Fund (IMF) and the World Bank. These would help ensure the further transnationalization and integration of the economies of the Third World into the world capitalist system. The EEC and its monopolies and conventions also assists in this process, enhancing the vertical integration of these economies to the detriment of horizontal and intra-Third World production and trade.

In short, the conclusion of such analysts as Nabudere is simply that regional economic cooperation in Africa (and Third World countries generally) is impossible in the era of imperialism and international finance capital. For Nabudere, the study of the EAC is illustrative of this.

What the study was saying was that regional integrated production and marketing was impossible in the face of the foreign ownership, management, and productive control over industry, commerce and agriculture. In short, the region was integrated externally so intra regional cohesion was impossible. (Ibid., p. 68)

But neo-colonialism also inheres an ideological framework within which the leaders of these African countries are incapable of understanding the true nature of the forces of imperialism and international finance capital. The neo-colonial states are thus unable to realize their complicity in the entire set-up. They are unable to design and develop regional organizations that can truly challenge the existing relations and structures of dependence and exploitation. They have neither the ideological, political nor economic capacity to establish the basis for sound economic cooperation.

In fact, the conclusion of such analysts as Nabudere is that even the SADCC and PTA cannot successfully resist the vertical integration pressures of transnational corporations and international finance capital. Besides, there is also the harassment of the World Bank and the IMF, who together ensure that developing countries adhere to new 'structural adjustment programmes' and 'conditionalities'.

Yet it would be both unrealistic and even ahistorical to conclude that Africa's efforts at regional economic cooperation are doomed to fail in the circumstances that she finds herself in at this historical conjuncture. There is the need not only to identify the positive way out of this apparent failure, but also to recognize that these efforts have developed a degree of political unity and coordination among African States, at both regional and continental levels. To many, such unity might appear fragile and even *ad hoc*. But given the nature of the African terrain and the history of the continent, political unity today might be the basis of the goal of economic cooperation and autonomous development tomorrow.

The question of interstate relations has often been cited as one other factor that undermines regional economic cooperation. Thus occasional assertions of sovereignty or the particular xenophobic reactions on the part of some member states could in the short- and long-term hinder the development of a regional organization. As Jinadu has pointed out, the sovereignty problem also expresses itself in the fear of domination by regional 'influentials'. (Ibid., p. 49.) These include Nigeria, Senegal and Ivory Coast in the case of ECOWAS; Zimbabwe with regard to the SADCC; and Kenya with regard to the defunct EAC.

Yet these are problems which cannot be viewed separately from the basic problem of the existing relations and structures of dependence, exploitation and domination. The problem of sovereignty arises out of the related issue of uneven and unequal development that is sparked off in the inception of colonialism. But, as we shall see in the following pages, the problem can be exacerbated during the neo-colonial era, not only undermining regional economic cooperation but even endangering the peace and security of African countries.

SADCC: Concept and Reality

The foregoing account of the history and development of regional organizations emphasizes the basic constraints on regional economic cooperation in Africa. It now seems that we were naive and over-optimistic in expecting so much of organizations like SADCC and PTA. Yet a brief analysis of the origins and historical development of SADCC in particular might assist us in drawing some perspectives on the likely developments in the Southern African subregion.

There are now numerous writings on SADCC but there is as yet no clear indication of the origins of the SADCC concept, though some of us have already pointed to its North American and Western European 'economic' roots: to the series of back-room diplomatic moves (between African and non-African personalities) that pre-date the inauguration of SADCC at Arusha in July 1979; and suggested that an analysis of the origins of SADCC might reveal an interesting aspect of North American and West European foreign policies, wherein SADCC is just another expression – akin to the *détente* exercise of the 1970s – of imperialist policy in Southern Africa. But the significance of such an analysis would be to ascertain whether there is today a close relationship between whatever those motives were and the manner in which SADCC has been operating ever since. If there is, this does not in itself mean that SADCC cannot be transformed into an organization that can truly reflect the aspirations of the African peoples and . thereby generate genuine regional economic cooperation in Southern Africa.

We shall show shortly why it has proved so difficult for most SADCC member states to disengage economically from South Africa. It will be argued that the reasons are the same as those which could make a liberated South Africa the centre of a possible viable and united Southern Africa regional economic union. But in the meantime the resultant *political* isolation of South Africa by the existence and development of SADCC is hardly matched by a corresponding level of disengagement at the *economic* level. This problem can best be understood through an analysis of the role of imperialism in Africa in general and Southern Africa in particular. For the purposes of this chapter, however, suffice it to state the main elements of this role and how, in the context of neo-colonial relations, the African states have responded within the framework of such organizations as SADCC.

At least such a brief analysis might explain why SADCC sees no contradiction in its policy of seeking economic assistance from the US and other Western capitalist countries as a means of reducing dependence on South Africa. This is in spite of the fact that many of these Western countries are themselves directly or indirectly supporting South Africa. Besides, there is even more than the possibility that, for the US and other Western capitalist countries, the SADCC has become a soft option, a face-saving commitment, a dubious counterbalance to their continuing involvement with South Africa. Indeed it is a situation within which the SADCC and frontline states have been mobilizing the Western world into a political and diplomatic isolation of South Africa, if only on the basis of common moral indignation to apartheid and racism.

But this can easily dovetail with the policy of the US (and its allies) in Southern Africa and what appears to be a plan for a neo-colonial South Africa.

Indeed it is difficult to find a favourable assessment of SADCC except, perhaps, the view which some of us share that the organization has attained a degree of success on the political level. As already pointed out above, this includes both the success with which it has mobilized the US and its allies into the deepening isolation of apartheid South Africa and the close relationship that is now developing between SADCC and the liberation movements of South Africa and Namibia. Admittedly it is difficult to isolate both these factors from the overall impact of the struggle in Southern Africa in general and in South Africa in particular. As such, SADCC might be seen as merely enhancing a pattern of political developments of which it is itself an outcome.

But the SADCC meeting in Harare in January 1986 was in some respects a good illustration of the growing diplomatic leverage of the frontline and SADCC states in their dealings with the US (and its allies) with regard to Africa's central objective of the decolonization of Namibia and South Africa. The meeting ended with the SADCC Chairman Mmusi criticizing the US for giving aid to UNITA in Angola. In general, however, observers noted that the meeting was a significant political and diplomatic victory for the frontline and SADCC states. It certainly enhanced the isolation of South Africa and possibly sounded the final death-knell for the latter's idea of a Confederation of Southern African States (CONSAS). But the meeting also embarrassed US policy in Southern Africa, marking thereby, perhaps, the gradual shift in this policy towards increasing pressure on South Africa. A recent (confidential) report on this meeting is an appropriate summary to this feature of US–SADCC relations:

> Though SADCC was fully aware that it risked a serious breach with the US, it decided that a clear message had to be sent to Washington. SADCC Executive

Secretary Simba Makoni noted that 'America cannot be friends with Savimbi and friends with Angola and SADCC at the same time', a view that was greatly strengthened by the unexpectedly political tone of speeches by donor country representatives. Even before arriving in Harare, the head of the Canadian delegation . . . condemned American support for UNITA and announced an increase in Canadian aid for Angola . . . A record 37 countries attended the Congress, and over half were represented by ministers or Secretaries of State. Eight socialist countries attended – more than before, including China and the Soviet Union. And 25 international agencies were there.

According to this same report, even the Lesotho coup 'actually seemed to strengthen SADCC's resolve' when the Lesotho Minister 'stressed that Lesotho remained committed to SADCC, and that it will continue to pursue an independent foreign policy'.

Furthermore, most donor nations supported the demand for sanctions against South Africa; and the EEC signed an agreement with SADCC recognizing the latter's primacy in regional development.

The liberation movements (ANC, PAC and SWAPO) were also represented for the first time since 1980. In a speech read on their behalf by SWAPO President Nujoma, the liberation movements expressed solidarity with SADCC:

It has become imperative that we translate our common recognition that SADCC and the national liberation struggle are two sectors of a single front into action. Only by harmonising our actions can both SADCC and the Liberation Movement realize our common cherished goals.

The speech also criticized 'the American, British and West German imperialist regimes' for 'condoning racist oppression in Southern Africa as well as providing assistance to armed bandit gangs trying to destabilize the legitimate governments of the front-line states, notably the People's Republic of Angola.'

In the next section an attempt is made to show the limitations of this strategy on the part of the frontline and SADCC states, in the context of the US policy in Southern Africa. For, the basic economic, political and military vulnerability of Africa in general and, in this regard, the frontline and SADCC states in particular, has generally meant that, individually and jointly, these states have had to operate within the ambit of the US policy (and imperialist hegemony) in Southern Africa.

However, other critics of SADCC have concluded that SADCC opposition to South Africa is nothing but rhetoric. In his chapter cited above, Thandika Mkandawire writes:

The high expectation and euphoria following Zimbabwe's independence gave further impetus to the political thrust of SADCC cooperation so that even Malawi could join in the condemnation of apartheid at the Blantyre SADCC conference in 1981. Yet surprisingly in a rather short span of time SADCC seems to have lost most of the political basis for its arguments. Under the guise of 'pragmatism' there is a growing tendency to 'keep politics out' of SADCC affairs, and to increasingly 'technocratize' dealings among SADCC states. One need not be a believer in some grand conspiracy theory to note that aid donors have contributed significantly to the depoliticization of SADCC affairs. Yet if experience elsewhere is anything to go by, this might spell the doom or at least the emasculation of SADCC. (Shaw and Tandon op. cit., p. 99.)

Perhaps, the politicization exhibited in the recent SADCC meeting referred to above might partly dispel this criticism. Similarly, also the fact that SADCC has since 1984 been under a new Executive Secretary, a former Minister of Government and a man who can hardly be described as apolitical. In both words and deeds, Simba Makoni has tried, within the immense constraints that face the organization, to push SADCC towards a pronounced anti-South African position that has tended to overlap with that of the frontline states. Unfortunately, the same cannot be said of all the SADCC member states.

It has been pointed out that, in contrast to the PTA which, for example, at its last summit meeting in December 1985, drew only four out of a possible fifteen heads of state, SADCC summits are almost always fully attended by the nine heads of state. Yet none of these nine states have so far tried to highlight the political significance of the SADCC beyond the officialdom of these summits and similar technical and donor meetings. Not surprisingly, therefore, SADCC so far remains quite divorced from the very masses that could provide the political basis and framework for both economic disengagement from South Africa and assistance to the liberation of Namibia and South Africa.

It is also on the basis of the political criteria that Tandon has drawn a contrast between SADCC and the PTA. Thus despite obvious constraints, 'the PTA is more openly nationalist, and therefore anti-imperialist, in its aspiration than the SADCC' (Ibid., p. 121). SADCC's strategy is based on the hope that with the help of Western capital, technical projects and foreign experts and consultancies, the region will be able to develop its industries and infrastructures and thereby decrease dependence on South Africa.

As Mkandawire has also noted, most of the SADCC projects are not only foreign-aid funded and technical in nature, but they are also purely national in character, therefore lacking both a regional framework and tending to 'divert the region from embarking on the more politically-loaded developmental and distributional issues'. (Ibid., pp. 108–9.) Because SADCC's definition of the enemy is 'geographically confined and conceptually limited', writes Tandon, 'it harbours the illusion that it can delink itself from South Africa with the assistance of Western capital aid' (Ibid., p. 131). Therefore it is more vulnerable to such agreements as Nkomati.

By contrast, states Tandon, the PTA has, at least on the basis of its elaborate document with twelve chapters and twelve annexes, a broader foundation and a detailed strategy for the ultimate objective of creating an Economic Community for Eastern and Southern African States. In particular, it seeks through its Treaty to promote intraregional trade and advocates 'nothing less than a complete structural transformation of the production, ownership and management control of the economies of the PTA countries'. (Ibid., p. 120.) It seeks to achieve this through three major instruments.

The first is its definition of 'Rules of Origin' with respect to goods if they are to be eligible for preferential treatment. The PTA insists on the economic criteria relating to such elements as value-added and import content of the commodities. But, according to Tandon, it also adds a 'political content' to these rules of origin by stipulating (under Rule 2, Annex III) that these goods will be accepted as originating in a Member state if

> they have been produced in the Member States by enterprises which are subject to management by a majority of nationals and to at least 51 per cent equity holding by nationals of the Member States or a Government or Governments of the Member States or institutions, agencies, enterprises or corporations of such Government or Governments. (Ibid.)

Second, there is the system of preferential tariffs for goods that enter into trade within the PTA area. The intention is that this system should within a period of ten years gradually lead to the establishment of a common union among the member states. Third, there is the system of multilateral payments, whereby member countries will in their trade with one another use their local currencies to settle accounts. Accordingly, the PTA has established a clearing house which is located in the Reserve Bank of Zimbabwe and designed to settle any outstanding payments in hard currencies every two months. (Ibid., p. 121.)

Perhaps one of the greatest sources of weakness of the SADCC lies in its loose structure. This is related to involvement of aid donors in the organization. Of course, it is no accident that the SADCC's structure is so loosely based, highlighting as it does the principle of the sharing of responsibilities or decentralization of functions. In the words of SADCC Executive Secretary Simba Makoni:

> This mode of operation guarantees us a direct involvement by our governments and their functionaries in the activities of the organization. It places primary responsibility and accountability for the organization's policies, programmes and projects on the member Government rather than on a distant, faceless and impersonal bureaucracy. Such a decentralized system demands of its members maximum political commitment to the ideals and objectives being pursued, as well as maximum confidence and trust in each other. These two attributes . . . are the hallmarks of SADCC: the explanation and vindication of how Marxist Mozambique and Capitalist Malawi or Republican Tanzania and Traditional monarchist Swaziland can work so well and effectively together.[2]

Without, however, wishing to be callous about these noble words by the SADCC Executive Secretary, most of the studies – including those in this anthology – on SADCC show that the organization has not been operating as effectively as its architects anticipated. Besides, the apparent lack of conflict between the nine members of the group of countries might be attributed precisely to the loose and therefore ineffective structure for coordination and intraregional development. (But as the next section will also help to explain, the nature of the historical, socio-economic and political development of the subregion has perhaps provided a greater basis for resolving potential conflict than would be the case with other regional organizations (ECOWAS).

Furthermore, the system of allocation of duties to member states has had less to do with the actual capacity of the respective countries to undertake such responsibilities than with the (politically expedient) need to ensure that each member state has at least been allocated something.

Given the legacy of uneven and unequal capitalist development between and within the economies of the member states of the subregion, there is potential for conflict. This is particularly so in the light of the tendency by donor countries to resort to a bilateral rather than multilateral approach to aid. In Chapter 1 Chitala cited the example of the US and how it favours a 'selective country strategy' based on its relations with a particular government. Chitala might be correct in his conclusion, though apart from Angola and Mozambique, it would be difficult to establish such a pattern of preferences on the part of the US in Southern Africa.

It should not be forgotten that there is often a close relationship between 'good infrastructure' and the high rate of investment. Also, one particular sector can attract more aid and foreign investment than another. Clearly, in this regard, the food and transport sectors of Zimbabwe and Mozambique respectively are doing much better than say the manpower and tourism sectors of Swaziland and Lesotho respectively. It is, of course, a great pity – and a source of additional criticism of the SADCC – that success or failure should be associated more with the level of foreign aid than with local and regional efforts.

But all this only helps to highlight the weakness of the SADCC structure and, as is evidenced by the small SADCC Secretariat, the absence of a strong supranational body that would in turn mobilize and coordinate local efforts at genuine regional cooperation. This has exposed SADCC members to the machinations of aid donors, who in many instances are able to exercise direct or indirect control of their economies. It is perhaps no exaggeration when Mkandawire states:

> There are probably more better-organized teams of experts and bureaucrats in Europe who are fully occupied with SADCC matters than we have in the region. This may explain why aid donors seem so pleased with the weakness of the SADCC Secretariat. In the absence of a strong supranational body, the foreign experts will hold sway in each speciality assigned to them with no corresponding regional expertise and institutional set up to 'interfere' in their work (Shaw and Tandon op. cit., p. 109).

More than that it would be no exaggeration to state that the Western countries in general have tended to view SADCC as their own institution. This is evidenced not only by what has been outlined in the foregoing with regard to the history and development of SADCC but also with respect to the extent and pattern of Western investment into SADCC and its various sectors. There is no need here to document the quantity and extent of such aid to SADCC: the various studies within this anthology have variously sought to establish this. But this might be illustrated with a reference to the $US276.5 million that was pledged at the Maputo SADCC Conference (SADCC 2) that was held in November 1980. All of it came from Western countries and their donor agencies but the largest came from the EEC ($US100 million), the US ($US50 million) and the bulk of the rest from the Scandinavian and Benelux countries.

The structure and general economic direction of SADCC is perhaps an adequate disincentive to the average member of the Socialist Bloc. But the dominance of such relations, 'hoping that moral suasion will result in winning concessions here and there, and in improving West Africa's relative position and advantage in international economic relations'. Thus ECOWAS has been concerned more with institution-building (within the framework of neo-colonialism) than with structural transformation (that would lead to autonomous development). (Ibid., pp. 46–7.)

In his account of the now defunct East African Community, Dan Nabudere has shown that the origins of this organization are to be found in British imperialist designs in East Africa at the turn of this century. Determined to exclude other imperialist competitors and thereby consolidate her economic interests in this region, British imperialism had established in 1907 a 'customs union' for Kenya and Uganda as 'one of the first steps . . . to protect its market in these two territories by imposing a tariff against the imports of other powers seeking markets'. (Ibid., p. 55.) Tanganyika was to join this British colonial structure in 1923, after the defeat of Germany in World War I. Tariffs and other mechanisms were subsequently introduced and together formed the basis for both the concentration of the productive powers of British capital and the establishment of white settler agriculture and semi-manufacturing. Included in this was the process of land-grabbing from the Africans, the consequent gradual proletarianization of the African peasantry, particularly in Kenya, and the development of a transportation and communication system, with preferential railway freight rates for settler farmers and therefore altogether designed to facilitate the exploitation of raw materials as required by British metropolitan industry.

With the emphasis on the railways as an important basis for development, there arose the East African Railways and Harbours which

> became the most important of the pillars of British integration of the region with its own finance capital. Upon this were added other institutions like the Currency Board, research institutes, the post office and telecommunications and these together were consolidated into a *system* supervised by the three governors jointly on directives of the Secretary for the Colonies of the British government through a *Governors' Conference*. (Ibid., p. 56.)

Subsequently, other institutions would be created, giving form and content to what became known as the East African High Commission.

Thus, Nabudere's main point is that 'the outlines of what came to be the East African Community' are to be found in these political, economic, and institutional arrangements by Britain, 'in the course of the competitive struggle to assert her interests in the region'. (Ibid., p. 55.) The difference, Nabudere would argue, between the colonial-inspired East African High Commission and the post-colonial East African Community that was formed in 1967, was 'no more than' the sentiment of Pan-Africanism that characterized the latter. But despite the good intentions of the African leaders of the East African Community, 'there were strong, compelling forces at work in the region that negated their honourable intentions'. (Ibid., pp. 58–9.) These forces included US-led multilateral imperialism.

In this new phase, the transnational corporation was becoming a new force of integration of production, distribution and finance on a world scale. The more dynamic of these finance capitals saw no particular value in regional arrangements. Indeed they saw these as old colonial structures advantageous to the former colonial powers only. (Ibid., p. 60.)

If this is true, then the post-colonial period – and the East African Community itself – in fact facilitated the transnationalization of the East African region, beyond the confines of British imperialism and its imperially protected markets. Indeed from the 1960s onwards, Africa began to experience more directly the influence of the US in the latter's objective of 'protecting' the former colonies from 'Communist' influence. As will also be outlined below, this US policy is many-faceted. But its main instruments have been 'aid', military assistance to client countries, and the development of such multilateral institutions as the International Monetary Fund (IMF) and the World Bank. These would help ensure the further transnationalization and integration of the economies of the Third World into the world capitalist system. The EEC and its monopolies and conventions also assists in this process, enhancing the vertical integration of these economies to the detriment of horizontal and intra-Third World production and trade.

In short, the conclusion of such analysts as Nabudere is simply that regional economic cooperation in Africa (and Third World countries generally) is impossible in the era of imperialism and international finance capital. For Nabudere, the study of the EAC is illustrative of this.

> What the study was saying was that regional integrated production and marketing was impossible in the face of the foreign ownership, management, and productive control over industry, commerce and agriculture. In short, the region was integrated externally so intra regional cohesion was impossible. (Ibid., p. 68)

But neo-colonialism also inheres an ideological framework within which the leaders of these African countries are incapable of understanding the true nature of the forces of imperialism and international finance capital. The neo-colonial states are thus unable to realize their complicity in the entire set-up. They are unable to design and develop regional organizations that can truly challenge the existing relations and structures of dependence and exploitation. They have neither the ideological, political nor economic capacity to establish the basis for sound economic cooperation.

In fact, the conclusion of such analysts as Nabudere is that even the SADCC and PTA cannot successfully resist the vertical integration pressures of transnational corporations and international finance capital. Besides, there is also the harassment of the World Bank and the IMF, who together ensure that developing countries adhere to new 'structural adjustment programmes' and 'conditionalities'.

Yet it would be both unrealistic and even ahistorical to conclude that Africa's efforts at regional economic cooperation are doomed to fail in the circumstances that she finds herself in at this historical conjuncture. There is the need not only to identify the positive way out of this apparent failure, but also to recognize that these efforts have developed a degree of political unity and coordination among African States, at both regional and continental levels. To many, such unity might appear

The success of the liberation struggles in Angola, Mozambique and Zimbabwe exposed the illusion of South African invincibility. All the same, it did not fundamentally change US policy in the subregion. Crocker's 'constructive engagement' strategy of the early 1980s remained reinforced in the belief that South Africa was an exception in that his policy

> was a product of his assessment that the Botha regime's secure domestic and regional position, deriving from the nation's relative economic and military self-sufficiency, limits the effectiveness of such pressures as economic sanctions or arms embargoes (Kitchen and Clough, p. 3).

But this was related to another assumption on the part of US policy-makers and one no doubt an outcome of the realization that Blacks could win political power through violence. I refer here to Crocker's belief that, on the basis of Prime Minister P. W. Botha's statement in 1979 that Whites must 'adapt or die', South Africa was really prepared to dismantle apartheid, accept Namibian independence, and develop good relations with South Africa's neighbours. In turn, Crocker hoped, Namibian independence thus attained 'would boost US credibility throughout Africa', deal a major diplomatic blow to the Soviet Union, and 'give the Botha government confidence to move faster with its internal reform programme, which would in turn confirm the merits of constructive engagement'. (Ibid., p. 5.)

It is easy to conclude now that Crocker's policy (and its expectations) have been a failure in the light of the recent developments in South Africa itself. The rising waves of mass unrest in South Africa no longer shore up the apparently invincible state machinery that was one of the bases of Crocker's policy assumptions five years ago. More than that, South Africa finds itself under increasing pressure from the international community, its economy is threatened and has already been subjected to some forms of economic sanctions and embargoes. South Africa is on fire and there is no prospect of violence subsiding; the liberation struggle is intensifying and apartheid is under siege. Besides, Namibia is not yet independent, the frontline states are not entirely without an initiative in the subregion and the South African military frontier is seriously stretched. The end is near.

Of great significance with regard to the US policy itself is the fact that the Reagan regime finds itself increasingly compelled to increase pressure against the apartheid regime. Hence Reagan's Executive Order of 9 September 1985; it

> bans bank loans to the South African Government, terminates the sale of Kruger rands, prohibits the export of computers or computer technology to that government's military, police, or apartheid-enforcing agencies, bars nuclear technology exports, and requires sizeable US subsidiaries to comply with a set of Fair Labour Principles that are similar to but not identical with the Sullivan Code.[8]

These were limited measures designed to try and stem the increasing pressure within Congress for sanctions and disinvestment in South Africa. Yet this is quite a far cry from Crocker's stance five years ago, not to mention the conventional US policy of the 1970s. It also reflected US Secretary of State George Shultz's earlier statement of 16 April 1985, acknowledging that the Blacks in South Africa were 'no longer willing to live under a system that denies them fair political participation; both demography and economics are on the side of those challenging the old order'.

More recently, Crocker himself virtually acknowledged the inevitability of Black majority rule in South Africa. Speaking to the members of the Foreign Affairs Committee in Congress on 12 March 1986, the Assistant Secretary of State stated the following with reference to South Africa: 'We want full political rights for everybody. We want a universal franchise. We want a democratic system' (USIS, Harare, 12 March 1986). He predicted that 1986 would be a decisive year in South Africa's history and said that South Africa 'cannot afford another year like the last one'. He warned that South Africa would be under increasing international pressure and scrutiny in 1986 by such bodies as the Commonwealth's Eminent Persons' Group, the European Economic Community, Western banks, and the US Secretary of State's South Africa Advisory Committee. He emphasized 'four issues': 'an end to violence, repression, and killing; getting dialogue and negotiations started; dismantling the existing apartheid legal structure; building a new system'. (Ibid.) He added that the State Department was keeping in constant touch with all groups in South Africa, 'across the political spectrum' and including 'a pattern of communication' with the African National Congress (ANC). He concluded with a call for the release of 'key individuals' (by implication Nelson Mandela) and for an end to bannings and detentions in favour of negotiations. (Ibid.)

As I stated earlier, there is the temptation to regard all these developments as a positive change towards Black majority rule, as the outcome of the struggles of the African peoples in Southern Africa. But let us conclude with some warnings against unguarded and unqualified optimism. First, US policy has not been such a failure after all. Southern Africa has suffered some very evident and far-reaching reverses in the course of the period that we have just described as giving birth to a new US policy in the subregion. In his speech on 16 April 1985, the US Secretary of State boasted about his country's ability to 'affect events' in the subregion.

Thus the US had had a positive influence on South Africa and brought about the Nkomati Accord of March 1984; had 'helped Angola and South Africa agree' on a plan for the withdrawal of South African forces from Angola and control of SWAPO and Cuban troops in Southern Angola; had 'helped bring about' understandings between Lesotho and Botswana on the one hand and South Africa on the other, thereby averting conflict; and

> helped move Mozambique away from heavy dependence on the Soviet camp and closer to true non-alignment. We demonstrated to Mozambique that its best interests are served by closer cooperation with the West, and by rejection of confrontation with South Africa. The trend of our relations with Mozambique is positive and needs further encouragement. (Ibid.)

Second, both Shultz's policy statement and this apparent shift in US policy would tend to reinforce the view that Southern Africa is part of the US sphere of influence. Related to this is the implication that the US will have to move quickly to 'reconcile' all antagonistic forces in the subregion, in the interests of US policy and in order to foreclose opportunities for the growth of Soviet influence. All the indications are donors as the EEC, the World Bank and the US itself might be construed as an additional assurance that the Soviet Union and the socialist countries will not gain a foothold in SADCC. If this is so, then it would be difficult not to view such a strategy – and with it, SADCC – as a reflection of US (and its allies') policy in Southern Africa. This is an issue to which I return in the next section. But suffice it to state at this stage that even some Africans have complained that SADCC is 'theirs not ours'. This is usually a reference also to the extent to which SADCC has, perhaps, become more an obsession among external forces than among Africans themselves.

However, there is no doubt that the SADCC Secretariat has since woken up to these and other criticisms about both SADCC's alignment to the West and the organization's lack of a sound framework for real regional economic cooperation and self-reliance. There are increasing efforts to involve regional experts and officials in the context of attempts to develop a series of regional institutional arrangements around and within given sectors. And even though SADCC will largely retain a structure based on decentralization of responsibilities, there is developing slowly a larger, stronger and more efficient Secretariat. The intention is to enhance the coordinative framework at the Secretariat level while not compromising the basic principles and structures upon which the organization has been founded. The Secretariat has also made efforts at interesting socialist countries in the work of SADCC.

More recently, SADCC has begun looking at the possibility of setting up a trade and finance network. To this end, SADCC has commissioned a *SADCC Intra-Regional Trade Study* by the Michelsen Institute in Norway. With the publication of the first SADCC *Macro Economic Survey 1986,*[3] the organization is clearly determined to develop an institutional framework similar to that of the PTA. Hopefully, SADCC and PTA will find ways of cooperating and merging into one effective organization that combines the positive aspects of both. I believe there have already been joint discussions between the officials of the two organizations. But, as is illustrated by both the Michelsen Institute Study and in the following section of this chapter, the problems of intraregional trade and development remain formidable, given the economic dominance of South Africa and also imperialist policy in the subregion.

In the political field, SADCC has sought to overlap with the frontline states. As had already been pointed out, SADCC has become increasingly overtly anti-South Africa in its official stance. But it has also recently established a Contingency Planning Committee to direct and coordinate a detailed examination of the effects of the deteriorating situation in South Africa, especially the impact of sanctions on the economies of member states, and to identify practical measures to counter them.

The major constraint in both this regard and in relation to the overall objectives of the organization remains solidly within the economic field. As the following section will illustrate, over the last five years there has been little disengagement from South Africa and hardly any evidence of increased economic cooperation among the member states. Tables in chapter 7 illustrate this quite adequately. Dependence on foreign aid has been almost total in its operations: SADCC has tended to reinforce rather than challenge the historical relations of dependence, exploitation and domination.

The next section begins with a brief account of the historical origins and development of Southern Africa as a subsystem of imperialism and international finance capital. This highlights in particular the central role of the South African economy in the subregion. But this is followed by a consideration of the possibility that political developments – particularly the liberation of South Africa itself – might lead to a new SADCC as a basis of genuine regional economic cooperation in Southern Africa.

SADCC and South Africa

The factors militating against SADCC are particularly formidable in that they constitute an historical, political and socio-economic reality from which by its very objectives SADCC wishes to disengage.

The main problem is rooted in the historical and socio-economic factors that have shaped Southern Africa and within which South Africa itself is central. Thus on the basis of mainly political considerations, SADCC has been designed to disengage economically from a country without whose economy, trade, and transport and communications infrastructure most of the SADCC member states are unlikely to survive, individually or even jointly.

The problem is exacerbated in that those external forces that support SADCC are also those which buttress the South African economy (and therefore also its military and political structures). Thus the existence of apartheid South Africa is viewed as the facilitating factor for SADCC and yet it also helps to blur the reality of imperialism and international finance capital as the main enemy of regional economic cooperation and autonomous development in Southern Africa. It is possible that the architects of SADCC envisaged a very long period before the liberation of South Africa. But the picture changes quite dramatically if it occurs within the next decade. This is particularly so if SADCC is viewed not as a permanently anti-South African union but one which ultimately sees its fortunes as reaching full fruition in the liberation of South Africa.

It raises both questions and suspicions about the immediate and long-term objectives of those forces that view SADCC as simply an extension of the economies of North America and Western Europe, regardless of the fact that many of these might be genuinely opposed to apartheid. But this might also render irrelevant and costly a strategy which in its considerations, plans and projects does not anticipate a liberated South Africa. Indeed SADCC has identified as crucial such sectors as transport and communications if only because South Africa is particularly dominant in these throughout the Southern African region. An alternative transport and communications network to be developed under SADCC might tomorrow be complementary to those of South Africa and therefore not undermine a liberated South Africa (as part of a united Southern Africa). But no doubt it would be more cost-effective and also therefore in the interests of long-term regional economic cooperation in the subregion if SADCC could currently include in its perspectives, plans and projects the probability that in the not too distant future South Africa will not only be part of it but the heart of it.

The other important point about what I have just stated is that the US and its allies accept the centrality of South Africa even while they support SADCC. The extent to which there appears to be no contradiction between their support for SADCC on the one hand and on the other the continued economic linkage with South Africa is in itself quite revealing. It indicates quite strongly that the founding objectives of SADCC cannot in the present conjuncture be met independent of a liberated South Africa.

But SADCC's own strategy, and the current political, ideological and economic trends that dominate it, tend to reinforce this. In the final analysis it helps to shore up the apparent economic indispensability of the South African hinterland. It reinforces the view that the future of SADCC itself is dependent on what happens in South Africa, and not, as some SADCC protagonists would like to believe, that SADCC will significantly affect the future of that country.

Besides, the economies of SADCC countries are quite underdeveloped and dependent, showing very little complementarity between them. The tables in chapter 7 illustrate this and underscore the fact that SADCC countries rely mainly on the export of raw agricultural and mineral products for which there is little demand in the region, while on the other hand they mostly import mineral fuels, capital goods and other manufactured products. There is little industrial development. The transport and communication system is still largely under-developed and therefore adversely affects intraregional trade and development. To all this should be added the problems resulting from the world economic recession, drought and the war situation and destabilization by South Africa.

Indeed the main and immediate problems that afflict and undermine SADCC are those that relate to the existence of South Africa. As already pointed out, it is difficult to understand the history and development of Southern Africa except in terms of the central position of South Africa. The origins of this subregional configuration are to be found in the European expansion, from the 15th Century onwards, in the context of which this subregion was recognized as constituting even then a vital strategic centre on the route to India and the rest of the Asian and the Far Eastern subcontinents. It was historically inevitable, perhaps, that South Africa should have featured prominently in this and other respects throughout the three successive stages of capitalist imperialism: mercantile imperialism, free trade imperialism, and modern monopoly imperialism. All these cover the modern history of Southern Africa, from 1652, when the first Europeans arrived at the Cape, to the present day.

But it is also usual to associate Southern Africa with those immense material and human resources that have also been the basis of its misfortunes in the form of the history and nature of imperialism and colonization in the subregion. Numerous studies have highlighted the extent of US and Western investment in subsequent decades: that between 1943 and 1973 US direct investments in South Africa grew from $US50 million to $US2 billion, an increase of 4,000 per cent; had reached $US7,200 million by 1980; that $US3,000 million are sent out of South Africa every year as profits and dividends for overseas international monopolies; that Britain and America account for about 70 per cent of the total foreign investment in South Africa; and that there are now 350 US companies involved in South Africa; and so on and so forth.[4]

There is also the relationship between such Western investment and the industrial and military build-up in South Africa. More recently, the emphasis has been placed upon the relationship between US and Western investment on the one hand, and South Africa's growing military technology and nuclear capability on the other. Therefore, it is also important to acknowledge the relationship between the rise of imperialism in the late 19th Century and the development in the Southern African subregion – particularly in Namibia, South Africa and Zimbabwe – of the historical phenomenon of white settler colonialism. The latter might be described as a particular expression of imperialism or colonialism *par excellence*. Elsewhere, I have sought to describe this spectre of imperialist hegemony resulting from this historical relationship between imperialism and Southern Africa; and how it affects both the development of the class structure in the colonial situation, the character of the struggle for national independence and the tendency towards neo-colonialism under the leadership of an African petty bourgeoisie.[5]

For the purposes of this study, however, it is important to mention two immediately relevant and interrelated aspects of relations between South Africa and SADCC. Both aspects are important also because they help to highlight what has already been described with regard to the enormity of the task that faces SADCC in its attempt to disengage from South Africa. But they also explain why in the highly unlikely event that the international community will impose sanctions on South Africa, most of the SADCC countries might find it not only virtually impossible to participate effectively but might themselves be very adversely affected by such measures. The analysis, however, also shows why the US and its allies might never impose such sanctions anywhere, except if such an action was designed to meet an objective consistent with its own strategic and economic interests in the subregion.

Indeed SADCC's Contingency Planning Committee referred to earlier was born out of the acceptance that the economies of most SADCC member states are substantially linked to that of South Africa, and that any deterioration of the South African economy will have adverse effects on its neighbours. The SADCC might consider such adverse effects as a worthwhile price to be paid for South African liberation and peace and security in the region. But the US and most of its allies have tended to underplay the latter point, highlighting the possibly worst scenario as a means of both justifying their own opposition to sanctions and deterring the SADCC countries from even considering such a course of action. There is considerable evidence of how the US and the British have been involved in overt and covert action in this regard. The point, however, is not so much about whether sanctions (if applied) will be effective. It is now a question of whether the SADCC countries will be able to initiate such measures when the US and Britain are against them.

The first aspect of SADCC–South Africa relations concerns the economic dominance of South Africa in the subregion, originating and developing as it does in the context of the history and development of Southern Africa as a subsystem of imperialism and international finance capital. Various studies – including some of those included in the present work – have highlighted the economic tentacles that bind most SADCC countries to South Africa.

These are most pronounced in the very sectors which SADCC has identified as the key areas of focus in its strategy of trying to disengage from South Africa. Thus the South African transport and communications system remains central to most SADCC countries in their import–export trade with those outside the African continent, in particular, with six SADCC countries landlocked and therefore almost entirely dependent on South Africa's route to the sea. Most SADCC countries are also dependent upon South Africa for the import of manufactured goods, particularly food, industrial machinery and equipment. South Africa has considerable investment in most SADCC countries, covering the various sectors of mining, manufacturing, railways and hydroelectric construction. In addition, as Chitala has reminded us in chapter 1, these dependence relationships in the field of South African investment in SADCC countries should not be confined to the formal volume in such terms as equity ownership shares. For the various informal mechanisms of economic control by way of management, sales and technical contracts and transfer pricing though less obvious, are actually more important.

There is also the question of migrant labour from the neighbouring SADCC countries to South Africa. According to Chitala's sources, there are about 600,000 such migrant labourers in South Africa. The important point to emphasize, however, is that such countries as Botswana and Lesotho are heavily dependent (economically) upon this 'export' of labour. These same countries depend heavily on their membership of the South African Customs Union. Thus, their economies are virtually extensions of South Africa's. In this category must also be included Namibia.

But even Zimbabwe is heavily dependent on South Africa. Indeed Chitala states that South Africa's investment in Zimbabwe is greater than in any other Southern African economy. Furthermore, five of Zimbabwe's top ten industries are either controlled by or associated with South African companies. Thus, although Zimbabwe has the strongest economy in the SADCC and has become the virtual centre and heart of the organization, it is nonetheless not only dependent on South Africa but also vulnerable to South Africa's destabilization programme.

The subject of South Africa's destabilization programme is so central to the future of SADCC that the organization has itself made the best available study of its impact in the region. According to an excerpt of the (confidential) document on the subject:

> South African aggression and destabilization has cost its neighbours in excess of $US10 billion in the five years since the founding of SADCC. This is more than all the foreign aid received by the SADCC States during this five year period; or: one third of all SADCC exports in the past five years.[6]

This South African aggression included such items as direct war damage, boycotts and embargoes, and smuggling; and the consequences (to SADCC states) of extra defence expenditure, higher transport and energy costs, lost exports and decline in tourism, refugees and reduced production and lost economic growth. It is also a clear reflection of the extent of the economic and military dominance of the South African state within the subregion.

US Policy in the Light of Revolutionary Pressures in South Africa

The second aspect with regard to this issue of South African dominance is the spectre of US policy in Southern Africa in general and towards South Africa in particular. This chapter has already indicated broadly the relationship between US imperialist policy and the rise of the South African social formation. Elsewhere,[7] I have outlined in some detail the main elements of this policy, beginning with the Nixon–Kissinger strategy of the 1970s, showing how this was succeeded in the 1980s by Chester Crocker's 'constructive engagement' policy framework.

US policy has since 1969 remained quite consistent with regard to two aspects. First, the need to maintain the Southern African subregion under the zone of influence of the US and its allies, and thereby also to keep the Soviet Union and its allies out of the area. It is a policy inspired by obvious strategic and economic considerations. Second, the view that South Africa is the central and predominant force in the subregion and that any 'solution' to the Southern African question will have to revolve around that 'fact'. The extent to which that 'fact' itself has in turn been buttressed and projected by this US policy stance is obvious.

For a long time US policy in Southern Africa was based firmly on the belief that Blacks could not gain political rights through violence and that only through a combination of persuading the Whites and influencing the Black states through economic aid could constructive and non-violent change be attained in Southern Africa.

This US position on South Africa and the latter's economic and military strength in the subregion have together helped to feed the view that South Africa is a 'sub-imperial' power. Thus a 'sub-imperial' power can be a regional centre for the maintenance of the economic, political and strategic interests of the imperialist centre. Yet the concept of sub-imperialism might also connote either a relative degree of independence on the part of the sub-imperial power; or that it enjoys the confidence of the imperialist centre in that its political, economic and military actions will in general coincide and reflect those of the imperialist power.

As the concluding pages of this chapter indicate, this is not entirely true with respect to South Africa. The South African state is devoid of a sound social base; and Black majority rule is inevitable. The latter prospect might not entirely undermine US policy objectives in the subregion. But there is, however, the danger for the US that the political ineptitude of the apartheid regime might at least incur high costs for maintaining and sustaining these objectives. It is within that context that one should not rule out the possibility of US intervention – against either the apartheid regime or a succeeding Black-ruled state – in the interests of US economic and strategic objectives. As long as this possibility exists, it is difficult to accept that South Africa is a sub-imperialist power. It might be that South Africa appeared to be so a decade ago; but this has changed immensely ever since.

The success of the liberation struggles in Angola, Mozambique and Zimbabwe exposed the illusion of South African invincibility. All the same, it did not fundamentally change US policy in the subregion. Crocker's 'constructive engagement' strategy of the early 1980s remained reinforced in the belief that South Africa was an exception in that his policy

> was a product of his assessment that the Botha regime's secure domestic and regional position, deriving from the nation's relative economic and military self-sufficiency, limits the effectiveness of such pressures as economic sanctions or arms embargoes (Kitchen and Clough, p. 3).

But this was related to another assumption on the part of US policy-makers and one no doubt an outcome of the realization that Blacks could win political power through violence. I refer here to Crocker's belief that, on the basis of Prime Minister P. W. Botha's statement in 1979 that Whites must 'adapt or die', South Africa was really prepared to dismantle apartheid, accept Namibian independence, and develop good relations with South Africa's neighbours. In turn, Crocker hoped, Namibian independence thus attained 'would boost US credibility throughout Africa', deal a major diplomatic blow to the Soviet Union, and 'give the Botha government confidence to move faster with its internal reform programme, which would in turn confirm the merits of constructive engagement'. (Ibid., p. 5.)

It is easy to conclude now that Crocker's policy (and its expectations) have been a failure in the light of the recent developments in South Africa itself. The rising waves of mass unrest in South Africa no longer shore up the apparently invincible state machinery that was one of the bases of Crocker's policy assumptions five years ago. More than that, South Africa finds itself under increasing pressure from the international community, its economy is threatened and has already been subjected to some forms of economic sanctions and embargoes. South Africa is on fire and there is no prospect of violence subsiding; the liberation struggle is intensifying and apartheid is under siege. Besides, Namibia is not yet independent, the frontline states are not entirely without an initiative in the subregion and the South African military frontier is seriously stretched. The end is near.

Of great significance with regard to the US policy itself is the fact that the Reagan regime finds itself increasingly compelled to increase pressure against the apartheid regime. Hence Reagan's Executive Order of 9 September 1985; it

> bans bank loans to the South African Government, terminates the sale of Kruger rands, prohibits the export of computers or computer technology to that government's military, police, or apartheid-enforcing agencies, bars nuclear technology exports, and requires sizeable US subsidiaries to comply with a set of Fair Labour Principles that are similar to but not identical with the Sullivan Code.[8]

These were limited measures designed to try and stem the increasing pressure within Congress for sanctions and disinvestment in South Africa. Yet this is quite a far cry from Crocker's stance five years ago, not to mention the conventional US policy of the 1970s. It also reflected US Secretary of State George Shultz's earlier statement of 16 April 1985, acknowledging that the Blacks in South Africa were 'no longer willing to live under a system that denies them fair political participation; both demography and economics are on the side of those challenging the old order'.

More recently, Crocker himself virtually acknowledged the inevitability of Black majority rule in South Africa. Speaking to the members of the Foreign Affairs Committee in Congress on 12 March 1986, the Assistant Secretary of State stated the following with reference to South Africa: 'We want full political rights for everybody. We want a universal franchise. We want a democratic system' (USIS, Harare, 12 March 1986). He predicted that 1986 would be a decisive year in South Africa's history and said that South Africa 'cannot afford another year like the last one'. He warned that South Africa would be under increasing international pressure and scrutiny in 1986 by such bodies as the Commonwealth's Eminent Persons' Group, the European Economic Community, Western banks, and the US Secretary of State's South Africa Advisory Committee. He emphasized 'four issues': 'an end to violence, repression, and killing; getting dialogue and negotiations started; dismantling the existing apartheid legal structure; building a new system'. (Ibid.) He added that the State Department was keeping in constant touch with all groups in South Africa, 'across the political spectrum' and including 'a pattern of communication' with the African National Congress (ANC). He concluded with a call for the release of 'key individuals' (by implication Nelson Mandela) and for an end to bannings and detentions in favour of negotiations. (Ibid.)

As I stated earlier, there is the temptation to regard all these developments as a positive change towards Black majority rule, as the outcome of the struggles of the African peoples in Southern Africa. But let us conclude with some warnings against unguarded and unqualified optimism. First, US policy has not been such a failure after all. Southern Africa has suffered some very evident and far-reaching reverses in the course of the period that we have just described as giving birth to a new US policy in the subregion. In his speech on 16 April 1985, the US Secretary of State boasted about his country's ability to 'affect events' in the subregion.

Thus the US had had a positive influence on South Africa and brought about the Nkomati Accord of March 1984; had 'helped Angola and South Africa agree' on a plan for the withdrawal of South African forces from Angola and control of SWAPO and Cuban troops in Southern Angola; had 'helped bring about' understandings between Lesotho and Botswana on the one hand and South Africa on the other, thereby averting conflict; and

> helped move Mozambique away from heavy dependence on the Soviet camp and closer to true non-alignment. We demonstrated to Mozambique that its best interests are served by closer cooperation with the West, and by rejection of confrontation with South Africa. The trend of our relations with Mozambique is positive and needs further encouragement. (Ibid.)

Second, both Shultz's policy statement and this apparent shift in US policy would tend to reinforce the view that Southern Africa is part of the US sphere of influence. Related to this is the implication that the US will have to move quickly to 'reconcile' all antagonistic forces in the subregion, in the interests of US policy and in order to foreclose opportunities for the growth of Soviet influence. All the indications are that the Soviet Union is not prepared to challenge the US in this regard. Besides, as has already been outlined earlier in this paper, the frontline and SADCC states themselves tend to reinforce the US position in the subregion while simultaneously 'keeping out' the Socialist Bloc. They will, of course, complain about aspects of US policy, particularly with regard to South Africa and in as far as it appears not in favour of Black majority rule in that country. But as a US diplomat explained to me, 'No one is saying to us get out of the region . . . No one has told us to pack our bags and go . . . They want the US to be constructively engaged in Southern Africa.'

Conclusion

Lastly, it is in the context of this chapter that we must reject the view expressed by some analysts with regard to US policy that Africa in general and Southern Africa in particular 'remains less central (despite mineral wealth) than the Middle East, South Asia, and the Central America Caribbean region'.[9] The US policy in Southern Africa is also a reflection of the US objectives in Africa. Addressing a State Department Foreign Policy Conference, in Washington, on 2 June 1981, Chester Crocker emphasized that Africa was a region of growing importance to US global objectives – 'economic, political, strategic, human and so forth'. The recent US attack on Libya (15 April 1986) might not be a good illustration of this policy, though it does highlight the madness of the 'Reagan Doctrine' as a philosophy and instrument for US intervention in various parts of the world. The US support for UNITA in Angola is similar to its support for the 'Contras' in Nicaragua. But it emphasizes the fact that the US will operate, however far from home, in pursuit of its global aims. In this respect, no place in the world is either too far or 'less central'. The world has become much smaller and almost entirely disposable at the hands of mad and modern imperialists.

Equally dismissed in this chapter is the related view that because Southern Africa 'is not a primary concern' to US policy, 'the movements of the region remain and will remain, relatively speaking, more on their own'. (Ibid.) If this statement implies a degree of indifference to Southern Africa on the part of the US then we have already illustrated that this is a misconception of the historical and political process in the subregion. Furthermore, the foregoing analysis shows that the US will at all costs seek to play a central role in the unfolding situation in South Africa. Unless the very drastic happens in the form of even more coordinated mass unrest and violence, we are on the verge of a 'settlement' similar (though, perhaps, not identical) to that which attended Zimbabwe in 1979–80.

That may not be a totally bad situation, given that such an outcome might be beyond the control of those waging the struggle. Much will depend on the relation of forces on Day One of South African Liberation: what alliances the African petty bourgeoisie is likely to forge in the pursuit of state power; and what the role of the US and its allies is likely to be in such a situation, and depending on how the US perceives its long-term interests, both regionally and globally.

As already indicated in the introduction to this chapter, the answers to these questions will also determine the future of such regional organizations as the

SADCC. Yet the analysis herein also emphasized that the struggle for genuine regional economic cooperation and autonomous development is both real, many-faceted and possibly very long. The challenge to imperialism and international finance capital requires more than the much-desired collaboration on the part of the oppressed and exploited peoples of a given region. There is the urgent need to draw up a political agenda that unites such regional organizations as the SADCC within a wider Third Worldist framework. For that will in the long run effectively challenge the existing relations and structures of exploitation and domination by the developed countries and international finance capital in the world.

Notes

1. See in particular the papers by Jinadu, Nabudere, Mkandawire, Tandon, and Mandaza in Timothy Shaw and Yash Tandon (eds) (1985).
2. Address by SADCC Executive Secretary to the African Association of Political Science (AAPS), Zimbabwe National Chapter, printed in *Monthly Forum*, Harare, July 1985.
3. Published by SADCC Secretariat, Gaborone, Botswana, September 1985.
4. Ibbo Mandaza, 'Conflict in Southern Africa' in Emmanuel Hansen (ed.) (1987) *Africa: Perspectives on Peace and Development*, Zed Books, London, pp. 101–19.
5. Ibbo Mandaza, 'The Post-White Settler Colonial State in Zimbabwe' in Ibbo Mandaza (ed.) (1986) *Zimbabwe: The Political Economy of Transition*, CODESRIA, Dakar.
6. SADCC, *An Illustrative Assessment of the Cost of Destabilization on the Member States of the Southern Africa Development Coordination Conference*, Confidential SADCC Paper, Gaborone, Botswana, 1986.
7. Ibbo Mandaza, 'Southern Africa: US Policy and the Struggle for National Independence', paper presented to AAPS Southern African Regional Workshop on *Whither South Africa*, Harare, 10–12 March 1986.
8. United States Information Services, Harare, Story AF 5030411, 11 April 1986.
9. See William Martin and Immanuel Wallerstein, 'Southern Africa in the World Economy 1870–2000: Strategic Problems in World Historical Perspective', paper presented to the *Colloquium on Security and Development in Southern Africa*, Paris, 24–25 February 1986.

Appendix: Tables

Table A.1

Basic Economic Indicators 1983

	Area km² 000	Population (million)	GDP per head ($US)	GDP ($US m)	Agriculture ($US m)	Industry ($US m)	Service ($US m)
Angola	1,246.7	7.2	576	672	739	994	333
Botswana	569.8	0.9	923	713	76	304	160
Lesotho	30.4	1.4	252	270	53	57	473
Malawi	118.5	6.5	208	1,234	505	256	1,875
Mozambique	771.1	11.0	407	4,204	1,654	616	135
Swaziland	17.4	0.5	1,064	432	156	141	1,231
Tanzania	945.1	19.1	221	3,825	2,107	488	1,303
Zambia	752.6	6.4	519	2,844	467	1,074	2,687
Zimbabwe	390.6	8.3	728	5,302	812	1,082	

Source: ECA, Survey of Economic and Social Conditions in Africa, 1983–84.

Table A.2
Structure of Industrial Production 1983 ($US m)

	Mining	*Manufacturing*	*Electricity and water*	*Construction*
Angola	549	102	18	71
Botswana	181	60	18	46
Lesotho	2	20	2	34
Malawi	—	160	22	74
Mozambique	18	330	70	258
Swaziland	14	105	7	15
Tanzania	12	282	45	149
Zambia	517	419	65	74
Zimbabwe	254	1,249	98	201

Source: ECA, Survey of Economic and Social Conditions in Africa 1983–84.

Table A.3

Mineral Raw Materials — Agricultural Sector

Sector	Subsector	Mineral Raw Materials	ANGOLA	BOTSWANA	LESOTHO	MALAWI	MOZAMBIQUE	SWAZILAND	TANZANIA	ZAMBIA	ZIMBABWE
AGRICULTURAL INDUSTRY	Fertilizer	Syenites								●	
		Carbonatites ⎤							•	●	
		Phosphate rock	●			•	•				•
		Veins-apatite ⎦									
		Phosphorite lake beds							•		
		Potash		•					•		
		Native sulphur	●								
		Pyrites-sulphur CU/FE	●			●	•	•	•	•	•
		Coal		•	○	○	•	●	•	•	●
		Natural gas	●	?			○		•		
		(Hydroelectric energy)					○	●		●	•
		Oil	•	?							
	Soil Conditioner	Limestone ⎤ Lime	•		○	•	•	○	•	●	●
		Dolomite ⎦				•				•	•
		Calcrete		•						○	
		Carbonatite (Ca)				•			•	•	
		Gypsum	•	•		○			•	•	
		Lignite								○	
	Pesticide Insecticide	Clay	•	•	•	•	•	•	•	•	•
		Talc	•	•					•	•	•
		Copper	○	•			○			●	•
		Cobalt		•						●	•
		Sulphur	●			●	•	•	•	•	•
		Phosphate rock	•			•	•		•	•	•
	Farm Implement	Iron ore	•				○	○	•	○	•
		Ferro alloy									•
		Manganese	•							•	

Large   Medium
●   • Indicated resource   ○ Inferred resource

Table A.4

Mineral Raw Materials — Industrial Sector

Sector	Sub-sector	Mineral Raw Materials	ANGOLA	BOTSWANA	LESOTHO	MALAWI	MOZAMBIQUE	SWAZILAND	TANZANIA	ZAMBIA	ZIMBABWE
INDUSTRIAL	Ceramics	Clays	●	●	●	●	●	●	●	●	●
		Kaolin	●		●	●	●	●	●	●	●
		Feldspar				●	●	●	●	●	●
		Fluorite						●		●	●
		Gypsum	●	●		○		●	●	●	●
		Talc	○	○					●	●	●
		Limestone	●	○	○	●	●	○	●	●	●
	Refractory	Kaolin	●		●	●	●	●	●	●	●
		Magnesite					○		●	○	●
		Kyanite	○	○		●		○		○	●
		Graphite		○		○	○	○	●	●	●
		Chromium		○			○				●
	Glass	Sand/silica	●	●		●	●	●	●	●	●
		Soda ash	○	●		○	○		○	○	
		Feldspar				●	●	●	●	●	●
		Lime	●			●	●		●	●	●
		Cobalt		●						●	●

Large Medium

● ● Indicated resource

○ Inferred resource

Table A.5

Mineral Raw Materials — Construction Sector

Sector	Sub-sector	Mineral Raw materials	SADCC Member States								
			ANGOLA	BOTSWANA	LESOTHO	MALAWI	MOZAMBIQUE	SWAZILAND	TANZANIA	ZAMBIA	ZIMBABWE
BUILDING & CONSTRUCTION	Cement	Limestone/marble	●		○	●	●	○	●	⬤	⬤
		Gypsum	●	●		○			●	●	
		Coal		⬤	○	○	●	⬤	●	●	⬤
		Clay	●	●	●	●	●	●	●	●	●
		Asbestos	○	○			●	⬤	○	○	⬤
	Bricks, tiles, stone	Sand	●	●	●	●	●	●	●	●	●
		Clays	●	●	●	●	●	●	●	●	●
		Aggregates	●	●	●	●	●	●	●	●	●
		Building stone	●	○	●	○		●	●	○	○
		Decorative stone	●	○			●			○	○
		Coal		⬤	○	○	●	⬤	●	●	⬤
		Cement	●				●		●	●	●

Large	Medium	
⬤	●	Indicated resource
	○	Inferred resource

Table A.6

Mineral Raw Materials — Communication Sector

Sector	Sub-sector	Mineral Raw Materials	ANGOLA	BOTSWANA	LESOTHO	MALAWI	MOZAMBIQUE	SWAZILAND	TANZANIA	ZAMBIA	ZIMBABWE
TRANSPORT AND COMMUNICATION	Roads & Railways	Stone/gravel	●	●	●	●	●	●	●	●	●
		Sand	●	●	●	●	●	●	●	●	●
		Calcrete	●	⬤					●	⬤	●
		Ferricrete	●	●	●	●			●	●	●
		Bitumen	●						○	○	○
		Steel (iron ore)	●				○	○	●	●	●
		Asbestos	○	○			●	⬤	○	○	⬤
		Cement	●				●		●	●	●
	Transmission	Copper	○	●			○			⬤	●
		Aluminium	○			○	○				○
		Steel (Iron Ore)	●				○	○	●	○	●
		Kaolin	●		●	●	●	⬤	●	●	⬤
		Magnesite				○		○	●	○	●
		Mica	○			○	●	○	●	○	●
		Graphite	●	○		○	○		●	●	●
		Manganese	●	○						●	

Large   Medium

⬤   ●   Indicated resource

○   Inferred resource

Table A.7
Number of Industrial Establishments by Branch

Branch	ISIC Code	Angola 1972	Botswana 1973	Lesotho 1975	Malawi 1974	Mozambique 1973	Swaziland 1982	Tanzania 1973	Zambia 1973	Zimbabwe 1973
Food	311	744	–	6	35	772	10	139	105	144
Beverage	313	45	–	0	4	18	4	11	42	34
Tobacco	314	6	–	0	7	6	0	3	0	13
Textiles	321	126	–	0	12	54	33	65	14	50
Wearing apparel	322	16	–	13	16	28	0	22	85	131
Leather & fur	323	6	–	1	0	26	0	5	6	0
Footwear	324	7	–	0	0	23	0	4	0	9
Wood	331	5	–	0	5	132	14	51	25	55
Furniture	332	12	–	2	9	41	0	31	32	55
Paper	341	7	–	0	12	9	11	9	7	18
Printing	342	52	–2	0	45	0	34	39	83	
Industrial chemicals	351	183	–	0	7	7	13	10	7	26
Other chemicals	352	0	–	0	0	31	0	21	18	47
Petroleum	353	2	–	0	0	1	0	10	3	0
Rubber	355	34	–	0	4	16	0	0	14	15
Plastic	356	14	–	0	0	12	0	5	9	37
Pottery	361	0	–	2	0	4	0	15	3	74
Glass	362	1	–	0	0	8	11	0	0	0
Other non-metallic	369	120	–	4	5	50	0	0	41	0
Iron & steel	371	3	–	0	0	3	0	4	3	21
Non-ferrous	372	0	–	0	0	0	0	0	3	12
Metal products	381	35	–	2	7	102	23	20	83	227
Non-electrical machinery	382	7	–	0	7	9	4	17	29	73
Electrical machinery	383	7	–	0	0	16	0	4	15	47
Transport equip.	384	32	–	0	0	16	0	16	18	48
Professional & scientific equip.	385	1	–	0	0	0	0	0	0	83
Other manufactures	390	5	–	4	0	9	7	8	11	0
Totals		1470	38	38	130	1438	130	503	612	1302

Source: UNIDO Vic Computer Centre, November 1985.

Table A.8
Principal SADCC Commodity Exports and Regional Cooperation

Commodity	Average value of regional exports 1976–78 ($US m)	Principal exporting countries	Share of export from developing SADCC countries (per cent)		World rank		Share of national regional exports (per cent)		Other producing countries	Share of national exports (per cent)
1	*2*	*3*	*4*	*5*	*6*	*7*	*8*	*9*	*10*	*11*
Single exporter dominant										
Copper[a]	963	all	100	24.3	16	4th	94	30	Botswana	29
		Zambia	89			4th	94		Zimbabwe	5
Petroleum	341	all	100	0.2	0.2		35	9.8		
		Angola	100							
Chromium[a]	61	all	100		5.6	4th	7			
		Zimbabwe	100							
Asbestos[a]	110	all	100		5.3	4th	11	3.4	Swaziland	12
		Zimbabwe	85						Angola	1
Sisal[a]	35	all	100	37.2	36.5	2nd	5	1.1	Mozambique	2
		Tanzania	75							
Sub total	1483							46.2		
Major foreign exchange earner for several SADCC countries										
Meat	107	all	100	6.7	1.2			3.3	Swaziland	5
		Zimbabwe	54				6			
		Botswana	41				3			
Tobacco*	263	all	100	17.6	8.1	5th	14	8.2	Zambia	1
		Zimbabwe	47			6th	49		Mozambique	4
		Malawi	35						Angola	0

Commodity	Value	Country	Share %			Rank		SADCC %	Country	
Diamonds[a]	171	Tanzania	11							
		all	100		18.5		6	5.3	Tanzania	6
		Botswana	37	4.2		4th	33		Lesotho	33
		Angola	41			5th	8			
Coffee	408	all	100		3.9		24	12.7	Zimbabwe	2
		Angola	51				35		Zambia	—
		Tanzania	45	5.8						
Tea	73	all	100		4.7		20			
		Malawi	51				4			
		Tanzania	26							
Sugar	123	all	100		1.6		34	3.8	Mozambique	8
		Swaziland	52	4			3			
		Zimbabwe	20				10		Tanzania	1
		Malawi	15							
Cashewnuts[a]	70	all	100				27	2.2		
		Mozambique	55				6			
		Tanzania	45							
Cotton	155	all	100		2.7		12	4.8	Angola	2
		Tanzania	39	5.3			7		Mozambique	9
		Zimbabwe	38							
Timber/wood pulp	65	all	100				23	2.0	Angola	1
		Swaziland	68						Mozambique	3
									Zimbabwe	0
Sub total	1435						74	47.7		
Total	2918							90.9		

[a] The SADCC region has a significant share in total world exports.

Source: Compiled from UNIDO (1985), Table 8.1.

Table A.9
Intra-SADCC Flows by Individual Commodities, 1980–81

Exports from 1	Products 2	Destination 3
	ISIC 31: Food, Beverage, Tobacco	
Angola	processed fish production	Mo, Swa, Za, Zi
	palm oil	Ta, Za
	dried beans and peas	Swa
	coffee	Bo, Mo, Swa, Za
	tobacco and products	Bo, Mo
Botswana	meat and by-products	Ang, Mo
	edible oils	Ang, Ta, Za
Lesotho	processed fruit and vegetables	Mo, Swa, Za, Zi
Malawi	processed fruit and vegetables	Mo, Swa, Za, Zi
	groundnuts	Bo, Swa
	dried beans and peas	Ang
	sugar	Ang, Bo, Le, Ta
	tea	Ang, Bo, Za
	tobacco and products	Bo, Mo
Mozambique	milk	Ang, Ta
	processed fish production	Swa, Za, Zi
	tea	Ang, Bo, Swa
Swaziland	meat and by-products	Ang, Mo
	edible oils	Ang, Ta, Za
	sugar	Ang, Bo, Le, Ta
	beverages	Ang
Tanzania	meat and by-products	Ang
	edible oils	Ang, Za
	coffee	Ang, Bo, Mo, Swa, Za
	Sugar	Ang, Bo, Le
	spices	Swa
	tea	Ang, Bo, Swa, Za
	honey	Le
	beverages	Ang
	tobacco and products	Ang
Zambia	groundnuts	Ang
	sugar	Bo, Le
	tobacco and products	Bo, Mo
Zimbabwe	edible oils	Ang, Ta, Za
	coffee	Bo, Mo, Swa, Za
	sugar	Ang, Bo, Le, Ta
	ISIC 32: Textiles, Garments, Leather	
Angola	sisal products	Zi
	hides and skins	Le, Ta, Za
Botswana	hides and skins	Le, Ta, Za
Lesotho	garments	Ang, Bo, Mo, Ma
	footwear	Ang, Bo, Ma, Ta

Malawi	textiles	Ang, Bo, Mo
	cotton	Zi
	leather goods	Ang, Bo
Mozambique	garments	Ang, Bo, Ma
	footwear	Ang, Bo, Ma, Ta
Swaziland	garments	Ang, Bo, Ma, Mo
Tanzania	blankets	Bo
	sisal products	Zi
	garments	Ang, Bo, Ma, Mo
	leather goods	Ang, Bo, Ma
Zambia	textiles	Ang, Bo, Ma, Mo
Zimbabwe	garments	Ang, Bo, Ma, Mo
	hides and skins	Le, Ta, Za⁻
	footwear	Ang, Bo, Ma, Ta

ISIC 33: Wood and Wood Products

Lesotho	furniture	Ang, Bo, Mo, Zi
	upholstery	Ang, Bo, Mo, Zi
Mozambique	wood and by-products	Ta, Za, Zi
	furniture	Bo, Za
Swaziland	furniture	Bo
Tanzania	wood and by-products	Za, Zi
Zambia	wood and by-products	Ang, Zi

ISIC 34: Pulp and Paper

Angola	wood and pulp	Za, Zi
Malawi	paper products	Ang, Bo, Mo, Ta, Za
Swaziland	wood and pulp	Ta, Za, Zi
	paper products	ang, Bo, Ma, Mo, Ta, Za
Tanzania	paper products	Ang, Za

ISIC 35: Chemicals and Products

Angola	PVC	Bo, Le, Ma, Swa, Ta, Za, Zi
	paint and varnish	Bo, Mo, Ta, Zi
	tyres and tubes	Swa
Botswana	soda ash	Za, Zi
	tallow and candles	Ma, Swa, Za, Zi
Lesotho	medicines	Ang, Bo, Ma, Swa, Ta, Zi
	tallow and candles	Ma, Swa, Za, Zi
Swaziland	soda ash	Ang, Ta
	paint and varnish	Bo, Mo, Ta, Zi
	tallow and candles	Zi
	explosives	Ta
Tanzania	fertilizer	Ang
	insecticides	Mo, Za
	soap and detergents	Ang, Bo
	tyres and tubes	Ang
Zambia	lime	Swa, Zi
Zimbabwe	chemicals	Swa, Ta

ISIC 36: Non-metallic Mineral Products

Angola	ceramic ware	Swa, Zi
	cement	Bo, Le, Swa, Ta, Za
Lesotho	ceramic ware	Swa, Zi
Mozambique	glass products	Ang, Zi
	cement	Swa, Ta, Za
Swaziland	ceramic ware	Ta, Zi
	glass products	Zi, Ang
Tanzania	ceramic ware	Swa, Zi
	glass products	Ang, Zi
Zambia	glass products	Zi
	cement	Bo, Le, Swa, Ta
Zimbabwe	cement	Bo, Le, Swa, Ta, Za

ISIC 37: Basic Metal Industries

Angola	reinforcing iron	Za
Mozambique	iron sheets	Bo, Zi
Tanzania	steel tubes and pipes	Ang, Bo
Zambia	copper and products, lead, zinc	Ang, Mo, Ta, Zi
Zimbabwe	steel ingots and bars, copper and products, lead, zinc	Ang, Ta

ISIV 38: Metal Products and Machinery

Lesotho	building materials	Bo, Ta, Zi
Malawi	structural fabrication	Ang, Bo, Zi
	industry machinery	Swa
Mozambique	building materials	Bo, Ta, Zi
	GLS lamps	Ta
	refrigerators	Ta
	agricultural pumps	Ang, Ma, Ta
	trailers	Ma, Ta
Swaziland	tractors	Ang
Tanzania	fabricated metal items	Ang, Bo, Zi
	agricultural implements	Ang, Ma
	building materials	Bo, Mo, Zi
Zambia	aluminium utensils	Ang, Zi
Zimbabwe	industrial machinery	Swa
	earthmoving equipment	Ang, Bo, Ma, Mo, Swa, Ta, Za
	car and parts	Ang, Bo, Ma, Swa

ISIC 39: Others

Lesotho	umbrellas	Ang, Mo, Swa
Tanzania	school materials	Ang, Ma

Key: Ang = Angola, Bo = Botswana, Le = Lesotho, Ma = Malawi, Mo = Mozambique, Swa = Swaziland, Ta = Tanzania, Za = Zambia and Zi = Zimbabwe.

Source: SADCC, *Industry*, Blantyre, 1981.

Table A.10

Structure of the Labour Force, 1960–80

	Labour Force in 1960				Labour Force in 1979/80				
	Total (000)	% in Agriculture	% in Industry	% in Service	Total (000)	% in Agriculture	% in Industry	% in Services	% Rate of Growth
Angola	1,465	69	12	19	1,917	59	16	26	1.4
Botswana	225	92	3	5	370	83	5	12	2.0
Lesotho	485	93	2	5	673	87	4	9	1.7
Malawi	1,598	92	3	5	2,484	86	5	9	2.3
Mozambique	2,814	81	8	11	3,953	67	17	16	1.8
Swaziland	162	54	4	42	247	52	9	39	2.2
Tanzania	4,851	84	4	7	7,328	83	6	11	2.2
Zambia	1,371	79	7	14	2,131	68	11	21	2.2
Zimbabwe	—	69	11	20	2,448	60	15	25	—

Source: ECA, Survey of Economic and Social Conditions in Africa, 1983–84.

Table A.11

Education Indicators

	1st Level		2nd Level		3rd Level			
	No. (000)	%	No. (000)	%	No. (000)	%	% Females	No. Teachers
Angola	1,178	—	141.7	—	2.6	—	16	374
Botswana	178	102	22.9	23	1.9	38	144	61
Lesotho	277.9	105	28.7	18	1.7	2.0	59	301
Malawi	809.7	59	20.4	4	1.8	0.3	20	323
Mozambique	1,162.6	90	121.0	—	2.3	—	25	247
Swaziland	125.3	111	23.6	42	1.7	—	41	1,068
Tanzania	3,512.8	102	77.4	3	4.0	0.4	17	717
Zambia	1,041.9	96	101.8	16	9.1	1.5	22	325
Zimbabwe	2,044	125	227.6	23	3.1	0.5	22	

Source: *South: The Third World Magazine*, August 1985.

Table A.12

Total Overseas Trade through the Regional Ports (tons m) 1981

	Angola	Botswana	Malawi	Mozambique	Swaziland	Tanzania	Zambia	Zimbabwe	Total SADCC	RSA	Total
Maputo				0.87	0.69		0.04	0.57	2.17	1.62	3.79
Matola				0.60	0.04			0.17	0.81	1.36	2.17
Beira			0.50	0.71			0.06	0.13	1.40		1.40
Nacala			0.33	0.28					0.61		0.61
Dar es Salaam						1.10	0.84		1.94		1.94
Lobito	NA						NA		NA		NA
Luanda	0.40						NA		NA		NA
Total SADCC *Ports*	0.40		0.83	2.46	0.73	1.10	0.94	0.87	7.33		10.31
RSA Ports	—	0.32	—	0.36	0.36	—	0.54	1.72	2.94		

Total overseas trade for Lesotho was 3,000 tons in 1981 pp. 138.

Source: SADCC – Maseru, 1983.

Table A.13

Total Overseas Trade on Railway Lines (tons m) 1981

Line	Botswana	Malawi	Swaziland	Zambia	Zimbabwe	RSA
Goba			0.73			
Limpopo				0.04	0.74	
Machipanda				0.06	0.13	
Sena		0.50				
Nacala		0.33				
Tazara				0.84		
Benguela						
Botswana	0.32					
	0.32	0.83	0.73	1.48	2.59	298

Source: SADCC – Maseru 1983, p. 137.

Bibliography

Adam, H., and Gidomee, H., *Ethnic Power Mobilized* (Yale University Press, New Haven, 1979).

Adedeji, A., 'Regional Economic Cooperation in West Africa', *Development Digest*, XI, 1, January 1973.

African Communist, no. 99, 1984.

Africa Research Bulletin, vol. 11, no. 5.

Allen, R. L., 'Integration in Less Developed Areas', *Kyklos*, 14, 3, 1961.

Allen, P. R., *Organisation and Administration of a Monetary Union* (Princeton Studies in International Finance, No. 38, 1976).

Amin, S. 'Development and Structural Changes: African Experience', in Ward *et al.* (1971).

—— 'The End of a Debate', UN African Institute for Economic Development and Planning, IDEP/ET/R 2558, Dakar (1973).

—— *Accumulation on a World Scale*, vols. 1 and 2 (Monthly Review Press, New York, 1974).

—— 'The Future of South Africa', *Journal of Southern African Affairs*, 11, 3, 1977.

—— *La Déconnexion* (La Découverte, Paris, 1985).

Arnold, G., and Weiss, R., *Strategic Highways in Africa* (J. Friedmann, London, 1977).

Balassa, B., *The Theory of Economic Integration* (R. Irwin, Homewood, Illinois, 1961).

Bhagwati, J., *International Trade* (Penguin Books, Harmondsworth, 1969).

Bienefeld, M., and Innes, D., 'Capital Accumulation and South Africa', *Review of African Political Economy* 7 (1976).

Bohning, W. R. (ed.), *Black Migration to South Africa* (ILO, Geneva, 1981).

Bostock, M., and Harvey, C., *Economic Independence and Zambian Copper: A Study of Foreign Investment* (Praeger, New York, 1972).

Botha, P. W., *Towards a Constellation of Southern African States* (Information Services of Southern Africa, Pretoria, 1979).

Bowman, L. W. 'The Subordinate State System in Southern Africa', *International Studies Quarterly*, vol. 12, no. 3, 1966.

Brandt Commission, *North–South: A Programme for Survival* (Pan World Affairs, London, 1980).

Breybenbach, W., *Migratory Labour Arrangements in Southern Africa* (Africa Institute of South Africa, Pretoria, 1979).

—— (ed.), *The Constellation of States: A Consideration* (South African Foundation, Johannesburg, 1980).

Brown, A. A., and Neuberger E. (eds.), *International Trade and Central Planning* (University of California Press, 1968).

Brown, R., 'The Theory of Unequal Exchange: The End of the Debate' *ISS Occ. Papers,* no. 65 (1978).

Burgess, J., *Interdependence, in Southern Africa: Trade and Transport Links in South, Central and East Africa,* Economic Intelligence Unit Special Report No. 32 (London EIU, 1976).

Burgess, S., and Wilson, M., 'Dependence and Limits to Regional Co-operation in Southern Africa', paper presented at SAUSSC V, Lusaka, Zambia 4–6 July 1983.

Castro, Fidel, *The World Economic and Social Crisis* (Office of the Council of State, Havana, 1983).

Cervenka, Zderek (ed.), *Land-locked Countries in Africa* (Scandinavian Institute of African Studies, Uppsala, 1973).

Chou, Yu-Min, 'Economic Integration in LDCs: the Case of Small Countries', *Journal of Development Studies,* July 1967.

Clarke, D. G., *Foreign Companies and International Investment in Zimbabwe* (Mambo Press, Gwelo, 1980).

Clarke, S., *Financial Aspects of Economic Sanctions on South Africa* (IUEF, Geneva, 1980).

Cohan, B., and El-Khawas, Mohamed A. (ed.), *The Kissinger Study of Southern Africa* (Spokesman Books, Nottingham, 1975).

Colclough, C., and McCarthy, S., *The Political Economy of Botswana* (Oxford University Press, 1980).

Collings, F. *et al.*, 'The Rand and the Monetary Systems of Botswana, Lesotho, and Swaziland', *Journal of Modern African Studies,* vol. 16, no. 1, 1978.

Commonwealth Institute, *SADCC: Development in the Region: Progress and Problems,* Conference Report, London, 18–20 July 1984.

Cooper, C. A. *et al.*, 'Towards a General Theory of Customs Union for Developing Countries', *Journal of Political Economy,* vol. 73.

Corea, G., 'New International Economic Order', *The Economic Times* (Bombay, 1977).

Crush, J. S., 'The Parameters of Dependence in Southern Africa: A Case Study of Swaziland', *Journal of Southern African Affairs,* vol. IV, no. 1, 1979.

Curry, R., 'US Aid's Southern Africa Program', *Journal of Southern African Affairs* (vol. V, no. 2, 1980).

Davidson, B., Slovo, J. and Wilkinson, A., *Southern Africa: The New Political Revolution* (Penguin Books, Harmondsworth, 1976).

Davies, R. H., and O'Meara, D., 'South Africa's Strategy in the Southern African Region: A Preliminary Analysis', paper presented to South African Development Research Association Conference, Lesotho, October 1983.

Davies, R. H., and O'Meara, D., 'The State of Analysis of the Southern African Region: Issues raised by Southern Africa strategy', *ROAPE,* no. 19 (1984).

Dell, S., 'Economic Integration and the American Example', *Economic Journal,* March, 1959.

Due, J. F., 'The Problems of Rail Transport in Africa, *Journal of Developing Areas,* vol. 13, no. 4, 1979.

ECA, 'The ECA Lusaka-Based MULPOC and its Role in the Establishment of the Eastern and Southern Africa Trade Promotion and Training Centre', paper for workshop held in Nairobi 20–24 May on 'Prospects and Problems of Intra-

Region Trade among ACP States in Eastern and Southern Africa WPR to Operation of the PTA (1985)'.

Economic Intelligence Unit, *Zimbabwe's First Five Years* (ETU, London, 1981).

Emmanuel, A., *Unequal Exchange: A Study of the Imperialism of Trade* (New Left Books, 1972) first published as *L'echange Inegal* (Francois Maspero, Paris, 1969).

Fair, D., 'Towards Balanced Development in Southern and East Africa', *Journal of African Affairs*, vol. 9, nos. 3 and 4, 1979.

First, R., *et al., The Southern Africa Connection* (Penguin, Harmondsworth, 1972).

Foxley, A., 'Development Alternatives Under Conditions of Reduced External Dependence', in Ruggles (1974).

Fransman, M. 'The Roots of South African Expansionism', 1976, unpublished mimeo.

Frobel, F., 'The Current Development of the World Economy' *HSDP–GPID Working papers series* 36/UNUP- 150, United Nations University (1980).

Furtado, C., 'Development and Stagnation in Latin America: A Structuralist Approach', *Centre Paper no. 95* (Economic Growth Centre, Yale University, 1966).

Gelden Huys, D., and Venter, D., 'Regional Co-operation in Southern Africa: A Constellation of States', *International Affairs Bulletin* vol. 3, no. 3, 1979.

Gifford, T., *South Africa's Record of International Terrorism* (SWAM, London, 1981).

Green, R. H., *South Africa: The Impact of Sanctions on Southern African Economies* (IUEF, Geneva, 1980).

—— 'Southern African Development Coordination: The Struggle Continues', in *Africa Contemporary Record* (African Publishing Company, London, 1981).

—— 'Economic Liberation and Economic Survival: SADCC 1980–1984', in *Commercial Banking in the SADCC Region: The Quest for a Role* – proceedings of the First Conference of Commercial Banks of the SADCC Region, 13–17 August, Arusha (1984).

Grundy, K., *Confrontation and Accommodation in Southern Africa: The Fruits of Independence* (University of California Press, 1973).

Guerke, A., 'Africa as a Market for South African Goods', *Journal of Modern African Studies*, vol. 12, no. 1, 1974.

Guma, X. P., 'The Rand Monetary Area Agreement', *South African Journal of Economics*, 53 (2) 1985.

Hazlewood, A., *Economic Integration: The East African Experience* (Heinemann, London, 1975).

Heard, K. A., and Shaw, T. (eds.)., *Cooperation and Conflict in Southern Africa: Papers on a Regional Subsystem* (Washington DC University Press of America, 1977).

Hymer, S. H., and Resnick, S. A., 'International Trade and Uneven Development', *Centre: Paper No. 178* (Economic Growth Centre, Yale University, 1972).

IBRD *Accelerated Development in Sub-Sahara Africa: An Agenda for Action* (Washington, 1981).

—— *World Development Report* (Washington, 1983).

—— *World Development Report* (Washington, 1984).

ILO, *Zambia: Basic Needs in an Economy under Pressure* (Addis Ababa, ILO (JBPA), 1981).

IMF *International Financial Statistics Year Book* (Washington, 1983).

Innes, D., *Anglo American and the Rise of Modern South Africa* (Heinemann,

London, 1984).

Isaken, J., and Faaland, I., 'Economic Dependence and Regional Cooperation', DERAP Working Paper no. 147 (1979).

Journal of African Marxists, no. 6, October 1984.

Kaldor, N., 'The Case for Regional Policies', *Journal of Political Economy* (November 1970).

Keren, P. B., *Capital Mobility and Financial Integration: A Survey* (Princeton Studies in International Finance, no. 39. 1976).

Kgarelse, A. (ed.) *SADCC 2* – Maputo (London: SADCC Liaison Committee, 1981).

Khonje, M., 'Financial Intermediation and Economic Development: Case Study of the Development Bank of Zambia', MA thesis, University of Zambia, 1984.

Killick, T., 'The Role of the Public Sector in the Industrialization of African Developing Countries' *Industry and Development* 7 (1983).

Kornegay, F. A., 'Dependency in Southern Africa and the SADCC: Selected Resources' *SADEX*, vol. 4, no. 3, 1982.

Kutnesov, V. I., *Economic Integration: Two Approaches* (Progress, Moscow, 1976).

Lamaswala, K., 'The Role of the Bank of Zambia and the Clearing House in the Furtherance of the Objectives of the PTA Treaty', *Zambia Journal of Business*, December 1984.

Landell Mills, P. M., 'The 1969 Southern African Customs Union Agreement' in *JMAS* vol. 9, no. 2, 1971.

Lanning, G., and Mueller, M., *Africa Undermined: A History of Mining Companies and the Underdevelopment of Africa* (Penguin, Harmondsworth, 1979).

Lazar, L., *Namibia* (Africa Publication Trust, 1972).

Legum, C. (ed.), *Africa Contemporary Record*, vol. 15 (African Publishing Company, New York and London, 1984).

Leistner, G. M. E., 'Towards a Regional Development Strategy for South Africa' *Journal of Economics* 49 (4), 1981.

Lenin, V. I., *Imperialism: The Highest Stage of Capitalism* (Progress Publishers, Moscow, 1975).

Leys, R., and Tostensen, A., 'Regional Cooperation in Southern Africa: The South African Development Co-ordination Conference', *Review of African Political Economy*, 23, 1984.

Linder, S. B., *An Essay on Trade and Transformation* (Almquist & Wicksell, Uppsala, 1961).

——*Trade and Trade Policy for Development* (Pall Mall Press, London, 1967).

Lindheck, A., 'The International Economic Environment and Industrialization Possibilities in Developing Countries', *Industry and Development*, 1984.

Maasdorp, G., 'Reassessing Economic Ties in Southern Africa' *Optima*, vol. 30, no. 2, 1981.

Mckinnon, R. I., 'Foreign Exchange Constraints in Economic Development and Efficient Aid Allocation', in Bhagwati (1969).

Makoni, S., 'SADCC – the Challenge', address to University of Botswana, 15 April 1985, mimeographed.

Mandaza, Ibbo, 'Conflict in Southern Africa', paper prepared for the UNU Project on Peace, Development and Regional Security in Africa, 1985.

—— 'Southern Africa: US Policy and the Struggle for National Independence', paper presented at the African Association of Political Science (AAPS) Southern Africa Region's Workshop on 'Whither South Africa?', Harare, 10–12

March 1986.

—— 'The Post-White Settler Colonial State in Zimbabwe', in Ibbo Mandaza (ed.), *Zimbabwe, The Political Economy of Transition* (Codesria Book Series, 1986).

Manuda, M., 'Problems and Prospects of intra-Region Trade – The case of the Preferential Trade Area'. Summary of Proceedings of Workshop by FES and Trade Promotion and Training Center of Eastern Southern Africa, Nairobi, 20–24 May 1985.

Mathews, J., 'South Africa's Trade Relations Foreign and Regional Interdependence', *International Affairs Bulletin*, vol. 4, no. 2, 1980.

—— 'Economic Integration in Southern Africa: Progress or Decline' *South African Journal of Economics*, 52 (3), 1984.

Mitrany, D., 'The Prospect of Integration: Federal or Functional' *Journal of Common Market Studies*, vol. IV, no. 2, 1963.

Mittelman, J. H., 'Mozambique: The Political Economy of Underdevelopment', *Journal of Southern African Affairs*, vol. 3, no. 1, 1978.

Molteno, R., *Africa and South Africa* (Africa Bureau, London, 1971).

Mosher, A. T., *An Introduction to Agricultural Extension* (Singapore University Press, 1978).

Msyua, C. D., 'The Quest for the Role of Commercial Banks in Fostering the Southern African Development Co-ordination Conference (SADCC) Initiative', in *Commercial Banking in the SADCC Region*, 1984.

Mtei, E. I. M., 'The Bank of Tanzania: Its Background and Functions', *Economic Reflections*, vol. 1, 1972.

Munslow, B. *et al.*, 'The Effects of World Recession and Crisis upon the Southern African Development Co-ordination Conference' *ROAPE Conference Paper*, University of Keele, September 1984.

Murray, R. *et al., The Role of Foreign Firms in Namibia* (African Publications Trust, 1974).

Myrdal, G., *Economic Theory and Underdeveloped Regions* (London, 1957).

Mytelka, L. K., 'Common Market in Central Africa', *Development Digest*, XI, 1, January 1973.

Nabudere, D. W. , 'Imperialism and the South Africa State', *IKWEZI*, no. 11, 1979.

Ndlela, D. B., 'The Development of the Capital Sector in Zimbabwe', *Zimbabwe Economic Journal*, vol. 1, no. 3, January 1986.

Ng'andwe, C. O. M., 'An Economic Argument for Political Unification in Africa', Lusaka, South African Social Sciences Conference Proceedings, 1982.

Nkonoki, S. R., *Some Aspects of Planning Industry and Energy for Self-Reliance in Southern Africa*, DERAP no. 189 (Chr. Michelsen Institute, 1985).

Nkosi, Z. 'South Africa's Imperial Expansion', *African Communist*, vol. 30, no. 7, 1967.

Nolutshungu, S., *South Africa: A Study in Ideology and Foreign Policy* (Manchester University Press, 1975).

Nomvete, B. D., 'The Role of the PTA in the Promotion and Facilitation of Sub-regional Trade', *Zambia Journal of Business*, December 1984.

Nsekela, A. J. (ed.), *Southern Africa Towards Economic Liberation* (Rex Collings, London, 1981).

Nyati, V. M., 'South African Imperialism in Southern Africa' *African Review*, vol. 5, no. 4, 1975.

Nye, J., *Pan Africanism and East African Integration* (Cambridge, Mass. Harvard

University Press, 1965).

Nye, J., 'The Extent and Viability of East African Co-operation', in R. G. Leys and P. Robson (eds.), *Federation in East Africa* (OUP, Nairobi, 1965).

Nyerere, J. K., *Unity for a New Order* (Government Printer, Dar es Salaam, 1979).

Nzioki-Kibua, T., *Regional Cooperation Development in Eastern Africa.* Summary of findings of a workshop held in Nairobi 15 May FES (1984).

OAU, *The Lagos Plan of Action for the Implementation of the Monrovia Strategy for the Economic Development of Africa Lagos*, April 1980.

Oden, D., *The Macroeconomic Position of Botswana*, 'Research Report no. 60 (Scandinavian Institute of African Studies, Uppsala, 1981).

Odle, M. A., and Arthur, O. S. (eds.) *Commercialization of Technology and Dependence in the Caribbean*, Caribbean Technology Policy Studies Project (University of the West Indies, 1985).

Olwa, 'Preferential Trade Area for Eastern and Southern African States (PTA)', in collection of papers presented in Nairobi at workshop on *Prospects for Increasing Trade in the PTA*, FES (1984).

Perroux, F., 'Multinational Investments and the Analysis of Development and Integration Poles', *Economies et Sociétés* 24, 1983.

Phillips, P., 'Review' of Arne Tostensen's 'Dependence and Collective Self-Reliance in Southern Africa: The Case of the Southern Africa Development Co-ordination Conference', *Review of African Political Economy*, 27/28, 1984.

Prebish, R., 'The Economic Development of Latin America and its Principal Problems', *Economic Bulletin for Latin America*, Vii (1) February 1962.

Puschra, W., 'Regional Integration and Development Cooperation: The case of PTA and SADCC', in *Regional Cooperation and Development* collection of papers presented at a FES-sponsored conference, Nairobi, May 1984.

Ross, A. R., 'Emmanuel on Unequal Exchange: A Marxist Contribution on Trade Relations Between Rich and Poor', *Journal of Economic Studies* 3 (1), 1976.

Sachs, I., 'The Significance of the Foreign Trade Sector and the Strategy of Foreign Trade Planning', in Sachs, K., *Studies in Political Economy of Development*, 1977.

Sachs, I., and Laski, K., 'Industrial Development Strategy' *Industrialization and Productivity Bulletin* 16.

Sachs K., *The Discovery of the Third World* (MIT Press, 1976).

—— *Studies in Political Economy of Development* (Pergamon Press, Oxford, 1977).

SADCC Record of the Southern Africa Development Coordination Summit Conference, Lusaka, 1 April 1980 (mimeo). Also in Nsekela, A. J. (ed.), *Southern Africa: Towards Economic Liberation* (Rex Collings, London, 1981).

—— Record of Ministerial meeting held in Harare, Zimbabwe on 11 September 1980 (mimeo).

—— Record of the Ministerial meeting held in Maputo, Mozambique on 28 November 1980 (mimeo).

—— Record of the Summit Conference held in Harare, Zimbabwe on 20 July 1981 (mimeo).

—— *Towards Industrial Coordination*, vol. 2 (Harare, 1980).

—— Regional Coordination in Food and Agriculture: SADCC 1981 (mimeo).

—— Industrial cooperation (SADCC, Blantyre, 1981, mimeo).

—— *SADCC Maseru* (Mambo Press, 1983).

—— Regional Annual Progress Report covering the period July 1983–June 1984 (mimeo).

—— *Current Status of Industrial Projects*, 1984.

—— *Five Year Strategy 1986–1990: SADCC Mining Sector* (Mining Sector Co-ordinating Unit, 1985).

Samuelson, P. A., and Stopler, U. F., 'Protection and Real Wages', *Review of Economic Studies* 9; also in Bhagwati (1969).

Schelling, T., *International Trade* (Allyn & Bacon, Boston, 1958).

Seidman, A., *Comparative Development Strategies in East Africa* (EAPH, Nairobi, 1972).

—— 'Towards Integrated Regional Development in Southern Africa', *Development and Peace*, N 1.2, 1981.

Seidman, A., and Seidman, N., *US Multinationals in Southern Africa* (Tanzania Publishing House, Dar es Salaam, 1977).

Senghaas, D., 'Friedrich List and the New International Economic Order', Worm, 1978.

Senghaas-Knobloch, E., 'The Internationalization of Capital and the Process of Underdevelopment: The Case of Black Africa', *Journal of Peace Research*, xii (4), 1975.

Senin, M. V., *Socialist Integration* (Progress, Moscow, 1973).

Shaw, T., 'Southern Africa: Cooperation and Conflict in an International Sub-system', *Journal of Modern African Studies*, vol. 12, no. 4, 1974.

Shaw, T. M., 'Southern Africa: Dependence, Interdependence and Independence in a Regional Sub-system', in Heard, K. A., and Shaw, T. M. (eds.), *Cooperation and Conflict in Southern Africa*.

Shaw, T. M., and Tandon, Y. (eds.), *Regional Development at the International Level: African and Canadian Perspectives*, vol. II (AAPS/CPSA Publications, London, 1985).

Simba, I., 'The Search for Payment Arrangement Mechanism in the SADCC Region', *Commercial Banking in the SADCC Region*, 1984.

Simons, H. J., and Simons, R. E., *Class and Colour in South Africa 1850–1950* (Penguin, Harmondsworth, 1969).

Sinare, H., 'The Implications of the Preferential Trade Area to Economic Integration in Eastern and Southern Africa' – paper for international conference on, *Peace and Security in Southern Africa*, Arusha, 24–31 May 1985.

Singh, A., 'The Interrupted Industrial Revolution of the Third World: Prospects and Policies for Resumption', *Industry and Development*, 1984.

Singh, T., 'Why World Capital Backs South Africa', *African Communist*, no. 99, 1984.

Sollie, G., 'Trade Patterns and Institutional Aspects of Trade: An Empirical Study of Trade in Southern Africa', *DERAP Working Papers*, no. 267 (Bergen: Chr. Michelson Institute, 1982).

Solow, R., 'Technical Change and Aggregate Production Function', *Review of Economics and Statistics*, vol. 39, August 1957.

South African Institute of Race Relations, *A Survey of Race Relations in South Africa*, 1966.

Spider, D. A., *Introduction to International Economics* (Richard D. Irwin, 1971).

Steel, W. F., *et al.*, *Energy Policy and Planning in Africa*, ADB Paper 1 (1983).

Stoneman, C., 'Foreign Capital and the Reconstruction of Zimbabwe', *Review of African Political Economy*, no. 11, 1978.

—— (ed.), *Zimbabwe's Inheritance* (Macmillan, London, 1981).

Tandon, Y., 'The Role of Transnationals and the Future Trends in Southern

Africa', *Journal of Southern Africa Affairs*, no. 4, 1977.

Thomas, W. H., 'A Southern African Constellation of States: A Challenge or Myth?', *South Africa International*, vol. X, no. 3, 1980.

—— 'South Africa and her Neighbours: Prospects for Cooperation', *International Africa Forum*, vol. 17, no. 1, 1981.

Thomas, C., *Dependence and Transformation* (Monthly Review Press, New York, 1975).

—— 'Neo-colonialism and Caribbean Integration', *Ratios: Discussion Journal of the Left*, 1975, pp. 1–28.

Thompson, C., 'Regional Economic Coordination for Planning: The Case of Zimbabwe in SADCC', paper presented at the Conference on Economic Policies and Planning under Crisis Conditions in Developing Countries, Harare, 2–5 September 1985.

Toler, D., 'Constructive Engagement: Reactionary Pragmatism at its Best', *Issue*, vol. 12, no. 3/4, 1982.

Tostensen, A., 'Dependence and Collective Self-Reliance in Southern Africa: The case of the Southern African Development Coordination Conference', *Research Report No. 62* (Scandinavian Institute of African Studies, Uppsala, 1982).

Turner, J., and Gervasi, S., 'The American Future in Southern Africa: An Analysis of an Agency for International Development Study on Zimbabwe and Namibia', *Journal of Southern African Affairs*, vol. III, no. 1, 1978.

UN ECA, *Treaty for the Establishment of the Preferential Trade Area for Eastern and Southern African States* (Addis Ababa, Ethiopia).

UNIDO, *Country Report: South Africa*, 1984.

—— 'The Capital Goods Industry in Africa: A General Review and Elements for Further Analysis', Sectoral Studies Series no. 14, UNIDO/IS. 502, 20 December 1984.

—— 'Industrial Cooperation through the Southern African Development Coordination Conference (SADCC)' UNIDO/IS. 570, 15 October.

UNO, *Bank Loans to South Africa: 1972–1978, 1979–1982*.

Vaitsos, C. V., *Intercountry Income Distribution and Transnational Enterprises* (Clarendon Press, Oxford, 1974).

—— 'Crisis in Regional Economic Cooperation (Integration) Among Developing Countries: A Survey', *World Development* vol. 6, no. 6, 1978.

Van Zyl, J. C., 'South Africa in World Trade', *South African Journal of Economics* 52 (1), (1984).

Viljeon, S. P., 'The Industrial Achievement of South Africa', *South African Journal of Economics*, 51 (1), (1983).

Wagao, J. H., 'Public Enterprises in LDCs: Reflections on Tanzania, *Daily News* (Tanzania) 21 and 22 December 1984.

Ward, B., *et al.* (eds.) *The Widening Gap: Development in the 1970s* (Columbia University Press, 1971).

Weisskoff, R., and Wolff, E., 'Development and Trade Dependence: The Case of Puerto Rico 1948–1963, *Review of Economics and Statistics*, 1975.

Wolff, R., 'A Marxian Theory of Trade', paper for a conference on New Approaches to Trade IDS, (Sussex), 1975.

Index